Also by Samuel G. Freedman

The Inheritance: How Three Families and America
Moved from Roosevelt to Reagan and Beyond

Upon This Rock: The Miracles of a Black Church

Small Victories: The Real World of a Teacher, Her
Students, and Their High School

Jew

SIMON & SCHUSTER

NEW YORK   LONDON   TORONTO   SYDNEY   SINGAPORE

vs. JEW

The Struggle
for the Soul
of American Jewry

SAMUEL G. FREEDMAN

SIMON & SCHUSTER
Rockefeller Center
1230 Avenue of the Americas
New York, NY 10020

Copyright © 2000 by Samuel G. Freedman
All rights reserved,
including the right of reproduction
in whole or in part in any form.
SIMON & SCHUSTER and colophon are
registered trademarks of Simon & Schuster, Inc.
Designed by Edith Fowler
Manufactured in the United States of America

10   9   8   7   6   5   4   3   2

Library of Congress Cataloging-in-Publication Data is available
ISBN 0-684-85944-0

CONTENTS

A NOTE ON HEBREW AND YIDDISH TERMS

This book necessarily includes many Hebrew and Yiddish words and phrases. Those that are deemed to have entered American English usage—in the form of *Merriam-Webster's Collegiate Dictionary*, tenth edition—are set in a roman typeface. Those that do not appear in the dictionary are set in italic type. As much as possible, I have used the dictionary as my authority for transliteration. For terms not transliterated there, I have consulted various scholars and rabbis to try to determine the consensus on any given word.

The Second Temple

I<small>N THE FIRST CENTURY</small> of the Common Era, as the Roman empire reigned over Judea, the tiny nation rose in revolt. For several years, Jewish revolutionaries drove mighty Rome into retreat, seating their own regime in defiance. Yet at the very time that the empire's counterattack demanded the utmost unity from the insurrectionists, they fell into a virtual civil war. The Jewish resistance fragmented between upper and lower classes, the priestly caste and the masses, fundamentalists and progressives.

As the Romans advanced through Judea, the Jewish forces guarding the holy capital of Jerusalem turned their swords against each other. Two high priests led a siege against Zealots encamped on the Temple Mount; the Zealots, victorious, executed their foes. Thus divided, the rebels could not even agree on how to defend Jerusalem. Titus and his troops reconquered the city and burnt the Second Temple to the ground.

The Romans intended for that act to warn their Jewish subjects against ever again resisting. But as the story was retold over centuries of exile and dispersal, the destruction of the Temple acquired a different meaning in collective memory. The First Temple had been razed by Babylonian forces; the Second Temple, Jews came to believe, was lost less to the Romans than to their own *sinat hinam*—pure hatred, groundless hatred.

Two NIGHTS before Rosh Hashanah of the Hebrew year 5758, on what the civil calendar designated as September 29, 1997, I visited a middle-aged couple named Jane and David Marcus, who had just moved out of Great Neck, Long Island, largely to escape their neighbors. The stories they told me of the family next door struck all the familiar notes of a suburban grudge— whose dog bit whose kids, whose guests made a racket. There was just one peculiar element. The Marcuses, both Jews with Brooklyn roots who had chosen to live in a quintessentially Jewish suburb, had fled it partly because their neighbors were, well, too Jewish.

For the first five years that the Marcuses shared a property line with Edna and Noam Guilor, they had considered them peers if not quite friends. They were all professionals— David an accountant, Janet a literature scholar, Noam an actuary, Edna an architect. They were all Jewish without being particularly religious. An Israeli by birth, Edna Guilor had grown up in Haifa steeped in secular Jewish culture. Janet Marcus had arrived at a similar position by an American route. The granddaughter of the *shammas*, or sexton, in an Orthodox synagogue, she had belonged in girlhood to a Conservative congregation and joined a Reform temple as a wife and mother in Great Neck. The Marcuses' two boys had both been bar mitzvahed, even if the rabbi complained they had missed Hebrew school too often. On both sides of the fence in Great Neck for those first placid years, the Guilors and Marcuses practiced what Janet called a "habitual kind of nondoctrinaire, nondogma" Judaism.

Then, in the early nineties, around the time Noam Guilor fell severely ill with cancer, the Guilors became fanatics. Or at least that was how the Marcuses saw it. Barely a Sabbath passed, it seemed, without the Guilors entertaining five or six other families from their synagogue. If the Marcuses drove down their own street on a Saturday morning, they would find their path blocked by a procession toward shul of husbands in suits, wives wearing broad-brimmed hats, children padding alongside or riding in strollers. "Like a game of chicken," David said. The day the Guilors started nailing together lengths of lattice, the Marcuses first thought it was some kind of home-improvement project and duly applauded. Then, when Edna and Noam started covering the wood with sheets of heavy blue plastic, the Marcuses realized this was the ceremonial booth for the Jewish harvest festival Sukkot. And not tucked discreetly in the backyard, but on the front lawn, for the world to see.

"Flaunting it," David told me.

"In your face," Janet added.

Those epithets recurred all through the next hour of my visit, as the Marcuses recounted all the ways Great Neck had grown suddenly alien to them. Their favorite butcher closed his shop because he lost too much business to competitors who met the stringent standard of glatt kosher. The local congregation of Lubavitcher Hasidim tried to erect a menorah in a municipal park. Then the Lubavitchers bought land within walking distance of the Marcuses' home for a $10 million Chabad center. David and Janet sensed themselves being surrounded, encroached upon, and implicitly judged. A few months before I met them, they had moved ten miles away from Great Neck, to a home filled with early American antiques on a private road in a town whose modest number of Jews were still mostly Reform.

At times, they spoke of the decision in idealistic terms. "I am an American," David said. "I live the American Dream." Janet equated the Orthodox emphasis on women maintaining the household with the sexism that decades earlier had quashed her dream of becoming a doctor. But there was a way, too, that the Marcuses had learned to delight in tormenting their Orthodox enemies. David regaled me with the story of being approached outside a hockey game at Madison Square Garden by a Hasidic teenager trying to convince him to put on *tefillin*, the phylacteries an observant Jew dons for weekday prayer. In the punchline, he screamed at the boy, "Get the fuck away!" Janet recounted an argument with an Orthodox man she believed had cut ahead of her in a supermarket's checkout line. When he refused to relinquish his place, she remembered the little bit she knew about the religious law requiring modesty between men and women, and hissed, "If you don't get behind me, I'm going to touch you."

When I spoke subsequently to Edna Guilor, I heard a drastically different version of events. She preferred not to address every specific complaint the Marcuses had about the sukkah or the Sabbath guests, saying the Torah forbade her from spreading *loshon hora*, hurtful gossip. Nor did she think of herself as a fundamentalist who had grabbed onto dogma as a life raft during family tragedy. It was true that her husband Noam had nearly died in 1990 from lymphoma. It was true that in the next two years his mother and father had both passed away. It was true that during the days of shiva, ritual grieving, the Guilors had been astonished to find a complete *Shabbos* dinner left on their doorstep by Orthodox families who had heard of their loss. "When you're faced with death," Edna told me, "something makes you get more in touch with the essence of what your life is all about."

She felt the same craving standing atop Masada on the Sabbath in 1992 when her daughter Yasmin celebrated the bat mitzvah. At the desert fortress, where Jewish soldiers had committed suicide rather than surrender to Rome, Edna feared that if Yasmin was a typical American Jew her religious experience would end that day. The pull of assimilation was too strong; or else the Guilors had too little force with which to push against it. Not long after returning home, Edna and Noam accepted an invitation to spend a weekend across the Hudson studying with an Israeli rabbi in the Orthodox community of Monsey, New York. On the drive back to Long Island, they resolved to live by the mitzvot. They began to worship both at the nearby Young Israel and a Lubavitcher shul. They indeed hosted many families on Saturday afternoons, because a houseful of grown-ups eating and talking about the Torah portion, a yardful of kids singing and playing, all that was the meaning of Shabbat.

There was just one thing about the Marcuses that confounded Edna. Several times she asked me the same question: Was Janet Marcus really Jewish? Was I sure? Edna never explained why she doubted it. It could have been the Southern accent Janet retained from some childhood years in Georgia. It could have been the fact she served ham. From another family in Great Neck, I heard that perhaps one of Janet's grandparents had not been Jewish. But why, I couldn't help wondering, was her authenticity even being cast in doubt?

Two HOURS before dawn on May 21, 1999, the holy day of Shavuot, I walked into the vine-draped courtyard of the Masorti synagogue in Jerusalem, already bustling with dozens of people studying, snacking, and pacing in anticipation. Like me, they were bound for the Western Wall for the traditional daybreak service to celebrate God's handing down of the Torah to Moses. It was my first trip to Israel and I had been advised not to miss the experience, in part for its tableau of faith in an ancient place and in part for its more recent history of religious strife.

The congregation in the courtyard belonged to one of the few Conservative synagogues in Israel, and each time its members had attempted to worship at the Wall with men and women together it had been attacked. On Shavuot two years earlier, ultra-Orthodox yeshiva students had rained soiled diapers on the minyan. Two months after that, on Tisha b'Av, the police had shoved and wrestled the worshippers off the limestone plaza facing the Wall in the name of protecting them from assault. Last Shavuot, the congregation managed to pray while being pelted with small rocks and plastic bags of chocolate milk. Of all this, the deputy mayor of Jerusalem, Orthodox himself, had said, "The very fact that the Conservative Jews, who symbolize the destruction of the Jewish people, came to this place that is holiest to the Jewish people is a provocation. They have no reason to be in this place."

Just now a lanky figure in khaki slacks and an oxford shirt gathered the crowd to within earshot. He was Andrew Sacks, a Philadelphia rabbi now leading the Conservative movement in Israel, and many of his listeners were Americans, too, students in the Conservative seminary and day school. "We'll probably daven very quickly," he told them, using the Yiddish word for "pray." "And if there is any threat of violence and the police ask us to leave, we will." Then he hoisted an Eddie Bauer duffel bag onto his shoulders. It contained a Torah. "Less conspicuous this way," Rabbi Sacks said as he led the congregation through the courtyard gate.

Already the streets leading to the Old City were thick with the reverent, moving seven or eight abreast toward the Jaffa Gate, and Rabbi Sacks's group slid like a tributary into the broad river—Jews in black hats and kerchiefs, Jews wearing skullcaps known proudly by the Hebrew term *kippot*, Jews trailing from their waists the fringes called *tzitzis* that remind them of the commandments, some of the Hasidim already singing and wheeling in joy. Down the crooked, zigzag lanes within the Old City went the thousands, passing over paving stones worn to icy smoothness by centuries of pilgrims. Finally, Rabbi Sacks's worshippers reached the rampart overlooking the *Kotel*, the wall built by Solomon, the holiest site in all of Judaism, and beheld a plaza filled to its last cubit with humanity.

"Why are we doing this?" an American high school student, suddenly fearful, asked Rabbi James Lebeau, Sacks's colleague.

"I know why I'm doing it," Rabbi Lebeau answered. "This is my place as much as anyone else's."

Officially, the *Kotel* remained under Orthodox dominion, and as a place of worship it subscribed to Orthodox rules. By design, the Conservative congregation assembled at a corner of the plaza far from the Wall itself. The police had erected a double line of metal barricades to demark a zone perhaps eighty feet by one hundred. Several dozen armed officers stood atop concrete pylons on the perimeter. Within this protective cordon, Rabbi Sacks hoped, men and women could worship in egalitarian fashion. The rest of the *Kotel* plaza, under Orthodox auspices, required the sexes to be separated by the partition called a *mechitzah*. As the sky altered slowly from black to faint purple, most of the worshippers passed the Conservative minyan without any more than a curious stare.

The congregation moved through the liturgy without incident—*Birkat Hashachar, Pseukei D'zimrah, Shacharit*, all led by men. Then, for the reading from the Book of Ruth, two women moved to the folding table holding the Torah, and the first heckling could be heard. It came from boys clad in the black of the ultra-Orthodox *haredim*, the tremblers, so named for the way they shake with awe before God. Less abashed in this setting, one gave the finger to the Conservative worshippers. Another hooted until he got some congregants' attention. "Why are you looking up," he then taunted in Hebrew, "when you're supposed to be praying?"

Gradually, as if bored, the *haredi* crowd around the barricades thinned from three-deep to one, even showing a few gaps. The moment of confrontation, it seemed, had safely passed. But as the Conservative service neared the Torah reading, the central element of any Jewish service, the nearby *haredim* once more raised their voices in derision. "Make an evil plan and it will be dissolved," they sang in a tune used on Purim for the villainous Haman. "Speak something evil and it will not come to pass, for God is on our side." Another song thanked God "for separating us from the goyim."

By now, the sound of ridicule had attracted a claque. The barricades grew more crowded than they had been all morning, and it was no longer just children, or just *haredim*, who led the catcalls. A young man in his early twenties—without sidelocks or fedora, and wearing a double-breasted suit—began shouting from the perimeter. "Are gorillas accepted by your conversions?" he asked. "At a homosexual wedding, who gives the ring to who?" He had been speaking, Rabbi Sacks's group abruptly realized, not in Hebrew but in English, and not in the thickly accented English of an Israeli but in the casual, easy English of an American.

Soon after that, bottles began to fly, plastic bottles of soda from the bag lunches that yeshivas had supplied their students. Every time one crashed into the Conservative minyan, the nearby *haredim* cheered. When the police waded into the crowd to grab assailants, the crowd cried, "Why are you taking civilians?" Some of the *haredim* ran deep into the throngs on the plaza, and from that safe remove hurled more bottles.

By then, nearly two hours into the service, half of the Conservative congregation was facing outward, chanting the liturgy while scanning the air for incoming rounds. The rest huddled tightly together, close to the Torah. Every time a bird swooped low, every time a *haredi* shouted a fake warning, the worshippers flinched as one. Some of them, quaking, headed for the gate. One young man, speaking in the cocky American English one might hear from a ballpark heckler, shouted as they passed, "Go back to Germany. Let the Nazis finish the job."

From somewhere in the fundamentalists' ranks, a plastic bottle of cola took flight, tumbling end over end through the bluing sky. Seconds later, the missile struck what its launcher surely would have considered a bull's-eye—the cheek of a woman named Tobie Strauss, a Jewish studies teacher from New Jersey who had read earlier from the Book of Ruth. As Tobie collapsed in a heap on the limestone plaza, a second bottle arrived. It, too, found an appropriate target, striking a rabbinical student named Shira Yisrael flush on the forehead, a few inches from her *kippa*. Shira recovered the bottle, this one containing orange pop. Her father was a rabbi. Her mother had been killed years earlier in their native Argentina in the terrorist bombing of a Jewish community center. Now she was being assaulted in the Jewish state by Jews. Clutching the bottle in her fist, she stalked to the barricades and began shouting at the nearest boys. "What are you doing with a yarmulke on?" one shot back in English.

As Shira retreated to apply an icepack and Tobie groped to her feet and into a friend's embrace, the Conservative service proceeded, with a woman chanting the Haftorah, the reading from the Prophets. And the attack proceeded, too, with more bottles, a few bags of ruggelah pastry, and a song whose Hebrew words translated as "You're desecrating the mitzvah place," the commandment place. As if in reply, a man in the Conservative group muttered, *"Sinat hinam,"* pure hatred.

Finally, a single wizened rabbi walked with police escort along the barricades, pleading with the young men to halt, even disarming one of a soda bottle. Several yeshiva girls began arguing with the boys, saying, "You're worse than they are." Ignored, the girls left in tears.

By the time the Conservative service was moving into its final section, the Musaf, a policeman, approached one of the worshippers.

"How much time is left?" he asked in Hebrew.

"Thirty minutes."

"See if the rabbi can hurry it up."

Based on past experience, Rabbi Sacks had been hurrying already, omitting the usual repetition of the *Amidah* section and pushing briskly through the rest of the service. At the end, he paused long enough to give directions in English and Hebrew on how to safely exit the plaza. Then the congregation sang the "Hatikvah," the Israeli national anthem. Two years ago, the *haredim* had booed it. This time, pushed back from the barricades by the police, they didn't respond.

Rabbi Sacks returned the Torah to the duffel bag and shouldered it for the mile-long walk back to the Masorti synagogue. The rest of his congregants staggered out, guarded by a corridor of police. As one of the Conservative worshippers, a teenager on a study trip from Maryland, passed through the gate, he encountered a *haredi* boy roughly his age whom he recognized from the barricades.

"*Hag sameach,*" the *haredi* said. Happy holiday.

The next day, the assault on the Conservative worshippers was barely mentioned in the Israeli media. And for that omission there was a logical explanation. Israel remains a country split between Orthodox and secularists, and its secular Jewishness is firmly rooted in citizenship, Hebrew language, and military service. To the degree that Israel's progressives cared about the Shavuot incident, they cared about it as proof of why the nation needs a separation of church and state, the removal of Orthodox authority from civil life. The legitimacy of Reform and Conservative Judaism was a matter for Americans.

Indeed it was. Andy Sacks, Tobie Strauss, James Lebeau, three-quarters of the Conservative minyan, and a good many of the *haredim* with their effortless English were American-born. As the service was ending, I spotted the cantor's wife from my own synagogue in New Jersey. Two other members of our shul, she told me, had retreated from the service earlier in terror. An American newspaper, the *Philadelphia Inquirer,* devoted more attention to the violence than did any Israeli periodical. The most expansive article in the Israeli press was a column in the *Jerusalem Post* by Jonathan Rosenblum, an American native, who equally castigated the assailants for misrepresenting the majority of *haredim* and the Conservative worshippers for having provoked them. In America, unlike Israel, the overriding issue of Jewish life was precisely the legitimacy of all branches, and the attack on a mixed congregation symbolized an attack on the authenticity of non-Orthodox Judaism. This particular skirmish may have occurred at the Western Wall, but when I considered who was fighting and what they were fighting about, it was plain to me that the larger war, the war over American Jewish identity, lay six thousand miles away.

FROM THE SUBURBAN STREETS of Great Neck to the foot of the Western Wall, I have witnessed the struggle for the soul of American Jewry. It is a struggle that pits secularist against believer, denomination against denomination, gender against gender, liberal against conservative, traditionalist against modernist even within each branch. It is a struggle being waged on issues ranging from conversion standards to the peace process, from land use to the role of women in worship. It is a struggle that has torn asunder families, communities, and congregations. And beneath each specific confrontation lie the same fundamental questions. What is the definition of Jewish identity? Who decides what is authentic and legitimate Judaism? And what is the Jewish compact with America?

This civil war, while building for nearly a half-century, has reached its most furious pitch in the final years of the millennium. In November 1995, a yeshiva student named Yigal Amir assassinated Israeli Prime Minister Yitzhak Rabin amid a climate of theological approval developed partly by American rabbis. In the wake of the killing, the peace process so divided American Jews that they could not agree on whether a rally in Madison Square Garden should commemorate Rabin for his negotiated settlement with the Palestinians or demonstrate Jewish cohesion despite the controversial Oslo accords.* In March 1997, an association of ultra-Orthodox rabbis, the Agudath Harabonim, declared that the Reform and Conservative

---

* The Oslo agreement, signed by Rabin and PLO leader Yasir Arafat in September 1993, began the process of Israeli withdrawal from the territories in the West Bank and Gaza that it had conquered in the 1967 war. The initial accord led to other agreements mandating the return of additional land to the Palestinian Authority; these agreements were widely considered the prelude to Palestinian statehood.

movements, which collectively represent about two-thirds of American Jews, were "not Judaism at all." Less than three months later, the first of the *haredi* attacks on egalitarian and mostly American worshippers at the Western Wall occurred. The religious parties holding the swing votes in Prime Minister Benjamin Netanyahu's governing coalition introduced legislation to formalize the Orthodox monopoly on conversion, marriage, and burial—which is to say the entire question of "Who is a Jew?" Such was the outcry among American Jews that Netanyahu promised a national convention of 4,500 fundraisers, educators, and community leaders, "There can be no such thing as a second-class Jew."

Still, the rage and rhetoric poured forth unabated. The chancellor of the Jewish Theological Seminary, a Conservative institution, called the Orthodox Chief Rabbinate of Israel "dysfunctional" and "without a scintilla of moral worth." When the president of Yeshiva University, the epicenter of Modern Orthodoxy, endorsed a compromise solution to the conversion issue in Israel, a spokesman for Agudath Israel of America, the powerful association of ultra-Orthodox groups, denounced him as a *soneh Hashem*, a hater of God. The national director of the Anti-Defamation League, a group devoted to protecting Jews from external enemies, resigned from his own synagogue to protest what he called the rabbi's "hate-filled rhetoric." The effort to conduct a census of American Jews in 2000 was riven by dispute among scholars over just who, in a population marbled by intermarriage, could even be counted as a Jew. The Jewish Federation/United Jewish Appeal, long unrivaled as the major communal charity, suddenly was being challenged by the New Israel Fund on its left flank and the One Israel Fund, Hebron Fund, and Jerusalem Reclamation Project on its right. Even in the pages of the weekly Jewish newspaper I read at my home in central New Jersey, I could watch the fissures widening between Jews. "My father was a soldier in World War II," wrote one non-Orthodox man in a letter to the editor. "He fought against Germans. He did his part to defeat

Nazism. I'd like to know what the Orthodox community did while Jews were being murdered in Europe. What battle did they fight in?" To which a man from the ultra-Orthodox community of Lakewood replied, "My parents were working in forced labor camps for the Germans."

The demographic truth offers little reason for any rapid or amicable resolution of that struggle. America's six million Jews are pulling toward the extremes. For one of the few times in Jewish history, the forces of assimilation and segregation, secularism and fundamentalism, are simultaneously ascending. On one flank, rampant interfaith marriage and declining religious observance leave a plurality of American Jews with that husk of identity that sociologist Herbert Gans has called "symbolic ethnicity"—"Seinfeld" and a schmear, one might say. On the other side, an assertive, charismatic, and increasingly purist Orthodoxy boasts the highest birth rate within Judaism and a sense of triumphalism to match. So while fewer than half of American Jews belong to a synagogue or temple in any branch and only one in six even lights Sabbath candles, according to the 1990 National Jewish Population Survey, the number of religious day schools operated or inspired by the Orthodox simultaneously booms. Every prospective solution to the Jewish identity crisis sparks a whole new set of problems. Is the solution to assimilation the "inreach" of deepening religious practice among existing Jews, or is it the "outreach" of proselytizing and converting gentiles? Is the answer to continuity numbers or quality? In the Jewish institutional world, that argument stops just short of turning physical. Caught between, flayed from both sides, are the congregations in suburbs and urban neighborhoods that once defined the Jewish entente with America as a belief one could be both sectarian and part of a greater whole.

American Jewry, then, is not going to vanish, as a particular style of alarmist analysis would have us believe. We do well to remember the scholar Simon Rawidowicz's famous essay, "The Ever-Dying People," in which he writes, "He who studies Jewish history will readily discover that there was hardly a generation in the Diaspora that did not consider itself the final link in Israel's chain." But it was the very fear of extinction, Rawidowicz continues, that stamped every effort at revival. And indeed American Jewry is being volatilely reshaped and destabilized by the countervailing trends of Jewish renewal and Jewish dissipation.

The present struggle sets two archetypes against one another. One is unity and the other is pluralism, and both are innocuous euphemisms for more controversial agendas. As invoked by America's Orthodox Jews, "unity" means unity if all Jews act and think as we do, accepting the inerrancy of Torah and the yoke of all 613 commandments, the mitzvot. As invoked by America's non-Orthodox Jews, "pluralism" means that any variation of Judaism must be accepted by everyone, no obligations required and no questions asked. The sociologist Steven M. Cohen had described the vying camps as "transformationalists" and "survivalists," with one faction seeing Jewish identity enriched by the influence of polyglot America and the other fearing that identity's erosion for precisely the same reason. Put another way, the dueling models might be expressed as "I am what I feel" versus "I feel what I am." I am what I feel: I define the terms of my Jewish identity. I feel what I am: Judaism defines the terms of my Jewish identity. I am what I feel: Jewish ethnicity exists independent of Jewish religion. I feel what I am: Jewish ethnicity arises from Jewish religion.

To recognize how irreconcilable are these versions of Jewish identity is to understand why the civil war promises only to deepen and worsen. The Modern Orthodox rabbi Irving (Yitz) Greenberg asked in a 1986 essay, "Will there be one Jewish people by the year 2000?" He predicted, "Within decades, the Jewish people will split apart into two mutually divided, hostile groups who are unable or unwilling to marry each other." And he continued, "In the past anti-Semites built their plans on the expectation and hope that Jews will disappear. We have come to the tragic situation where good and committed

Jews are predicating their survival strategies on the disappearance of other Jews."

For six thousand years of slavery, exile, oppression, persecution, and genocide, the Jewish people endured out of a nearly sacred devotion to the concept of *Klal Yisrael*, the community of Jews. Indeed, whatever shatters Jewish community is described as a *chillul Hashem*, a desecration of God's name. At the most practical level, a succession of gentile enemies from Pharaoh to Hitler threatened Jews as an undifferentiated mass. The Marxist, the boulevardier, and the shtetl rabbi died alike in the gas chambers, and the lesson, as the renowned American Orthodox rabbi Joseph Soloveitchik expressed it, was that in a hostile world all Jews were joined by a *brit goral*, a covenant of common fate.

Why is it, then, that the ancient bond no longer holds in modern America? Why is it that the most comfortable, secure, and prosperous Jewish community in history is also one of the most fractious? Three causes emerged during my research, and they underlay much of the human conflict I will describe in these pages.

First, far from unifying American Jews, Israel now divides them on both political and religious grounds. Israel's own schism over the peace process is mirrored in this country, provoking anguished debate, philanthropic competition, and violent acts of terror. Simultaneously, the issue of who is a Jew has become more contentious than ever, as both Benjamin Netanyahu and his successor Ehud Barak have relied on Orthodox parties for the pivotal votes in their Knesset majorities. By accepting continued Orthodox dominion over Jewish status in exchange for support on political issues, both Labor and Likud governments have estranged and antagonized the non-Orthodox Jews who comprise about 90 percent of American Jewry.

Second, neither America nor the larger world presents Jews with a single foe against whom to coalesce. Egypt and Jordan, two of the aggressors in the wars of 1948, 1967, and 1973, have established diplomatic relations with Israel. Even Yasir Arafat, the despised guerrilla, is now a partner in the peace process. The former Soviet Union, for twenty-five years the Jim Crow South in American Jewry's equivalent to the civil rights movement, has allowed more than seven hundred thousand Jews to emigrate. Disowned by his former allies in Republican and conservative circles, Patrick Buchanan has moved outside the two-party system entirely with his complaints about Israel's "amen corner" in Congress and criticism of America for fighting Hitler in World War II. The Christian Right, largely for millennialist reasons of its own, stands as a bulwark of support for Israel. When white supremacists burned synagogues in Sacramento and opened fire on a Jewish community center in suburban Los Angeles, Christian churches instantly rose in condemnation. Which leaves Louis Farrakhan, blustering out all the old canards about Jewish conspiracies, and lacking both the support and the power to do anything more than bluster.

Third and finally, America has genuinely accepted Jews—not simply tolerated them as court physicians or expedient bankers who could be jettisoned in times of crisis, but literally loved them to such a degree that the intermarriage rate for American Jewry now stands at 52 percent. The 1998 election left eleven Jews serving in the Senate and twenty-three in the House of Representatives, while two others held lifetime appointments on the Supreme Court. Nothing in the diasporic past of ghettos and oppression, and nothing in the Israeli present of forming a majority culture, has prepared Jews for the phenomenon of being embraced by a diverse society. Least of all did they expect that the modern American model of cultural pluralism, a product of liberal thinking, could embolden not only the less observant Jew to join the mainstream but the fervently Orthodox Jew to resist it.

I aspire to tell the human story of the struggle for the soul of American Jewry and to tell it by the traditional Jewish means of the parable. From the Torah and Talmud, from Hasidic folktales and Borscht Belt shtick, Jews have looked to stories for insight, guidance, and even divine truth. In the past three years, I have traveled throughout America and to Israel as well, visiting synagogues and households and neighborhoods, conducting hundreds of interviews to capture the bitter battles pitting Jew against Jew. I make no claims for this book to be encyclopedic, all-encompassing. By design, I look at the tremendous discord in Israel only insofar as it bears on the American Jewish dilemma. Still, the parables in this book constitute something larger than their sum. They span nearly a half-century of modern history and take place in congregations and communities from Los Angeles to Jacksonville, from Cleveland to Denver, from Yale University in Connecticut to New York's Catskill Mountains. They consider the most urgent and divisive issues afflicting American Jewry, and it is my hope they do so with fairness and compassion. The current turmoil has not lacked for partisans and polemicists, but I have no desire to add to the decibel level. My goal is to fulfill a peculiarly Jewish mission, the mission of bearing witness.

THE STRIFE wracking American Jewry, unique though it is in many respects, also reflects a history of discord among the Chosen People. As modern Jews, we may joke of our disputatious nature: "Two Jews, three opinions." Yet this humor attests to a war between the impulses toward assimilation and separation, parochialism and universalism that goes back literally to the dawn of Jewish nationhood.

The Book of Exodus describes Moses descending from Mount Sinai with the Ten Commandments only to discover that his brother Aaron has fashioned a Golden Calf for the Jewish encampment to worship. Moses shatters the tablets and orders the faithful Levites to "put sword on thigh, go back and forth from gate to gate throughout the camp, and slay brother, neighbor and kin." Centuries later, with the Jewish land newly partitioned into southern Judea and northern Israel, the Israeli king Jeroboam reestablishes worship of the Golden Calf. His dynasty is destroyed in divine retribution. Eight hundred years after that, the Jewish people fragment into more than twenty competing sects, and the Roman army destroys the Second Temple in punishment for *sinat hinam*.

The Hebrew words for pure hatred have remained part of Jewish parlance and Jewish thought for two thousand years because events have conspired to keep them timely. The entire religion of Christianity arose from a Jewish sect that rebelled against the legalism and ritual of rabbinic Judaism and considered Jesus the Messiah whose coming Isaiah had prophesied. The lesser-known faith of Karaism began evolving in the eighth century among Jews who accepted only the Torah, not the Oral Law as formalized in the Talmud.

Three particular periods of Jewish history—the Hellenistic era, Moorish Spain, and Enlightenment Europe—provide the most striking parallels to the present moment in America. Then as now, religious tradition collided with provocative and potent secular culture, and the impact fractured the Jewish community. Many Jews in Palestine and Egypt adopted language, philosophy, and notions of civic life from the Greek colonists who settled in the wake of Alexander the Great's conquest. Under Islamic rule, Spain saw a flowering of Jewish poetry, science, and scholarship, as embodied most famously by Maimonides. The Enlightenment brought Jews in Western Europe emancipation to join larger society and the stimulus to develop a particularly Jewish hybrid of modernism and heritage called the *Haskalah*, after the Hebrew word for "understanding" or "reason." Both Reform Judaism and Modern Orthodoxy emerged from the cultural and intellectual ferment, as did the prototype of the irreligious Jew in such figures as Spinoza, Kafka, and Freud.

All of these golden eras had their own bitter internal battles, not so unlike those cracking apart American Jewry today. The Maccabees of ancient Judea, celebrated at Hanukkah for saving the Temple from Greek desecration, were a fervidly religious faction with contempt for hellenized Jews. Rabbis banned Maimonides' books for their rationalism. The yeshiva aristocracy of eighteenth-century Europe excommunicated devotees of the burgeoning Hasidic movement as "worthless and wanton men" who "worship in the most insane fashion."

Every fragile paradise, however, ended the same way— with the blood of persecution. Pogroms ravaged Alexandria early in the Common Era, destroying the most worldly and acculturated Jewish community of the ancient world. The Christian capture of Spain in the thirteenth century led to the Inquisition and the expulsion of as many as two hundred thousand Jews. On the cusp of the twentieth century, the Jews of the *Haskalah*, the Enlightenment, and the supposedly modern world learned like their ancestors in Alexandria and Spain that however they might physically escape the ghetto they would never be permitted to escape the gentile hatred that the ghetto symbolized. Their bitter lesson was the Dreyfus case—the arrest, trial, and public humiliation of a French captain named Alfred Dreyfus, the only Jew on the general staff, for having passed secrets to the Germans. Among those who attended the trial and who later saw Dreyfus in the courtyard of the Ecole Militaire as his sword was broken and uniform shorn of decorations was a young Viennese journalist, Theodore Herzl. He wrote the following year in his Zionist manifesto, *The Jewish State*, a summary of what the Diaspora had taught Jews:

> We have honestly endeavored everywhere to merge ourselves in the social life of surrounding communities and to preserve the faith of our fathers. We are not permitted to do so. In vain we are loyal patriots, our loyalty in some places running to extremes; in vain do we make the same sacrifices of life and property as our fellow-citizens; in vain do we strive to increase the fame of our native land in science and art, or her wealth by trade and commerce. In countries where we have lived for centuries we are still

cried down as strangers, and often by those whose ancestors were not yet domiciled in the land where Jews had already had the experience of suffering.

Extolling unity, the Talmud calls the Jewish people *chativah achat,* one entity in the world. Surveying history, Herzl expressed a similar idea rather more pragmatically. "Our enemies," he put it, "have made us one people without our consent." If any Jew on the globe doubted him, then the Holocaust provided the tragic proof. When the Nazis slew the secular Jew and the fundamentalist Jew with indiscriminate efficiency, they left in mass graves the evidence of what exile had meant and forever would mean for Jews. Except, of course, for the Jews in one particular nation.

AMERICA WAS ALWAYS different. It had no state religion, no medieval past. It had a constitutional commitment to equality, at least for white men, and a practical need for minds and bodies to build the nation. Free to practice their religion from the birth of the Republic, Jews achieved full political rights throughout America within decades. "For the first time," writes Marshall Sklare, the noted sociologist of American Jewry, "the fact of Jewishness became irrelevant in the public sphere." The United States elected its first Jewish governor in 1801 and its first Jewish senator in 1845. Less than a decade later, the rabbi of a Reform temple in Charleston, South Carolina, proclaimed, "This country is our Palestine."

For their part, Jewish immigrants were a self-selecting breed—united not by class or language or national origin but by the willingness to sever themselves from the theocracy of rural shtetl and urban ghetto. The first major wave, the German Jews of the mid-nineteenth century, ranged from merchants and petty tradesmen who rose by pluck to American affluence to a small, influential rabbinical elite that propounded Reform Judaism's self-conscious modernism. For the

Eastern European Jews who thronged to America more than two million strong between 1880 and 1924, immigration and with it modernization was a two-stage process. In the first step, many left their villages for cities like Warsaw and Minsk, where they often worked in factories or as merchants and tradesmen. Unlike the peasantry simultaneously streaming into America from Italy, for instance, the vast majority of Jews reached Ellis Island with literacy and urban skills, preparing them well for the pursuit of upward mobility. And a substantial, important minority, already radicalized by the pogroms, poverty, and proletarian upheavals shaking the Czarist empire, arrived here committed to various strains of Jewish socialism and in the process of developing the culture later to be dubbed *Yiddishkeit.*

The Eastern European immigrants treated religion as part of Jewish folk life, something remembered and periodically practiced, but not the organizing principle of Jewish existence. The Orthodox establishment acutely understood that, as the historian Arthur Hertzberg would later write, "Modernity is the solvent of tradition." The Christian governments of Europe, by segregating Jews, had arrogated to Jewish religious authorities much control over communal life, and such dominance could not possibly be reestablished across the ocean. It was simple enough in the shtetl, for instance, to close all Jewish shops for the Sabbath, but American cities expected Jews to work on Saturday. So while the immigrants called America the *Goldene Medinah,* the Golden Land, the rabbis who stayed behind disparaged it as the *Treif Medinah,* the Unkosher Land. Jacob David Wilkovsky, the famous rabbi of Slutzk, even traveled to New York in 1900 to plead with its Jews to come back. "It was not only home that the Jews left behind in Europe," he maintained in a speech. "It was their Torah, their Talmud, their yeshivot . . . their entire Jewish way of life."

His appeal failed utterly, and his fears were in certain respects confirmed. Contrary to the popular notion that religious observance has fallen precipitously among American Jews since the fifties, the decline occurred soon after immigration. Between 1899 and 1910, as the American Jewish population rose by one million, a mere 305 rabbis entered the United States. And on American ground, Jews flocked to college, not to the handful of rabbinical seminaries. The immigrant father clinging to synagogue and Talmud study became in the eyes of children like the novelist Anzia Yezierska an anachronism worthy of pity or ridicule. When New York's Orthodox Jews reached out to the scholarly center of Vilna in 1887 to import a chief rabbi, Jacob Joseph, his authority was so routinely ignored that when he died impoverished in 1902 he was never replaced. By 1930, only a third of American Jews belonged to a synagogue, and only a quarter of Jewish children received any religious instruction. Only a fraction of Jewish households by that time bought kosher meat or owned a kiddush cup for the Sabbath blessing. It was nearly impossible to find a *mikvah*, a ritual bath, outside New York City.

Meanwhile, it was a Jewish writer, Israel Zangwill, who coined one of the signature phrases of the American experience when he entitled a 1908 play *The Melting Pot*. Nowhere was the Jewish embrace of America more apparent than in education. Unlike their immigrant predecessors, the Irish Catholics, who created a system of parochial schools as their bulwark against Protestant acculturation, Jews consciously submitted themselves to the crucible of public education. In 1917, there existed only five religious day schools for a population of 3.5 million American Jews. A generation later, Jews comprised more than half the teaching corps in New York's public schools and 80 percent of the students at the elite City College. The first Hillel center was inspired not by a Jew but a Christian, a professor of biblical studies at the University of Illinois who was disturbed that his Jewish students knew so little of the Hebrew Bible.

Decades ago, then, the religious establishment was already confounded by the seeming indifference of American Jews. What we think of as the modern phenomenon of the "two-day-a-year Jew," who attends synagogue only on Rosh Hashanah and Yom Kippur, had attracted the indignant notice of the *American Hebrew* as early as 1905:

> They are evidences of that wretched state of religion which is symptomatic of the life of so many Jews. They are the outward display of the two-sided attitude of Jews who, all the year around, have no use for congregational worship, may even deride it, and yet when the fall holidays arrive, are not manly enough to persist in their indifference. . . . Religious indifference with them is not the result of deep and serious thinking. It is due to chronic mental and spiritual deadness.

What that editorial considered dead was actually alive and thriving. But it wasn't religion. It was ethnicity, Jewishness, a way of life that eventually came to be called *Yiddishkeit.* Born in Eastern Europe and carried to America in steerage with the immigrants, *Yiddishkeit* was less an organized movement than a sensibility. And that sensibility, as the historian Gerald Sorin has put it, "had to do with language, style, values, and behavior more than with belief." *Yiddishkeit* did not reject Judaism as much as appropriate it, treating religious tradition not as the ultimate expression of Jewish identity but as part of the raw material for it. "In our striving toward secularism, toward the separation of the national idea from religion," the historian Simon Dubnow wrote, "we aim only to negate the supremacy of religion, but we do not wish to eliminate it altogether from the people's cultural treasures." The literary critic Irving Howe described the typical Yiddishist as a "self-educated worker-intellectual still bearing the benchmarks of the Talmud Torah . . . yet fired by a vision of universal humanist culture."

Yiddishkeit possessed the combination of tools any culture needs to transmit and perpetuate itself. It had a language shared by millions of Jewish immigrants and American-born children that was so beloved they called it their *mamaloshen,* their mother tongue. It had means of communication, with some one hundred different Yiddish-language publications emerging during the peak decades of Eastern European immigration, most famously of all the *Forward.* It had social and political institutions. While immigrant Jews were abandoning their synagogues early in the twentieth century, they were flocking by the hundreds of thousands into trade unions, Zionist groups, the Workmen's Circle. Summer camps dotted the Catskills and Pennsylvania's Poconos. Yiddish theater flourished along Manhattan's Second Avenue. Two thousand of the mutual-aid societies known as *landsmanschaften* had sprung up by 1910. The Socialist party drew up to 40 percent of the presidential vote in certain Jewish districts of the Bronx and the Lower East Side. So if the affluent German Jews had counted the financiers Jacob Schiff and Felix Warburg as their heroes, then the Eastern European newcomers could point to a pantheon of their own—the writers Sholom Aleichem and Abraham Cahan; the labor leaders David Dubinsky and Sidney Hillman; the actors Jacob Adler and Maurice Schwartz.

The great paradox was that the Yiddishists depended every bit as much on the enforced cohesion of the ghetto as did the Orthodox against whom they rebelled. In the late twenties, fully 85 percent of American Jews lived in a handful of Northeastern and Midwestern cities, and usually within the same neighborhoods. The Jewish anarchist who tormented his Orthodox neighbor by carousing at a Yom Kippur ball was statistically no more likely than he to marry a gentile. The literary critic Alfred Kazin, son of a freethinker father, wrote of his childhood in the Brownsville section of Brooklyn: "We always had to be together: believers and non-believers, we were a people; I was of that people. Unthinkable to go one's way, to doubt or escape the fact that I was a Jew."

Events outside the ghetto left immigrant Jews little choice. The size and suddenness of the Eastern European influx provoked an anti-Semitic backlash that impeded Jewish progress toward the American mainstream. The decades between 1900 and 1940 saw the resurgence of the Ku Klux Klan, the lynching of Leo Frank by a Georgia mob on the mistaken belief that he had murdered a Christian girl, the virtual ending of legal immigration by Congress, and the rise of bigoted populists like Father Charles Coughlin and Gerald L. K. Smith. Covenants barred Jews from elite neighborhoods and clubs, and quotas harshly limited their presence in Ivy League colleges and white-shoe law firms.

For all that, America provided incomparably the most secure and welcoming home Jews had known since their forced dispersal by Rome after the destruction of the Second Temple. Looking across the ocean to their former homelands, American Jews saw Joseph Stalin ruling Russia and Adolf Hitler conquering Europe. Anti-Semitism in America, however noxious, remained an aberration, not a first principle. American Jews understood as much when they gave Franklin Delano Roosevelt the whopping majority of their votes, when one Bronx mother demanded that the rabbi at her son's bar mitzvah parade through the sanctuary holding a portrait of FDR alongside the Torah scrolls.

Nearing World War II, America's Jews were a liberal, city-dwelling, lower-middle-class people. The institutions of the Modern Orthodox movement were in their infancy. The movement into suburbia that would nourish Reform and Conservative congregations had not yet begun. The dominant mode of American Jewish existence, in influence if not numbers, was *Yiddishkeit*. It had shown the way to be Jewish, uncompromisingly Jewish, without being religious.

IF ONE HAD TO DATE the beginning of the current struggle over American Jewish identity, then it might well be Passover eve in 1941. On that day, an Orthodox rabbi named Aaron Kotler reached New York as a refugee from the cataclysms in Europe. The scion of a renowned rabbinical family, the head of the yeshiva in Slutzk, Poland, and the youngest member of the

Council of Sages and Scholars, the preeminent body of East European Orthodoxy, Kotler had fled into Lithuania seeking escape from both the Russian and German armies. Only the ceaseless lobbying of Orthodox Jews in America secured for Kotler one of the precious emergency visitors visas issued by President Roosevelt himself.

Kotler typified the Orthodox clergy and laity who considered America the *Treif Medinah*, who had persevered in Europe through pogroms and expulsions, survived the hatred of Christians who believed that Jews not only had killed Christ but slew little babies to use their blood in Passover matzoh. For them, a golden age was not one that offered liberation but one that afforded peaceful isolation; their homeland was not a place but what the Talmud called "the four cubits of *halakhah*," the body of Jewish religious law. Were it not for the impending Holocaust, in other words, Aaron Kotler might never have touched these shores. But he did, and he stayed, and he entered the atmosphere of American Jewry like a charged ion, challenging and discomfiting the established community by a principled refusal to compromise. "Torah is above time and space," he said once, "and if the American context is not cause for undermining Torah's integrity, neither does it give reason to alter the character of the yeshiva."

Within two years of arriving in the United States, Kotler opened a yeshiva on the classic European model called the Beit Medrash Gevoha in the fading resort town of Lakewood, New Jersey. From an initial dozen students, the academy grew to 450 in 1971 and 760 from 22 states and 14 countries by 1979. His alumni went on to lead yeshivot and rabbinical colleges of their own in Philadelphia, St. Louis, and Denver, and to help establish Talmudic centers in Los Angeles and Detroit and operate several Orthodox publishing houses. Like the religious minorities that had founded America, Rabbi Kotler and his followers used its freedom to segregate themselves and preserve their ways.

Nor was Kotler alone in reviving the yeshiva world on American ground. From the remnants of European Jewry, other Orthodox scholars and rabbis emigrated with the same fierce, desperate passion to recreate in the New World what the Nazis had sought to incinerate in the Old, and thus to prove it was God and Torah that once more had permitted Jews to survive. In Brooklyn neighborhoods, Abraham Kalmanowitz established the Mirrer Yeshiva, named for his former academy in the Russian town of Mir, and Joel Teitelbaum replanted the Satmar Hasidic dynasty he led as grand rabbi. Chaim Mordechai Katz and Elijah Meir Bloch, driven from their yeshiva in Telz, Romania, founded in Cleveland a successor they called Telshe.

All told, fewer than a hundred thousand Orthodox Jews entered the United States in the generation after the war, and yet their effects were profound. "Only the religious believers had a clear and unshakable answer to the question of why be a Jew," Arthur Hertzberg has written, and these particular believers "asserted the most uncompromising, separatist version of the Jewish religion." The effect of the refugee influx on Orthodoxy is a subject to be treated at length later in this book. For now, let us consider its influence more generally in the aftermath of World War II and the Holocaust. For the first time in modern American history, the secular, humanistic impulse of American Jewry, as expressed most powerfully by *Yiddishkeit*, faced the challenge of a vibrant, charismatic, and almost completely antithetical belief system with institutions and folkways of its own. The Yiddishists and most other American Jews surely thought they had left all that behind in Europe decades earlier.

At the same time, *Yiddishkeit* was being undermined by another unexpected factor: affluence. The postwar economic boom lifted millions of Americans into the suburban middle class. For Jews, the passage was speeded by the collapse of anti-Semitic quotas and covenants, which looked positively un-

American after the Holocaust. Between 1940 and 1957, the share of Jews in white-collar jobs soared from 10 percent to 55 percent. One-third of the American Jewish population moved from cities to suburbs in the twenty-year period after World War II. In the process, they spent an estimated $1 billion building a thousand new synagogues, the overwhelming majority of them in the Conservative and Reform branches. The Conservative movement in 1950 bent religious law to demographic reality and allowed members to drive on the Sabbath. Sixty percent of American Jews were affiliated with a synagogue in 1960, three times the level in 1930, even as religious observance remained static at the low level it had sunk to in the twenties. With their clubs and sisterhoods and fund-raising dinners, these institutions were updated, polished versions of the immigrant *landsmanschaften* as much as they were houses of worship. Yet if in many ways the burgeoning style of Judaism was "belonging without believing," in the Reform scholar Eugene Borowitz's phrase, then it is also true that, as the sociologist Chaim Waxman argues, synagogue membership was an acknowledgment that religion was what conferred identity on a Jew. And that proposition, of course, stood in counterposition to *Yiddishkeit*.

Beneath its placid surface, then, postwar American Jewry was roiling. Philip Roth captured the turbulence in his 1959 short story, "Eli, the Fanatic." The Eli of the title is a lawyer who has just moved into a largely gentile suburb, only to discover to his shock that two Holocaust survivors are operating a yeshiva in a tumbledown house. One of them, even worse, strolls through town in the black garments of a Hasid. On behalf of the suburb's Jews, all of them ashamed at this vestige of the shtetl past, Eli tries to persuade the survivors to comply with local laws, if not move out altogether. Ultimately he settles for donating a business suit that the old man can wear on his strolls. Shortly thereafter, Eli finds a bundle of Hasidic clothing on his porch. After he puts it on, strangely drawn to its ancient integrity, he is whisked off to a mental hospital.

What Roth rendered as farce, the Jewish movement into the suburban mainstream, Irving Howe perceived as tragedy. In the final pages of his masterpiece, *World of Our Fathers*, he wrote:

> America exacted a price. Not that it "demanded" that immigrant Jews repudiate their past, their religion, or their culture; not that it "insisted" they give up the marks of their spiritual distinctiveness. American society, by its very nature, simply made it all but impossible for the culture of Yiddish to survive. It set for the east European Jews a trap or lure of the most pleasant kind. It allowed the Jews a life far more "normal" than anything their most visionary programs had foreseen and all it asked—it did not even ask, it merely rendered easy and persuasive—was that the Jews surrender their collective self. This surrender did not occur dramatically, at a moment of high tension. It took place gradually, almost imperceptibly. . . .

It took place, among other settings, at a Labor Zionist summer camp in the Catskill foothills. There, as much as anywhere, the paths of Orthodoxy and secularism crossed, the one asserting itself, the other deteriorating. And in those dynamics lay the essential preconditions for the coming civil war.

CHAPTER ONE

Camp Kinderwelt, New York, 1963

O<small>N THOSE LAST STIFLING NIGHTS</small> of June 1963, Sharon Levine found herself wakeful in a familiar way. She left her bedroom in the Newark house shared by several branches of her extended family and repaired to the glider on the back porch, a Howard Fast novel in hand. The temperature had hung in the nineties all week, prompting kids all over the city to pry open hydrants, stirring Sharon's father Jack to install the window fans. Sharon herself thought the heat almost comfortable. Heat meant summer. Summer meant Camp Kinderwelt. And the prospect of two months at Camp Kinderwelt, as always, made her sleepless with anticipation.

She was seventeen now, a week out of Weequahic High School, skinny and dreamy and often ill at ease as the daughter of Old World parents, immigrants with accents they weren't about to lose in middle age. Even in a Jewish enclave, her friends were the children of salesmen and doctors, people who played Perry Como records and served Twinkies for dessert. Her boyfriend, Richie, was a detective in his early twenties. It

was Kinderwelt that reconciled Sharon to her parents' world—
its Yiddish, its Zionism, its sense of Jewishness without religion—and instilled in her something like direction. "The
summer was my life," she would put it later. "The rest of the
year was the time between summers."

On the last morning of June, Jack packed his used
Chevy for the trip to camp. He angled Sharon's footlocker into
the trunk, tying down the hood with twine. In the back seat, his
wife Pauline settled herself and a plaid cooler full of tuna sand-
wiches. Sharon took the front seat, next to Jack, her favorite
place on these drives. She loved when he pushed the speed,
making her mother cry over the rushing air, "Slow down, slow
down." In such moments, Sharon glimpsed the Jack Levine beyond the struggling wholesaler of candy and cigarettes, beyond
the mourning son of a family he could not save from Hitler.
She saw the would-be pioneer who subscribed to *Yidisher Kem-
fer*, the Jewish Fighter.

The trip to Kinderwelt, though, was usually a fitful affair, sixty miles that could take four hours. First Jack stopped by
his warehouse in Down Neck, across the city. Then he tried out
the back roads through North Jersey, anything to avoid the
crawl toward the mountains on Route 17. Eventually there was
no choice but to join it, stopping halfway for ice cream and the
bathroom at the Red Apple Rest, then climbing along narrow
twisting roads into the Catskill foothills, past dairy farms and
through hamlets like Central Valley and Highland Mills. Amid
such unlikely environs sprawled 250 acres owned by the Farband, the Labor Zionist Order, with the land split between
Kinderwelt and the adults' Unser Camp. Scattered along the
fringes of Unser Camp, in turn, were bungalow colonies
named Tel Aviv and Ra'anannah in solidarity with Israel.

When the Levines' car pulled between the stone pillars
and up the long driveway beneath arching trees, Sharon looked
for the landmarks. The green shingled building—that was the
Casino, Unser Camp's stage for Yiddish theater stars like Ben
Bonus and Mina Bern. A couple hundred yards later, the old

stone water tower came into sight, marking the entrance to Kinderwelt. From there, in a hillside meadow, Sharon spotted the social hall called Beth Sholom, the arts-and-crafts building with a map of Israel painted on the roof, the bunkhouses white-washed and perched on cinder blocks, and the asphalt path separating the boys' side from the girls' that was called "the Mason-Dixon Line."

Five, six, seven buses idled back in the Unser Camp parking lot, disgorging forty or fifty campers apiece. As a junior counselor, Sharon waded into the mob, helping to sort the kids by bunk, finding her own contingent of nine-year-old girls, then trying to march the ragged line off to its quarters. There the scrambling began—for the trunks piled on the porch, for the cot with the softest pillow, for the movable cubbie instead of the nailed-in kind. By three o'clock, the entire camp, nearly four hundred strong, was thronging to the chestnut tree for afternoon milk and then racing to the lake for general swim. Gazing on the joyful chaos, the grown-ups shrugged and muttered *Hefker-pefker,* anything goes.

In the hubbub, Sharon sought her cherished friends, her bunkmates from the last six summers. Tami Heringman had come again, all the way from Terre Haute, Indiana, and Myra Graubard from the West Bronx and Gloria Freed from Sheepshead Bay and Merry Levy from Kew Gardens and Judi Schulman from Merrick, Long Island. They had been the core, these five girls and Sharon, leading the volleyball team and setting their hair in curlers and harmonizing on "In the Still of the Night." They had learned the facts of life together as twelve-year-olds, getting a whispered lesson after lights-out from their daring counselor Zena. They all remembered the time Judi's mother had caught them smoking the summer they were fourteen and Judi calmly offered, "Have a Kent?"

Much more than the usual teenage rites tied them. "The same values, the same ethos, the same upbringing," Sharon would later say. All their families had been Labor Zionists for generations. Tami's grandfather Hyman had helped found Kinderwelt in the twenties; he still summered in a bun-galow nearby with his petite wife Minnie, whom everyone called "Rocky." Myra's parents had met as Kinderwelt campers. Sharon's older sister Lorelei and her future husband, Milt, began courting as camp waiters. And Judi's father, a longshore-man before he went into labor law, had raised money for Pales-tine among his companions along the docks.

They were being raised for the cause, these girls, for the Zionist enterprise. Each summer at Kinderwelt followed a theme; two summers ago, on the thirteenth anniversary of Jew-ish statehood, it had been "Israel's bar mitzvah." Sharon learned the folk dances of the kibbutzim, all about tilling the soil and wringing water from the desert. *Ahlay uvnay*, went one chant, arise and build. In the *Makelah* chorus, she sang not only the Yiddish lullabies like "Rozhinkes mit Mandlen" ("Almonds and Raisins") but the Israeli army anthem, "Shir Hapalmach," with its vow in reborn Hebrew:

> *Mimetula ad hanegev*
> *Min hayam ad hamidbar:*
> *Kol bachur vetov laneshek*
> *Kol bachur al hamishmar*
>
> *From Metula to the Negev,*
> *From the sea to the desert:*
> *Every boy is good with a gun,*
> *Every boy on his guard duty.*

For now, Sharon would not see any guard duty beyond her occasional stint of *vacht*, night patrol against curfew viola-tions and panty raids. Still, the idea of making *aliyah* informed the very atmosphere of Kinderwelt, and if not actually emigrat-ing then of serving as some kind of American partner. So many of the leaders of Israel—David Ben-Gurion, Itzhak Ben-Tzvi, Golda Meir—had emerged from the same cluster of Labor Zionist groups as had the Kinderwelt community. Parents of

Jack Levine's age had heard Israel's founders speak at the camp. And now, with Israel a secure state and America a country of proven tolerance, what stood in the way of the triumph of a new Jewish culture, secular and liberal and enlightened?

Just a few weeks before taking Sharon to Kinderwelt, Jack had attended a vast rally in Newark to celebrate the fifteenth anniversary of Israeli statehood. Six thousand people filled the Sussex Avenue Armory, and many weren't even Jewish. There were Marines, black civil rights leaders, a Catholic church's drum and bugle corps. The mayor, both senators, and the governor attended. And they all heard the Israeli ambassador to the United Nations declare, "Nobody's going to put us out of business."

The actors once limited to the Yiddish theater were breaking into the mainstream, being discovered by an audience far beyond Second Avenue's. The summer of 1963 found Morris Carnovsky essaying King Lear at the American Shakespeare Festival, Zero Mostel winning a Tony for *A Funny Thing Happened on the Way to the Forum*, Menasha Skulnik mugging his way through *Come Blow Your Horn* in Westchester, Wasp Westchester of all places. *Seventeen* magazine, that bible of pop culture for teenage girls, had even recommended a record of Yiddish folk songs.

Sharon Levine had surprised herself by convincing three of her girlfriends from Newark, all Jewish but none of Farband lineage, to pass up the traditional Weequahic summer at Bradley Beach for the quirkier charms of Kinderwelt. So if Sharon felt there was no reason to choose—between Israel and America, between Jewish identity and American birthright, between "Runaround Sue" and "Mayim, Mayim," between the fantasies of marrying Richie the cop or that handsome Rishon Bialer, her Kinderwelt boyfriend last summer, who always played Theodore Herzl in the camp's historical pageants— then she was just understanding the world around her. On the morning after arriving at Kinderwelt, after all, she had lined up with the rest of the camp to pledge allegiance to two flags, first the Stars and Stripes and then, hanging ever so imperceptibly lower, the Israeli blue and white.

ALL THROUGH Sharon's childhood, her father insisted on little. If anything, Jack struck her as compliant to a fault—living in his in-laws' house, working for their wealthy relatives, dismissing any hint of vanity by remarking, "Why do I need two pairs of shoes for one pair of feet?" He reminded Sharon of the character in the Y. L. Peretz story "Bontsche Shvayg," the humble man summoned to heaven to sit at God's side and offered by the Almighty any wish. He asks only for a hot roll every morning, and God and the angels hang their heads in sorrow at what life had done to him.

On the subjects of Zionism and *Yiddishkeit*, though, Jack Levine suffered no hesitation. Each time Sharon entered the kitchen, she reached into her pocket for coins, and dropped them in the slot of the blue-and-white tin of the Jewish National Fund. Five afternoons a week, she attended a *folkshul* called Bet Yeled, the House of Children, where she learned Jewish culture, conversational Hebrew, and Zionist ideology. She resisted the place, a rickety frame house with crooked stairs, and she resisted the classes, so different from the conventional Hebrew schools her friends attended in preparation for splashy bar or bat mitzvahs. Yet, she would say later, some learning stayed with her by a function of osmosis, or perhaps by the force of a will Jack otherwise kept well hidden.

He had embraced Zionism soon after emigrating from the Polish shtetl of Butka at the age of fifteen in 1920, leaving behind the Orthodox ways he had learned both at home and in the one-room religious school called a *cheder*. He returned to his family once in the thirties, pleading with them to join him in America. Too irreligious, they replied. Their deaths in the Holocaust deepened Jack's belief in the necessity of a Jewish homeland. And Pauline's family, inclined toward the Communist party, brought into his life a fierce critique of religion.

After the Nazi genocide, Jack didn't have to be Marx to wonder what had happened to God.

The Levines believed in art and ideas. Jack quoted from Maimonides in Hebrew, and on the Saturdays when observant Jews went to synagogue, he set the family radio to the Metropolitan Opera. Pauline educated herself about vitamins and health foods, sneaking pureed green beans into her children's orange juice. Her brother David prepared for *aliyah* by training in agriculture at the *hachsharah*, the preparation camp in South Jersey. Molly Gen, matriarch of the extended family, was no *bubbe* in a babushka but a modern woman who flourished a cigarette holder and presided over a monthly salon in the living room. The Levines may have strained to pay the rent, needing money both from Jack's candy orders and Pauline's cottage industry peddling pajamas at flea markets, but they held themselves above the *proster menschen*, the common boors.

In Newark, the Levines had company in their passions, particularly Jack's Labor Zionism. Known as the "Workshop of the Nation," Newark was a union town, populated by smelters and fur cutters, electricians and garment workers and leather tanners. And Newark was a Jewish town, home in 1948 to 56,000 Jews, the seventh-largest such community in America. Newark's Jews supported institutions ranging from two Yiddish weeklies to a rabbinical college to Tabatchnik the Herring King. At Weequahic High, the alumnus and novelist Philip Roth recalled, the football backfield consisted of Weissman, Weiss, Gold, and Rosenberg.

"All the ingredients were there," the historian William Helmreich has written about Newark's concentration of leftist Jewish groups, which included active branches of the Bund and the Workmen's Circle as well as Labor Zionists. "Poverty, conflict between labor and management, Jewish intellectualism, and the well-known Jewish passion for social justice."

Four generations enlisted in the Labor Zionist cause: the children in the Habonim youth movement, the young adults in the Dorot Zion, and the parents and grandparents in the Poale Zion. Wives and daughters joined their own chapters of the Pioneer Women. The Farband functioned as a communal parallel to the politicized Poale Zion, providing members with insurance and burial plans and, of course, the chance to vacation at Unser Camp and Kinderwelt. It did what the mutual-aid societies called *landsmanschaften* had long done for Jewish immigrants, but in this case what bound the constituents together was not a common birthplace in Europe but a common cause in Palestine.

Jack Levine served as secretary for the Habonim in New Jersey, a board member of the Bet Yeled school, a regular in a Yiddish literature discussion group, and a mainstay of the Farband, Sholom Aleichem Chapter 59. His contemporaries counted themselves among the Labor Zionist elite, the men who proudly called one another *chaver*, comrade. Ralph Wechsler was an intimate of Ben-Gurion's. Ralph Goldman assisted the Israeli prime minister on his visits to the United States. When Israel mounted a trade exhibition in America in 1963, it held the exposition at the Chancellor Avenue YMHA, a block from the Levines' house.

For a dollar a year, Jack absorbed the Labor Zionist creed from the pages of *Jewish Frontier*, the movement's English-language magazine. He read essays on Zionism by Ben-Gurion, Chaim Weizmann, and even Albert Einstein. Poems rhapsodized about "The Blooming Desert," and photos celebrated the *chalutzim*, the pioneers, erecting tent cities and taking spades to the earth. *Jewish Frontier* went beyond Palestine and purely Jewish issues, too, publishing Mahatma Gandhi on apartheid, Claude McKay on civil rights, Reinhold Niebuhr on anti-Communist liberalism. On paper at least, the parochial and universal aspects of Jewish radicalism coexisted under the banner of the working class.

Once Israeli nationhood and American pluralism had been achieved in the wake of World War II, however, the tone of *Jewish Frontier* turned oddly cautionary. An article in the

March 1953 issue, by a mother abashed enough to hide behind the byline "Anonymous," bemoaned her son's impending interfaith marriage, one of ten in her extended family. The following year, Ben-Gurion dismissed Zionism without *aliyah* as merely a fund-raising operation, unworthy of "the name of a Movement of Redemption." *Jewish Frontier* itself filled column inches with advertisements for Israel Bonds, imprecations to "Convert Commitments Into Cash."

A decade later, as Sharon was nearing her summer as a junior counselor at Kinderwelt, *Jewish Frontier* chronicled a movement—indeed, a way of life—in the midst of an identity crisis. The magazine, once a beacon of secularism, began writing approvingly of religious practice. It reported that Yiddish, earlier in the century the language of two-thirds of the world's Jews, was now spoken by only one-tenth of Jewish students. Immigration to Israel had failed to replace that lost culture, at least for American Jews. These days, Labor Zionists organized not settlers' brigades but tours on El Al. "The builders of the Land and the State are only those who dwell and live within it," Ben-Gurion insisted in a letter marking his seventy-fifth birthday. "In the Diaspora, Jews as Jews are human dust, whose particles try to cling to each other."

But as a writer named Yaacov Morris put it, "Middle-class Americans are not likely to become farmers and miners in the Negev." And the advertisements in *Jewish Frontier* in the summer of 1963 showed just how middle-class American Jews, even the Farband sort, were becoming. The fancy Catskills resorts touted "Free Golf," "New Elevator," "Catalina Pool and Health Club," "Solarium," "Supervised Children's Day Camp." Newark's own Jerry Lewis declared Brown's "my favorite hotel." While Labor Zionists understood the word *aliyah* to mean immigration to Israel, it literally translated as "ascent." And ascending they were, toward the good life in the Golden Land.

• •

FROM THAT FIRST MORNING in July 1963 when Sharon joined all of Kinderwelt in singing "The Star-Spangled Banner" and then "Hatikvah," "The Hope," camp slid into its predictable, comforting rhythms. From reveille at seven to taps at nine, from mail call to milk time, tradition guided her days. The first week of summer was dominated as always by swimming tests to see which children merited their deep-water badge. The fourth would end in visiting weekend, with all its parental kibitzing. And in the last weeks of August would come Color War, with the camp divided into *Kachol* and *Lavan*, blue and white, like the Israeli flag.

Meanwhile, the brilliant July sun of a drought summer browned the campers like the kibbutzniks they emulated. The Kinderwelt Knesset, named after the Israeli parliament, took office to weigh such matters as the relative merits of field trips to West Point and Hyde Park. Each day an imitation newscast over the camp loudspeaker brought Kinderwelt dispatches from the Jewish Telegraphic Agency—Egypt and Syria forming the United Arab Republic, Israeli farmers being murdered in border ambushes, the army shelling in retaliation.

As for Sharon, she danced to "El Ginot Egoz" in Beth Sholom, the social hall named for Tami Heringman's late uncle. She led her campers to the summit of Schunnemunk Mountain. She anchored the volleyball team in its matches against Kindering, the Workmen's Circle camp, and Habonim—always an easy win for Kinderwelt because the kids there were too busy raising crops and livestock in preparation for *chalutz* life to spend much time practicing a sport.

In the several hours each night between bedtime for her nine-year-olds and the counselors' eleven-thirty curfew, Sharon joined Tami and Gloria and Myra in putting their curlers to use on the flips and bouffants that were the season's vogue. They turned their transistor radios to Murray the K's Swingin' Soiree and turned their a cappella talents to the summer's first hit, "It's My Party." They walked into nearby Woodbury for movies, hitched to Monroe for ice cream at the diner, went to Newburgh on their day off for *David and Lisa*, a sensitive teenager's kind of romance.

Still, Sharon and her friends could not avoid noticing some disquieting changes at Kinderwelt. There were empty bunks, as many as four or six in a cabin built for twelve, in the younger groups, like the five-year-olds Gloria oversaw. Grass sprouted through cracks in the tennis courts, and the asphalt buckled on the basketball court where Sharon watched the college guys play pick-up games. Kinderwelt's maintenance crew had always been less than fastidious, so now the camp director's wife followed in their wake, scrubbing and sweeping and disinfecting. A ten-year-old camper named Joel occasionally fixed toilets. Sharon and her cheekier companions sang the camp hymn with a twist. Where the words were supposed to be "Kinderwelt iz shayn un sunik," Kinderwelt is nice and sunny, they made it "shayn un schmutzik"—nice and dirty.

The satire poked at an uncomfortable truth, one that had much to do with the empty bunks in Myra's cabin. Kinderwelt was starting to lose its clientele, and with it the fees that paid for upkeep. The Farband had split along generational lines in apportioning its budget, and the greatest infusion of money went to Unser Camp, to build a hotel meant to compete with Brown's and Grossinger's. No longer able to fill its beds by word of mouth, Kinderwelt had resorted to shooting a promotional film and sending a recruiter door to door among the families of Holocaust survivors. Whatever their feelings about Zionism and secularism, they at least spoke Yiddish.

For Sharon and her crowd, the city was still home—Weequahic, with Wigler's Bakery and Halem's candy store and the Chancellor Avenue Y. But she was the youngest daughter of parents nearing fifty, the urban remnant of a Jewish population climbing, like Neil Klugman in Philip Roth's *Goodbye, Columbus*, into the once-gentile suburbs. The allrightniks' ambitions exceeded a camp with Second Avenue schmaltz and a lopsided softball field. In any issue of the *New York Times Magazine* in the spring of 1963, they could have found pages of advertisements for camps named Iroquois, Beaverbrook, and Lincoln Farm, camps with horseback riding, water skiing, indoor basketball courts, scuba diving, French lessons.* Every time Sharon played volleyball against Camp Monroe, the one member of Kinderwelt's league not operated by a secular Jewish organization, she saw in its facilities a competitor in more than sporting terms.

Sharon had to admit that some of Kinderwelt struck even her adoring eyes as dated. For years, campers had spent an hour each day in *sicha*—Hebrew for discussion—learning about the shtetl or Jewish art or Zionist heroes like Herzl. Sharon found the sessions sheer tedium. Every few weeks, she had to herd her unwilling charges to a shaded grove in Unser Camp to hear some *alter kocker*, some old-timer, fulminate in Yiddish few of the children understood. In earlier decades, Kinderwelt's youngsters had listened to Abba Eban and Golda Meir orate in the *Literarisher Vinkl*, the Literary Corner, and been exhilarated by the experience. Sharon and her peers, who could not remember a world without Israel, dismissed the place as the *Narrish Vinkl*, the Foolish Corner. Ironically, they were using a variation of the same Yiddish term—*narrishkeit*, foolishness—that their parents hurled at their taste for *Gidget* movies and rock and roll.

What exactly was there beyond the confines of Jewish life? Six weeks shy of her eighteenth birthday, Sharon still wasn't sure. "Everything in my family was related to being Jewish," she would say years later. "If Adlai Stevenson was running for president, was it good for the Jews? If there was a murder in Newark, then it shouldn't be a Jew who committed it. You knew you'd marry a Jewish person. You knew you'd have a Jewish life."

---

* In one of his most famous and most trenchant jokes, the comic Henny Youngman observed, "Camp Hiawatha, Camp Seneca—that's where the Jewish kids go for the summer. Camp Ginsburg is where the Indian kids go."

But last summer, when she kept company with Rishon Bialer, Sharon had begun to glimpse other possibilities. In some ways, Rishon was consummately Jewish, educated in a yeshiva, now majoring in premed at Brandeis. Yet he and his buddies among the waiters and athletic staff—Artie Eisenberg, Hesh Josephson, Vic Fershko—possessed a sophistication that impressed Sharon. Instead of the typical camp play like *The King and I*, in which Sharon had played a secondary role, they put on Edward Albee's *Zoo Story*. They listened to Tom Lehrer records, watched "That Was the Week That Was," knew enough to call it "TW3" in the Morse code of hip.

This year, with Rishon no longer at Kinderwelt, the intellectual crowd centered around Vic Fershko, Gloria Freed's boyfriend, and his single room in the rafters of the old social hall. Peter, Paul and Mary, whose folk music was already a staple of Kinderwelt campfires, had just covered Bob Dylan's "Blowin' in the Wind," sending a protest song high enough on the charts to challenge "Surf City." President Kennedy negotiated a test-ban treaty with Khrushchev. Buddhist monks cremated themselves in the streets of Saigon to protest the South Vietnamese regime. The civil rights movement was building toward a rally outside the Lincoln Memorial on August 28, a few days after Kinderwelt's season would end. Myra Graubard and her friend Marty Greenfield planned to be there. Here was a bigger vision, Sharon would later put it, "than the Zionist idea of brotherhood."

As the wider world enticed Sharon in one direction, religion beckoned from another. The call came in the person of the camp director, Eli Gamliel. By almost any measure, he was an outsider to Kinderwelt's culture, which was rooted in the radical movements of Eastern Europe. Gamliel hailed from Yemenite stock, the Sephardic side of Jewry, and had grown up in Israel and America deeply observant. He had attended the Talmudical Academy high school and Yeshiva University, both Orthodox institutions, and had taught in day schools and Hebrew schools affiliated with synagogues. Though he had married into a Labor Zionist family and spent summers emceeing shows at the Unser Camp Casino, he cut a drastically different figure from such predecessors as Zvi Schooler. Gray-haired and thickly bearded, Schooler had acted in Yiddish theater and hosted a Yiddish-language radio show called "Der Graumeister," "The Storyteller." The closest he would ever get to organized religion was playing a rabbi in the film version of *Fiddler on the Roof.*

Gamliel, in contrast, presented himself as a modern man, clean-shaven, handsome in creased slacks and a white oxford shirt. And he was moving Kinderwelt in the direction Labor Zionism itself was going, however reluctantly—toward reconciliation with religion. To any Orthodox Jew, even to many Reform Jews, the practices Gamliel brought to Kinderwelt would have qualified as mere whiffs of observance. Among secular Jews, though, they represented major concessions.

From its beginnings, Kinderwelt had honored certain rituals, in the same way that even militantly atheistic Jews could not bring themselves to eat ham. The camp separated both its dishes and its meals by meat and milk, an homage to the spirit if not every letter of the dietary laws of kashrut. Each Friday pointed toward sundown and Shabbat, starting with bunk cleanup in the morning and continuing with the procession of campers, all clad in white, into the dining hall for a traditional chicken dinner. Kiddush was spoken over the grape juice, and in Sharon's time Artie Eisenberg always sang "Lecha Dodi," "Welcome Bride," the bride being the Sabbath. But nobody wore a yarmulke, and on Saturday morning instead of davening, Kinderwelt shed its shoes and whirled across the meadow in Israeli dances. "You didn't think of it as holy," Sharon's friend Judi Schulman would recall years later, "but as something clean and special and fun."

Now Gamliel gathered the camp in Beth Sholom every Saturday morning for a distilled service—the Shema, Judaism's declaration of faith; excerpts from the *parsha*, the weekly Torah portion; and the sermon known as a *d'var Torah*. "Why do we have to do this?" parents occasionally complained. He had his answer: He wouldn't subscribe to any Zionism that denied religion. Besides, the faction of campers from Holocaust survivor households tended to be quite observant. Even some of the American-born kids came from families that had returned to Judaism's rituals, if not exactly fervent faith. Sharon had always sensed that her own father longed in some unspoken way for the synagogue and the connection it offered to his vanquished family in vanished Butka. As it was, he settled for worship on the High Holy Days.

Sharon didn't even know about Tisha b'Av, for instance, until coming to Kinderwelt. There the holiday commemorating the destruction of the First and Second Temples was becoming yet another measure of religion's renewed claim on Labor Zionism. Well into the fifties, Tisha b'Av had consisted of little more than a handful of Unser Camp adults fasting and the Kinderwelt children forgoing swimming for the day. Then, toward 1960, a ritual emerged. The campers would congregate at dusk along the lake shore and watch as a wooden model of a temple was set aflame and set adrift.

By the time Tisha b'Av was commemorated on July 30, 1963, Gamliel had devised a more elaborate pageant. As the entire camp settled on the hillside between the boys' and girls' cabins, floodlights struck stage flats painted with scenes of the First Temple being destroyed by Babylonian conquerors. Then the assemblage, having rehearsed for weeks, sang "By the Rivers of Babylon" and recited verses from Psalm 137:

> If I forget thee, O Jerusalem, let my right hand wither.
>
> Let my tongue stick to my palate, if I cease to think of you, if I do not keep Jerusalem in my memory, even at my happiest hour.

More flats appeared—the Romans ravaging the Second Temple, the martyrs at Masada choosing death before captivity, and finally the modern pioneers working the land. The campers' voices rose again, this time in "Hatikvah," Israel's anthem.

In one respect, Gamliel was doing exactly what Zionists since Herzl had done, conflating Biblical symbolism with secular politics. Hadn't Ben-Gurion himself called Zionism a "Movement of Redemption"? But Ben-Gurion also was a leader who once issued a press statement announcing that he hadn't fasted on Yom Kippur, who boasted to a convention of American Orthodox rabbis that he'd been married by a justice of the peace. There had long existed a religious Zionist group, the Mizrachi. The Reform and ultra-Orthodox Jews who had opposed Zionism prior to statehood now, for the most part, adopted it. So why did the Farband, which had been right about Zionism all along, have to bend to religion? Never before had Kinderwelt's leftists and laborites sought clerical cover.

Any such concern got lost in the last dizzying weeks of camp. Just after Sharon turned eighteen on August 17, Color War broke out, splitting Kinderwelt into armies of *Kachol* and *Lavan*. Over the next four days, the teams competed in events from riflery to water polo to "Name That Tune." Bunk inspection counted for points. So did a ready knowledge of Jewish history. Neither team entered the dining hall without delivering, by way of a chant, proof that this was not any camp's version of Color War:

> *Out of exile came the Jews,*
> *Back to their land ascending,*
> *Built a state as a Jewish home,*
> *Determination unending.*
>
> *Farmers, man your guns, then return to the soil,*
> *For fighters you must be to preserve Yisrael.*
> *Elijah's spirit is here to incite us.*
> *Rise and conquer those who'd defy us.*

Color War always made Sharon feel defiant. Straining till her arms ached in the tug-of-war, swimming the winning leg of a relay race, she exulted in physicality. And Kinderwelt put her physicality in the service of something grander than mere sport; she was part of the Zionist mission to forge a new kind of Jew, the robust rejoinder to the pale, cowering product of *Galut*, the Exile.

Sharon had been rewarded over the years, not only as a teammate but as an individual. Her most precious keepsakes included five felt patches, given in the awards ceremony Kinderwelt held in its final week. Four of the patches were for achievement in music and sports and for excellence in cooperation. The fifth, larger than the rest, commended her as the outstanding camper in her bunkhouse. Its insignia bore the Yiddish letters *mem* and *kupf*, the initials for *Machnay* Kinderwelt, Camp Kinderwelt. But Sharon's friend Judi Schulman liked to say that the *mem* stood for "mensch."

Kinderwelt closed the summer of 1963 with an all-camp social, the Victory Dance. For one night, Beth Sholom doubled as a high school gym. Paper lanterns and crepe-paper ribbons dangled from the ceiling. Beneath them couples in crinolines and penny loafers slow-danced to "Theme from *A Summer Place*," one more siren song from America, one more invitation to leave the tribe and join the nation.

As the dance wound down, Sharon left Beth Sholom and walked back to her cabin in a cool drizzle. There was nothing *hefker-pefker* about camp's end. She wanted it to linger. At the foot of each bed sat a trunk, ready to be hauled back home. A few campers stopped by the arts-and-crafts building to pick up a Popsicle-stick basket or ceramic bowl that was just drying. Others hunted through the cabins for artifacts—a keychain, a necklace, a hairband. Judi Schulman always did that, cupping each find in her palms like a talisman.

Overnight, the wind picked up from the northwest, driving the clouds off the Catskills and dropping the temperature into the forties. The morning of August 24, 1963, Sharon's last at Kinderwelt, dawned with an autumnal chill. The weather told her it was time to go back to Weequahic, to start her freshman year at the Newark campus of Rutgers, to face the prosaic reality of living at home and riding the city bus to a commuter school. All she knew about her longer-term plans was that, based on her experience as a junior counselor, she didn't have enough of a disciplinarian's streak to be a teacher, the job a bright Jewish girl was supposed to take.

By the chestnut tree of Kinderwelt, not the rivers of Babylon, Sharon wept as she prepared for her own exile. "Call me," she heard people saying. "See you in the city." As buses pulled out of the Unser Camp parking lot, hands reached out every window, waving, grasping. Bitter as Sharon's parting was, she expected it to last only ten months, until next summer at Kinderwelt. To Tami and Myra and Merry and Gloria and Judi, Sharon promised, "We've all got to get together." Thirty years would pass before they did.

After a listless freshman year at Rutgers, Sharon spent the summer of 1964 not at Kinderwelt but in Israel itself, with Gloria and Judi on a Labor Zionist program. More even than touring the sights, she loved the demanding life on a kibbutz. Rising at four, riding a tractor to the fields, weeding peanuts by the hour, she craved the compliment that she worked like an Israeli, not a soft American with a checkbook. She contemplated *aliyah*, filled with an ardor for Israel so strong it made her feel almost disloyal to America. And in Israel, secular Judaism flourished; it was the culture of the land. But Sharon's boyfriend Richie was staying in Newark. She returned and ultimately married him. Rishon Bialer, having graduated from Brandeis with honors and begun Harvard Medical School, died in a car accident.

Tami Heringman, to all appearances the straight girl from Indiana, the one who used no more makeup than pale pink lipstick, prepared to give birth in early 1964. Throughout the previous summer, she had managed to hide her pregnancy, if not the fact that her boyfriend, a marine, was not Jewish. She gave up her baby girl for adoption and ultimately married an Is-raeli whom she met while living in Tel Aviv in 1968. Frightened by a series of terrorist attacks on Israel over the next several years, she decided against making *aliyah* and wound up settling with her husband in Texas.

Myra Graubard, forbidden by her mother to attend the March on Washington, married a non-Jew, a half-Spanish, half-Finnish Lutheran named Joseph whom she was set up with on a blind date. In the summer of 1972, she brought him to Kinderwelt, to show him what all the ballyhoo was about. The camp, she discovered, had closed the previous summer. Now Unser Camp was limping through its own final weeks. She took Joseph to the Casino, where they heard a comic tell jokes with Yiddish punchlines.

Later that day, as Myra was getting ready to leave, a waiter vanished while swimming. He was twenty years old, a former Kinderwelt kid. Eli Gamliel called the police, who fruitlessly dragged the lake. The next morning, the body floated to the surface. In the dining hall, three-quarters empty, the campers compared memories. No, nobody could recall any other death here, not in all forty-six years, not unless, of course, one counted Kinderwelt's own.

ONE AFTERNOON IN 1984, Myra Graubard, now a teacher and mother living about ten minutes from the abandoned site of Kinderwelt, went searching for plastic bags. She had an oddly shaped garbage can, and standard-size bags didn't fit the rim. Her husband had spotted an ad in the local paper, though, from a wholesaler open to the public. Myra checked the address and nodded with a certain recognition.

"Where are we going?" asked her daughter as they climbed into the family car.

"To the Middle Ages," Myra replied.

A few miles later, she pulled into Kiryas Joel, a village entirely populated by Satmar Hasidim. Myra had never actually been there before, but she knew well enough that the sect's members had been moving into the area by the thousands. She remembered a particular Friday at the eye doctor's, hearing a Satmarer mother who'd shown up without an appointment demanding that her son be seen before *Shabbos*. Whenever a gentile mocked the Hasidim, Myra reflexively defended them. Privately, however, she blamed the Satmarers and their clannish ways for giving anti-Semites ammunition.

Now, waiting in the car while her husband bought the garbage bags, she shuddered with self-consciousness. On both sides of the street, apartments clung to hillsides, packed tightly as pueblos carved into a cliff. Mothers in cuffed blouses and wigs nudged boys trailing *peyes* and tzitzis. The men, each a study in black, stepped toward synagogue. And here sat Myra, married to a gentile man, a *shaygetz*, wearing a sleeveless dress, thinking back to 1968 in Mea Shearim, the ultra-Orthodox section of Jerusalem, and the black-hats shoving her aside for wearing a mini-skirt. "I feel I don't belong," she told herself now. "I know I don't belong."

Most incredible of all, and most maddening, Kiryas Joel stood just two miles from Kinderwelt. As a camper, Myra had hitched to Monroe along Forest Road, which now ran right through Kiryas Joel. And while Kinderwelt lay empty, a paradise overgrown and rotted, Kiryas Joel flaunted its continuity with strollers and swing sets and station wagons. Yiddish, once the language of secular strongholds like Kinderwelt, was the lingua franca here, the characters on every billboard, the type in every newspaper, the sound in every chat. Kiryas Joel was doing the very thing at which Kinderwelt had finally failed—transmitting its culture from one generation to the next. That culture centered on religion and deemed Zionism blasphemy. Kiryas Joel embodied everything Kinderwelt was and everything it wasn't.

The village had its origins in 1972, the year after Kinderwelt closed, when a Canadian importer wearing a business suit and a baseball cap appeared in Monroe to buy land.

Though not Hasidic himself, he was the brother-in-law of a Brooklyn man named Leibush Lefkowitz, who was a close aide to Rabbi Joel Teitelbaum, rebbe of the Satmar Hasidim. And though the Canadian spoke of wanting to purchase real estate for investment purposes, he was acting in fact on behalf of the rebbe's wish to build a shtetl far from the immoral city, to create a place, as a Satmar leader later put it, "where you can live in the way you lived in Europe a hundred years ago."

The need for subterfuge was understandable, at least to the Satmarers. A decade earlier, they had spent nearly a million dollars on 250 acres of land in New Jersey, all aboveboard. The community had fought them on every last permit and regulation, and the Satmarers filed suit before finally giving up. So when they saw an appealing 170 acres near Monroe, they sent a trusted outsider willing for the day to wear a baseball cap instead of his usual yarmulke.

Over the next two years, other intermediaries bought more land—fifty-seven acres, then forty-four, then fourteen. Plans were drawn for eighty garden apartments and twenty-five single-family homes. A particular design feature distinguished the units; each would have dual sinks and stoves to allow for strict separation of meat and milk. Various basements would house a yeshiva and a *mikvah*, and the garage of Rabbi Teitelbaum's home would serve as a *shtibel*, an intimate synagogue. A construction company run by Leibush Lefkowitz broke ground early in 1974, and by Sukkot that fall, the first dozen families moved into Kiryas Joel, Joel's Town.

Those early arrivals included Abraham Wieder, a contemporary of Sharon Levine and Myra Graubard from the far side of the Jewish universe. Wieder's parents had lived near the Satmar capital of Satu-Mare, Romania, until the Nazis and their Hungarian collaborators decimated the region. Like Rabbi Teitelbaum, the Wieders were among the handful of Satmarers to survive the Holocaust and try to reconstitute shtetl life in the alien cities of North America. As the rebbe settled in Brooklyn, they immigrated to Montreal, and when

Abraham was fourteen they sent him to Williamsburg to study in the rebbe's yeshiva.

There Abraham steeped himself in Talmud and Torah and *halakhah* and the Hasidic literature and philosophy known as *Hasidut.* He basked in the wisdom of his rebbe. Rabbi Teitelbaum received the faithful each afternoon as they presented him with the petitions called *kvitlech,* and he married them beneath a *chuppah* outside his own home. So when Rabbi Teitelbaum sought pioneers for Kiryas Joel, Abraham Weider, by then a father of three and the director of a job-training program, considered it *zachir,* good fortune, to fulfill the rebbe's wish. On the *Shabbos* mornings of that first autumn, he wound through the reddening trees to the *shtibel,* first to daven and then to enjoy *shalashidis,* the afternoon meal, a feast of fish and challah and song. "It was," he later recalled, "heavenlike."

The residents of Monroe, whose boundaries included Kiryas Joel, recoiled at the Hasidim in their midst. The town government charged that the Satmarers had flouted zoning laws by converting houses for religious uses and dividing one-family homes into apartments. But the most severe reactions, by all accounts, came from the local Jews. The owner of the Tel Aviv bungalow colony, unofficially part of the Farband compound, refused to sell property to the Satmarers. "I drive a car on Saturday, I smoke on Saturday," one man told a local newspaper. "What will they do to me?" A woman whose bungalow bordered Kiryas Joel announced, "They are the most horrible people that God put breath in."

Kiryas Joel solved at least its legal problems by incorporating as a village in 1977. The next year, the central synagogue opened. The year after that, the rebbe's new residence was completed. And when Rabbi Teitelbaum died the following year, he was interred in the village cemetery, and his home was turned into a maternity center for a booming community. Families moved into Kiryas Joel at the rate of a hundred a year, pushing the population from 525 in 1977 to 5,500 in 1986 and 12,000 in 1998. Households had nearly seven children apiece on average, and the village's median age of 13.8 years was the youngest in New York state.

The more populous Kiryas Joel grew, the more isolated it became, the more protected from *ausgegrunt*—literally, "the green wearing off"; colloquially, acculturation. Kiryas Joel forbade television, radio, home videos, and English-language newspapers. It supported its own florist, pizza parlor, shoe store, matzoh factory, slivovitz distillery, and sewage treatment plant. Its men commuted to jobs in Manhattan's diamond district on buses fitted with *mechitzah* to allow for davening the morning service of *Shacharit* inbound and the evening liturgy of *Maariv* on the drive home. More than anything, Kiryas Joel poured its resources into inculcating the next generation with the Satmarer way, creating a system of thirteen schools overseen by four hundred teachers and administrators and teaching five thousand children. "There is not a generation gap," one Satmar spokesman boasted. "The only generation we are missing is the one that was lost in the concentration camps, in the gas chambers, and the suffering of the post-Holocaust period. Our youth is more intensely Hasidic than their elders."

Scornful as it was of American culture, Kiryas Joel embraced American politics. In 1986, after six hundred yeshiva boys refused to board buses provided by the Monroe school district because they had women drivers, Kiryas Joel sued the local school board. It lost, started its own bus service, and set about creating its own school district altogether, primarily to allow handicapped boys and girls to be educated separately. In recognition of the village's voting bloc, New York governors and legislators of both major parties passed laws allowing Kiryas Joel to form the district. Court after court struck down the various laws, and each time Kiryas Joel appealed, driving a wedge between Orthodox and non-Orthodox Jewish groups.

Abraham Wieder, meanwhile, was elected mayor. He also learned how to manufacture wire and cable and bought a factory in Monroe. By Kiryas Joel standards, he was a worldly man. He posed for photographs in the company of governors and congressmen, received letters from them extolling the village. His business won contracts from the navy, and he traveled as deep into the Bible Belt as Alabama to meet customers. For many years, though, he never knew that a Labor Zionist summer colony had once thrived just up the road from Kiryas Joel. Once he learned of it, he was not surprised to hear that it had failed. "Secular Judaism," he said, *"is* failure."

SHARON LEVINE stepped into a Manhattan apartment one evening in October 1998, carrying her past in a stationery box. It contained her *mem kupf* award, a 1962 staff roster, the Color War schedule from 1957, a sign-out sheet for visiting day in 1963, snapshots of her bunkmates in matching tennis sweaters and Bermuda shorts. On the box top she had written simply, "Kinderwelt."

She placed the carton delicately on a coffee table beside a tray of mixed nuts and an array of yellowed, curling photographs—formal portraits of particular bunks, casual shots of shirtless boys rolling their eyes and puffing their cheeks. Already a crowd had gathered around the exhibit, reminiscing about the camp laundry and necking sessions under the Beth Sholom stage.

"See her?" one woman said, tapping a photo. "That's Zvi Schooler's daughter."

"Was Vinny your counselor?"

"You know Phyllis? This is her brother."

"Hannah Weingarten went to Israel?"

There were thirteen guests in all, representing four decades of Kinderwelt. In a room of bifocals, iron supplements, and tinted hair, Sharon was the youngest by nearly a decade, tanned and fit. Still, she was fifty-three, the mother of a son in high school and a daughter in college, a middle-aged graduate student in social work after a career in fashion design, and twenty-three years into her second marriage, to a real estate developer named Tom Elghanayan whom she'd met at Club Med.

Manny Azenberg, a theater producer, hosted the reunion. He had spent every summer from 1941 through 1954 at
Kinderwelt as a camper and counselor. His father Charles had
managed both Kinderwelt and Unser Camp before retiring to a
bungalow on the camp's fringes in Ra'anannah. Azenberg wore
a ring with the Farband insignia that his father had received in
recognition of his work as a driver for the Second Zionist Congress.

Something more complex than sentimentality had
spurred the gathering. A few months earlier, Azenberg had visited the former Kinderwelt with his camp buddy Yudi Rosen. It
was depressing enough to find the whole place razed, replaced
by a housing development called Highland Lake Estates. But
then, driving to the Monroe Diner, retracing the route they
had taken decades earlier as counselors on their days off, Azenberg and Rosen stumbled into Kiryas Joel. "Theirs is blossom-
ing," Azenberg had muttered in shock that August afternoon,
"and ours is dead."

Indeed there was an aspect of shiva to the reunion, jovial
as it was. Sharon, her sister Lorelei, her brother-in-law Milt,
and all the rest seated themselves in a living room overseen by a
Ben Shahn drawing of Gandhi. They helped themselves to a
buffet of chicken cacciatore and pasta with cheese, casually
nonkosher. They talked about their children and their choices.

"I sent my daughter to Kinderwelt and it didn't work,"
Milt Kaplan said.

"I sent my son and it didn't work," Rosen added. "I
think it was Israel. The two-thousand-year dream came true.
And we lost our reason to be."

Overhearing the exchange, Azenberg joined in.

"It was American camps," he said. "We wanted our children to be Americans. They lived in a more mixed environment than us."

Sharon perched on the edge of the conversation. How
many hours and days had she spent trying to find the equivalent
of Kinderwelt for her kids? Jessica wound up at a religious

camp with children from Conservative and Orthodox day schools. Jacob tried a Reform camp and pulled out after two weeks, bored with singing Jewish songs. From then on, he spent summers at a sports camp with friends from his private school, Dalton.

"We wanted them to have good tennis instruction," Sharon told Azenberg and the others. "We wanted them to have water skiing. We wanted them to be able to compete." She paused. "We tried to pass along something. But it was inexplicable."

Just then the front door opened and Azenberg's wife Loni and their two daughters arrived, the girls' hair still in tight buns from ballet class. Loni, a former dancer, was Azenberg's second wife. She accompanied him on the annual trips he led to Israel for theater people and had learned enough Hebrew to converse there. Still she, unlike the first Mrs. Azenberg, the one Manny had met at Kinderwelt, was not Jewish. And Azenberg, proudly secular, had not insisted she convert.

"Everything I got, I got from Kinderwelt," he said now. "And the trips I take to Israel—I make people into Zionists. But my wife isn't Jewish and, halakhically, my children aren't Jewish. And I have to take that from some rabbi with a beard down to his *pupik*? You know what my answer is?" He bent his arm ninety degrees, fist aiming upward.

Across the room stood the only parent at the reunion with reason to be sanguine about the next generation's Jewish identity. Judy Polisar had grown up Labor Zionist and raised her son Daniel in the Reform movement. When he attended Princeton, though, he adopted Orthodoxy. And after spending a year at yeshiva in Israel, he moved permanently to a settlement in the occupied West Bank. As far as such settlers were concerned, they, with their right-wing politics and Orthodox theology, were the true carriers of the Zionist creed. The Labor crowd had gone soft in north Tel Aviv, jetting to Paris for shopping weekends, raising children the West Bank pioneers ridiculed as "Hebrew-speaking gentiles."

Toward nine o'clock, dessert was served with decaffeinated coffee. Two cousins, David Diness and Josh Weiss, mentioned that they had recently visited the Kinderwelt site and come upon Kiryas Joel. Comparing dates with Azenberg and Rosen, the men realized that they had been there the same week.

"Just think of what our parents would've thought of the Satmarers," Azenberg mused.

Judy Polisar let out a rueful laugh.

"Farshmolstene Yiddin," Diness said. Greasy Jews.

"Shmecht vie a cholerye," Azenberg added. They smell like cholera.

"Why am I bitter?" Rosen asked everyone and no one. "I'm not a bitter person. Because they're the kind of people who are against everything I stand for."

"It's like we lost our land," Azenberg said wistfully. "We had so many people there, so much life. How could it be empty?"

Azenberg's housekeeper began clearing the dessert plates, the cups and saucers. The clock showed nine-thirty, late enough on a weeknight. Sharon packed her Kinderwelt papers back in the box. Her own trip home would be a short one, to the Upper East Side of Manhattan. Judi Schulman from Kinderwelt, now Judi Lederer, lived across the street. Lorelei and Milt Kaplan had an apartment a few blocks away. With this reunion over, the perimeter of Kinderwelt in Sharon's life would shrink back to those borders.

"Remember the song?" Rosen asked as the guests reached for their coats. They all knew which one he meant. The last time Sharon had heard it was on the final night of camp, back in August 1963.

> *Friends, friends, friends*
> *We will always be.*
> *Whether in fair or in dark stormy weather,*
> *Kinderwelt will keep us together.*

The blue and white
Is our guiding light.
The camp that unites us, the camp that delights us,
We're friends, friends, friends.

A few nights later, Sharon sang again in a different sort of reunion. Every Tuesday she rehearsed with the Workmen's Circle Chorus, a Yiddish ensemble affiliated with what was left of the Socialist group. She had first heard the chorus perform at a Reform temple eight or nine years earlier, and it had taken her two full years to work up the nerve to ask if she could join. Not that the chorus had the luxury of holding auditions. It was glad to have new blood, and, then in her mid-forties, Sharon qualified as new blood by thirty or forty years.

Which was part of the appeal for her. Ever since her father Jack had died in 1980, Sharon had felt hollowed out, less by sorrow than regret. She thought of the whole world of *Yiddishkeit* he had tried to give her, through Bet Yeled and Kinderwelt and the Farband and the Jewish National Fund collection box on the kitchen table, and she excoriated herself for not having devoured every bit of it. Why had she been so damned embarrassed about a father who spoke Yiddish, a father who had an accent?

When Sharon cast her gaze across the chorus, though, she saw Jack reincarnated in the collection of Yiddish teachers and garment workers, retired now, age-spotted and poor, making the gloriously guttural sound of shtetl songs. "Maybe this," she said at one point, "is an atonement."

There was only one problem. Each time the chorus added a song to its repertoire, a member needed to explain it to Sharon. She knew how the words sounded. But she didn't know what they meant.

Who Is a Jew?

WHEN CAMP KINDERWELT shuttered its bunkhouses for the final time, closing after nearly a half-century, it conceded something larger than one corner of the Catskills to observant Jewry. The more that secular Judaism declined as a force in American Jewish life, the more it abdicated the task of defining Jewish identity to religious authorities. And once the debate became a religious debate, it was conducted on Orthodox Jewry's ground. The Reform and Conservative movements might hold the allegiance of the vast majority of affiliated American Jews, but the Orthodox by their refusal to compromise *halakhah* with modernism seemed to embody authenticity, and they were not timid about dictating the terms of it to every other branch. With their common foe, secularism, now spent, the Jewish denominations turned against one another.

"Judaism the religion had existed in tandem with this other thing we might call Jewishness as ethnicity, Jewishness as peoplehood," says the historian Hasia Diner. "If you asked someone in 1910 what made them Jewish, it might be going to the Yiddish theater, belonging to a Jewish union. They didn't sit around asking what it meant to be Jewish. They lived in a Jewish world. But when that life disappeared or evolved into nostalgia, the religious core that was always there was revealed. And as it was revealed, the religious struggle was exposed."

Nowhere was that struggle more divisive than in the so-called "Who is a Jew?" issue. The phrase actually covered several related elements of Jewish status—intermarriage, conversion, the legitimacy of the non-Orthodox rabbinate. While none of these conflicts was unprecedented in Jewish history, rarely if ever had they imperiled communal unity. Jewish tradition had long held that any prospective convert be turned away three times from the synagogue door. *Halakhah* rejected intermarriage so completely that when such unions failed, the Jewish spouse was not even required to obtain the rabbinical divorce decree known as a *get*. Only in modern America did disputes over status reach a critical apogee. For when it came to whom a Jew loved and married and had children with, the interest of America in a common national culture and the interest of Judaism in tribal continuity were diametrically opposed.

During the Jewish emancipation in Europe, the poet Heinrich Heine had described baptism as "an entrance ticket" to the larger society, but even those like him who chose it remained ineffably alien to their host country. In the United States, a nation without a state religion, a pioneer land that allowed every citizen to reinvent himself, the ultimate act of belonging took place at the wedding altar. When Jews intermarry, as the historian Jack Wertheimer has written, "they are embracing the American way."

During the heyday of secular Judaism, the rate of intermarriage between Jews and gentiles barely exceeded that between whites and blacks. From the early twenties through the late fifties, the share of such marriages crept up only from 1.7 to 6.6 percent; such shame attached to "marrying out" that Jewish parents often observed the mourning ritual of shiva for a child who did so. Then, with the opening of suburbia and private colleges to Jews and the retrenchment of anti-Semitism, the percentage of interfaith marriages nearly doubled in the early sixties and almost tripled during the late sixties and early seventies, reaching about one-third. The kind of Jewish-gentile union that had qualified as a novelty early in the century with the hit play *Abie's Irish Rose* looked more like documentary realism in the television sitcom "Bridget Loves Bernie."

The alarms about Jewish survival rang at several junctures. In 1964, the mass-circulation magazine *Look* published a major article on "The Vanishing American Jew," which gravely discussed the intermarriage rate. In the early seventies, the first National Jewish Population survey showed the intermarriage number at its highest level yet, 31 percent. Twenty years later, the next such survey put the figure at 52 percent. Strictly speaking, a Jew marrying another Jew was now the exception rather than the rule in America. Even those scholars and journalists who disputed the 1990 survey's accuracy placed the intermarriage rate at around 40 percent.

And marriage connoted children, most of whom were adrift from Jewish identity. Only 28 percent of intermarried couples were raising their children solely as Jews; only 13 percent of intermarried couples were affiliated with any branch of Judaism. One in six households that called itself Jewish in the 1990 survey had no member who was a Jew by birth or formal conversion; for those families, evidently, Jewish identity was not something to be earned or inherited but merely declared. Some 664,000 children under eighteen were not uniformly recognized as Jewish.

One hopeful line of reasoning saw in conversion the solution to Jewish continuity. The demographer Egon Mayer found that parents in a "conversionary" marriage were far more likely than those in a mixed marriage to provide their children with Jewish education and observance. Leaders of Reform Jewry in the late seventies began promoting the search for converts as a fulfillment of God's injunction that Jews be "a light unto nations." In an evolving corpus of memoirs—Paul

Cowan's *An Orphan in History*, Stephen Dubner's *Turbulent Souls*, and Gabrielle Glaser's *Strangers to the Tribe*—writers who had been reared as gentiles rediscovered their Jewish heritage.

At the same time, however, conversion only deepened the schisms over Jewish identity. Each branch of Judaism maintained separate standards for conversion and no branch accepted the converts of a less observant branch. In the decades of mass immigration, when Orthodoxy dominated American Judaism, these disparities mattered little. In the postwar suburban era, though, the Reform and Conservative movements boomed, representing eighty percent of all affiliated American Jews by 1990, and conducting an even greater share of all conversions. The Reform and Reconstructionist branches both departed from the traditional standard of matrilineal descent. Under their new definition, it didn't matter which of a child's parents was Jewish as long as the child was being brought up exclusively as a Jew. And more than one-third of Reform rabbis by the late nineties were performing interfaith weddings.

The distress in Orthodox circles was profound. "A Holocaust of our own making," Sol Roth, a philosophy professor at Yeshiva University, termed intermarriage in 1980. Over time, his phrase was shortened and coarsened to "Silent Holocaust," and that term enjoyed widespread use among both Modern Orthodox and *haredim*. Whether or not Jewish intermarriage constituted autogenocide, it contributed, along with low birth rates and a sharp decline in Jewish immigration, to the shrinking of American Jewry. While the raw number of American Jews rose slightly from decade to decade after World War II, their proportion of the American population fell from 3.6 percent in 1940 to 2.3 percent in 1990. And even if all 180,000 converts were instantly, magically accepted by Orthodox authorities, these self-proclaimed "Jews by choice" comprised less than 5 percent of the American Jewish population, hardly a foundation for continuity.

The love story of Jews and gentiles in America, though, supplied only part of the combustibility of the "Who is a Jew?"

issue. The rest resulted from the tangle of religion, politics, and law in Israel. In both real and symbolic ways, American Jews looked to Israel for their cues, and Israel exacerbated American frictions more often than it ameliorated them. Ironically, as the Israeli legal scholar Asher Maoz has pointed out, much of the discord arose from the very law meant to enshrine Jewish unity.

The Israeli parliament, the Knesset, unanimously adopted the Law of Return in 1950. While guaranteeing all Jews the right to immigrate to Israel and receive immediate citizenship there, it deliberately avoided defining Jewish identity by any religious measure. Secularists dominated both of Israel's major political parties, the rightist Herut as much as the leftist Mapam, and for both, the law fulfilled the Zionist promise of homeland and refuge from a gentile world that had just finished demonstrating its hatred in the Holocaust.

Yet conflicts underlay the law, too, because of the Zionist tradition of conflating religious authority and civil affairs. Decades before Israel achieved statehood, Theodore Herzl drew the religious Mizrachi movement into the Zionist cause by promising autonomy to Orthodox rabbis in a Jewish state. Under both Ottoman and British rule in Palestine, for that matter, Jewish religious leaders had enjoyed similar power. It was no coincidence that Israel, once established, chose a prayer shawl as its flag and the seven-armed candelabra of the Second Temple as its symbol. Arch-secularist though he was, David Ben-Gurion, the founding prime minister, granted rabbinical courts sole jurisdiction over marriage and burial, provided state support for religious schools, and permitted military exemptions for yeshiva students. In part, Ben-Gurion was practicing smart coalition politics; in part, he was acting on the belief that Orthodoxy would soon wither away.

It did not, of course, and under the pressure of intermarriage and conversion in the Diaspora, the inherent contradictions of the Israeli system exploded. A series of cases forced the Israeli Supreme Court to begin answering the question that the Law of Return had studiously avoided: Who exactly is a

Jew? In the so-called Brother Daniel case of 1962, the court sided against a Carmelite monk who had been born Jewish and imbued with Zionism before converting to Catholicism in a concentration camp. As a professed Christian, the court decided, Brother Daniel could not simultaneously claim still to be an ethnic Jew. The next major case, however, involved a gentile woman from Scotland who had married an Israeli man and was raising their children in Israel. Rebuffed by the Israeli Ministry of the Interior when they tried to register the children as Jewish, Ruth and Benjamin Shalit in 1970 won a reversal from the nation's Supreme Court.

The Knesset responded with an awkward, troublesome compromise, amending the Law of Return to be simultaneously more lenient and more strict. For purposes of immigration, anyone with a Jewish grandparent would receive immediate citizenship; but for purposes of national registration, Jewish identity was defined by matrilineal descent or "legitimate" conversion. To add to the confusion, the amendment avoided specifying the criteria for a legitimate conversion. No longer was the question of status simply, "Who is a Jew?" Now it was also "Who is a convert?" and "Who is a rabbi?" In Israel, a homogeneous country with an overwhelmingly Orthodox rabbinate, these fine points of debate mattered little. In America, with its boom in both intermarriage and Reform and Conservative affiliation, they could hardly have mattered more.

Initially at least, American interests prevailed. After the Interior Ministry refused to register as Jewish an immigrant named Susan Miller, who had converted under Reform auspices in Colorado, the Israeli Supreme Court in 1986 ordered the recognition of conversions conducted "in any Jewish community abroad." In a later case, the high court criticized the Interior Ministry for denying Jewish recognition to a Brazilian immigrant who had been converted by Reform authorities in Israel, though it did not order a reversal.

But what looked like the triumph of American-style pluralism instead provoked an unprecedented split between

American Jewry and the Jewish state, as well as rifts between American Jewish branches. In the late eighties, the ultra-Orthodox bloc in the Knesset held the balance of power between Labor and Likud. Courting the religious parties' support for his hawkish stance on the peace process, Prime Minister Yitzhak Shamir promised in May 1987 to introduce an amendment to the Law of Return requiring the Chief Rabbinate to approve all conversions. This meant essentially that only Orthodox conversions would pass muster. In both July 1987 and June 1988, the Knesset debated and defeated the measure. In November 1988, just after the Orthodox bloc had added several seats in the most recent Knesset elections, rumors swirled that Shamir would cut a political deal to ensure passage of the conversion amendment.

Much of American Jewry reacted with fury and panic. "Israel is the battlefield, but the war is in America," said Ismar Schorsch, the chancellor of the Jewish Theological Seminary, a Conservative institution. As the United Jewish Appeal dispatched an elite delegation to lobby Shamir against the conversion bill, the UJA's chairman, Martin Stein, declared, "This issue goes right to the kishke." The American Jewish Congress branded the legislation "a betrayal of Israel's partnership with Diaspora Jewry." Yet American Jews were themselves divided. The Lubavitcher Hasidim had poured millions of dollars from their Brooklyn headquarters into support for the amendment. In a full-page advertisement in the *New York Times*, an array of American Orthodox groups, from the *haredi* Agudath Israel of America to the centrist Rabbinical Council of America, blamed the Reform and Conservative movements for breaking with "a clear definition of Jewish identity that was universally accepted among all Jews for thousands of years." Citing the intermarriage rate in America, the ad went on, "The floodgates of disintegration and demise are beating down our very doors."

The crisis over conversion law subsided when Shamir chose to form a national unity government with Labor, depriving the religious parties of their leverage. But the underlying conflict never went away, any more than intermarriage in America ceased or the Reform and Conservative movements disappeared. In 1997, in fact, the "Who is a Jew?" issue returned with a vengeance. The ultra-Orthodox parties, now part of Benjamin Netanyahu's ruling coalition, introduced a bill to give the Chief Rabbinate control over conversion. Like Shamir before him, Netanyahu was torn between his religious constituency and an inflamed American Jewry; unlike Shamir, he also faced the task of integrating into Israel two hundred thousand Russian immigrants who were not Jewish according to *halakhah*. Israel now had a reason of its own for reconsidering conversion standards.

Netanyahu appointed a commission led by a cabinet minister, Yaakov Ne'eman, to seek a compromise. Its seven members included one apiece from the Reform and Conservative movements—just enough for those branches to denounce their seats as tokenism and for the ultra-Orthodox to object to the mere presence of other branches. Twice, first in the summer and then in the fall of 1997, the commission missed its deadline for delivering its recommendations. When word leaked in October that the Ne'eman Commission would propose a conversion institute operated jointly by all three denominations, the ultra-Orthodox Shas party threatened to bolt from Netanyahu's coalition, toppling his government.

Finally, in January 1998, the commission unveiled its plan. Indeed, it called for rabbis from all three major branches to jointly educate the conversion candidates in a powerful symbol of collaboration and mutual respect. The task of officiating at the actual conversion ceremonies, however, would rest with the Chief Rabbinate, and the Chief Rabbinate made it instantly clear it had no intention of doing so. "There can be no cooperation" with those "who try to shake the foundation of the Jewish religion," the rabbinate declared in a formal resolution. The Reform and Conservative movements, it continued, have "brought about disastrous results of assimilation among Diaspora Jewry." In slightly more refined language, then, the Chief Rabbinate was decrying the Silent Holocaust.

The disparagement of non-Orthodox Judaism and the continuing controversy over Jewish identity weighed far more heavily on America than on Israel. When the news magazine *Jerusalem Report* asked its readers in 1998 to name Israel's most important issue, only 7 percent pointed to conversion standards. Even Tommy Lapid, a politician and commentator known for his flagrant Orthodox-bashing, accused the Reform and Conservative movements of meddling in Israeli affairs. The Ne'eman Commission's institute opened in early 1999 with a mere thirty-seven candidates, all Russian immigrants.

Few of the American Jews who hoped Israel and the Ne'eman Commission could solve their own identity crisis realized that the conversion institute had been modeled on an experiment in the United States. It had taken place in Denver more than twenty years earlier, deliberately hidden from view. And what happened then and there showed just how maddeningly difficult it was for three different strains of Judaism to agree upon a single answer to the question, "Who is a Jew?"

CHAPTER TWO

Denver,
Colorado,
1977–1983

Nᴏᴛ ʟᴏɴɢ ᴀғᴛᴇʀ the High Holy Days in the autumn of
1978, Dr. William Pluss glanced up his caseload of pneumonia
and abdominal pain on the internal medicine floor of University Hospital in Salt Lake City to find a pharmacy graduate student observing his selection of medications. He looked back at
her approvingly, and not simply because among the residents
Bill had that rare quality of treating nondoctors as humans.
Something more visceral was at work. Blonde-haired, green-
eyed, graced with a feathery Southern accent, the student embodied those traits Bill had craved in women from the moment
puberty hit, what he described succinctly as "the cheerleader
type, the shiksa."

Just back from spending Rosh Hashanah and Yom Kippur with his family in Denver, Bill had been reminded yet again
how problematic that aesthetic was on the home front. His father, Julius, had managed to stay not only Jewish but Orthodox
while growing up in the archipelago of Jewish enclaves strewn
80 across the Rockies. Now, settled in a booming postwar city

with a Jewish community sizable enough to have once been nicknamed "Brooklyn," he was watching the young generation marrying out at a rate topping 70 percent. And here was Bill, eyeing Miss Anne Davis of Raleigh, North Carolina, and asking her out for dinner and a movie.

They laughed together on the night of their first date about having to bring their own cocktails to the restaurant in the form of airline bottles. Well, that was Utah, Mormon Utah, with its screwy liquor laws. They both felt alien there, as itinerants in the hospital where neither intended to stay, and as a Jew and a Southern Methodist in the inland empire of Brigham Young. It showed how much they had in common.

Their affinity grew fast. They were a couple within three weeks of meeting. Soon after, they were talking of marriage. Hundreds of miles from his family, thousands of miles from hers, flush with both love and desire, Bill and Anne populated a planet of two, where all that mattered was what they could share.

In the hospital, Anne came to know one part of Bill, the doctor revered by colleagues for his talent and by patients for his manner. At his apartment, fingering the souvenirs from his trips to Hawaii and Mexico and Europe, she touched a worldliness she envied. Those wide vistas appealed to her, the liberal apostate in a family that esteemed Jesse Helms. Bill saw Anne as a peer, an athlete who would ski and bike with him, an imminent Pharm.D. who understood not just the nomenclature of medicine but the devotion and strain of a doctor's life.

At Thanksgiving, much enthralled, Bill went home to Denver to tell his family about Anne. Julius Pluss was not unfamiliar with the appeal of gentile women. Growing up in the tiny Jewish community in Greeley, a cattle town fifty miles from Denver, he had dated a few himself, as much out of necessity as allure. But there had been no question about how a Jewish person should live, no question about what was truly important, even at what seemed like the far edge of the Diaspora.

The dozen Jewish families in Greeley had turned a house into a synagogue, and each year they hired a rabbinical student to prepare their boys for bar mitzvah. Whenever a Jewish merchant from town journeyed to Denver with scrap metal or livestock, he also carried the entire congregation's orders for the kosher butcher, so the Jews of Greeley could observe *kashrut*. In marrying its children, too, Greeley looked to the city with the largest Jewish community between the Great Plains and the Pacific. Julius's wife, Rose, had grown up a grocer's daughter in oil outposts like Borger, Texas, and Hobbs, New Mexico, places with too few Jews to attract even a circuit-riding rabbi. For the High Holy Days, the family trekked hundreds of miles to Lubbock, taking rooms in a hotel. When Rose reached her teens, her father shut down his store and moved to Denver to find her a suitable beau.

"Just because you love her doesn't mean we'll accept her," Julius told his son of Anne. Realistically, Julius knew he wouldn't disown Bill for a mixed marriage; wrath would only drive him even further away. Still, he believed sameness—common values—held a marriage and a family together. Bill had to grant the point. A few years earlier, fourteen of his relatives had vacationed together. At the time, Bill was essentially living with his college girlfriend, another one of his cheerleader idylls. She did not go on the trip, and not long afterward they broke up.

Before Thanksgiving ended, Julius offered his son a less absolute option with Anne. "If she's the love of your life, if you're sure of it, and if she's willing to convert," he said, "then Mother and I will accept her with open arms."

Anne, meanwhile, met her mother, Ellen Davis, in Las Vegas in early 1979, ostensibly for a pleasure trip, but more importantly to tell her about Bill. Anne knew better than to expect approval. She had grown up under a parental command not to get serious with a Jew or a Catholic, and even as the family rebel, the freethinker, the only daughter among five to leave the South, she had never before put the edict to an empirical test. "You know we're not going to like that," her mother said now of the relationship. "It can't work. You're too different. It goes against the way you were brought up."

Anne had been brought up in the Edenton Street Methodist Church. For her and her four sisters, a typical Sunday began with worship at eight-thirty and proceeded through religious school at nine-thirty, a second service at eleven, children's choir practice in the early afternoon, and youth fellowship until dinner. On Wednesday evenings, the Davises took part in family fellowship at church, and on other occasions they studied the Bible together at home.

The elder Davises were by no means cartoonish Holy Rollers. Their denomination was notable for self-restraint and good works, typified by its tradition of temperance. They both held college degrees. Charles Davis was an architect. They simply believed, not unlike Julius Pluss, that shared religion belonged at the center of matrimony.

Anne agreed, too. She and Bill wanted to have children soon, so any decision they made would either give or deny their family a broader community. The phrase "mixed marriage" sounded to both of them uncomfortably like "mixed message." "Who are we going to be?" Anne asked. "And who are our kids going to be?" Bill had made it abundantly clear that he had no intention of accepting Jesus Christ as his Lord and Savior. The burden of choice rested on Anne alone.

Nearly a year after the Las Vegas trip, she went home to Raleigh for Christmas, bringing with her the prospect not merely of marriage but also conversion. It became, as one of the Davis sisters would later recall, "the line in the sand." The mere mention of conversion sent Anne's mother out of the room. Why was Anne betraying her family? Why was she turning her back on her way of life? And why was she, not this Jewish boyfriend of hers, the one being asked to make all the sacrifices? Anne's parents, like Bill's, set their terms. If she went ahead with conversion and marriage, they would refuse any contact with her husband.

Anne told herself that becoming Jewish wasn't such a big deal. In more than a year together in Salt Lake City, neither she nor Bill had gone to a religious service of any kind. As a Methodist, she already believed in the Old Testament, and she worshipped God as part of the Trinity. Judaism, Christianity— they had sprung from the same tradition. Yet she had a nagging question, one that she finally asked Bill outright: What exactly did it mean to be Jewish?

The answer was, well, complicated. In deference to his wife, who had never received much religious instruction, Julius Pluss had joined a Reform temple as well as an Orthodox synagogue. The Plusses' daughter, Jane, followed Rose to Temple Emanuel, while Bill and his brother Dick accompanied Julius to Beth Joseph. Julius revered the rabbi there, Daniel Goldberger, for his gentle pastoral ways. And he counted on Beth Joseph's conventional brand of religious education to make his boys, if not fervent believers, then "Jewish enough."

Bill dreaded the Tuesday and Thursday afternoons devoted to Hebrew school, all dogma and mumbo-jumbo, and when he wasn't skipping the homework, he was cutting class entirely to hang out at the soda fountain of Del-Mar Drugs. The Sabbath service struck him as "a little bit of a joke," the way the regulars wandered in and out at will and chattered away during the prayers. Worst of all, the combination of synagogue on Saturday and still more Hebrew school on Sunday meant Bill could not ski. And for a teenager in Denver not to ski meant sticking out as surely as if Jews really did have horns.

In 1964, Bill Pluss mounted the altar at Beth Joseph to become a bar mitzvah, a son of the commandment, a Jewish man. He promptly put his autonomy to use by switching his allegiance to Temple Emanuel. Much to his own surprise, Bill found himself estranged from Reform practice, with its organ music and English liturgy. He missed the sight of tallit and *kippot* in the congregation, the tight wrap of tefillin around his own arm, the incantatory cadences of Hebrew. Still, there was one good thing to be said for Emanuel: Its major service was on Friday night. Bill took up skiing.

If Judaism as a faith offered little to Bill, Judaism as a culture suffused him. His best friends were Jewish—Chet Stern, David Zuckerman, Robert Davidson. He spent summers at JCC camp. His family lived, as Julius never failed to mention, across the street from a neighborhood called Crestmoor that for decades had been forbidden to Jews. During the Six-Day War in 1967, Julius had spent hours putting through calls to cousins in Jerusalem, Holocaust survivors, and when Israel triumphed mightily, Bill, then fifteen, felt by association a little bit mighty himself.

More than anything, Jewish culture meant *Shabbos* dinner with Aunt Nellie and Uncle Lou. Childless themselves, they doted on Bill and his siblings. Aunt Nellie always made gefilte fish or chopped liver or brisket, and also the dishes that harked back to childhood poverty—*miltz*, which was spleen, and a sweet-and-sour cow's foot called *fees*. Then came peach pie and a stroll through the neighborhood and finally Uncle Lou's home movies. So what if Julius Pluss had drifted far enough from his own Orthodoxy to work on most Saturdays; so what if Rose Pluss periodically sneaked bacon onto the family menu. What were rules compared to all the heart the Plusses put into their Sabbath table?

When Bill tried to explain it to Anne, the answer sounded feeble and formulaic. "It's doing the High Holy Days," he said. "Having a seder. Being with the family." The only way to really learn was by immersion. After Bill finished his residency in Salt Lake City in the summer of 1980, Anne moved back to Denver with him.

Julius Pluss greeted her with more than the promised open arms. He had a plan for her conversion. His old friend Rabbi Goldberger had told him about a program in Denver in which Reform, Conservative, and Orthodox rabbis jointly prepared candidates for conversion, and the actual ceremony was performed to Orthodox specifications. Julius knew all the *mishagas*, the mess, that Judaism's varying standards had caused. He'd followed the controversy in Israel a decade earlier over the Law of Return and recognized, rightly, that the issue was by no means resolved. His daughter Jane had married a divorced man only to discover that her husband had never received the religious divorce decree called a *get*. After he obtained one, he and Jane had to go through a second, Orthodox ceremony with Rabbi Goldberger. And Jane's husband had been Jewish to begin with. So here was the chance for Anne to become Jewish in a way nobody could challenge, to ensure that her children, Julius's grandchildren, would be Jewish by anybody's definition. Besides, Julius figured, if Anne went through the program, maybe it would help make Bill a little more religious, too.

Just before conversion classes began that fall, Anne went with her future family to Temple Emanuel for Rosh Hashanah and Yom Kippur. She strained to find similarities with her old heritage in order to gain a foothold in her new one. The Reform prayer book had been assembled jigsaw-like, with chunks of text from different biblical books fitted together into a liturgy; still, she remembered many of its passages word for word from Sunday school. And she appreciated how passionately the rabbi, Steven Foster, sermonized about social justice, so different from a Methodist minister's calming, fatherly advice. "This is the right path," she told herself. "This isn't going to be so difficult."

ON THE FRIDAY AFTERNOON in July 1970 when Steven Foster arrived to become assistant rabbi at Temple Emanuel, his boss greeted him with an assignment. "You have an appointment with a young woman," Rabbi Earl Stone said, "and you should convert her." Too flummoxed by the command to question it, Foster kept listening as Stone added, "I'm officiating at her marriage in August."

From that moment through the rest of the summer, Foster saw a retinue of prospective converts, maybe twenty or twenty-five in total, almost all of them young women seeking to placate a Jewish fiancé's family. He spent four or five hours a day running what felt like an assembly line, and even at that pace fielded calls from future in-laws demanding, "When's this gonna be done? You had her last week, didn't you?"

An hour after Rabbi Foster reached Denver, another new rabbi had entered the city. Bernard Eisenman, taking over the pulpit at Rodef Shalom, soon discovered intermarriage creeping into his Conservative congregation. Often the parents were too ashamed to tell him. In one case, an official of the congregation, adamant to sanctify his daughter's interfaith ceremony, sneaked into Rodef Shalom to steal the wedding canopy, the *chuppah*.

Then there was Rabbi Stanley Wagner of Congregation Beth HaMedrash Hagadol, for nearly a century a linchpin of Orthodoxy in Denver. In 1977, a longtime member who had just donated $50,000 to the synagogue came for premarital counseling with her daughter, who was engaged to a Jewish man. Rabbi Wagner asked one of his stock questions—"Are there any divorces or conversions in the family?"—and the mother surprised him by saying that she had been converted under Conservative auspices, with immersion taking place in a swimming pool. Which meant neither mother nor daughter qualified under Orthodox standards as a Jew. So Rabbi Wagner cobbled together an Orthodox conversion ceremony for both women at a local *mikvah*. "You're telling me my marriage is a lie?" the mother cried. "That our children are not Jews? That we've been living a lie?"

In different ways, the three Denver rabbis were encountering the explosion of interfaith marriages. More importantly, they were being forced to confront the crisis of legitimacy within Judaism. As friendly and respectful as they were, the three presided over congregations affiliated with branches of Judaism that held irreconcilably different definitions of conversion, of Jewish identity itself. For all that they recognized of each other's criteria, the rabbis might as well have been practicing different religions entirely and saved their socializing for ecumenical prayer breakfasts. Their realization that interfaith marriage presented a deeper dilemma than parental unhappiness ultimately convinced them and six of their colleagues to create an experimental program in joint conversion. To liberals in all the branches of American Jewry, the Denver system offered the hope of forever answering the question "Who is a Jew?" and answering it for Israel and the Diaspora alike. As for the more traditional forces, particularly within Orthodoxy, from them it was supposed to be kept secret.

Both for creating and solving the Jewish identity crisis, Denver proved an ideal petri dish. Its soaring rate of intermarriage reflected the openness of a frontier city in a frontier society: Denver was America italicized. At the same time, the mutual support among the city's rabbis reflected the isolation and modest size of the city's Jewish community. Denver Jewry could not indulge in the luxury of rancor.

The first Jews had come to the region with the 1859 gold rush, less to pan for nuggets along the Platte River than to provision and outfit those who did. One walked six hundred miles from Kansas; another traded his hobnail boots for moccasins on his odyssey from St. Louis. By September 29 of that year, enough Jewish men had arrived to form a minyan, and a grocer named Julius Mitchell conducted High Holy Days services in the shadow of Pike's Peak.

As a trading center called Auraria formed further north, where the Platte met Cherry Creek, and evolved into Denver, Jews settled into frame shacks on the floodplain. In a city just being born, prejudices had no time to calcify. So while Jews built their own institutions by the 1870s—a B'nai B'rith chapter, the Hebrew Ladies Benevolent Society, Temple Emanuel—they also found acceptance in public life. A Jew named Wolfe Londoner won election as mayor in 1884. Another Jew, Simon Guggenheim, represented Colorado in the

U.S. Senate. Fred Salomon, a Jewish businessman, presided over the Denver Board of Trade. It seemed nothing but normal when the local chapter of the National Council of Jewish Women traveled by wagon train to an all-kosher picnic. "We should marvel not at persecution," one Jewish commentator said in 1881, "but at toleration."

True, Jews were barred from the "Sacred Thirty-six," the social elite, and from the clubs, neighborhoods, and hospitals it established and dominated. But such bias was inconvenient more than devastating; Jews simply created parallel institutions—the Town Club, General Rose Hospital, the Jewish district along West Colfax. The only serious challenge to Jews occurred in the 1920s, when the Ku Klux Klan controlled the city government. Led by an Orthodox rabbi, Charles Kauvar, and an attorney, Philip Hornbein, Denver's Jews allied with their Irish Catholic neighbors to rout the racists from office. "I love you for the enemies you have made," one Catholic priest said of Denver's Jews, "for my people have made the same enemies."

In such fertile soil, the Jewish population steadily grew, from 260 in 1877 to 4,000 in 1905 and then 17,000 in 1927. The early residents, mainly Reform Jews of German stock, many of them transplanted from the American Reform capital of Cincinnati, found themselves outnumbered at the turn of the century by Eastern European Orthodox. Some had traveled directly from the shtetl, sponsored by relatives, while others had come from American slums to receive free tuberculosis treatment at the Jewish charity hospital. One short-term resident, Golda Myerson, left for Palestine and changed her surname to Meir.

Packed together on a square mile of Denver's West Side, the divergent Jews coalesced in a manner uncommon in larger cities. A German Jewish lodge brought nearly a thousand refugees to Denver in the decade after the 1903 Kishinev pogrom. "No one has better powers of adaptability than the Russian Jew," one Reform rabbi enthused, while elsewhere in

America German Jews were coining the racial slur "kike" for their coreligionists from the Pale. The rare Orthodox rabbi to devote a Yom Kippur sermon to denouncing "our so-called radically reformed brethren" who "don't want it known they're Jews," had to slink out of town a year later after he was discovered eating pork on *Shabbos*.

More often, Denver's rabbinate abided by the principle of *shalom bayit*, peace of the house. When Rabbi Manuel Laderman was installed in 1932 at the Hebrew Educational Alliance, the ceremony included the patriarch of Reform Jewry in Denver, Rabbi William Friedman of Temple Emanuel, and the Orthodox dean, Rabbi Charles Kauvar, the product of a Vilna yeshiva. A generation later, Denver's rabbis collaborated on publishing ventures, an adult-education program, and the Soviet Jewry campaign. After the murder of eleven Israeli athletes and coaches by Palestinian terrorists during the 1972 Olympics, two thousand mourners from all branches filled Temple Emanuel for a memorial service.

There was just one challenge all this unity had failed to address: Denver's tolerance, indeed its literal love, of Jews. In the years after World War II, the Anti-Defamation League pried open the exclusive Crestmoor district, and the once gentile East Side, with its leafy parkways, drew thousands of Jews from the confines of West Colfax. A 1953 analysis of Denver's Jewish community found that more than half its working adults were business owners or professionals. Upward mobility enabled outward mobility. A 1981 study calculated that 72 percent of Denver Jews in their twenties were marrying gentiles, only a few of whom later converted. The rate of intermarriage had leaped fivefold in a generation. Of the 42,500 members of Denver's Jewish community in 1981, 4,000 were the Christian spouses and children of Jews. Maybe it was prophetic that a Jewish woman from Denver had invented that shiksa totem, the Barbie doll.

Rabbi Steven Foster, for one, had always wondered why his predecessor, Earl Stone, refused to perform interfaith wed-

ding ceremonies but routinely signed off on the most perfunctory sort of conversions. Foster had attended rabbinical school
during the resurgence of ethnic pride and roots-consciousness
in the 1960s and observed the dietary laws of kashrut even
though Reform doctrine deemed them atavistic. He wanted to
make Reform conversions "as halakhic as possible." But he
could not do it alone.

Foster knew that Jerome Lipsitz, his rabbinical neighbor in an Orthodox shul three blocks from Emanuel, brought
the occasional candidate for conversion to the West Side *mikvah*. Would he be willing, Foster asked, to conduct the *mikvah*
ceremony for a Reform candidate? Would he do it if Foster
guaranteed that the person was serious about leading a Jewish
life and making a Jewish home? Lipsitz consented and quietly,
through the mid-seventies, complied.

In 1976, Foster and Lipsitz divulged their private
arrangement to the Denver Rabbinical Council, whose members ran the gamut from Reconstructionist to Modern Orthodox. Some were appalled; here were two rabbis, each flouting
his own denomination, improvising rites as they went along.
And yet, the central idea glowed with appeal. Establishing a
common set of conversion standards seemed the very essence
of serving *Klal Yisrael*, the Jewish people. The question was
how. Orthodoxy required of a convert *kabbalat ol mitzvot*, accepting the yoke of the commandments, all 613 of them. "If a
proselyte is prepared to accept the Torah, bar one religious
law," the Talmud instructed, "we must not receive him." Conservative converts accepted only some of the mitzvot, however,
while Reform converts treated them as guidelines rather than
rules.

Then two major figures from Modern Orthodoxy happened to appear in Denver in 1977, each speaking both at the
adult-education program and to the rabbis' council. Eliezer
Berkovits, a professor emeritus from Hebrew Theological
College, warned that the "Who is a Jew?" debate was destroying Jewish unity. And shouldn't Jewish unity be the greater

good, the greatest good? *Halakhah* itself held that in times of crisis one need not insist on *lechatchila*, a convert's embrace of all the commandments at the outset, but on *bedi'avad*, the level of observance a convert would achieve over time. Steven Riskin, the rabbi of Manhattan's renowned Lincoln Square Synagogue, spoke in Denver about Judaism's teachings on the mitzvot. Both the Talmud and the Rambam held that a prospective convert should be instructed not only in several *mitzvot hamurot*, difficult requirements, but also a few *mitzvot kalot*, lenient commandments. To Stanley Wagner, among others, Berkovits and Riskin had offered theological justification for conversion as an ongoing process, not a contract signed as a condition of admission. An Orthodox rabbi could convert someone who professed adherence to the Torah's laws even if his present life revealed *umdena demuchach*, a compelling indication of breaking some of them.

One morning a few weeks later, seven Denver rabbis rented a conference room in a hotel along the interstate. They placed an order for a kosher lunch and vowed not to leave until they had forged the framework of a joint conversion program. After ten hours of the negotiation called *masa umatan*, literally, "burden and giving," they emerged with a plan.

Each prospective convert would take a twenty-week class in Basic Judaism, with various lessons taught by rabbis from all the branches. The sponsoring rabbi would conduct personal instruction and counseling. Then a panel of three rabbis—one apiece from the Reform, Conservative, and Orthodox denominations—would evaluate the applicant for conversion. Finally, three Orthodox rabbis would convene as a religious court, a *bet din*, to make a formal decision. Male converts would undergo either actual circumcision or *hatafat dam brit*, the symbolic drawing of blood, and both men and women would submit to *tevilah*, full immersion in the *mikvah*. Only afterward would the officiating Orthodox rabbi sign the *te-uda*, the conversion certificate.

To earn conversion, an applicant also had to subscribe to a list of duties pointedly called the Ten Commitments. These included such specific acts as fasting on Yom Kippur, joining a synagogue, lighting candles on the Sabbath and holidays, and placing a mezuzah on the doorpost of one's home. They included such broadly held Jewish ideals as devotion to Israel and the giving of charity called *tzedakah*. But they also included language about maintaining dietary laws and keeping a Jewish household that remained deliberately vague. Eating matzoh on Passover was a dietary law. Was that sufficient? Did a Jewish household have to be *shomer Shabbos*, Sabbath-observant? Was it permissible to drive or watch TV on a Saturday?

It had always been a rule of the rabbinical council, a foundation of its comity, not to discuss *halakhah*. Whenever the subject arose, Stanley Wagner would say, "We're getting right on the cusp here." And so rather than crack apart the fragile construction that was the joint-conversion program, its participants left a vast, unmapped middle ground in the requirements, a vacuum to be filled by goodwill and best intentions.

Such compromises left all of the Denver rabbis vulnerable to attack. The Reform rabbis, part of a denomination that had denounced much ritual as "altogether foreign to our mental and spiritual state" in its founding document, the Pittsburgh Platform of 1885, not only were acknowledging the sanctity of *mikvah* rites but granting sole control over them to the Orthodox. The Orthodox rabbis, in turn, were departing from their movement's established benchmark of *kabbalat ol mitzvot* in favor of the Ten Commitments, which had been hashed out at the Regency Hotel, not handed down at Mount Sinai.

A fissure already ran through Denver Orthodoxy, separating Hasidic and ultra-Orthodox congregations from those led by Daniel Goldberger, Jerome Lipsitz, and Stanley Wagner. While all three men had been ordained by Orthodox institutions, belonged to an Orthodox rabbinical association, and led synagogues affiliated with an Orthodox union, they permitted mixed-gender seating and the use of microphones during worship. This strain of Orthodoxy, known as Traditional, had thrived for decades in the western United States. But as American Orthodoxy as a whole moved to the right, Traditional rabbis were becoming marginal even without covertly experimenting on conversion standards. The Denver contingent decided to hide its involvement from its own governing body, the Rabbinical Council of America.*

"Guilt, guilt, guilt," Rabbi Goldberger would say later of the decision. "Guilt about acting apart from the movement. Doing something that wouldn't be approved of. Not being loyal."

"I felt like a person walking the middle line of the highway," Rabbi Wagner said. "You could get hit by a car going in either direction."

Steven Foster, on the Reform flank, girded for reproach from his own liberal colleagues. "How dare you stand back and not sign the *te-uda*?" he imagined them asking about the conversion certificate. "You're denying who you are. You're giving in to an Orthodoxy that doesn't recognize us. You're selling us out."

But a common despair about the fragmenting of American Jewry overrode their fears. "Why have two separate types of Jews?" Jerome Lipsitz would later say. "We want to create a Jew all of us can recognize as being Jewish."

IN THE AUTUMN OF 1980, having just fulfilled the requirements for her doctorate in pharmacy, Anne Davis commenced a different sort of education. She enrolled in the Basic Judaism class at Temple Emanuel, the first step toward conversion. Every Tuesday evening for five months, she brought her pen and

---

* Rabbi Goldberger had resigned his pulpit to work full time as a marriage counselor at the time the Denver plan was created. But when he returned to a synagogue in 1979, he participated fully in the program, abiding by the decision by the Orthodox rabbis to obscure their involvement from denominational leaders.

notebook to the Sisterhood Lounge, her curiosity piqued as much by her classmates as the teacher. She saw who was pregnant. She saw who had no wedding ring. She saw who, tremulous in alien surroundings, clutched a partner's hand. And from those physical details, she extrapolated history and motive—who was turning Jewish for the sake of a child's identity, who was doing it as part of a spiritual search, who, like herself, was making the change for love.

The joint-conversion class had been running for three years by now, teaching about forty prospective converts annually, from the lawyer who'd been seeking a spiritual home since her counterculture days living in a teepee to the Chilean immigrant hoping to win over in-laws who still hung a picture of her husband's ex-wife. From afar, meanwhile, the Denver program had attracted the selective, confidential attention of progressive rabbis such as Irving (Yitz) Greenberg and Haskel Lookstein in the Modern Orthodox camp and Jules Harlow and Wolfe Kelman of the Conservative movement. Anne Davis had no idea just how closely, and with what sense of import, conversions like hers were being observed.

A volunteer named Max Frankel—"Uncle Max" to the students—presided over her class, and week by week he brought in local rabbis in a sort of Judaic chautauqua. From Rabbi Foster, Anne heard a lecture on Judaism as religion, culture, and nationality; from Rabbi Lipsitz, she heard a lesson on the laws of kashrut. Holidays, history, customs, and the Bible filled various sessions. With all the time she had spent around doctors and hospitals, Anne found herself fascinated with the Jewish rituals that marked life and death—the *bris* for a baby boy, the naming ceremony for a baby girl, the seven-day mourning period of shiva. Even Bill, who had always thought of religious instruction as a form of punishment, enjoyed revisiting this familiar ground by choice.

Max Frankel knew just how to ease Christians into Judaism. He opened the first class with a prayer of support and empathy for the converts on their journey, a far cry from the

Talmudic teaching that a prospective convert be spurned three times. He spoke of Jesus as a great teacher, though not the Son of God, and of the Last Supper as a seder. It didn't rattle him when one student, having been reared with anti-Semitic canards, innocently asked, "What's the blood ceremony?" About the only time Frankel suffered a few dropouts was when he made it clear that a Jew couldn't keep a Christmas tree.

That Christmas tree rule was going to be a tough one, Anne realized, but Christmas was still a few months off. Meanwhile she savored the rituals of a new identity, lighting candles at sundown every Friday and worshipping in the vaulted sanctuary at Temple Emanuel. The routine touched the sensememory of her Methodist childhood, when piety and its obligations had guided her diurnal life. For his part, Bill grated under the Denver program's mandate that he, as Anne's fiancé, attend temple every week, a frequency he had abandoned as a teenager. Once Anne was converted and they were married, he could return to being Jewish the way he preferred to be Jewish, the way of Aunt Nellie and Uncle Lou. For now, he told himself of the Denver rabbis, "You play in their game, you play by their rules."

Just one thing confounded Anne. The Denver program prided itself on including rabbis from the three major branches and presenting their denominations' beliefs as equally legitimate. Yet all of this effort to be scrupulously evenhanded only managed to confuse her. How could a religion that talked so much about unity be so divided? The reason Anne was taking this class wasn't to satisfy Bill or her in-laws; they would've been content with a Reform conversion that didn't require the Ten Commitments or the *mikvah*. Bill's mother had never even been to the *mikvah*. In the Protestant world of Anne's upbringing, you could go down the aisle at some lowborn Baptist church to accept Jesus and the snooty Episcopalians would have to accept you as Christian, no questions asked. So why wasn't any Jewish conversion good enough for all Jews?

She took her question to Julius Pluss and then to Steven Foster and they gave her the same answer. "Look, you're in love, you're going to get married, you're going to have children," the rabbi said. "And just suppose one of your children grows up and wants to marry an Orthodox Jew. Don't you want your child considered Jewish all along?"

Her protective instincts aroused, Anne forged ahead with the class. And as fall proceeded, with the snow line dropping down the Rockies and her wedding date drawing closer, she and Bill entered counseling sessions with Rabbi Foster. He intended to measure her integrity as a convert, and Anne had enough friends in town whom the rabbi had refused to convert to feel queasy herself.

"Do you know what you're giving up?" Rabbi Foster asked her at the outset.

"I'm giving up the Methodist religion," Anne answered quite literally.

"Are you sure you can do that?" he persisted. Give up Christmas and Easter? Give up raising her own children with youth choir, family fellowship, summer Bible school, and the other staples of her own girlhood? Give up the common bond of faith with her parents and sisters?

While Rabbi Foster didn't know just how deep the animosity of Anne's family ran—she and Bill hadn't told him—he knew the general pattern all too well. Once, a bride's mother had confronted him in the midst of a wedding reception to proclaim that her daughter would forever be a Catholic. Anne tried to allay the rabbi's concerns. For her, converting was no act of impulse made in new love's thrall; she and Bill had been together for two years by now. She spoke of Jesus as no more than a great teacher, as Max Frankel had taught, and of her faith in God rather than the Christian Trinity. All that put her far ahead of the conversion candidates who were struggling with belief itself, like the divorce lawyer who insisted on calling God the "cosmic administrator."

Once Anne and the rabbi had established what she would give up, the discussion turned to what she would take on. Going to services, lighting candles, celebrating major holidays, joining a temple or synagogue—Anne could readily assent to all of these responsibilities since she was complying with them already. She would fast on Yom Kippur because Bill fasted. As for the rest of the Ten Commitments, particularly those addressing dietary laws, Sabbath observance, and the concept of a Jewish household, they remained nebulous, deliberately nebulous.

Anne knew that the whole point of her conversion was to be authentic in Orthodox eyes, but she couldn't imagine being Orthodox herself. She had attended services with Julius Pluss a few times at the Hebrew Educational Alliance, where Daniel Goldberger now was the rabbi, and grown quietly indignant at limits, both imposed and self-imposed, on the role of the women. What struck her was not only their enforced absence from the *bimah*, the altar, but their reluctance to take part in responsive readings from the pews. "Aren't they here to worship?" she asked with a mixture of naïveté and censure. Even the Southern Methodists, no band of rebels, gave female laity prominent roles. So for Anne, accepting the Ten Commitments meant agreeing to build a Jewish life based on general precepts more than specific directions: a Jewish life with wiggle room. Bill consented to the commitments out of pragmatism. To have his marriage and his family, he needed to meet Rabbi Foster's criteria, and he had to respect the man for not giving approval easily. "You may think you're ready to convert," went one of the rabbi's refrains, "but you won't be ready until I know you're ready." Back home after the sessions, both of them shaken, Bill often assured Anne, "The Torah tells you what to do, but you adapt it for your own family."

A few weeks later, having been approved by Rabbi Foster, the conversion panel, and the Orthodox *bet din*, Anne drove across Denver from the East Side's Jewish present to the West Side's Jewish past. The stretch of Colfax where the Star Bakery, the Pelish Theater, and Radinsky's Rags once thrived had degenerated into a strip of pawnshops, convenience stores, and budget motels. Of twenty-six synagogues, only three remained. But down at the corner of Fourteenth and Quitman, next to the Yeshiva Toras Chaim, hunched a one-story tan brick building that housed Denver's sole remaining *mikvah*.

Anne stepped tentatively into a waiting room, unadorned except for two shelves of books on kashrut and *halakhah*. Rabbi Goldberger greeted her, tried to put her at ease. Presently, a female attendant guided her down a cinder-block hallway and into a changing room with a shower, a Styrofoam head for wigs, and a checklist of reminders—brush teeth and floss; cut toenails; remove scabs if not painful. Anne had been told in advance the rules of ritual cleanliness, so she had spent the previous night scrubbing off every last bit of nail polish and makeup. Even so, when Anne emerged from the shower now, the attendant inspected her hands yet again.

Through a door Anne came upon the *mikvah* itself, a tub of gray pebbled tile about four feet deep. "Like a baptismal font," she told herself, trying to render the alien familiar, "like a hot tub." Anne disrobed and tiptoed down seven steps into the water, grasping the brass handrail to quell her nerves. Then the attendant knocked on the door to the men's changing room, alerting Bill, Rabbi Goldberger, and two witnesses to crack it open wide enough to speak and listen.

By Rabbi Goldberger's standards, Anne's was a meaningful conversion. He had known Julius Pluss for decades and bar mitzvahed Bill. He took the pastoral side of ministry so seriously that during most of the seventies he had abdicated the pulpit in favor of marriage counseling. Still, his role on this day, as on many others at the *mikvah*, was not to inquire beyond the limits of his script.

"Are you doing this of your free will?" he began, reading from a rabbi's manual. "Have you given up any former faith or severed any other religious affiliation? Do you pledge loyalty to Judaism and the Jewish people amidst all circumstances and conditions? Do you promise to establish a Jewish home and to participate actively in the life of the synagogue and the Jewish community?" He reached the last question, the one that mattered to Anne perhaps most of all. "If you should be blessed with children, do you promise to rear them in the Jewish faith and have the male children circumcised?"

Anne said yes, dropped her head beneath the surface and lifted her feet off the tile, allowing water to touch every cell of her skin. Emerging, she recited the blessing she had learned phonetically and practiced almost nightly. *Barukh attah Adonai, Eloheinu Melech ha-olam, asher kid'shanu b'mitzvotav v'tzivanu al hatevilah.* Praised are You, O Lord our God, King of the Universe, who sanctified us with Your commandments and commanded us concerning immersion.

Now, as a Jew, Anne immersed herself twice more in the *mikvah.* Then, together with Bill, she prayed the *Sheheheyanu,* thanking God for having "enabled us to reach this moment." Moving through his manual, Goldberger read from the thirty-sixth chapter of Ezekiel, the passage culminating in the divine promise: "You shall be My People and I will be your God." He intoned the *mi-sheberach* prayer, which seeks divine blessing even as it sets forth a Jew's ethical obligations, and with its centuries-old words conferred upon Anne the Hebrew name Hannah *bat Sarah imenu,* Hannah daughter of Sarah our mother. The suffix was used for all female converts. As for Hannah, Anne had chosen it for the sound, so close to the name with which she'd been baptized.

Officially a convert *al pi haHalakhah,* according to *halakhah,* Anne felt no revelation, just the satisfaction of having completed a process. Rose Pluss, soon to be her mother-in-law, was waiting in the dressing room to congratulate her. Even Bill, who thought the whole episode "a little bugga-bugga-boo, like they were throwing the bones for somebody," had to admit to a certain sense of moment.

It was clearer than ever to Anne and Bill what conversion had cost her. A few weeks before the *mikvah* ceremony, they had traveled together to North Carolina, hoping to win the approval of Anne's parents, or at least to defang their opposition. From the Raleigh airport they called the Davis home— no answer. That was odd, considering Anne had told her folks of the visit. She and Bill drove to the house, only to find the doors locked and the rooms dark. Anne called her sisters and none knew where their parents had gone.

Back in Denver, Anne began shopping for a wedding dress with Rose Pluss. Julius stepped forward to pay for the reception.

As December arrived and the wedding loomed, Anne installed a tiny Christmas tree in the basement of the house she and Bill shared. That way, he didn't actually have to see it. He knew it was there, of course, and he kept reminding Anne that there was no place in a Jewish home for a Christmas tree. But that lonely Yuletide of 1980 Anne sat beside it, wrapping presents for her estranged family, listening to carols she would never again sing, and, as she later put it, "just saying good-bye to it all and grieving."

On January 17, 1981, Anne donned the ivory princess gown with lace appliqué that she had chosen with her mother-in-law. She put on a string of pearls Bill had given her, fixed her veil into place, and clutched a bouquet of orchids, her favorite. Then she descended the staircase of the Town Club, a converted mansion that was the zenith of Reform social life in Denver, to a *chuppah* decorated with sunbursts of flowers. She descended alone. Neither of her parents was attending the wedding. Two of her four sisters had stayed away. "Their loss," Anne told herself.

As Anne joined Bill beneath the *chuppah*, two rabbis awaited. In the spirit of the Pluss family's dual affiliation, and also of the meticulous balancing act required by the joint-conversion program, both Daniel Goldberger and Steven Foster officiated. At Rabbi Goldberger's request, the men in the wedding party wore yarmulkes, even though they are not required in a Reform ceremony. The couple received two separate *ketubot*, marriage contracts, inscribed with the divergent Reform and Orthodox texts.

At the reception, Anne danced a graceful hora. She urged Bill on as he squatted and kicked his way through the shtetl dance called the kazatzky. She posed for photographs with Bill's relatives and friends, who comprised nearly all of the eighty guests. And when Julius and Dick Pluss, her new father-in-law and brother-in-law, hoisted Anne toward the heavens in a chair, she was not surprised. She had seen the ritual before, in a production of *Fiddler on the Roof.*

EARLY IN 1982, Rabbi Daniel Goldberger received a progress report on the joint-conversion panel. It listed the number of candidates sponsored by each local rabbi—twenty-four from Raymond Zwerin, thirty-six from Steven Foster, seventeen from Richard Shapiro, and so on. Rabbi Goldberger saw the list as confirmation of his own growing disenchantment with the program. Of the 130 converts on it, 94 had come through Reform rabbis and just 8 from Orthodox clergy. Yet who was it except the three Orthodox rabbis in the program—Goldberger, Stanley Wagner, and Jerome Lipsitz—who had put the ultimate imprimatur of Jewish legitimacy on the candidates?

Wagner often met a convert for the first time at the *mikvah*. He and his Orthodox partners, straining to coordinate their own schedules with the availability of the ritual bath, commonly wound up performing three or four ceremonies consecutively. Pressed for time, they might skip one of the most touching parts of the liturgy, the verses in which Ruth, the first convert in Jewish history, says, "For wherever you go will I go, and wherever you lodge I will lodge. Your people will be my people and your God my God." Occasionally, they even bypassed the Shema, the declaration of God's oneness that is among the most sacred passages in all Judaism, in the interest of keeping to the schedule of thirty minutes per convert.

Recently, Rabbi Goldberger had attended a fund-raiser for a Jewish organization and been thanked by a stranger. He squinted in return, as if focusing on a blurry object, and the young woman added, "Remember, you took me through the *mikvah*." But the rabbi-cum-counselor, who prided himself on knowing each congregant or patient by name, could not conjure this one. "What should've been a beautiful, individual experience," he would later say, "had become an assembly line."

Impersonality was just part of the problem. All the Orthodox rabbis had begun to feel theologically fraudulent. The provisions of the Denver program left the men with no true autonomy in their role as a rabbinical court, a *bet din*, no right to poke and probe a convert with follow-up questions. An Orthodox conversion, for instance, demanded that a candidate *kasher* her kitchen—ridding it of *treif* foods like pork, separating meat and milk, even tossing out pots and pans if necessary. A Denver convert submitting to the Ten Commitments might construe obeying the dietary laws to mean eating challah on Friday night. All the Ten Commitments specified about Sabbath observance, for that matter, was that a convert light candles. Did a convert intend to work on Shabbat? To drive? To watch television? The *bet din*, for the sake of the program, the national experiment, the ideal of Jewish unity, withheld any such inquiries.

"*Mikvah* dunkers," a Reconstructionist rabbi called the Orthodox clergy, as if that were their only role. Rabbi Goldberger preferred a different metaphor. A rabbi validated a food product as kosher by awarding it a *hechsher*, a stamp of approval. "And we," Rabbi Goldberger told his Orthodox colleagues, "are giving a *hechsher* for Reform converts."

Outside forces, too, shook Denver's delicate latticework of compromise. In December 1982, the president of the national association of Reform temples came to Denver to announce that it would serve as the trial city for Project Outreach, a $5 million campaign to educate gentiles about Judaism and invite their conversion. "Our program has to be tested," explained Rabbi Alexander Schindler of the Union of American Hebrew Congregations. "You just can't dream these things up in an office." And what city could be more appropriate than Denver, with its soaring intermarriage rate and rampant assimilation? Even better, Schindler suggested, Project Outreach could operate through the Basic Judaism class that was already a linchpin of the joint-conversion program.

Ever since the Reform union had approved the project a year earlier, it had set off raging protests in Conservative and Orthodox circles. Proselytizing had been anathema to Jewish tradition since the Roman era. And outreach was the antonym of "inreach," the concept of raising the level of observance among existing Jews. "Our supreme missionary obligation is to retain Jews within the Jewish community," wrote Rabbi Sol Roth, president of the Rabbinical Council of America, to which the Denver panel's three Orthodox rabbis belonged. "To be prepared to give up Jews who strayed from Judaism in order to secure the privilege of converting non-Jews who strayed from other religions is an exchange of dubious value."

More in Denver than anywhere, Conservative and Orthodox rabbis reacted with alarm. The issue, as they saw it, came down to quantity versus quality. The joint-conversion program sought to elevate the seriousness and thus the Jewish status of converts. Project Outreach, in comparison, had all the selectivity of a block party. Its message, Rabbi Wagner complained, was: "Anybody want to convert? Just go to a conversion program." Bernard Eisenman, the Conservative rabbi who chaired the joint-conversion panel, called Project Outreach "a nail in the coffin."

In March 1982, with the Project Outreach controversy still fresh, the national Reform movement again widened the rifts in Denver when the Central Conference of American Rabbis (CCAR) adopted patrilineal descent as a basis for Jewish identity. For 2,500 years, since the time of the prophet Ezra during the Babylonian exile, Judaism had accepted only matrilineal descent as valid. At a historical level, Reform leaders argued, matrilineality was less a hallowed concept from antiquity than a pragmatic answer to diasporic life, a way to ensure that even the child of an abandoned or unwed mother would be accepted by the Jewish community. More to the contemporary point, adopting patrilineality meant formally acknowledging what Reform rabbis had long tacitly tolerated—the prevalence of interfaith marriage and the presence in congregations of children born to gentile mothers.

"I don't think it's honest," Rabbi Foster said a few months after the vote, "to say that on a de facto level we will accept these children but on the de jure side we will opt for *Klal Yisrael*. I think patrilineal was an important decision—to say, finally, that this is what Reform Judaism stands for." He went on, "Religious identification is not whose sperm and whose egg goes into the making of this particular child."

Idealism aside, the Reform vote in practical terms created a caste of Jews whom neither Conservative nor Orthodox authorities recognized. For that matter, Reform rabbis in Israel refused to follow the American lead. A major American Reform scholar, Jakob Petuchowski of Hebrew Union College, decried the patrilineality decision as "a conscious step . . . to establish Reform Judaism as a sect on the periphery of Judaism." Even two Reform rabbis from the Denver area, Herbert Rose and Raymond Zwerin, abstained from the CCAR vote. But it was a decisive vote. Patrilineality won by a three-to-one margin, and, coupled with Project Outreach, the stance had a decisive effect in Denver.

"It was so flagrant!" Rabbi Jerome Lipsitz said several months later. "It was so obvious what they were doing because they knew that both of these concepts we could not live with. So why introduce them? Why impose them when they knew we were going to have to reject them?"

Steven Foster had an answer. "Now we live in an assimilated world," he argued, "and the only way we are going to guarantee people marrying Jews is to go back to a ghetto mentality or go back to the ghetto."

• •

SEVERAL MONTHS into her new life as a wife and a Jew, Anne
Davis asked her husband Bill a question. Why was it that three
thousand people had packed Temple Emanuel during the High
Holy Days but no more than a hundred had come to any of the
Shabbat services since then? On many Friday nights, Bill him-
self begged off, explaining that he was on call or just worn out.
It all mystified Anne. During her childhood, Edenton Street
Methodist had filled to capacity twice every single Sunday. And
when she followed the liturgy at Temple Emanuel, recent
Christian though she was, she had the sense that she knew
more of what the Methodists called "the Old Bible" than did
the Jews around her whose sages had written it.

"I don't understand," she confessed to Bill. "Where is
the commitment?"

Lots of Jewish people, he replied, don't think of the synagogue as the center of Jewish life. It's not even required for a
rabbi to lead a service. Jewish life is based on the family and the
home.

So Anne and Bill celebrated all the bar mitzvahs and
naming ceremonies and *bris*es a large extended family could
muster. They ate Rosh Hashanah dinner at Bill's parents'
house, and held the Passover seder and broke the Yom Kippur
fast at his sister's, where Jane made *bilkes* and *pireshkes* for
dessert from Aunt Nellie's recipes. Bill and Anne went to temple only for the High Holy Days.

"A revolving-door Jew"—that was what Rabbi Foster
sometimes called Bill, the kind who comes twice in the fall and
then is gone again. Bill didn't appreciate the joke. Regardless of
what promises he had made or implied in the joint-conversion
program, now that it was over he intended to "lead the life I always led, which was not observant." And where he led, at least
in matters Jewish, Anne followed.

An arrangement like theirs was the underside of the
Denver program, and of Jewish conversion as a whole. While

halakhic authorities fulminated about what standards a convert should meet, congregational rabbis knew that in conversionary marriages the less observant partner was frequently the born Jew. And the born Jew, by squatter's rights, set the tone. When Rabbi Foster thought about some of his converts, the ones he barely saw after the ceremony, he remembered how as a Boy Scout he had strived for an athletics merit badge. It required him, among other things, to high-jump, but his pudgy body refused to rise above the bar. When he finally managed to clear it, he felt less satisfaction from the achievement than from the knowledge that he'd never have to high-jump again.

Sure, there were exceptions in Denver. About the time Anne Davis converted, a psychiatrist named Jean Guthery started the Basic Judaism class. Born into the stern preachments of Calvinism, she had felt herself drawn to Judaism ever since a Jewish doctor eased her grief at watching a patient die when she was in medical school. Her marriage to the son of German Jewish refugees only added a practical motive to her spiritual stirrings. Ultimately she and her husband Peter sang together in their temple choir, traveled to Israel, sent their daughter to day school. The Guthery family embodied all that was most promising in the Denver program, and all that was most rare.

Still, Anne and Bill stayed faithful to their own sense of Jewish identity. Unable to have children, they began trying to adopt a child in 1985. The pregnant girl who approved them as parents was a gentile, and she insisted that her child be raised with Christmas. Without the threat being uttered, Anne knew the stakes: Agree or risk not getting the baby. She finessed the issue by pointing out that her family in North Carolina was Christian and surely would include any grandchild in its celebration. But at a deeper level, she refused any compromise. She had already made her decision. She'd gone over the hurdles. No way was she going to justify who she was all over again. She was a Jew.

Shortly after receiving an infant daughter, Alyssa, in early 1986, Anne and Bill brought her to Temple Emanuel to be given the Hebrew name Pessie Esther, after Bill's grand-mothers. When Alyssa was eighteen months old, Rabbi Gold-berger performed an Orthodox conversion ceremony for her. He did the same after Anne and Bill adopted a son, Andrew, in 1990.

The children, as they grew, drew their parents into a new round of Jewish activities—Hebrew school, Purim carnivals. They also provided the means and motive for thawing relations between Denver and Raleigh. Accompanying six-month-old Alyssa on a visit to the Davises, Bill met his in-laws for the first time, five years into his marriage. A routine developed. While Anne's parents never came to Denver, they hosted her family twice each year, for a week over Christmas and a week during the summer.

From both a physical and psychic remove, Anne and Bill followed the bitter debates in Israel about the Law of Re-turn. Bill's parents had visited Israel four times, and his sister Jane had won a local award for Jewish involvement named for Golda Meir. But Bill and Anne couldn't imagine making *aliyah*, and they doubted their children ever would. What they cared about was Denver, and beyond that America, and, as Anne put it, "protecting myself and my children from rejection, the re-jection of the Orthodox."

ON JUNE 17, 1983, six years after the Denver Rabbinical Coun-cil had sequestered itself in a hotel to engineer the joint-conversion program, the group convened for a regular business meeting. On paper, all that distinguished this session from any other was that it was being held thirty miles away in Boulder in deference to one member whose temple was in the college town. For months leading up to the meeting, however, the three Orthodox rabbis on the council had been secretly con-vening on their own, gradually drafting a statement to be issued this day.

Facing the entire body, Daniel Goldberger announced that the Orthodox rabbis were withdrawing from the conversion program. Privately, he had described it as "onerous" and "embarrassing" and "Kafkaesque." In the cause of diplomacy, even at this moment of its failure, he spoke more temperately of too many converts and too many compromises. He promised that the Orthodox rabbis would fulfill their obligations to any conversion candidates already being processed.

Then Rabbi Goldberger distributed copies of a letter drafted by Stanley Wagner, who was not present. It brought up Project Outreach and the patrilineality vote, both familiar causes of friction in Denver, and drove right to the essence of the conversion program. "The compromises," Wagner maintained, "were really uneven." A Reform rabbi, given a candidate uninterested in the joint program, enjoyed the "out" of performing his own conversion ceremony. The Orthodox, meanwhile, labored under the mandate to convert anyone who completed the program, even those who "fell so far below traditional standards." In the next paragraph, in capital letters, appeared the word for koshering meat: HECHSHER.

"I feel discounted," Steven Foster told the group. He felt ambushed besides. Before pulling out of the program, killing it really, the Orthodox had not even given their Reform partners the chance to discuss a solution. "And who says the compromises are unequal?" Foster thought. Why was it that liberal rabbis never got credit for their concessions? Here he was, asking his own candidates to obey at least one dietary law when the Reform movement as far back as 1885 had dismissed kashrut as "altogether foreign to our mental and spiritual state." Here he was, encouraging his candidates to submit to *hatafat dam brit* and *tevilah* when the Reform movement had disavowed both in 1891. Weren't those compromises?

With the joint program moribund after six years and 175 conversions, the veil of confidentiality slipped off. The *Intermountain Jewish News*, a weekly based in Denver, devoted a twelve-page section to the program in December 1983. The coverage could hardly have been more balanced or judicious, consisting almost entirely of transcribed interviews with the participating rabbis—an oral history, in effect. But as copies of the section gradually made their way through Orthodox circles, from centrist groups like Young Israel to Hasidic sects, a backlash gathered.

Rabbi Meir Kahane, the founder of the Jewish Defense League, fumed in his column in the weekly *Jewish Press* that the Denver rabbis were being paid "stupendous wages" to "calmly and without 'furor,' preside over the death of a community." Rabbi Moshe Sherer, leader of the ultra-Orthodox coalition Agudath Israel of America, disparaged the conversion process as "mind-boggling." The *Algemeyner Dzornal*, a Yiddish-language paper popular with Hasidim, called the program *gemeynzamer*, a double-edged adjective meaning "joint" but containing the root for "base" or "vile." Less elliptically, it likened the conversions to a "plague." An editorial in the *Jewish Observer*, a magazine of *haredi* Orthodoxy, declared that "compromise is actually a sell-out" and charged that the Denver Orthodox rabbis "have been party to an outrageous fraud."

"We have no choice but to draw the line, clearly, as to who is a Jew and who is not, as to what limits and basic standards of elementary Jewish identity and personal conduct we must insist upon," wrote Harold Jacobs, president of the American Council of Young Israel. "It is time that Orthodoxy put the rest of the Jewish community on notice: no longer will 'Jewish unity' be bought at the expense of Jewish identity. For *Klal Yisrael* today, that is too high a price."

The most significant assault of all came from the Rabbinical Council of America—the group that the Denver Orthodox rabbis had sworn allegiance to and then kept in the dark. Addressing the council's entire membership in February 1984, President Gilbert Klaperman declared that by participating in the joint-conversion program, Goldberger, Lipsitz, and Wagner had "raised serious questions as to their reliability, credibility, and integrity as rabbis."

Soon after, the council mounted a formal investigation, separately summoning rabbis Goldberger and Wagner to New York to defend themselves. A panel of council officers peppered each man with questions: Why had they surrendered Orthodox standards? Why had they collaborated on theology with Conservative and Reform clergy? Why had they kept it secret? Had they been paid? "We took part in an exciting, historical experiment," Rabbi Goldberger offered, not very convincingly. "Maybe it will pave the way for something in the future."

After several hours of interrogation, the Denver contingent retreated to the airport. Stanley Wagner felt relieved that things hadn't gone worse. Facing an ad hoc committee was far better than the *Vaad Hakavod*, the Honor Council, which held the power to expel. The committee hadn't even issued a formal censure. Daniel Goldberger, though, cringed at the humiliation, the public shame. The whole program, he now thought, had been a mistake. Of nearly two hundred Denver converts, the rabbinical council accepted as Jewish fewer than a dozen sponsored by Orthodox rabbis. It had delivered a message, indelibly and unmistakably, to the very mainstream of the Orthodox rabbinate: *Don't you dare try anything like Denver.*

In the years ahead, as the "Who is a Jew?" issue flared anew in Israel and America, Rabbi Wagner tried futilely to revive the Denver model. He raised money to commission two Modern Orthodox scholars in Jerusalem to write a halakhic basis for a joint-conversion program. He carried the campaign to the Modern Orthodox group Edah and to the organization of Conservative congregations, United Synagogue of America. He testified before the Ne'eman Commission.

The memory of how Wagner and his Denver colleagues had been pilloried, however, scared off nearly every potential ally in the Orthodox world. "Let it drop, Stanley," one colleague in the Rabbinical Council of America pleaded. "We got you out of this mess once." Steven Riskin, who by 1984 had left Manhattan's Lincoln Square Synagogue to become the chief rabbi of the West Bank settlement of Efrat, denied having inspired the Denver program with his lecture on conversion and mitzvot.

There were exceptions who viewed Denver in retrospect as the great missed opportunity. "It is a sad commentary on Jewish religious life today that those who favor unity are on the defensive and must keep their efforts secret," Rabbi Irving Greenberg wrote in an essay entitled "Tragedy in Denver." He went on, "The threatened outcome is a *kulturkampf* in Israel and communal divisiveness and increased assimilation of nonobservant Jews in America." Rabbi Haskel Lookstein struck a similar tone, writing to Jerome Lipsitz: "The fact that the effort in Denver collapsed is, I believe, a tragedy for American Jewry. While I am very upset at what the Reform are doing, I do feel you and Stanley and Daniel were trying to find a way to solve a problem which most Orthodox rabbis are ducking outrageously."

In Denver, time rendered its own verdict. The intermarriage rate for young adults in 1997 stood at 72 percent, virtually the same number as when the joint-conversion program had begun. Rabbi Steven Foster threw his efforts into an outreach program called Stepping Stones, aimed at building Jewish identity in the children of mixed marriages. Stanley Wagner, after retiring as the rabbi of Beth HaMedrash Hagadol, took to worshipping in its chapel, which unlike the main sanctuary has a *mechitzah*. He turned down a $5,000 honorarium one year rather than lead Yom Kippur worship for his former congregation, with its mixed seating.

Various theories, none of them correct, laid the blame for the Denver program's demise on different factions. One version condemned the ultra-Orthodox for their ferocious criticism; but that criticism had come only after the fact. Another indicted the Reform movement for having adopted patrilineality; but that ignored problems inherent in the Denver system from its genesis. The joint-conversion panel collapsed under the weight of its own contradictions, fundamental differences in doctrine that no amount of belief in *Klal Yisrael* could wish away. "The lesson that we learned from this six-year experiment," Rabbi Wagner said in 1984, "was that it's erroneous to build the idea of Jewish unity on religious or ideological compromise." Put another way, Denver discovered it was easier to change a Jew's status than a Jew's soul.

ON THE SATURDAY MORNING of August 14, 1999, more than twenty years after Bill Pluss and Anne Davis had first exchanged admiring glances on the internal medicine floor, they looked upon their daughter Alyssa becoming a bat mitzvah. Rabbi Foster, who had guided Anne through much of the conversion process, officiated. And when the time came to open the Ark, that honor went to Anne's father, Charles, who was making his first visit from Raleigh. Two of Anne's sisters also participated in the ceremony. Their mother did not attend because she had to care for two infirm relatives in North Carolina. Or so Anne was told.

For Bill, the ceremony confirmed the wisdom of Anne's conversion. His family was Jewish. His children were Jewish. The heritage was being passed on to another generation.

Bill knew, of course, how the Denver program had failed in the end. And he knew that, more recently, the Ne'eman Commission in Israel had similarly failed to gain recognition from the nation's Chief Rabbinate for its joint-conversion program there. After all the efforts Anne had exerted to satisfy any standard for Jewish identity, her conversion, like the vast majority of the 175 in Denver, had never been accepted by Orthodox authorities. Ironically enough, Andrew and Alyssa stood on firmer ground as adoptees who had been converted solely under an Orthodox rubric than they would have as the biological children of a mother whose own Jewish credentials could be impeached.

With her bat mitzvah, though, Alyssa entered a period of life when Jewish children famously stray from observance, as had her own father. The phenomenon has even spawned its own joke. A rabbi has mice in his synagogue and asks advice from a colleague on how to get rid of them. The second rabbi says he has a foolproof system. Every time he finds a mouse, he makes it a tiny *kippa* and tallit and gives it a bar mitzvah. After the ceremony, the mouse never comes back to shul.

Anne and Bill had already talked about what they would do if their children, now thirteen and nine, fell in love with Christians. Bill was adamant that they marry Jews. Anne, the one who had sacrificed so much to turn Jewish and been so baffled at times about what actually constitutes Jewish identity, was less absolute.

"It's going to be hard for me to tell Alyssa not to date whoever she wishes," Anne told Bill one day. "I can't stand up and say, 'Don't marry out of your faith.' It would be hypocritical. Because I did."

Judaism and Gender: Revolution toward Tradition

"WHO IS A JEW?" was a question with more than one meaning as American Jewry grew ever more fractious through the seventies and eighties. While Denver tried futilely to answer in the language of conversion standards, the female half of the American Jewish population was asking in terms of religious and social equality. Literally speaking, Jewish women were considered just as Jewish as men; under *halakhah*, in fact, a child's identity as a Jew descended entirely from the mother. But in practical terms, whether in worship or religious education or fulfillment of the commandments called mitzvot, Jewish women in the feminist era saw discrimination under patriarchy. When one couldn't be a rabbi or read from the Torah or study the Talmud, when one couldn't pray or sing beside a man under religious law lest his mind be turned to base desires—when all that was true, women wanted to know, then who indeed was a Jew?

The gender issue was unique among all the collisions between modernism and traditionalism in American Judaism because it represented a drive toward deeper observance rather than away from it. Whether as Reform Jews creating liturgy, Conservatives seeking ordination, or Orthodox joining in prayer groups, women pressed for more observance, more participation. "I do not want to reject the basics," the Orthodox activist Blu Greenberg has written. "All I ask is that women have equal access to them." That imperative has allowed Jewish women to ally across the usual dividing lines between the major branches or separating political liberals from conservatives. The spectrum of Jewish feminism stretched from the left-wing lesbian Reform rabbi at a Seven Sisters college to the Orthodox woman covered for modesty from neckline to ankles while learning Talmud in a yeshiva on the West Bank.

"Has there ever been a greater social and religious revolution in any century such as Jewish women have achieved in this last one?" the journalist Jonathan Mark marveled in the *New York Jewish Week*. Rabbi Mordechai Breuer, an award-winning Torah scholar in Israel, contends that only the Enlightenment and Zionism reshaped modern Judaism as dramatically as the "revolution on the status, rights, and role of women." Secular Jewish life, too, was shaken by the feminists' critique of conventional family roles.

But the revolution, precisely because it *was* a revolution, provoked strife at every turn. To create a Jewish woman equal in her position to a Jewish man was to challenge both religious law and communal custom. In both real and symbolic ways, *halakhah* erected a *mechitzah*, a partition, between the sexes. It stipulated that women cannot serve as rabbis or cantors, cannot be called to the Torah to read or recite blessings, cannot be divorced without a husband's consent, cannot perform any mitzvot that might absent them from their domestic duties. In his prayers each morning, an Orthodox man thanked God for *shelo asani isha*, not making me a woman.

And while only Orthodox Jews consider *halakhah* the immutable word of God, for decades males held nearly as complete a monopoly on congregational and clerical leadership in the Reform and Conservative branches, too. The famous Jewish support for liberalism and social justice, including such feminist causes as legal abortion and the Equal Rights Amendment, effectively ceased at the synagogue door. For all their political progressivism, Jewish men created the stereotypes of the Jewish American Princess, with her nose job and mink coat, and of the sacrificing, suffocating Jewish Mother. Even when Jewish women achieved equality on paper outside Orthodoxy, equality in practice came fitfully and against backlash, cracking apart individual synagogues and the entire Conservative denomination along the way.

Jewish women themselves are hardly immune from the tension between doctrine and custom on one side and the modern American belief in gender equality on the other. The writer Adrienne Rich has called herself "split at the root" between her allegiances as a Jew and a woman. Letty Cottin Pogrebin, one of the founders of *Ms.* magazine, chose the image of "a double agent." As an Orthodox feminist, Blu Greenberg likened herself to a passenger forced to choose between two cars, one parked and the other pulling away. Staying still feels like "moving backward," yet going ahead feels like "losing connection."

The roots of Jewish feminism reach back to antiquity. The Bible tells not only of wives and mothers but also of Deborah, the judge and prophet and warrior. Esther saves Persia's Jews in the Purim story, and in one Hanukkah legend, a woman named Judith inspires the rebellion against Hellenistic rule. The immediate history of Jewish feminism and the conflicts it wrought can be traced to the Breslau Conference in 1846, when the German leaders of Reform Judaism called for women to undertake all of the mitzvot. On American shores in succeeding decades, Reform created "family pews," mixed choirs, and confirmation ceremonies for girls and boys alike, all of them ruptures with *halakhah* and tradition. The massive immigration of Eastern European Jews offered women careers, whether paid or as volunteers, in the burgeoning field of social work; the National Council of Jewish Women was formed in

1893, Hadassah in 1912. It was Hadassah's founder, Henrietta Szold, who in 1903 became the first woman admitted to the Jewish Theological Seminary in New York.

Szold won entry, however, on the promise that she would not use the knowledge she acquired there to seek ordination. Her experience typified the distance between the rhetoric of equality and its enactment for much of the twentieth century. Mordecai Kaplan, the Conservative maverick who inspired the Reconstructionist movement, gave his daughter Judith the first bat mitzvah in history in 1922, but the ceremony remained rare until after World War II. In 1955, the religious law committee of the Rabbinical Assembly, the major association of Conservative clergy, voted to allow women on special occasions to take an *aliyah*, ascending the altar to bless the portion of Torah being read; a minority opinion, which congregational rabbis were permitted to accept if they wished, held that women could take an *aliyah* under any circumstances. Even with such theological sanction, a survey in 1962 discovered that barely 3 percent of Conservative synagogues gave women *aliyot* without restrictions.

The very next year, the revolution began, with the publication of a book that superficially had nothing to do with Judaism. Betty Friedan's manifesto, *The Feminine Mystique*, described the frustration and anomie of educated, motivated women penned into suburban domesticity. Perhaps not coincidentally, Friedan was Jewish and the product of quintessentially Jewish left-wing politics. Many of the women who rose to feminist leadership in her wake, such as Gloria Steinem and Bella Abzug, were Jewish as well. While they expressed their activism primarily through the secular domain of politics, their campaign for equality reached the ears of religious listeners, too. Blu Greenberg, a self-described "mild-mannered yeshiva girl," read Friedan and felt the "click" of feminism in specifically Jewish ways—the Talmudic education she never got, the religious rituals her daughters were denied, the way she herself cleaned the household of leavened products before Passover while her husband was the one allowed under Jewish law to declare the home ready for *Pesach*. "Once I had tasted the tree of knowledge," she wrote, invoking the biblical Eve, "there was no going back."

Jewish women were stimulated as much by feminism's flaws as its attributes. In feminist circles, they sometimes found themselves attacked by blacks for clinging to white privilege, and even by certain Christians for participating in a religion that had destroyed goddess worship in ancient times. The moment of reckoning for Letty Cottin Pogrebin, among others, occurred at the 1975 United Nations conference inaugurating International Women's Decade. When the assembly passed a resolution parroting the UN's notorious declaration equating Zionism with racism, Pogrebin went from being a feminist who coincidentally was Jewish to a feminist Jew.

The Jewish feminist movement, in fact, had been building for nearly a decade already in one corner of the counterculture. The late sixties and early seventies saw the creation of the first *chavurot*, groups that prayed and studied together without rabbinical leaders or denominational ties. While the *chavurot* scorned the mainstream Judaism of suburban synagogues as vapid and materialistic, they aspired to reclaim the religion instead of reject it. The do-it-yourself ethos of the *chavurot* demanded a laity steeped in liturgy, ritual, and Torah, much like the typical Orthodox congregation; yet as products of the Left, the *chavurot* accepted the principle of equal participation by women, however imperfectly they practiced it.

From the *chavura* movement emerged some of the most important Jewish feminists—the scholar Paula Hyman, the theologian Judith Plaskow, the editor Elizabeth Koltun. It gave rise to *The Jewish Catalogue*, an anthology of Jewish observance and lifestyle for the baby-boom generation, as well as the influential magazine *Response*. But the single most influential product of the religious and social ferment was Ezrat Nashim, a women's study group founded in 1971. The name literally meant "succor for women," and it wryly punned on the Hebrew term for the segregated women's gallery in a traditional synagogue—precisely the existing order Ezrat Nashim aimed to demolish.

In March 1972, ten of Ezrat Nashim's members descended on the Rabbinical Assembly's convention to present a "Call for Change" demanding full equality for women in Jewish law and worship. It was no accident that the group chose to direct its appeal to the Conservative movement. The tiny Reconstructionist branch had already agreed to ordain women as rabbis, and the Reform branch was about to similarly act. Not even the wildest optimist expected the Orthodox to follow. So the Conservative movement, as the center of the Jewish religious spectrum, provided the arena for the clash of modernism and heritage. And the women of Ezrat Nashim were the elite of Conservative Judaism, the products of its Camp Ramah system and United Synagogue Youth groups. "To educate women and deny them the opportunity to act from this knowledge," the "Call for Change" argued, "is an affront to their intelligence, talent, and dignity."

That challenge resounded through both Jewish and feminist circles. Within a year of Ezrat Nashim's declaration, the Conservative movement had voted to count women in the minyan, the quorum of ten adults required for a prayer service, and to read from the Torah and take *aliyot* without restrictions. Jewish feminism simultaneously began to spread across denominational lines. Five hundred delegates attended the National Jewish Women's Conference, where the keynote address was delivered by Blu Greenberg. "Where there's a rabbinical will," she later implored the Jewish community and Orthodoxy in particular, "there's a halakhic way."

Indeed, the revolution of rising expectations reached even the more tradition-bound quarters of Jewish life. In the late seventies, the monumental rabbi of Modern Orthodoxy, Joseph Soloveitchik, delivered the first Talmud lecture for women at Stern College, the female division of Yeshiva University. With Soloveitchik's powerful approval thus signaled,

Orthodox Jews opened the Drisha Institute in New York to provide women with advanced religious study. A Modern Orthodox rabbi in the Bronx, Avi Weiss, permitted a women's *tefillah* group, so named for the Hebrew word for "prayer," to meet regularly in his synagogue. In the Conservative branch, meanwhile, the Jewish Theological Seminary had remained resistant enough to egalitarian practice through the seventies that its own synagogue still had a *mechitzah*. After four years of bruising debate among its faculty, the seminary voted in 1983 to admit women for rabbinical training. The first female Conservative rabbi, Amy Eilberg, was ordained two years later.

To outward appearances, Judaism was proceeding inexorably toward sexual equality through the late eighties and into the nineties. Women ultimately formed half of the rabbinical class at Hebrew Union College, a Reform institution, and nearly 40 percent at the Jewish Theological Seminary. Despite resistance in the Northeast and industrial Midwest, most Conservative congregations accommodated full participation by women. The poet Marcia Falk produced an entire liturgy in gender-neutral English* in her *Book of Blessings*, published in 1996, while both the Reform and Conservative movements began to revise passages in their prayer books presenting God as a male. Mainstream temples and synagogues routinely held naming ceremonies for newborn girls as a ritual comparable to a baby boy's circumcision. Women's Talmud study and *tefillah* groups flourished within Orthodoxy, and several particularly daring synagogues hired women to conduct pastoral duties as "congregational interns."

Far from settling the gender war in American Judaism, however, this progress in many ways intensified it. Feminism raised a question that discomfited Jews, including some women, in every branch: Was religious tradition merely raw

---

* It is grammatically impossible to use gender-neutral language in Hebrew, so in the Hebrew version of the liturgy, Falk alternated between masculine and feminine forms.

material to be cut to modern fashion? In a protest against their movement's acceptance of female rabbis and egalitarian worship, about 250 rabbis and 3,000 families broke from the Conservative movement in 1990 to form a new body called the Union for Traditional Judaism. The union later established its own seminary under the leadership of David Weiss Halevni, a renowned scholar who had resigned from the Jewish Theological Seminary in protest against female ordination. At the Western Wall in Israel, Orthodox men and yeshiva students disrupted the mixed-gender services of Reform and Conservative congregations, as well as the all-female Torah readings of a trans-denominational group called Women of the Wall that was led by an American Orthodox rabbi's wife, Rivka Haut. Within the Reform branch, consternation grew about a "feminization" of Judaism, brought on both by the increasing number of female clergy and the trendiness of "spirituality," with its emphasis on mysticism, meditation, and divine healing.

The bitterness seeped into individual congregations. Leaders of the East Midwood Jewish Center, a Conservative synagogue in Brooklyn, literally locked out a faction opposed to egalitarian worship. A similar rift at the Hillcrest Jewish Center in Queens wound up in court. A Conservative synagogue in Passaic, New Jersey, allowed a homeless Orthodox congregation to use its sanctuary, only to discover the guests had erected a *mechitzah*. When the synagogue president tried to tear it down, he was arrested. At a 1985 convention of *chavurot* Jews, who had in many ways developed Jewish feminism, traditionalists demanded for the sake of "pluralism" that egalitarian worship services be augmented by those using a *mechitzah*.

To the Jewish women who had pressed for an equal role in their own religion, however, their revolution seemed, if anything, to have accomplished too little by the late nineties. Even with three hundred female rabbis in Reform Judaism, only three led congregations with more than a thousand families. Of the fourteen hundred Conservative rabbis in America, fewer than one hundred were women, and fewer than thirty headed a synagogue. A *Los Angeles Times* poll in 1998 found Jewish women twice as likely as Jewish men not to have received any religious education. Even among Jews born in the sixties and seventies, nearly two-thirds of men had been bar mitzvahed, while fewer than half of women had been bat mitzvahed. While two thousand women flocked to an international conference on feminism and Orthodoxy, women's *tefillah* groups remained concentrated on the Modern Orthodox fringe. The president of the Rabbinical Council of America, a centrist body by Orthodox standards, personally solicited a halakhic opinion from a panel of Yeshiva University scholars, who denounced the prayer groups as a "total and apparent deviation from tradition" that could only contribute to "licentiousness." Even the Modern Orthodox rabbi Shlomo (formerly Steven) Riskin, a firm supporter of *tefillah* groups, worried aloud, "When you're one step ahead of the crowd, you're a genius. When you're two steps ahead, you're a crackpot."

The gender issue in Judaism, then, was a study in gaps—the gap between principles and practice, the gap between political ideals and religious tradition, the gap between a biblical past and an American present. The major branches of Judaism could stipulate policies but not dictate individual conscience, and for that reason the struggle over sexual equality in the synagogue proved so intractable, even among comrades of goodwill. Few congregations abounded more in camaraderie and Jewish knowledge than the *minyan* that met every Saturday on the Westside of Los Angeles. And few were plunged more deeply into study, contemplation, and conflict by the prospect of reconciling ancient ways to modern mores.

CHAPTER THREE

Los Angeles, California, 1987–1989

Early on the Sabbath morning of April 25, 1987, Rachel Adler strode along the empty boulevards where Los Angeles borders Beverly Hills, bound for a stucco chapel tucked amid the glass towers and gallerias, where she would lead worship for her new congregation. With each step, she cut a doubly unlikely figure. She was a walker in this most automotive of cities, and she was a Jewish woman carrying a tallit, the prayer shawl reserved throughout centuries for men.

Not quite an hour later, standing at a reading table fronted and flanked by pews, Rachel moved into the heart of the morning service called *Shacharit*. She chanted the promise of godly deliverance that ends the *Shema*, Judaism's declaration of faith, and then she waited momentarily for the faithful around her to rise and face east for the *Amidah*, the series of benedictions so essential to Jewish observance it is called *ha-Tefillah*, The Prayer.

This congregation, filled with clergy and educated laity, was not the sort that needed to be cued. Before taking its current name, the Library Minyan, it had been called the Rabbis' Minyan. A member for one year, a graduate student in a sanctuary of the ordained, Rachel had begun volunteering to conduct services, as Judaism allowed a learned congregant to do. Many of the regulars, though, already knew her reputation, and the rest could read the Hebrew lettering on her crocheted *kippa*. It spelled *apikoros*—heretic.

Rachel prayed the first words of the *Amidah* silently, for they were meant to be absorbed quietly, privately, to focus a worshipper's mind on the blessings ahead. *Adonai siphatai tiftach u'phi yagid tehilatecha*, Open my mouth, O Lord, and my lips will proclaim your praise. Then Rachel's lips parted to praise "the God of Abraham, of Isaac, and of Jacob," words that derived from the Book of Genesis. And then she inserted a phrase found nowhere in the Torah: *Elohay Sarah, elohay Rivka, elohay Rachel v'elohay Leah*, God of Sarah, God of Rebecca, God of Rachel, and God of Leah.

Now a rustle rose from the pews, a wave of murmurs and grumbles. The Library Minyan was accustomed to all manner of distractions, from the thrum of traffic outside its doors to the sight of children playing with the Ark; it so prided itself on a history of informed disputation that one Yom Kippur a member had sermonized about how much the congregation loved to argue. This was different. Rachel Adler, people instantly realized, had just changed the *Amidah*. She had taken a passage of liturgy codified for more than a millennium and inserted a blessing created only a generation ago. It was called the *Imahot*, the Matriarchs.

As the worshippers absorbed the first shock, Rachel proceeded, oblivious to the stir, to close the first blessing. *Barukh attah Adonai, magen Avraham*, Praised are you, Lord, shield of Abraham. To which she added, *u'foked Sarah*, Rememberer of Sarah.

"What's this la-di-da Judaism?" Mitch Miller, head of the minyan's steering committee, asked himself.

"You can't just put in whatever you want," Jeff Rabin, a member of the minyan since its founding sixteen years earlier, heard a neighbor mutter.

"I'd love to have done it," whispered a friend to Fran Grossman, who had spent her entire life in Los Angeles's Jewish community.

When night fell and candles burned in the *havdalah* ceremony that ends Sabbath with its pleasures and proscriptions, the telephone wires sizzled with hours of pent-up indignation. Who was Rachel Adler to act by fiat? Where'd she get those blessings? Did religious law, *halakhah*, allow them? Had she run them by the Ritual Committee? Did you hear the way she slowed down when she said them? It was so in-your-face.

The next morning the phone rang in Rachel's apartment, the one she had chosen specifically to be within walking distance of the Library Minyan. Looking up from a pile of schoolwork on the kitchen table, she grabbed the receiver off the pass-through. A representative of the Ritual Committee informed her that it was forbidden to make changes in liturgy without prior approval. From now on, she had to stick to the words in the prayer book. No *Imahot*.

"Then I won't lead services," Rachel replied, "until I can pray the way I want to."

She had been invoking the *Imahot* for more than a decade already at the *chavurot* and conferences of Jewish feminists like herself. She could've sworn she'd spoken it while leading the Library Minyan on some other Sabbath. The *Imahot* brought the Torah's women back into the liturgy, gathered in the foremothers from theological exile. Rachel did not think of herself as a confrontational person but as one who chose the battles that mattered.

Until this weekend, the minyan had always enjoyed its battles, confident that beneath them lay a bedrock of shared convictions. Everyone honored in Jewish tradition. Everyone accepted in egalitarian worship. Everyone believed they could reconcile the patriarchal past and the equal-rights present, could square the circle of heritage and modernism. Now Rachel Adler had shaken the equilibrium.

Before hanging up, Rachel asked just one dispensation from the Ritual Committee. She wanted to make her own case for the *Imahot* to the congregation. It was agreed. Each week in the Library Minyan, a member delivered a *d'var Torah*, a mixture of exegesis and moral lesson drawn from the weekly Torah portion. Two Sabbaths hence, it would be the *apikoros*'s turn.

RACHEL ADLER had grown up as Ruthelyn Rubin, a heretic against not religion but atheism. The matriarchal line of her own family stretched back from the West Rogers Park neighborhood of Chicago to Bohemia and Germany and to the headwaters of Reform Judaism. Little of that faith remained during Ruthelyn's childhood in the fifties. Her parents, a guidance counselor and an insurance executive, never held a seder. They spoke the noun "ritual" only when preceded by the adjective "mindless." As for Yiddish, her maternal grandfather called it "degenerate."

Drawn in some inchoate way to God, Ruthelyn learned at age five how to cross herself from a Catholic playmate named Patsy Doyle. "I want to be the first Jewish nun," Ruthelyn told her mother soon after. A few years later, Lorraine Rubin caught her daughter in the backyard trying to set fire to a steak as an offering to Athena.

Ruthelyn ultimately found the Almighty through her paternal grandmother, Ida Rubin, who was still practicing Orthodoxy amid the gritty graystones and six-flats of her Albany Park neighborhood. The epiphany came one Yom Kippur. Ruthelyn and Ida were in the women's balcony of the shul, gazing down on the men prostrating themselves before the Ark, a tide of reverence in black and white tallitot. "If having a mystical experience is feeling a compelling truth you can't articulate," Ruthelyn would later recall, "then I was having a mystical experience."

Ida Rubin died when Ruthelyn was ten, but she lived on

for her granddaughter partly through her candlesticks, which Ruthelyn inherited early in her teens. As her own parents ate dinner oblivious in the kitchen, Ruthelyn kindled the *Shabbos* candles in the deserted dining room every week. Through high school, even as she aspired to follow her mother into education, Ruthelyn took part in a Reform temple's classes and youth group, ultimately winning a scholarship to a Reform summer camp. There, for the first time, she laid eyes upon a page of Talmud, albeit in English translation. By the time she entered Northwestern University as an English major, she had learned enough Hebrew to worship at an Orthodox synagogue, untroubled by the *mechitzah* and all that the partition symbolized, moved instead by the eloquence of ritual and gesture and liturgy. And she had dropped "Ruthelyn" in favor of her Hebrew name, Rachel.

During her freshman year, Rachel met an Orthodox rabbinical student named Moshe Adler who was teaching a course at Northwestern's Hillel center. Three years later, she married both the man and the way of life he embodied. Moshe Adler knew Jewish texts as Rachel wished to know them. He resided in an Orthodox section of West Rogers Park that, more than a neighborhood, was a community. On Shabbat afternoon, you could leave a house key where your minyan friends knew to find it, take a leisurely stroll, and return to find company in the living room sipping tea.

After ordination, Moshe Adler became a Hillel rabbi and Rachel followed him through campus postings in Wisconsin and Southern California before settling at the University of Minnesota. Working on her dissertation on the language of madness in Renaissance drama, Rachel doubted that a university job awaited in a glutted market. Besides, there was a field that attracted her even more than English literature. With advanced religious education closed off to Orthodox women, she learned Talmud and *halakhah* from Moshe at the kitchen table.

Meanwhile, she was studying other texts as well, particularly Simone de Beauvoir's *The Second Sex*, with its critique of how women are treated as "the Other." Rachel thought back often to an event in her sophomore year of college. Her maternal grandmother had died, leaving no male survivor to say kaddish, the prayer a pious Jew is required to recite daily during the twelve months of formal mourning. Rachel asked an Orthodox rabbi whether, given the circumstances, she could say the prayer. No, the rabbi told her, not as a woman. But for $350 she could hire a man to do it.

At the time, as Rachel was falling in love with Moshe and Orthodoxy, the rejection had stung in a personal way. Now, nearly a decade later in 1971, the rebuke struck her as more systemic. How could the prayer of a woman, of the woman who had nursed her grandmother through the last days, please God less than the prayer of a hired male stranger? How could *halakhah* override right and wrong? Was it really divine? Or was it just a kind of power controlled by the privileged?

By coincidence, the editor of a small local Jewish magazine called *Davka*, a Hebrew word that connotes a sort of principled contrariness, was then planning an issue on women. Since Rachel was both a Hillel *rebbetzin*, a rabbi's wife, and a graduate student in English literature, he asked her to submit something. She sat at the same kitchen table that was the closest thing she had ever known to a yeshiva desk and began to write about life as a "peripheral Jew," denied learning and responsibilities because of her gender. After the essay had been accepted, she begged the editor to return it, certain that she was merely, like one of the characters in her abandoned dissertation, "a solitary madwoman."

Instead, the article appeared under the title "The Jew Who Wasn't There." And when the issue of *Davka* attracted such a wide readership that it had to be reprinted and distributed nationwide, Rachel found herself quite unexpectedly one of the foremothers of Jewish feminism and its rebellion toward tradition:

> The halakhic scholars . . . must make it possible for women to claim their share in the Torah and begin to do

the things a Jew was created to do. If necessary we must agitate until the scholars are willing to see us as Jewish souls in distress rather than as tools with which men do mitzvot. . . . There is no time to waste. For too many centuries, the Jewish woman has been a golem, created by Jewish society. She cooked and bore and did her master's will, and when her tasks were done, the Divine Name was removed from her mouth. It is time for the golem to demand a soul.

It was easier to call for revolution, though, than to live it. In 1975, Rachel helped found a women's minyan in the University of Minnesota's Hillel center. The group contravened Orthodoxy simply by counting women in the quorum for prayer. Compounding the apostasy, women read Torah, took *aliyot*, uttered the mourning prayer of kaddish and the *kedushah* that proclaimed God's holiness. Rachel herself wore a tallit. Yet all the while she remained married to an Orthodox rabbi and obedient to the mitzvot. While many Jewish feminists denounced the halakhic law on family purity for considering a menstruating woman as unclean, Rachel wrote an essay for *The Jewish Catalogue* defending it as "one of the few major Jewish symbolisms in which women had a place."

The dichotomy tore at her soul. She longed for the ecstasy of a Hasidic *shtibel* even as she refused to submit to its dogma. She could no more envision praying in a Conservative synagogue than in a mosque. To buy kosher meat on Friday and no longer be dispatched by the butcher with "Shabbat Shalom" was to be cast into the wilderness. She wanted her three-year-old son educated in an Orthodox day school, yet she feared he would learn sexism there. Her public stances left her beloved husband open to ridicule, she wrote in an essay, as "the rabbi who can't convince his own wife . . . the man who can't control his own wife."

In 1984, the awkward balance tipped. Rachel and Moshe Adler divorced. Rachel joined a Conservative synagogue. It never felt like home, but it never felt like a mosque either. On most Sabbaths, Rachel sat next to Michael Goldberg, an ordained rabbi with a doctorate who taught her theology. She studied Bible and Talmud with professors at the University of Minnesota. The hunger for more learning, for the formal Jewish education so long deferred, led Rachel to apply for a joint program in religion and social ethics at the University of Southern California and Hebrew Union College.

When she was admitted in 1986 and had moved to Southern California, Rachel faced one last question: where to daven? One of her Minneapolis friends, an anthropologist named Riv-Ellen Prell, had done fieldwork in a *chavura* in Los Angeles. Many of its members, she told Rachel, now belonged to something called the Library Minyan, which had a participatory style and no formal leader. That appealed to Rachel. "I'm allergic," she would later say, "to having rabbis tell me what to do."

Now, drafting her *d'var Torah* in the early days of May 1987, Rachel was trying to tell the rabbis what to do, the rabbis and the rest of the Library Minyan. She realized she had underestimated the consequences of introducing the *Imahot*. It was one thing to seek more access for women as worship leaders, Torah readers, even rabbis; that spoke to liberal democratic values deeply embedded in the congregation. But letting the presence of women transform the tradition, altering the words that were the pathway to God—well, that was a frightening prospect, if you saw yourself as the custodian of a fragile heritage.

The price of change grew even clearer as Rachel consulted the Torah portion she would interpret. It was *Acharay Mot*, a section of Leviticus read both in spring and on Yom Kippur because of its instructions about the Day of Atonement. Rachel focused, though, on the opening verse: "The Lord spoke to Moses after the death of the two sons of Aaron who died when they drew too close to the presence of the Lord." The sentence referred to an incident six chapters earlier:

Now Aaron's sons Nadab and Abihu each took his fire pan, put fire in it, and laid incense on it; and they offered before the Lord alien fire, which He had not enjoined upon them. And the fire came forth from the Lord and consumed them; thus they died at the instance of the Lord.

How many times Rachel had heard that passage preached in her Orthodox years. The rabbi would exhume Aaron's sons as object examples of the price of defying divine law. Here was the proof of what God thought of Conservative and Reform Jews and their so-called innovations of mixed seating and driving to shul. Yet here, for Rachel, was the defense of her own alien fire.

She rose to address the congregation on May 9, 1987, with no small trepidation. She was now engaged to a civil rights lawyer named David Schulman, but he was hundreds of miles away, attending a conference on AIDS discrimination. Without David, her closest ally, Rachel had invited half a dozen Jewish feminist rabbis and scholars, much like a Broadway producer who "papers the house" with friends on opening night, hoping their certain applause will affect the critics.

"The offering we make with our words," Rachel now declared, "is grounded in our personal integrity. . . . What prayer demands of us therefore is not only the stylized and symbol-laden choreography of ritual but also sober comprehension and scrupulous truthfulness to our own experience of God. A pressing enough reason to change the language or content of liturgy is the demand upon us to speak truthfully to God out of our own reality."

In her own reality, Rachel had abandoned hope that Orthodoxy would ever fully admit her. Literally and otherwise, she had left the *eruv*, the wire boundary that demarked sacred ground, and she had suffered a kind of homelessness ever since. It harrowed every hallowed Sabbath. She tried to fill the void now with a belief in the morality of risks, terrible risks. The *Imahot* was one. This *d'var Torah* was another.

"The half truth of 'God of Abraham, God of Isaac, God of Jacob,' " she said now, "can only be a whole truth if we add 'God of Sarah, God of Rebecca, God of Rachel, God of Leah.' The half truth *magen Avraham* is only a whole truth if we add *u'foked Sarah*, Rememberer of Sarah. Unless we acknowledge both men and women as parts of the historic Jewish community, just as we acknowledge both as contributing members of our community, we will be making our female community members invisible and punishing our foremothers with the ultimate Jewish curse—erasing their names."

As Rachel sat down, a woman named Sharon Kushner rose to lead the *Musaf* service. Kushner faced the Ark, then turned to the congregation. "I don't want to go against the Ritual Committee," she said, "but I want you to know I'd prefer to add the *Imahot*."

Ripples of nervous laughter wafted up from the pews. Rachel's sermon had discomfited the congregation enough, and now Sharon Kushner was abandoning the liturgy to put in her two cents. Even after she returned to the prayer book and completed *Musaf*, the congregation remained jarred. During the time usually reserved for announcements, members spontaneously rose to speak about the *d'var Torah*, as if the Library Minyan were a New England town meeting, or a black church in the full throat of testimonies.

"How can anyone impose their style of prayer on us?"

"Is the Ritual Committee the last word?"

"Is making things even the only way to make them right?"

There was no one to quell the cacophony. By design, the Library Minyan had no rabbi to serve as *mara d'atra*, literally "teacher of the place" and in practice a congregation's halakhic authority. Its peculiar approach to theological disputes called for communal study, a staple of the yeshiva and *beit midrash*, followed by that most American endeavor, a democratic vote.

THE LIBRARY MINYAN had begun with *imahot*—not biblical matriarchs but contemporary mothers. Each Saturday they accompanied their husbands to Beth Am, a Conservative synagogue on the Westside of Los Angeles, and they brought their young children into the sanctuary rather than miss worship altogether. A tangle of strollers often blocked the building's front steps. Mothers nursed infants in the pews. Toddlers ambled up and down the aisle. The rabbi, Jack Pressman, never objected, but many of the faithful complained.

In a brainstorm of pragmatism, Pressman offered the young families the use of Beth Am's library, which adjoined his own office. Already many of the husbands met there early on Shabbat morning for study. The room could serve just as easily as the setting for a minyan, and the kids could yelp and drool without anybody kvetching.

In more ways than the familial, the young worshippers formed a distinct generation. Beth Am was a conventional and conventionally accomplished synagogue, with its Sisterhood and Men's Club, its Golf Outing and Hawaiian Night. A talented enough pianist to sit in with bands at bar mitzvah receptions, Pressman had earned the nickname "Rabbi to the Stars." Monty Hall of "Let's Make a Deal" emceed a testimonial dinner for Pressman's twenty-fifth anniversary in the pulpit in 1976, and five years later Beth Am honored Sammy Davis, Jr., at a Candy Man Ball. Appropriately enough, Beth Am held its High Holy Day services in a movie theater, the Fox Wilshire.

The several dozen men and women in the library, though Angelenos themselves, bore little resemblance to their half-million coreligionists in Southern California. The region's Jewish community was a study in diffusion and denial; a 1986 study found that two-thirds of its members belonged to no synagogue, four in ten intermarried, and the most famous, the

Hollywood stars, anglicized their names. In the archetypal Los Angeles captured by the literary critic David Klinghoffer in his memoirs, families waited for a Santa Claus equivalent named "Hanukkah Charlie" to leave presents under a "Hanukkah bush," and rabbis cracked that the ram Abraham sacrificed instead of Isaac wasn't a Los Angeles Ram.

Upstairs at Beth Am, amid the leather volumes of Talmud, gathered a Jewish elite. Its members had learned Hebrew and religious Zionism in the Camp Ramah system, earned ordination as rabbis at the Jewish Theological Seminary, and taught either at the Conservative movement's University of Judaism or Hebrew Union College, the Reform rabbinical seminary. They were also, many of them, products of the Jewish counterculture, committed to applying the New Left's ideal of participatory democracy to religious practice. Their models were not the institutional synagogues afflicted, as they saw it, with the edifice complex, but religious communities like the Boston area's Chavurat Shalom; their "sacred text," as one historian put it, was the do-it-yourself compendium *The Jewish Catalogue*. They aspired to paradox: being an alternative that was *more* traditional than the mainstream it was providing an alternative to. By personal choice as much as halakhic command, the minyan's founders conducted 90 percent of their service in Hebrew, and most kept their households *shomer Shabbat*.

The group informally dubbed itself the Rabbis' Minyan and later the Library Minyan. For ten years, it continued meeting there, growing from the initial dozen families to four or five times that many, and in the early eighties moving to the larger quarters of Beth Am's chapel. The minyan also acquired a certain Jewish version of star appeal, with members such as the Holocaust historian Deborah Lipstadt, the scholar of mysticism Jonathan Omer-Man, and the historian of ideas, David Ellenson, a Reform rabbi who had grappled with Modern Orthodox theology in his doctoral dissertation. For learned Jews on the spectrum from neotraditional Reform to liberal Orthodox, the Library Minyan gained a reputation as *the* place to daven, like an all-night jazz club where the best musicians meet after their separate gigs to jam.

Only in matters of gender did the Library Minyan pointedly depart from both *halakhah* and local custom in a leftward direction. At the time of the minyan's founding, only one Conservative synagogue in greater Los Angeles counted women in the prayer quorum and let them fully participate in the Torah service. The Library Minyan had adopted both reforms by 1976. Years before the Jewish Theological Seminary agreed to ordain women as rabbis, years before any temple or synagogue in Los Angeles installed a woman as chief rabbi, the minyan gave women prominent and visible responsibilities in the role of *sheliach tsibbur,* worship leader.

The term had another meaning, too, "agent of the community," and it suggested how much more the Library Minyan was than a forum for worship. It considered itself also a *beit k'nesset,* a house of assembly. Instead of moving over the Hollywood Hills into the San Fernando Valley, the promised land of suburbia, members bought Spanish Revival bungalows in Carthay Square, a Westside neighborhood otherwise being depleted by white flight. On Sabbath mornings, when the air was fragrant with jasmine, they walked together to Beth Am. After services, they picnicked together in La Cienega Park. The harvest festival of Sukkoth brought a tour of local sukkahs each autumn, and on the second night of Passover a University of Judaism professor named Hanan Alexander hosted sixty or seventy people for the *birkat hamazon,* the grace after meals, and a thunderous rendition of the song *"Chad Gadya."*

In the early years, the Library Minyan had managed to resolve its disputes in the amicable fashion of friends. Whether the issue involved women's role in worship or the right of children to read Torah or the precise wording of the prayer for the state of Israel, the members could sit in the same living room, study together from the same texts, and find a way to justify what was contemporary or simply practical within the confines of *halakhah*. Not subordinate to a rabbi, not officially members of either Beth Am or the Conservative movement, the minyan's faithful owed allegiance primarily to one another. "In Los Angeles, there was a vacuum of tradition," Elliott Dorff, a University of Judaism professor, put it. "There was no sense of, 'You have to do this because it's always been done this way.'"

But by the late spring of 1987, the Library Minyan had grown too large to parse *halakhah* in a living room. The Ritual Committee appointed a subcommittee to study the *Imahot* matter. And from the very first meeting, it became evident that this issue would not yield readily to consensus.

"This is a whole new thing," warned Joel Rembaum, a longtime member of the minyan who had replaced Jack Pressman as Beth Am's rabbi several years earlier. "This isn't women reading Torah, women in the minyan. This has transcendent implications. The *Amidah* is a prayer that is used worldwide. The ramifications are global."

Three times during the summer of 1987, twenty members of the subcommittee gathered to study Jewish law, history, and liturgy, seeking some precedent that would provide a solution. Instead, the dividing lines deepened, because now each side was more informed. When had Jews ever changed a prayer as essential as the *Amidah*? Revising a blessing from the sixth century couldn't be compared to tinkering with the prayer for modern Israel. And weren't there doubts in the Torah itself about whether all of the matriarchs believed in one God? But hadn't that same Torah insisted on the full humanity of women, even in the ancient world? Hadn't it been interpreted as providing their rights to food and clothing, lovemaking in wedlock, and remarriage after divorce? And if prayers were so immutable, then how had the Conservative movement back in 1945 edited its *siddur*, its prayer book, to no longer call for the resumption of animal sacrifice in the restored Temple?

Each question put pressure on the existing fissures in the minyan. They were like the cracks beneath Los Angeles itself in the San Andreas Fault, imperceptible until the tremors

start. One of the minyan's founding members, a professor of religious studies named Fredelle Spiegel, had been doing her version of seismology all along, though. In one of several academic
papers she wrote about the Library Minyan, she warned of the
"internal contradiction" in its "conflicting desires and principles," most specifically its twin missions to be "traditional yet
egalitarian." Precisely because of that struggle, she wrote, "it
offers a picture of contemporary American Judaism and indeed
of contemporary American religion."

In November 1987, the *Imahot* subcommittee decided it
could not produce even a potential solution for the minyan's
vote. Already several members who were firmly against any
change had pulled out of the subcommittee. On the national
stage, the Union for Traditional Judaism was heading toward its
final break with the Conservative movement over egalitarian
worship. Wary of such fractures, the subcommittee arranged
for a series of six *divrei Torah* to be delivered by members of the
congregation. In a minyan untethered to any larger authority,
nobody's position was preordained. Every one of the speakers,
and the two hundred worshippers who would listen to them,
would have to synthesize heritage and modernity in a personal
way and figure out, to paraphrase the old labor anthem, which
side they were on.

All around the Library Minyan in the late eighties
swirled the seemingly larger issues of world Jewry—the trial of
Klaus Barbie, the Gestapo chief in Lyons, France, for crimes
against humanity; the sentencing of an American intelligence
analyst, Jonathan Pollard, to life imprisonment on charges of
spying for Israel; the beginnings of the *Intifada* in Gaza and the
West Bank. One minyan's debate over the *Imahot* looked in-
significant. Yet that debate dealt with forces more eternal than
any war or genocide—past and present, men and women, tradition and change.

"This entire discussion has its roots in approximately
eight words," the historian Deborah Lipstadt would say a few
weeks hence in her *d'var Torah*. "There will be those who might

say, 'What a strange, legalistic people this is. So much discussion over such a little thing.' But those people miss the point of this and so much else in Judaism and Jewish tradition."

HANAN ALEXANDER steadied himself at the *shulchan*, the raised table normally reserved for reading Torah, on the Sabbath morning of February 13, 1988. He straightened his notes for the first of the *divrei Torah*, then looked up to regard the congregation. In the dozen rows of pews before him and the several that flanked him on each side not a space was empty. Folding chairs filled the aisles. The rear door swung open briefly as parents hurried their toddlers outside toward the Hebrew school playground, knowing that on this day not even the Library Minyan would tolerate the giggles and gurgles of its young.

The sanctuary had known so much joy in Hanan's years with the minyan—newlyweds pelted with almonds and raisins, kids costumed as Mordecai and Esther for Purim, grown-ups in propeller hats and feathered headbands on Simhat Torah. And as one of the Carthay Square pioneers, Hanan knew just how deep the sense of community ran. A few years earlier, during a wave of muggings and burglaries, Hanan and his minyan friends had formed a neighborhood patrol rather than be driven away.

Now the chapel grew as still as on the Days of Awe. In the ten months since Rachel Adler had spoken the *Imahot*, Hanan had heard the tensions rising. After David Ellenson had helped the subcommittee study liturgy, the minyan's traditionalists griped, "We're not Reform. What are we listening to a Reform rabbi for?" Some of the congregation's liberals, meanwhile, privately described their foes as "Neanderthals." Rabbi, philosopher, college dean, a man admired in the congregation for his ruminative style, Hanan stood in the breach.

"Let this," he began, almost pleadingly, "be a *machloket l'shem shamayim.*" In the pews before him, the listeners understood without translation: an argument for the sake of heaven.

In his own mind, however, Hanan admitted unity wasn't quite so simply achieved. He was one of the Neanderthals. If the *Imahot* entered the minyan, Hanan would have to leave.

He spoke at first about the literary and historical aspects of the issue. The phrasing of the *Imahot* appeared nowhere in biblical text; there was reason to believe that Rachel, even as Jacob's wife, persisted in pagan worship; if the minyan's women wanted and needed a role model, then why not choose Deborah? All these arguments, though, amounted to a preamble. Hanan's real subject was *Klal Yisrael*, the Jewish people.

"The form with which we pray is not only an expression of our relationship to God," he said, "but also an expression of us as a community within the Jewish people. What other communities are there that have made these changes? With whom would we be affiliating ourselves if we pray this way? And from what portions of the Jewish people would we be disaffiliating ourselves?"

In the broad sense, Hanan meant that the Library Minyan would separate itself from nearly every other congregation in the world. Only a scattering of feminist *chavurot* prayed the *Imahot*. But in his appeal to commonality, Hanan was also making a personal plea. He couldn't bear being severed from Orthodoxy, and he dreaded being forced into a choice.

Hanan had been raised as Henry and introduced to Judaism in the pallid atmosphere of a Reform temple. Growing up in Berkeley in the sixties, he and his sister Irene often eased the tedium of household chores by mocking the operatic style of the temple's choir. Most of its members were Christian, hired to do a job. Up and down Telegraph Avenue, meanwhile, and across the paving stones of Sproul Plaza, Hanan encountered the advocates of ethnic roots and group rights—for Chicanos and the Black Panthers, for Native Americans and Palestinians. The atmosphere led him to search for a more genuine Judaism. During high school in 1970, Henry adopted the Hebrew name Hanan and began attending a sixty-year-old *shtibel* presided over by a young Orthodox rabbi.

That man, Saul Berman, was himself a disciple of Joseph Soloveitchik of Yeshiva University, the towering figure of Modern Orthodoxy. Like his mentor, Berman espoused a Torah Judaism that engaged the secular world and was enhanced by the process. Hanan, heading toward a college major in philosophy, appreciated how Rabbi Berman wove Enlightenment thought, even modern psychology, into homilies. When it came to matters of gender, Rabbi Berman struck a tone that was similarly progressive within the confines of Orthodoxy. He was not about to tear down the *mechitzah* or amend *halakhah*, but he argued for Jewish women to be provided with rigorous religious education and encouraged them to form prayer groups. "Relegating women to the back of the synagogue, both physically and spiritually," he wrote in a 1973 essay, "will only assure their gradual disappearance from religious life."

When Hanan studied in Israel for year-long stints before and during college, others reinforced the same ethos. He lived with a religious Zionist family on a *moshav*, a collective, and he took classes from the Modern Orthodox rabbi David Hartman. Returning to the United States, he earned bachelor's degrees from both UCLA and the University of Judaism. Delivering the graduation address at UJ, an institution inspired by the Reconstructionist patriarch Mordecai Kaplan, Hanan instead extolled *Rav* Soloveitchik.

"The Orthodox model," he would say later, "was how I formed my religious identity. These were the people who were my influences. I knew no other authentic Judaism."

Coincidence as much as choice brought him into the Conservative fold. He started in the rabbinical program as a UJ graduate student partly to remain near his wife-to-be, Shelly, and partly because the Modern Orthodox seminary, Hebrew Theological College, never answered his request for an application. And the rationalist in Hanan, the part that craved logic, grew uneasy with the certitude of Orthodoxy.

Still, all through the eighties, he felt the strains of trying to accommodate himself to any other kind of Judaism. He transferred to the Jewish Theological Seminary and earned his rabbinical credentials as the battle about ordaining women convulsed the school. Moving back to Los Angeles to become a professor of education and later an assistant dean at the University of Judaism, Hanan joined the Library Minyan despite his misgivings about its egalitarian style. His own wife declined to read Torah from the *bimah* or take an *aliyah*. At one point, he attended a conference on Jewish women and spirituality and recoiled at all the factual errors and mispronounced Hebrew. Hanan had to appreciate the women's fierce desire to participate as Jews, but it seemed to him that what they needed more than an equal role in synagogue was a first-rate yeshiva education—essentially the Modern Orthodox formula. The Conservative movement, he feared, was evolving away from him.

Hanan confessed his discomfort with egalitarian worship to a Conservative rabbi he had known since his student days. "It's a matter of what you're used to," the rabbi advised. Indeed, as the years passed and Hanan became entrenched in the largely Conservative domain of the Library Minyan and the University of Judaism, he sensed his theology moderating to meet his observance.

The *Imahot*, though, upset his internal diplomacy. Invoking the God of the Matriarchs, however well-intentioned an idea, meant a drastic, public break with Orthodoxy, and, down to his soul, Hanan believed that Orthodoxy was the truest Judaism. It didn't matter that he himself no longer practiced it. It didn't matter that only 10 percent of American Jews did. It didn't matter if what he felt for Orthodoxy, when he was really honest with himself about it, was nostalgia.

"I, for one," he now told the Library Minyan, "want my children to be able to walk into any shul and be able to daven. I would like them to be able to recognize the liturgy with which we pray in our synagogue as being used all over the world."

In the spirit of *l'shem shamayim*, and against his own personal wishes, Hanan closed by proposing a compromise. Perhaps the Library Minyan should seek a ruling on the *Imahot* from the Conservative rabbinate's law committee. Then, if the minyan altered the *Amidah*, it might not be acting in complete isolation. The isolated one, though Hanan didn't say so, would be he himself.

In her pew, Deborah Lipstadt seethed. Hanan Alexander, so knowledgeable, so esteemed, had sided against the *Imahot*. Worst of all, he had nearly convinced her. His warning about the loss of community resonated with her own upbringing—fourteen years of day school, religious summer camp, the whole vertical enclave of Modern Orthodoxy on Manhattan's Upper West Side. "Damn it," Lipstadt told herself, "why'd he have to have such good arguments?"

And she would have no chance to answer those arguments for another five weeks, when her own *d'var Torah* was scheduled. As for the next Sabbath, it belonged to Joel Grossman, quite possibly the minyan's most articulate traditionalist.

EMBARKING ON MARRIED LIFE in 1980, Joel and Fran Grossman chose the Library Minyan before they chose their house. They retained a real estate agent, bought a street map, and drew a circle in a one-mile radius around Beth Am. It was more than convenience they sought. Joel and Fran lived *shomer Shabbat*—walking to shul, not using electricity, neither cooking nor answering the phone. Before joining the Library Minyan, they had tried out Young Israel in Century City, an Orthodox congregation.

Joel had grown up in Pennsylvania as the son of a rabbi who was both Conservative and conservative. Although the Rabbinical Assembly had voted in the fifties to allow women to take *aliyot* on special occasions, Rabbi Grossman saved his *bimah*, his altar, for men. He sent Joel to an Orthodox day school and later to Yeshiva University's high school, while an older son earned ordination as an Orthodox rabbi. Only as a college student did Joel veer in the liberal arts direction of his mother, a drama teacher, ultimately proceeding through all of his graduate coursework for a Ph.D. in English at the University of California–Santa Barbara before entering law school.

He met Fran, appropriately enough, at the UCLA Hillel center. The daughter of parents who stubbornly remained in the South Central neighborhood until theirs was nearly the last white family on the block, Fran embraced both religion and Zionism through the Conservative movement's youth program, spending her eighteenth year in Israel with a hand-picked group of "young leaders." Enough of a feminist to earn a master's degree in library science and a position as a law librarian, Fran in synagogue wore a hat instead of a *kippa* and refused the chance to serve as *sheliach tsibbur* because she didn't think her voice carried well (or tunefully) enough.

The very nearness of the Library Minyan to Orthodoxy—in its passion about religion and its depth of community—had in large part attracted Fran and Joel. Shortly after joining the minyan, they ran into another member, a Jewish educator named Gail Dorph, at the supermarket. Instantly they had an invitation to *Shabbos* dinner. After the Grossmans missed a Saturday service, Gail phoned them to ask, "Gee, where were you guys?" Fran thought of such concern as much more than neighborliness. There was a phrase for it in Genesis. When Abraham and Sarah are visited in their tent by three strangers, who are actually God's angels, they immediately offer them food and drink. *Hachnasat orchim*, the Torah called it, the welcoming of guests and newcomers. So Joel and Fran had taken seriously Hanan Alexander's fear that the Library Minyan might alienate itself from *Klal Yisrael* by adopting the *Imahot*.

Now Joel, poised at the *shulchan* on February 20, 1988, opened his *d'var Torah* by speaking about the tradition of the mitzvot. "I pray because I have no choice," he said. "I am commanded to pray as I am commanded to keep kosher and give charity." Maimonides, Joel continued, wrote that the mitzvah of prayer applied to both men and women, because it was not time-bound. Even in saying so, however, Joel was tacitly acknowledging that women were denied many mitzvot—wearing tallit and tefillin, hearing the shofar on Rosh Hashanah, eating in the sukkah, praying at the three daily services—to avoid any interference with their domestic duties. And for Jewish feminists like Rachel Adler, that provision consigned women to inferior status as Jews and thus underlay the *Imahot* debate.

"All sides should be respected accordingly," Joel said of the issue, not taking a stand. "We are, after all, debating how best to observe a mitzvah."

He paused for a moment. A lawyer who had clerked for a federal judge, an experienced litigator, Joel usually exuded calm on his feet, and more than mere calm a kind of élan. People in the minyan still talked about the *d'var Torah* he'd given years ago about commitment to worship, the one he had begun by asking, "What do you want in a really good shortstop?" The idea had come to him in mere seconds when he heard Cal Ripken mention that he wanted every ball hit to him. In preparing this address, though, Joel had spent a lot of mornings on solitary walks, three or four miles through the Westside and Beverly Hills, starting in the dark and finishing just as easterly light was silhouetting the San Gabriel Mountains. Now, with nothing close to a joke on his lips, he gathered himself.

"I must tell you that I would be no less uncomfortable if I were standing before the congregation and asked to talk about my relationship with my wife," he said. "My relationship with God is intensely personal and hard to talk about."

In fact, he was about to talk about both God and his wife.

Three years into their marriage, Joel and Fran Grossman decided to have children. They began by abandoning birth control and waiting for nature to take its course. A year later, in 1983, they went to a fertility doctor, who found a varicocele in Joel's scrotum and removed it surgically. Certain he had solved the couple's problem, the specialist never checked Fran, though she herself had been a DES baby and was thus a likely candidate for gynecological problems. Seven months passed, seven menses arrived.

A friend in the Library Minyan recommended a second doctor, an expert in in-vitro fertilization. His ultrasound exam revealed that Fran wasn't producing eggs during ovulation. He put her on medication, and Fran formed eggs, but they didn't burst to allow conception. Twelve more cycles came and went, each month's lovemaking governed by a thermometer and the temperature inside Fran, the miracle of creation reduced to digits and decimals and routine.

The doctor then scheduled Fran for a laporoscopy, and in doing an ultrasound check before the procedure he found inside her thirteen eggs, thirteen chances at a child. His plan was to bring on ovulation with drug injections and harvest the eggs at the optimal moment for Joel to fertilize them with sperm. Then they would be replanted in Fran. But on the appointed weekend in January 1986, Joel developed an infection. The doctor told Fran, "No go."

Her patience dashed by three years of futility, her emotions magnified by fertility drugs, Fran withdrew to her bedroom. She was so sick of it all. Getting cysts from the drugs. Going off the drugs to get rid of the cysts. Going back on the drugs and feeling so damn weepy that a radio report on the anniversary of the Apollo moon landing could loose her tears. Meanwhile, downstairs, Joel lost himself in the Super Bowl. Or tried to. He and Fran, a floor and a chasm apart, thought of every newscast they'd seen about abortions and unwed mothers and child abuse, all the things that made them wonder where was God. All they were trying to do, after all, was fulfill the first mitzvah, to "be fruitful and multiply."

In the winter of 1988, as Joel took his lonely morning walks and drafted a *d'var Torah* in his head, he remembered not just the medical agony but the metaphysical kind. He remembered most of all the trip he and Fran had taken to Israel in 1984. They had gone, at least officially, to visit Joel's relatives. But the reminders of infertility came constantly. First Joel's Aunt Chani pleaded with him and Fran to seek a blessing from the Ger Hasidim's rebbe. Then, while the couple was visiting

Joel's brother Danny at his air force base, the all-important thermometer fell to a tile floor and shattered. By the time Joel had borrowed a car and driven to a pharmacy and back, it was too late to try.

They had one more hope. Joel's brother Tuvia, an Orthodox rabbi on the West Bank, urged them to pray for fertility at the Tomb of Rachel. He would accompany them there, daven himself, and he was the holiest person Joel knew.

So one scorching summer day, Tuvia drove them through the checkpoint in the hills south of Jerusalem and a few dusty kilometers down the main road to Bethlehem. They parked next to a Christian curio shop outside a low stone building; this, so unassuming, was the tomb. Past a fountain at the entry, they walked down a corridor of polished limestone and reached the spot where men and women diverged, each sex granted one side of the tomb. A blue velvet cloth covered the monument itself, and on both faces it bore the same biblical inscription:

> Thus said the Lord: Restrain your voice from weeping, your eyes from shedding tears; for there is a reward for your labor, declares the Lord: They shall return from the enemy's land.

Fran began to daven amid women pressing their cheeks to the tomb cover, women wailing up to the arched, white-washed dome. Her own cries, all smothered within, would have been for unrewarded piety. Each month she had immersed herself in the *mikvah*, as the Torah commands, and abstained from sex while impure. Didn't God care that she had stayed obedient, accepted the risk that the *mikvah* waters and abstinent days posed to conception? Yes, if she didn't have psalms to read, she could have howled.

The women's shrieks echoed down to Joel's side of the tomb. So raw, so naked, they unnerved him, and yet he understood all they implied. Just before driving to the tomb, he and

Tuvia had studied the story of Rachel. From his earliest years of day school, of course, Joel had known how Rachel, Jacob's beloved, is barren, while his other wife, unloved Leah, bears seven children. On this day, though, he read the verses in Genesis as the analogue to his own crisis, identifying utterly with an anguished woman's plea:

> When Rachel saw that she had borne Jacob no children, she became envious of her sister; and Rachel said to Jacob, "Give me children or I shall die." Jacob was incensed at Rachel, and said, "Can I take the place of God, who has denied you fruit of the womb?"

Then, after Rachel has given Jacob her servant Bilhah as a fertile surrogate, and after Leah has borne the last two of her children, Joel read in the Torah:

> Now God remembered Rachel; God heeded her and opened her womb. She conceived and bore a son, and said, "God has taken away my disgrace."

Driving back from the tomb a half-hour later, Joel and Fran experienced a comfort that stunned them. For all the logic of their world, the logic of a lawyer's briefs and a librarian's catalogues, the tomb had connected them to Rachel, and through Rachel to what Fran would later call "not just a global God but a personal God, a God who revives the dead."

That God did not open Fran's womb, at least not then. A few days after the fiasco of Super Bowl Sunday in 1986, she had the thirteen unfertilized eggs replanted inside her, and, on a tip from a nurse, made love with Joel on the off chance. Three weeks later, she learned she was pregnant. On the morning of Yom Kippur 5747, otherwise known as October 13, 1986, David Grossman was born.

Even with a son, Joel clung to the insight of Rachel's Tomb. He, a man, had found communion with one of the Matriarchs. And not just one, as he realized in drafting his *d'var Torah*. Sarah and Rebecca, too, had been barren and heartbroken and only late granted children by God. The Torah portion on the first day of Rosh Hashanah begins with the verse about God remembering Sarah and allowing her to conceive. In the second day's Haftorah, its reading from the Prophets, Jeremiah invokes the image of Rachel crying as the Jews are led into Babylonian exile, and God reassuring with the same words Joel had read on the velvet cover of Rachel's Tomb. No man in the Bible bore Joel's pain, only the women, among them three of the four *Imahot*.

"For me," Joel now told the Library Minyan, as his sixteen-month-old son frolicked on the playground, "the God of Joel Grossman today is not the God I prayed to yesterday, nor the God I will pray to tomorrow. Not because He has changed but because I have changed. It is in this light that I approach the question of adding a reference to the *Imahot* in the *Amidah*.

"Many of you know that before Fran and I were blessed with David we tried unsuccessfully for years to conceive a child. During our long struggle with infertility, I prayed not to the God of Abraham but to the God of Sarah. Infertility was not Abraham's problem, just as in the Bible it is never the man's problem; men merely take a concubine or their wife's serving women and can sire a child. It is the woman who struggles with this problem. Faced with Sarah's problem, I prayed to her God, just as she did to ask for God's pity. On so many occasions, it is to this God of these great women that I need to address my prayers."

With those words, Joel Grossman threw his influence behind the *Imahot*. There were members of the Library Minyan, especially some of the newer ones with less learning, who resorted to autobiography in *divrei Torah*. They were the object of the founders' condescension, not even worth the effort of scorn. Joel, though, wore his religious knowledge with quiet confidence. He prayed with that quality of intention called *kavvanah*. So when for a rare instance he preached from the depths of personal experience, no one could dismiss it as self-absorption.

Certainly Jeff and Amy Rabin couldn't. Joel left them crestfallen. They considered him and Fran, like them, stalwarts of the minyan's right wing. They had expected Joel to lend his eloquence to the sanctity of liturgy. Now that he had shocked them, even though there were four more *divrei Torah* and a congregational vote ahead, they wondered if opposition to the *Imahot* was futile. And if so, where did futility leave them?

AMY RABIN at twenty-six had prayed the *Amidah* only one way as far back as she could remember. She had prayed it in her grandfather's shul in San Francisco, in the wooded groves of Camp Young Judea, in the Hillel center at UCLA, in the Great Synagogue of Jerusalem, and in a *shtibel* in Safed, Galilean city of the kabbalists. She had prayed it on Sabbaths for nearly five years in the Library Minyan, which felt more like a Jewish community to her than any place ever had.

Maybe it was easy, if you had grown up in Fairfax or the Upper West Side or West Rogers Park, if you had always been surrounded by Jewish people and things, if you could just assume their constancy and comfort, to believe that adding the *Imahot* made Judaism even richer, more inclusive. To Amy, though, once her minyan spoke words no other congregation did, she was cut adrift from *Klal Yisrael*. And from her childhood in Salt Lake City, she knew too well the pain of dislocation.

Her father had moved the family there after buying a company that manufactured construction materials. And overhearing the laments of her mother, the displaced daughter of a big-city rabbi, Amy Bernstein first grasped the sense of isolation. During Amy's youth in the early 1970s, Jews constituted only 1,800 of the Salt Lake City metropolitan area's half-million residents, or barely three-tenths of one percent. There were not enough to form a Jewish neighborhood, to support a kosher butcher, to keep the Reform temple and Conservative synagogue from having to merge. Amy took Hebrew school courses with as few as two or three classmates. She watched as her friend Alysse Eisen's father wasted four years in a failed effort to run a delicatessen. Had he not gone nearly broke, it would have been amusing to see the way the customers asked what a blintz was and ordered—what was that Oriental dish?—*pastrami*.

Amy's loneliness reflected more than the Mormon dominance of Salt Lake City. Somehow, it seemed, the Mormons wanted to be the Jews, wanted to seize the birthright from Amy. They considered themselves the House of Israel, traced their lineage through Aaron and Joseph back to the Patriarchs, and referred to Jews as "gentiles." During junior high school, Amy was called a "Christ-killer," informed that "all Jews are rich," and accused of having had a nose job because "yours isn't big." She pleaded with her mother to register her at a high school in another neighborhood, and there, with a different set of classmates, she experienced a more innocent and so more devastating kind of bias.

An editor of the yearbook and school newspaper, a member of the speech team, a young woman with the slender, dark-haired looks of a folksinger and the attentions of a number of duly smitten boys, Amy appeared to have soared above the self-doubts of any teenager, much less a member of a minority. She had triumphed in a school whose leaders had all-American names like Bud Brown and Becky Romney, a school so homogeneous its foreign exchange student came from England. When Amy graduated from East High School in 1978, page after page of her yearbook bore parting messages from classmates. Many of them paused to comment on her difference.

"Yid," wrote one boy. "Boinstein," began another. "Amy my Yid," a third penned. And: "Being Yiddush [*sic*] you'll go far in life, you pervert." And: "I really am glad that I got to know you this year (even though you're Jewish)." And: "You've got a very special spirit about you, only too bad your spirit's not Latter-day Saints." No wonder, then, that on the inside cover of the yearbook, next to Amy's middle name, Joy, someone scratched in a question mark.

"I got my Jewish identity because I felt different," Amy would say years later. "I got it because I had to defend myself."

All through her childhood, though, she wanted a self-hood based on more than enemies. She touched it for ten summers at Camp Young Judea and Camp Ramah, with folk dancing and Holocaust study and Hebrew lessons and Shabbat dinners. As each season neared its end, she cried for days at the prospect of returning to Utah. In high school, she talked cease-lessly to Alysse Eisen about growing up and getting out, as Alysse's two older brothers had, and her conviction went well beyond the typical teenager's bluster about escaping a boring hometown. She drove herself academically with one goal in mind: winning admission to UCLA, a daunting task as an out-of-state applicant. When cynics called it "Jew-C-L-A," they actually made the right point. Los Angeles held the largest Jewish community in the entire West. There Amy would be an outsider no more.

For her first several years on the Westwood campus, bagels and Mel Brooks movies and Israeli dancing at Hillel satisfied Amy's craving for Jewish life. Her dorm was so homogeneous that she and others called it "Jew Hall." One fall she didn't even attend Yom Kippur services. It was reassuring enough, after Salt Lake City, just to live in a place that marked Yom Kippur on the calendar. But in the autumn of 1981, entering her senior year as a political science major, Amy roomed with a woman who had begun keeping kosher in deference to an observant boyfriend. The effort carried Amy along—to Sabbath dinners of meatless lasagna, to volunteer fund-raising for the United Jewish Appeal, and finally to a year of study and worship in Israel under the aegis of the Jewish Theological Seminary. Returning in the summer of 1983 to finish the last courses for her degree, Amy started attending the Library Minyan. Friends from Camp Ramah went there. So did one of her college professors, Elliott Dorff.

On Amy's first Shabbat in the minyan, she received an *aliyah*. There, standing beside the Torah scrolls, was a young attorney named Jeff Rabin. She recognized him instantly as a fellow counselor at Camp Ramah five years before. And when he looked quizzical, she reminded him it was her, Amy, just with that waist-length hair now cut to the shoulder. By Purim of 1984, they were engaged. They married that September.

Jeff instantly deepened the communal bond that Amy felt in the minyan. His parents had wed at Beth Am, he had become a bar mitzvah there, and at age fourteen in 1971, he had worshipped with what would become the Library Minyan on its very first Shabbat. The young rabbis, perhaps seeing in Jeff their teenaged selves, let him lead *Shacharit* and *Musaf*. When he mistakenly read the wrong Torah portion one Saturday, they indulged the blunder. And over the coming years, even as he proceeded through college and law school and launched his career, Jeff kept adding to his knowledge of Judaism. When he told people, as he often did, that "being Jewish is my hobby," he didn't mean there was anything casual about it; he meant that he put every free moment into learning how to be a better Jew.

By the time the *Imahot* controversy arose, though, the minyan was sixteen years old, quadruple its original size, and, in Jeff's view, worse for the growth. The original core of rabbis and scholars and educated laity had been padded out, he fretted, with newcomers who believed "alternative" was a synonym for "experimental." Jeff tired of *divrei Torah* that concerned politics, social issues, or anything but Torah. He endorsed the minyan's decisions to have women fully participate in worship because he believed in the equality of the sexes. Amy, after all, had held jobs ranging from development officer for a Jewish high school to administrative assistant for an industrial machinery broker. Besides, they would have felt hypocritical insisting on strict obedience to *halakhah*. On some Sabbaths, they drove to the minyan, and one Saturday afternoon, Amy awoke from a nap to find Jeff watching a ballgame on TV.

But when they thought of Rachel Adler, the self-proclaimed *apikoros*, imposing her own prayer on the minyan, inflicting it, the Rabins drew the line. Eliminating discrimination was one thing; promoting a political agenda was something else. Amy was well acquainted with the argument that the language of Jewish liturgy disenfranchised women. Personally, she worried far more about the minyan revising that language and disenfranchising *her* by alienating her from other Jews. "You don't change the most important prayer to advance feminism," Jeff insisted. "Tradition ought to trump." But how could you expect a heretic to respect tradition?

Stunned by the *Imahot* that Sabbath morning in April 1987, Jeff had told Amy, "We're out of here." They were just being flippant. Surely this was just one troublemaker on her soapbox; surely the hubbub would quickly pass. It didn't, of course, and in late 1987 the *Imahot* subcommittee scheduled Jeff to deliver one of the *divrei Torah*. He begged off, preferring to watch and listen from the periphery. And when he and Amy heard Hanan Alexander, they heard their own voices. Hanan raised Jeff's objection to altering the language of blessings; he raised Amy's concern about splintering off the minyan from the Jewish whole. The next week, though, Joel Grossman spoke, and his poignant speech struck Jeff and Amy as "a betrayal of principles."

So they listened to the last four *divrei Torah*, every one arguing for the *Imahot*. They received Rabbi Joel Rembaum's written opinion pushing for incorporation of the prayer, which he would also present to the Rabbinical Assembly's law committee. As precedent for the change, Rembaum cited discrepancies between the wording of the *Amidah* in the classical *siddur* and in the so-called Cairo Genizah fragment, which dated back to between 700 and 1000 C.E. but was only discovered in the late nineteenth century. None of the examples, though, involved gender. Finally, in early March of 1989, nearly two years into the controversy, the Rabins received a written ballot from the Library Minyan. It posed two questions: Should including the *Imahot* be permitted? And, if so, should saying it be mandatory, or optional at the discretion of the *sheliach tsibbur*?

Several weeks later, the votes were tallied, and the results confirmed what the Rabins had feared since Joel Grossman's address. By a two-to-one margin, the congregation approved the use of the *Imahot*. Even Hanan Alexander, as it turned out, had been privately persuaded by Rachel Adler to abstain from the voting and to remain part of the congregation. Less than a year later, in March 1990, the Rabbinical Assembly's law committee voted to allow the *Imahot* in Conservative services.

Outnumbered in their congregation, contravened by their movement, Jeff and Amy took little solace that the *Imahot* at both the local and national level remained an option rather than a mandate. The minyan, in fact, had decided by a four-to-one margin to leave the actual decision on speaking the revised *Amidah* to each Sabbath's worship leader. Still, "sometimes" was too often for the Rabins. Whenever the *Imahot* was uttered, Jeff clamped his hands over his ears. Amy pressed her lips tight. "Why do they have to butcher a central prayer?" she asked later. "It's not the place to prove your feminism."

Just after the *Imahot* vote, Amy had given birth to a son named Daniel. With him in infancy and their first child, Max, only two, the Rabins found themselves driving to synagogue nearly every Sabbath and feeling more and more guilty about it. They lived in Pico-Robertson, a neighborhood with a growing Modern Orthodox contingent centered around the B'nai David Judea synagogue. And B'nai David, under the leadership of a young rabbi named Daniel Landes, was itself turning more observant, erecting a *mechitzah* after forty years of mixed seating. One Shabbat afternoon, a few neighbors from B'nai David invited Jeff to study with them; ironically enough, Amy drove him there. The subject was Maimonides' Mishnah Torah, the first codification of Talmudic law, and to Jeff the erudition was oxygen. A few weeks later, in the wake of the Los Angeles race riot of 1992, Jeff went back to the Library Minyan. The *d'var Torah* was about buying a gun. The contrast sealed things for Jeff and Amy Rabin.

They joined B'nai David Judea. They became *shomer Shabbos*. A few years later, having had two more children, they bought a larger home on a two-block stretch that was home to seven rabbis, all Orthodox. Their immediate domain ran perhaps a half-mile along Pico Boulevard, home not only to B'nai David but the Mitzvah Store, Jerusalem Market, Negila Dairy restaurant, and a kabob house whose marquee proclaimed, "We Now Carry Only Lubavitch Meat."

To Jeff's relief, the *mechitzah* at B'nai David bothered Amy not at all. She had never read Torah or led worship at the Library Minyan, so she could hardly miss those roles. And she had always felt uneasy with women clad in tallit and *kippot*, as if they were seeking not equality as much as the trappings of manhood. The women of B'nai David held jobs, but when Amy's daughter Yael was born in 1992 they hurried over to the house with brisket and chicken and kugel. So if the *mechitzah* carried a price, Amy gladly paid it in exchange for the solidarity, the continuity that the Library Minyan had ruptured in adopting the *Imahot*.

While the Orthodox population of Los Angeles was actually declining through the eighties and nineties, it was becoming more active and visible in areas like Pico-Robertson and Hancock Park. Even the entertainment industry—so steeped in sex, violence, and profanity that Orthodox Jews like the film critic Michael Medved assailed it for undermining religious values—included a sprinkling of Orthodox producers, composers, managers, performers, and writers. Kirk Douglas, who had followed the Hollywood norm by Christianizing his name from Issur Danielovitch, emerged as a booster of the ultra-Orthodox organization Aish HaTorah. These days, the Rabins wound up on the liberal side of most disputes. After the new rabbi at B'nai David, Yosef Kanefsky, allowed seventy women to meet as a prayer group in the synagogue, the statewide association of Orthodox rabbis showed its displeasure by dropping him from the committee certifying food as kosher.

Curiously, the Rabins retained their membership at Beth Am. Jeff chaired its Education Committee. Amy worked as facilities manager. Their son Max started attending the day school named for Rabbi Jack Pressman, where he was one of two boys in a student body of several hundred to wear *tzitzis* out, the banner of unapologetic Orthodoxy. For Jeff, practical reasons explained only part of why he maintained ties to the Library Minyan even after he had left it. When he mulled over the subject, he sounded like nothing so much as a Reagan Democrat who, even while voting Republican, can't quite bring himself to switch his party registration.

"I wasn't leaving the Library Minyan I'd known," he said in retrospect. "I was leaving a different place, not the place where I'd read from the Torah at fourteen, fifteen. It wasn't that I'd changed. The minyan changed and the movement changed and the doctrine changed. I guess all of us small-*c* conservatives feel the same way."

NEARLY TWELVE YEARS after Rachel Adler had first spoken the *Imahot* in the Library Minyan, she moved to the *shulchan* to deliver the latest in her periodic *divrei Torah*. By now, she was an established figure in the congregation and in Jewish intellectual life—a professor with a joint appointment to Hebrew Union College and the University of Southern California, a nominee for the National Jewish Book Award in both the women's studies and Jewish thought categories for her latest work, *Engendering Judaism: An Inclusive Theology and Ethics.* When she won the prize a few weeks later, she would say in her acceptance speech that it "indicates that women have finally talked their way in and become equal partners in the enterprise of thinking and rethinking Judaism." And here in the Library Minyan, the *Imahot* had been permitted in worship for nearly a decade.

Still, Rachel had prepared this sermon with a sense of disquiet. She would be speaking on the Sabbath before Purim, February 27, 1999, and because of the impending holiday, tradition called for a second Torah portion to be read. It contained three verses from Deuteronomy:

> Remember what Amalek did to you on your journey, after you left Egypt—how, undeterred by fear of God, he surprised you on the march, when you were famished and weary, and cut down all the stragglers in your rear. Therefore, when the Lord your God grants you safety from your enemies around you, in the land that the Lord your God is giving you as a hereditary portion, you shall blot out the memory of Amalek from under heaven. Do not forget!

With Purim approaching, Amalek was meant to represent Haman, who sought to slay all the Jews of ancient Persia. For in the Torah, the Amalekites were both actual enemies of the Jewish people and the archetype for all foes. The verses from Deuteronomy referred to a battle in the seventeenth chapter of Exodus, after which God tells Moses, "I will utterly blot out the memory of Amalek under heaven." In the Haftorah that accompanies the reading from Deuteronomy, the prophet Samuel instructs King Saul to annihilate Amalek: "Spare no one, but kill alike men and women, infants and sucklings, oxen and sheep, camels and asses!" When Saul refuses, sparing young children and choice animals, Samuel strips him of his crown for disobeying the Lord.

All these accounts disturbed Rachel partly because she had invited a group of graduate students from a Catholic university to visit the Library Minyan on this particular Sabbath. And what would they hear but a description of Jews in murderous fury. What Samuel and thus God had demanded of Saul was called *cherem*, the act of consecrating something to the Almighty by destroying it utterly. Were these grad students going to leave Beth Am feeling like Amalekites?

So Rachel turned the Torah portion on its head and made it a lesson not in memory but "the abuse of memory." She talked about how on Purim five years earlier Baruch Goldstein had massacred twenty-nine Muslims in a Hebron mosque as modern-day Amalekites. She talked about how the *haredim* of Israel disparaged Reform and Conservative Jews as Amalekites. And she had one more point to make about the term *limcho zekher*, blotting out the memory.

"Women's names are routinely erased," she told the minyan. "By Tanakh, by rabbinic literature, and by liturgy. We erase them ourselves. Even though the minyan voted ourselves the option of mentioning the *Imahot* in the *Amidah*, approximately two-thirds of our service leaders choose to blot out the names of our foremothers."

With that declaration, Rachel dispelled a cherished assumption of the Library Minyan. Its members had believed, had wanted to believe, that in adopting the *Imahot* on a voluntary basis they had achieved an equilibrium between past and present, between tradition and change. Jeff and Amy Rabin, people pointed out, had been the only congregants to leave in dissatisfaction, and even the Rabins themselves acknowledged that the *Imahot* was only one of several reasons. The center had held.

Or had it? Nobody maintained statistics, but by some estimates only 5 or 10 percent of the worship leaders recited the *Imahot*. Rachel herself had noticed the frequency dropping with each year, the same way she noticed young female rabbinical students beginning their sentences, "I'm not a feminist, but . . ." "I wanted people to put some moral weight into naming the foremothers," she said. "I wanted them to risk their *kavvanah* to be more truthful. Instead I get a feeling of 'Oh, we experimented with that for awhile, but we really don't read it.' "

If anything, Rachel and the other feminists in the minyan now thought they had settled for much too little. Even making the *Imahot* mandatory would not have sufficed. In her new book, Rachel dared Jews to "grow a prayer language that is authentic and inclusive and powerful," not simply gender-balanced or gender-neutral. In a paper for a Reform Jewish journal, Fredelle Spiegel of the minyan rued the absence of liturgy and rituals "geared to women." She distilled her disappointment into an aphorism from Jane Wagner's one-woman play for Lily Tomlin, *The Search for Signs of Intelligent Life in the Universe:* "All my life I've always wanted to be somebody. But I see now I should have been more specific."

Nothing better epitomized the intractability of gender, even at the center of the Jewish spectrum, than the publication of a new Conservative prayer book in late 1998, after seven years of deliberation. The *Siddur Sim Shalom,* revised for the first time since 1985, now included two versions of the *Amidah,* without the Matriarchs on page 3a and with them on page 3b. Jewish feminists were galled that the *Imahot* had been tacked on merely as an alternative. Meanwhile, the editor of the previous edition of the *siddur,* Rabbi Jules Harlow, expressed the indignation of traditionalists when he wrote in an essay that "changes based upon gender language referring to God disrupt the integrity of the classic texts of Jewish prayer, drive a wedge between the language of the Bible and the language of the prayer book, and often misrepresent biblical and rabbinic tradition." He went on to assail those who "worship at the altar of inclusiveness, which for them is essential in ways that principles of liturgy and language apparently are not."

Rachel Adler had another way of depicting the unrelieved tension. On the door to her office at Hebrew Union College, she had posted a "Peanuts" comic strip back in the autumn of 1993. It was still hanging there on the Monday in March 1999 when she resumed work after her *d'var Torah.*

As the strip begins, Marcie and Peppermint Patty are eating lunch at recess when a boy intrudes. "Move over, little girls," he says. "Let a man sit down." In the next frame he continues, "Girls take up too much room. Girls are always in the way."

Marcie replies, "Miriam was Moses' older sister. In chapter twelve of the Book of Numbers, she asks, 'Has the Lord spoken only through Moses?' "

"What's that supposed to mean?" the boy shoots back.

Peppermint Patty turns to Marcie, says she'll do the explaining, and knocks their antagonist to the ground with a punch.

Israel and America: The Price of Peace

AMERICAN JEWRY'S WAR of the sexes, however bitterly it was prosecuted, remained finally a figurative version of combat. It had no blood, no death, no prisoners. When Rachel Adler preached about Amalek to the Library Minyan, she was invoking Amalek as a metaphor, not an armed reality. Modern Israel faced an enemy that was all too real in the form of the Arab nations that went to war against the Jewish state four times in its first twenty-five years of existence and the Palestinian refugees who waged their campaign for a homeland through terror. If any force bound American Jews together despite their fundamental conflicts, both cultural and theological, it was support for Israel. Instead of religion or culture or language, Israel served as what the historian Arnold Eisen has called "the principal symbol and prop of Jewish identity."

So when the traditional unity collapsed over the 1993 Oslo accords between Israel and the Palestine Liberation Organization, and indeed over the entire principle of trading land 162 for peace, the effect on American Jewry was massive. The assassination of Prime Minister Yitzhak Rabin two years later by an Orthodox law student named Yigal Amir offered terrible proof not only of the conflict among Israeli Jews but among their American brethren as well. In the past, the unswerving support of Israel absolved American Jews of their internal rancor. Increasingly over the past generation, however, during the very years that Israel has struggled toward peace with most of its Arab neighbors, American Jews have divided ever more sharply over it.

To say American Jews differ on the issue—recent polls find about two-thirds favoring the land-for-peace formula—is to see only the surface of a widening chasm. The poll numbers in many ways mask the reality. Aside from an energetic and visible leadership, the Jews who support the Oslo agreement are largely those disengaged from Israel in all but sentimental ways. The opposition, resting disproportionately in the Orthodox population, is the segment of American Jewry most involved with Israel, most committed to it in concrete actions. This passionate minority has dominated the peace issue, influencing events from the halls of Congress to the settlements of the West Bank, arguing on grounds of both security and Torah that Israel must never surrender the lands won in 1967. And while the right wing of American Jewry has expressed itself primarily through political activity, its fringe elements have repeatedly turned to inflammatory rhetoric and violent acts both in the United States and Israel. Yigal Amir's trail to the murder of Yitzhak Rabin, it might be said, was one partly blazed by American Jews.

American Jewry's solidarity with Israel was born, in a sense, on May 15, 1967, when the Egyptian president Gamal Abdel Nasser mobilized his army for invasion. Within three weeks, Nasser had ordered United Nations peacekeeping troops out of the Sinai Peninsula, throttled Israel's shipping lanes through the Straits of Tiran, and enlisted Arab nations from Algeria to Iraq as financial and military allies in a "holy war." For the nineteen years of Israel's existence up to that point, American Jews had offered it a steady if modest stream of philanthropy. Barely a thousand Americans emigrated to Israel in a typical year, and barely a hundred American Jewish leaders even bothered to visit; the Israel lobby in Washington was small and timid. When Dwight Eisenhower in 1956 ordered Israel to withdraw from the Egyptian land it had just conquered during the Suez invasion, his administration squelched American Jewish complaints by threatening to revoke the United Jewish Appeal's tax-exempt status. But this image of Arab forces massing to destroy the Jewish state, this impending reenactment of the Holocaust, drove American Jewry into unprecedented activism. On June 5, the morning Israel launched its devastating preemptive attack, the renowned scholar Saul Lieberman of the Jewish Theological Seminary proclaimed, "This day is our great opportunity, one that may never repeat itself, to save *Klal Yisrael.*"

The United Jewish Appeal's "emergency campaign" raised $307 million within six months, more than doubling the amount taken in for the entire year before. In the largest rally of American Jews in history, 150,000 people gathered in New York to declare their bond with Israel. A thousand American Jews volunteered in Israel during the summer of 1967, and in the years immediately after the war the number of American Jews settling or studying there more than quadrupled. The American Israel Public Affairs Committee, better known by its acronym, AIPAC, began its growth from a three-man lobbying operation to a multi-million–dollar powerhouse as influential in Washington as the tobacco and gun lobbies. Along with the Conference of Presidents of Major Jewish Organizations, a coalition of about fifty nonprofit groups, AIPAC ensured that American Jews spoke with a single voice in unquestioning advocacy for Israel.

Yet in the euphoric wake of the Six-Day War, the historical moment when the relationship of American Jews to Israel appeared most simple and salutary, the largest community in the Diaspora was being drawn more deeply than ever into the internal battles of the Jewish state. In their ardor for Israel, American Jews readily embraced the Zionist mythology of a nation built by plucky kibbutzniks with farm tools and folk dances. The reality was far more complicated and contentious. Even before its founding, Israel had been violently torn between two competing strains of Zionism. The socialistic Labor Zionism of David Ben-Gurion emphasized tactical restraint against Palestine's British rulers, even calling its nascent army the Haganah after the Hebrew word for "defense." The militaristic Revisionist Zionism inspired by Vladimir Jabotinsky and led in the forties by Menachem Begin envisioned the homeland as *Barzel Yisrael*, Iron Israel. The Irgun militia, as well as its more ruthless offshoot, the Lehi,* conducted bombings and assassinations of British and United Nations targets to achieve it.

The Revisionist narrative of Israel's birth, the one few American Jews heeded, presented Labor as not merely incorrect but undeserving. This was the Labor movement that had secretly negotiated with the Nazis to ransom Jews who would settle in Palestine, that had betrayed Revisionist soldiers to the British during the Mandate period. Most of all, the Revisionists indicted Labor for its attack on the *Altalena*, a ship carrying volunteers and arms to Irgun forces in June 1948, a month after Israel had declared statehood and supposedly joined its various militias into a single army. The vessel was shelled and sunk off a Tel Aviv beach on Prime Minister Ben-Gurion's personal order.

All this history, latent in Israel and little known in America, mattered anew in the wake of the Six-Day War. For the first time in its existence, Israel now held a buffer of land around its borders, and that land begged a question: Should it be swapped in peace negotiations, or should it be held and even

---

* The name is an acronym from the Hebrew words for Israel Freedom Fighters. More pejoratively, the group was called "the Stern Gang," after its leader, Abraham Stern.

settled? Israeli society, as the political scientist Ehud Sprinzak has put it, started to cleave into feuding camps of territorial "minimalists" and "maximalists," which closely subscribed to the contours of Labor and Revisionism. Even more importantly, the maximalists came to include a previously apolitical population of ultra-Orthodox Jews, conflating political and theological conservatism in Israel more potently than ever before.

From the early days of Zionism until the Six-Day War, a sizable share of Orthodox Jews inside and outside Israel had refused to recognize the legitimacy of the state, maintaining that Zion could be created only by the Messiah. The competing cosmology, as expressed most notably by Jerusalem's chief rabbi, Avraham Yitzhak ha-Cohen Kook (1865–1935), held that Zionism even in its secular, socialistic trappings formed part of a divine plan for redemption. The lightning triumph of 1967—the capture of the biblical lands of Judea and Samaria on the West Bank and of Jerusalem's Old City with the Temple Mount and the Western Wall—seemed to validate Kook's mysticism. His son and successor at a Jerusalem yeshiva, Rabbi Tzvi Yehuda Kook, preached in the war's aftermath that the Torah considered every inch of biblical Israel holy ground, where Jews were commanded to live. His protégé, Rabbi Moshe Levinger, moved with a small band of followers into Hebron in 1968, and six years later a group of Rabbi Kook's former students formed a movement to settle the West Bank, calling themselves Gush Emunim, the Bloc of the Faithful.

As much as Gush Emunim drew on messianic faith, it also harked to Zionist history. Many of the settlers were products of the religious Zionism of the B'nai Akiva youth movement and the *hesder* yeshivot, which combined religious study with military service. They had grown up on stories of the early Zionists defying British authorities in Palestine by erecting the fences and guard towers of their new settlements under cover of night. Religious and conservative as they were, the Gush pioneers consciously linked themselves to their secular, left-wing forebears when they referred to their settlements by the old Zionist term of "facts on the ground." Their cause was enhanced in 1977, when Israeli voters ended nearly thirty years of unbroken Labor rule by electing a Likud coalition led by Menachem Begin, the former Irgun commander. While Begin's Labor predecessors had grudgingly allowed limited settlements, Begin emotionally embraced the concept of *Eretz Israel*, the Land of Israel, as defined by the Bible, not modern armistice lines. The Arab world, for its part, had offered Israel nothing but ceaseless hatred—the Palestinian massacre of Israeli athletes at the 1972 Olympics, the Egyptian attack on Yom Kippur of 1973, the 1974 oil embargo against the United States in retaliation for its alliance with Israel.

Then, in the fall of 1977, just months into Begin's term as prime minister, the new Egyptian leader, Anwar Sadat, flew to Jerusalem to declare himself ready to negotiate. In March 1978, a group of Israeli war veterans formed Shalom Achshav, Peace Now, the first grass-roots group to call for territorial compromise. Six months later, Sadat and Begin signed the Camp David agreement, and six months after that a peace treaty. Israel agreed to return the entire Sinai Peninsula, abandoning all its settlements and setting the precedent of trading land for peace.

When tens of thousands of settlers and their supporters rallied in early 1982 against the Israeli government and army at the Sinai outpost of Yamit, it was the first sign of the conflicts to come both in Israel and America. A half-dozen political parties prepared to run for Knesset seats on prosettlement platforms, making Gush Emunim the most dynamic force in Israel's electoral politics. Then, in September 1982, Israeli forces invaded Lebanon on a mission to destroy the PLO's Beirut base, and the nation's left wing rose to its feet. One hundred fifty thousand Peace Now supporters marched in opposition to the invasion, and some 400,000 protested the massacre of Palestinian refugees in the Sabra and Shatila camps by a Christian militia associated with Israel. Five years later, in 1987, Palestinians on the West Bank and Gaza launched the *Intifada* uprising, ending any Israeli illusions about a bloodless dominion over the occupied territories.

The deep schism in Israel created a crisis of allegiance for American Jewry. The venerable formula of supporting Israel no longer applied because there were two Israels vying for that support—Peace Now's and Gush Emunim's, Labor's and Likud's—and the votes in most Knesset elections split almost equally between them. In the years immediately after the Lebanon invasion, polls by the respected sociologist Steven M. Cohen found, a plurality of American Jews began favoring "territorial compromise" in the West Bank and Gaza. Amid the *Intifada*, the American Jewish Congress took the extraordinary step of making the private disagreement public, buying a full-page advertisement in the *New York Times* favoring a land-for-peace settlement with the Palestinians. Individual Jews from the historian Arthur Hertzberg to the comic Woody Allen criticized Israeli policy in print.

Yet this apparent assertion by American Jewish liberals was deceptive in several ways. The heart of the communal establishment—AIPAC, the United Jewish Appeal, the Conference of Presidents—continued to place its collective financial and political might behind Israel's elected government. And, however narrow their mandates, the Likud prime ministers Menachem Begin and Yitzhak Shamir led Israel for all but two years from 1977 through 1992, meaning that Israel's eternal right to Judea and Samaria was government policy backed by American Jewish clout. Meanwhile, attitudes toward peace among American Jews took on an increasingly denominational cast. In 1991, Steven Cohen's polling showed, nearly 61 percent of Orthodox Jews termed themselves "hawkish" on Israel, twice the rate for Conservative Jews and three times the rate for Reform and unaffiliated Jews. These lines hardened even more with the election of Yitzhak Rabin's Labor coalition in 1992, his negotiation of the Oslo accords in 1993, and the subsequent waves of Hamas terrorism aimed at destroying the peace process.

Superficially, then, American Jewry presented the mirror image of Israeli Jewry in its split between Orthodox hawks and secular or less observant doves. There was, however, one essential difference. America's doves on the whole did not care about Israel nearly as deeply as did its hawks. Asked general questions about their emotional tie to Israel in various polls, the doves did proclaim it. But in specific measurements of the bond—multiple trips to Israel, study in Israel, friendships with Israelis, Hebrew fluency—the liberals showed far less connection than the conservatives. By some estimates, Orthodox Jews have constituted half the American immigrants to Israel since 1985, though they make up less than one-tenth of the American Jewish population.

Thus the conservatives have dominated Jewish organizational life, not only shaping policy in groups like AIPAC but also creating philanthropies devoted to the most controversial Jewish settlements in the West Bank and East Jerusalem. Shortly after his election, Yitzhak Rabin publicly rebuked AIPAC for its partisanship. During the tenure of Benjamin Netanyahu, the Likud prime minister who greatly slowed the Oslo process, AIPAC took a sterner stand against Palestinian statehood than even he. One of the major liberal groups, the New Israel Fund, raised $9 million in 1993, the optimistic year of Oslo. That was half of what a single right-wing donor, Irving Moskowitz, gave for Jewish housing developments and yeshivot in the occupied territories. So even as Ehud Barak won election in Israel in 1999 on a platform of peacemaking, liberal American Jews had already lost the peace issue to their conservative foes, less through defeat than by lassitude and abdication.

Elections, fund-raising, and lobbying tell only part of the story of the discord wrought by the peace process—the nonviolent part. Alongside it, blood was being shed. At the same time in the late seventies that the patriotic mainstream of Gush Emunim was operating within the electoral system, a radical fringe centered in the settlement of Kiryat Arba outside Hebron began challenging the legitimacy of the state itself. To surrender any territory in Eretz Israel meant more than endangering national security, by this line of argument; it meant contravening the divine plan for messianic redemption. "Those who want to withdraw from Judea and Samaria will be cursed by the Almighty," Rabbi Tzvi Yehuda Kook declared in one speech. "We are commanded by the Torah, not by the government."

Such rhetoric, added to decades of festering hatred between Laborites and Revisionists, provided a theoretical framework for political violence. Some of the actual violence was committed by Americans, who absorbed the bitter feuds of Israeli Jewry but not the shared national revulsion at civil war. In 1980, a terrorist band known as the Jewish Underground and including an American émigré named Era Rapaport tried to assassinate three Arab mayors of West Bank towns with car bombs. Two years later, another American, Alan Goodman, opened fire on Muslim worshippers at the Dome of the Rock, killing one Palestinian and provoking rioting. And two years after that, Israeli police discovered that the Jewish Underground had been plotting to blow up the Temple Mount.

The murderous atmosphere both fed and was fed by Rabbi Meir Kahane. A self-proclaimed admirer of Vladimir Jabotinsky, Kahane had begun his career of political agitation and vigilante violence by founding the Jewish Defense League in his native Brooklyn in 1968. He immigrated to Israel in 1971, only to lose in his first race for the Knesset and be rejected as an unstable outsider by Jabotinsky's Israeli disciples and the settlers whose cause he claimed to champion. Kahane settled in the far-right outpost of Kiryat Arba, reviving his political fortunes with a party named Kach and a platform of expelling all Arabs from Eretz Israel. It would require more than settling Judea and Samaria to hasten the Messiah, Kahane believed; the way to sanctify God's name was with "a Jewish fist in the face of an astonished Gentile world." This was not the reactive violence of the vigilante but the premeditated violence of the provocateur.

The lineage of American extremists led directly to Kiryat Arba's doctor, a former New Yorker named Baruch Goldstein. Goldstein studied with Meir Kahane. He closely followed Alan Goodman's attack at the Dome of the Rock. And on February 25, 1994, he enacted a more successful version of it, shooting to death twenty-nine Muslim worshippers at a mosque in Hebron before being killed himself in retaliation. An American Hasidic rabbi in the West Bank city of Nablus, Yitzhak Ginsburg, oversaw the publication of a memorial book glorifying Goldstein as "the Saint, may God avenge his blood." One of those who read it was Yigal Amir.

It would be falsely simplistic to ascribe all the political violence in Israel to Americans, of course. The Jewish Underground, which perpetrated the most important acts of anti-Arab terrorism in the eighties, consisted primarily of Israelis. An Israeli threw the grenade that killed a Peace Now supporter at a 1983 rally. After the Oslo accords and the wave of Hamas terror, Israeli political foes printed posters of Yitzhak Rabin wearing Yasir Arafat's trademark, a *khaffiyeh* headdress, and with blood dripping from his hands. Israeli rabbis placed a ritual curse on the prime minister and openly debated whether the Talmud justified sentencing him to death as either a *moser* (one who turns over innocent Jews to gentiles) or a *rodef* (one who is pursuing a Jew in order to kill him).

Still, several American rabbis devised similar arguments. A figure widely respected in Orthodox circles, the Talmud scholar Herschel Schacter of Yeshiva University, asserted that Rabin hated God and Torah. Another Yeshiva professor, the rabbi and medical ethicist Moshe Tendler, delivered the eulogy at Meir Kahane's funeral. On the same morning in early 1994, extremists placed bombs outside the Manhattan offices of two liberal groups, the New Israel Fund and Americans for Peace Now. And when the Conference of Presidents and several other pillars of the American Jewish establishment scheduled a memorial service for Rabin at Madison Square Garden in December 1995, they were pressured by Oslo foes to ban any reference to the "peace process" in the event's program or speeches. Even at that, both the Zionist Organization of America and Agudath Israel of America boycotted the event.

"When you have two views," Rabin's successor, Shimon Peres, told 15,000 listeners at the memorial service, "you don't have to become two peoples." Exactly such a separation had already occurred, however, and not even the assassination was sufficient to shock American Jewry back into its unanimous romance with Israel. For American Jews who had grown up dropping coins into the tins of the Jewish National Fund or donating dollars for trees to be planted in the reborn Zion, Israel had become and would remain the cause of communal tension, not the antidote to it. Instead of bridging the gaps between denominations, or between secularist and fervent believer, Israel deepened them. The rift ran all the way from Jerusalem to Jacksonville, in the person of a kosher butcher named Harry Shapiro.

CHAPTER FOUR

Jacksonville, Florida, 1993–1997

N EAR TWO O'CLOCK one morning in October 1996, during the joyful middle days of Sukkoth known as *chol hamoed,* the telephone woke Harry Shapiro in his apartment in Jacksonville, Florida. His rabbi was on the line with dire news and a favor to ask. Several hours earlier, a van carrying a family of Orthodox Jews home from a vacation in Disney World had crashed along an isolated stretch of interstate sixty miles away. A boy lay dead in the hospital, his mother was heading into surgery, and his father, a Russian immigrant named Leibov, was marooned in an emergency room with five children, one just two years old. He had called his rabbi in the ultra-Orthodox community of Monsey, New York, who called Harry's rabbi, who called Harry.

It was three o'clock when Harry reached the hospital. He packed the father and children into his car, stopped by the disabled van to get them clean clothes, and brought the Leibovs to his home. Later that day, Shapiro bought the children's favorite cereals and fed them breakfast. The next morning, he 173 drove the Leibovs to the airport for their flight home. When Harry discovered that the dead child's body was not being sent on the same jet, he flew with it at his own expense and remained in Monsey to assist in *tahara*, the ritual washing of a body that *halakhah* requires for funeral and burial. The little boy's name was Yudi, and Harry wanted to help him toward *olam haba*, the next world.

Back in Florida later that week, Harry returned to the wrecked van and salvaged the family's belongings. He washed some clothes, sent others for dry cleaning, and shipped them all to Monsey. A month later, after the Leibovs had finished shiva and were alone in their grief, Harry visited them again. *Kol Yisrael areyvim ze la ze*, says a famous passage in the Talmud, all Jews are responsible one for the other.

A FEW MOMENTS past noon on Saturday, February 22, 1997, the Sabbath falling on the fifteenth day of the Hebrew month of Adar I, Aliza Morris completed the ceremony of bat mitzvah. Normally, three hundred members attended Shabbat service at the Jacksonville Jewish Center. But Aliza's father, Jeff, was a former president of the Conservative synagogue, and her mother, Robin, taught in its religious day school, and so seven hundred fifty friends had crowded the sanctuary to see her ascend to the *bimah*, hear her chant the Haftorah, and witness her elevation to womanhood. Now the guests were passing through the portal into the adjoining social hall, congratulating Aliza and her parents, then diving into the deli platters.

In a hallway on the far side of the sanctuary, just outside the smaller chapel where Junior Congregation services for several dozen children had been held, the Levenson brothers were playing around several floor-to-ceiling panels that held brass memorial plaques. The synagogue's kids loved that spot. About a foot of space separated the bottom of the panels from the wall, providing an ideal nook to stash a backpack or to secret yourself in hide-and-seek. Just a week or two earlier, one youngster had discovered a cache of Kit-Kat bars there.

Adventurous as any other eleven-year-old just liberated from coat, tie, and piety, Eric Levenson peeked behind the fourth panel. He spotted something long and rounded, sort of like the barrel of a baseball bat, and covered in masking tape. Eric picked it up and showed it to his brother, hefting its seven pounds, and then began to unravel the tape. Each twist revealed the internal gadgetry—a watch, some wires, a nine-volt battery, all of it seemingly connected to the gray metal of a pipe.

An eight-year-old girl named Melanie Dale Jolson wandered down the hall, drawn to the buzz of activity. Eric handed her the contraption.

"That looks like a bomb," she blurted and threw it down.

At that moment, a grown-up, Steven Greenfield, turned the corner from the lobby and came up the hall. Picking his way through the children, he gazed at the device on the floor.

"Shit," he said, too alarmed to censor himself in deference either to the young or the house of God. "This looks like a bomb."

As gently as a mother with her infant, Greenfield carried the device outside the synagogue and through the parking lot, finally laying it in a drainage culvert at the edge of the Jewish Center's property.

Then, at 12:12 P.M., he called 911.

A patrolman arrived, inspected the device, and called his supervisor, who summoned the bomb squad and then drove to the synagogue.

Evan Yegelwel, the president of the congregation, was just leaving the men's room when someone told him about the cops and the bomb. Yegelwel introduced himself to the police supervisor, who said, "Look, you've got to evacuate the building."

Yegelwel and Jeff Morris hurried to the altar. Using the same microphone that Aliza had in delivering the verses from

Ezekiel prophesying the New Jerusalem, Morris announced, "The Jacksonville Sheriff's Office has told us to evacuate the building."

Looking up from their plates in the social hall, people asked, "What's going on?"

"You just have to leave," Morris and Yegelwel ordered.

Suddenly alarmed, parents searched for their children, hunting through the rooms and corridors of the 100,000-square-foot building whose sprawling size was normally a matter of congregational pride. One ten-year-old checked each bathroom for stragglers. A little boy was discovered cowering in the library. It took fifteen minutes before the last of the 750 celebrants, some still clutching half-eaten tuna pitas, squeezed through the clogged front door and into the chilly drizzle.

Far in front of the congregants, three men from the bomb squad hunched over the object in the ditch. It was made of an eight-inch length of galvanized steel pipe two inches in diameter, the sort commonly used for household plumbing. A steel end-cap closed off each end. The officers could not tell if the device included a blasting cap, too, but they were not going to risk unraveling the tape any further to find out. Instead, one expert delicately attached a countercharge to the pipe and at 1:27 P.M. proceeded, in bomb squad parlance, to "render it safe."

White smoke billowed from the blast. An end-cap slammed into the exterior wall of the synagogue's day care center, ninety feet away.

From those results, the officers deduced several facts. First, the device had been a real bomb, not a hoax. Second, it had been packed with black powder, the most volatile of the four types of gunpowder. Third, only luck had kept the bomb from blowing up earlier—either from the friction created when the boys began unwrapping it or from the concussion when the girl dropped it. The same force that sent the end-cap flying could just as easily have shot scraps of shrapnel into a hallway filled with children.

Nobody, however, thought those children were the target. Flush against the other side of the wall behind the memorial plaques stood the chairs on the sanctuary platform set up for the Jewish Center's rabbi, David Gaffney, and various dignitaries. Nine days earlier, one of those chairs had held Shimon Peres, the Nobel laureate, former Israeli prime minister, and architect with Yitzhak Rabin and Yasir Arafat of the Oslo peace accords.

Rabbi Gaffney, among a handful of synagogue leaders, knew that the police had received a bomb threat just three hours before Peres's speech:

> OPERATOR: Jacksonville 911, Lesnick.
> CALLER: Is this being recorded?
> OPERATOR: It is.
> CALLER: I am calling from the American Friends of the Islamic Jihad. We have placed two bombs in the Yahudi temple on Mandarin, where the dog Shimon Peres is speaking tonight.
> OPERATOR: Where is it at?
> CALLER: One is at the front hallway. Find it and you will know we are serious. You will not find the other.
> OPERATOR: What's the name of the business?
> CALLER: This will be your only warning.

A sweep of the synagogue in the early evening had turned up nothing, and Peres had addressed a capacity audience of thirteen hundred without incident. Now the Jacksonville police led several bomb-sniffing dogs back into the Jewish Center. They found the scent of gunpowder behind the fourth panel, but no evidence of any other bomb.

And though the 911 call remained unknown to most congregants, the suspicions of many of them turned to the Arab community. Jacksonville was home to about 35,000 ethnic Arabs, ranging from second-generation Americans to recent immigrants from the West Bank and Syria. Over the last forty years, the synagogue had endured several attacks—a 1958 bombing that was part of a wave of violence by white supremacists against synagogues assumed to be sympathetic to civil rights; windows shot out during Friday night services in the early seventies; swastikas painted on the exterior walls during a spate of anti-Semitic vandalism in 1989; telephone threats in 1994, one day after several Arabs were convicted of bombing the World Trade Center in New York City. These episodes sufficiently disturbed the congregation that it installed a house-trailer on synagogue property as the residence for a police officer. During the Gulf War in 1991, the Jewish Center even arranged for an out-of-use patrol car to be parked out front to give the appearance of vigilance.

As far as the authorities knew, none of the previous incidents had involved Arabs. But for Jews who had lived through the massacre of Israeli athletes during the 1972 Olympics in Munich, the drowning of elderly, wheelchair-bound Leon Klinghoffer off the hijacked cruise ship *Achille Lauro*, and the recent campaign of bus bombings in Jerusalem and Tel Aviv by Hamas, not even the Oslo treaty, not even an appearance by Shimon Peres himself, could undo the reflexive fear of Arab fanatics.

On the Monday evening after Aliza Morris's bat mitzvah, Evan Yegelwel was reading some transcripts he had brought home from his law office. His wife had gone to a meeting of the Jewish Center's teachers, and he was minding their daughters, aged seven and thirteen. Just past eight o'clock, the phone rang.

"Evan, we know who did it," said a friend.

"You know who planted the bomb?"

"Can you come right over to Etz Chaim?"

Etz Chaim was an Orthodox synagogue. Its property abutted the Jewish Center's, and its faithful often took a scenic walkway across the Jewish Center's shaded, landscaped property on their way to Sabbath worship. In Jacksonville's community of just ten thousand Jews, a number of families had members in each congregation.

Still in his sweatpants, Yegelwel drove to Etz Chaim. Just inside the synagogue stood his friend, three other members of an adult-education class, and the rabbi, Avraham Kelman, who had been teaching it. Midway through the session, the rabbi had collapsed into sobs and started talking about the bomb at the Jewish Center. That was when one of the students called Yegelwel.

Now, twisted with anguish, Rabbi Kelman sputtered out an explanation. Harry had said he was going to do something. He didn't think Harry would really do it. He'd been trying to reach Harry tonight. He couldn't find him.

Yegelwel needed no further information to summon the man in question from memory. Harry Shapiro had grown up in Jacksonville and after periods in New York and Israel returned there to open a kosher butcher shop. Evan could still remember Harry's black fedora, one sign he was *frum*, rigorously observant. Shapiro's sister Juli belonged to the Jewish Center; his nephew attended its preschool. He had always struck Yegelwel as a misfit, a loner, a different kind of guy. Still, what kind of Jew would try to bomb a synagogue?

Yegelwel rushed over to the Jewish Center, pulled Rabbi Gaffney out of a meeting, and called an FBI agent he knew, who immediately headed for the synagogue. At nine-thirty, the temple administrator, Bruce Horovitz, phoned Detective W. R. Baer of the Jacksonville police to say he had information about the identity of the bomber. Baer arrived moments later with his case file and the 911 tape from the day of Peres's speech.

Yegelwel and Gaffney listened: . . . *two bombs* . . . *Yahudi temple* . . . *that dog Shimon Peres* . . . Beneath an amateurish version of an Arab accent, the voice was unmistakably Shapiro's.

"How could he do such a stupid thing?" Rabbi Gaffney cried. "How could he do such a stupid thing?"

If only there were some way to keep Shapiro's identity a secret, the rabbi thought, some way to punish him just within the community. Surely Harry couldn't have intended to destroy a synagogue and kill fellow Jews. To have an arrest and a trial with cameras and headlines would be a *shande far der goyim*, a disgrace in front of the gentiles.

"Shmuck," Yegelwel muttered. "Could've put on a sandwich board and got plenty of publicity."

Instead, Harry Shapiro had planted a bomb in a synagogue filled with children and their parents. During the ten days between the Peres speech and the Morris bat mitzvah, the Sisterhood had convened, the Men's Club had run a Sabbath service, the Kadima youth group had hosted a regional convention, basketball teams had competed in the gym, and hundreds of pupils, including Harry Shapiro's two-year-old nephew Seth, had attended preschool, elementary school, or Hebrew school.

As Detective Baer interviewed the synagogue's leaders, Rabbi Kelman reached Shapiro's older sister Juli, who then called a longtime family friend, a prominent criminal defense attorney named Barry Zisser.

"Uncle Barry," she said in a familiar endearment, "it's about Harry."

"Not on the telephone," Zisser commanded. "Get Harry right down here."

Juli's husband Scott presently delivered Harry to Zisser's home, which was about halfway between downtown Jacksonville and the Jewish neighborhood called Mandarin in the southern part of the city. In a family room decorated with menorahs and a bust of Moses, Harry, a stocky figure who sported a goatee and aviator glasses, fidgeted under Zisser's gaze. Around his neck hung a medallion of the Magen David, the Jewish star, that had belonged to his late father; in his pants pocket, unseen by Zisser or anyone else, lay a plastic vial of pills.

Shortly before ten-thirty, Zisser drove Shapiro to the sheriff's office. As he guided his sedan north along San Jose Boulevard, FBI and police cars roared past, sirens wailing and roof lights whirling, heading south to Harry's apartment.

At one minute past midnight on Tuesday, February 23, 1997, the Jacksonville police arrested Harry Shapiro, a thirty-one-year-old gas station cashier, for the felonies of placing a destructive device and making a threat to place a destructive device. Or, to put it another way, he was charged with pure hatred, *sinat hinam*.

HARRY SHAPIRO had never known an Israel without the West Bank, and he had never known an Israel unthreatened by its enemies. The Six-Day War occurred when he was not quite two years old, much too young to experience the swaggering confidence the swift victory imparted to Jews in Israel and throughout the Diaspora. Harry had formed his bond with Israel after the surprise attack by Egypt on Yom Kippur of 1973, those frightful days when the Suez Canal was crossed and the Bar-Lev Line broken and it seemed that the Jewish state might be vanquished. There was a bulletin board in the lobby of Etz Chaim, the Orthodox synagogue Harry attended, and it listed the names of all the dead and wounded Israeli soldiers. Now seven years old, he scanned it grimly each day, praying he would not find one name in particular—Shelly Wachsmann, the son of Etz Chaim's rabbi. The young man had made *aliyah* a few years earlier and was now fighting in the army, and Rabbi Wachsmann was to Harry Shapiro more of a teacher than his teachers and perhaps even more of a father than his father.

Clean-shaven, hair Brylcreemed, always in a charcoal gray suit, Haskel Wachsmann cut an American figure. Only when he spoke in a Hungarian accent did his ancestry become clear. And to young Harry that voice was the sound of honey. He had begun studying with the rabbi at age five, learning to read Hebrew, mastering the major prayers and the order of service, being introduced to the dense pages of Talmud. Rabbi Wachsmann even taught Harry to play chess. And always the rabbi was patting Harry on the back, laying an approving hand on the boy's shoulders. Harry chanted an entire Haftorah in Etz Chaim by the time he was nine, with an adult supplying the accompanying blessings, and for his bar mitzvah he led virtually the entire service. By then Rabbi Wachsmann had retired from the pulpit, but he returned to watch his pride, his prodigy.

Both Harry's parents, Philip and Sandy, had clung to observance, he in the isolated Jewish enclave of Augusta, Georgia, and she in the community of several thousand Jews in Jacksonville. A Southern city by geography but a port city by temperament, Jacksonville generally accepted Jews, as it did other white newcomers, without much bother. The rare expressions of anti-Semitism made news precisely because they were rare. Over three generations, Jews moved steadily from apartments downtown to bungalows and brick ranches set amid palms and mossy oaks along the banks of the St. John River. Philip Shapiro, an executive with a supermarket chain, appeared to accommodate himself to the good-ol'-boy style of Southern manhood, boating and hunting and collecting guns. But he and Sandy kept a kosher home and avoided shopping, driving, and watching television on *Shabbos*. Philip served on Etz Chaim's board and helped raise money for its new building. At any business outing or neighborhood picnic he would quietly find out which dishes were *treif* and steer his family to the safety of cole slaw. When Juli Shapiro once went to a temple that in the interest of Americanism used a trumpet instead of shofar to herald Rosh Hashanah, she wept at the betrayal of tradition.

"I had a taste at that early age of the love that true Orthodoxy can bring," Harry later reflected. "Love of Torah, love of life, love of all things around you. And I took to the structure and discipline of learning, the idea there was an answer for everything."

He found those same pleasures in mechanics. At age six, Harry took apart and reassembled his mother's vacuum cleaner. He performed the same trick a few years later with the family lawn mower. On his own, Harry planted and tended a garden of nasturtiums for his mother.

All of which made it more vexing for the Shapiro family that Harry was faltering in school. By first grade he had been put in special-education classes due to outbursts of temper that included holding his breath until he passed out. For junior high school, with Harry now diagnosed as hyperactive and medicated with Ritalin and Dexedrine, Harry's parents cobbled together tuition for the Bolles School, Jacksonville's most elite and expensive. Harry got C's and a reputation for being disruptive. Philip and Sandy Shapiro, weary of Harry's misbehavior and enduring turbulence in their own marriage, shipped him off to a military academy. Instead of self-control, Harry discovered marijuana. Back in Jacksonville for tenth grade in the fall of 1980, he begged for another chance at Bolles.

Philip Shapiro, loving and affable at times, could also be rigid, a man of absolutes. As much as Harry had once pleased him by embracing Orthodoxy, which to Philip was genuine Judaism, Harry now enraged him with his costly misadventures in school. Philip laid down the terms. He would put up the tuition for Bolles again only if Harry agreed to himself pay $500 for each B on his report card and $1,000 for every C. Harry protested by failing every course, even turning in a statewide standardized test blank. On the day he got his report card, he showed off the straight F's to his aunt, Charlotte Greenburg, who could only sigh, "You really have to try to do that."

All through his teenage years of boredom in classes and hostility with his father, Harry found solace and support in only one part of his life, the Jewish part. He had slipped away from observance since his bar mitzvah, but he was attending Hebrew high school classes and United Synagogue Youth meetings at the Jacksonville Jewish Center, and his leader in both endeavors, Rabbi Dov Kentof, did for Zionism what Haskel Wachsmann had done for Judaism. Robust as a kibbutznik, Kentof could fell trees and pilot a white-water raft. He turned a USY campout into a simulated mission with the Israeli army, ending with anthems around the bonfire. Week after week in the classroom, he narrated the Jewish epic of persecution and resistance, from Masada and Bar Kochba through the Warsaw ghetto uprising and the Final Solution, covering one wall with photographs of Jewish corpses.

"These were totally new reasons to be Jewish," Harry recalled years later. "Being Orthodox spoke to actions—do the mitzvot, follow God. This was more about feelings and emotions—being proud you're Jewish, not letting a Holocaust happen again. It affected my soul. It made me feel being Jewish is worth fighting for. It's worth dying for."

By coincidence, Philip Shapiro soon reified that lesson for his son. In March 1982, he and Sandy joined a two-week tour of Israel led by David Gaffney, rabbi of the Jacksonville Jewish Center. Theirs was to be a conventional tourist itinerary—the Old City and Yad Vashem in Jerusalem, nightlife along Dizengoff Street in Tel Aviv, folklore at several kibbutzim, mud baths beside the Dead Sea. A vacation together, the Shapiros hoped, would shore up their marriage. But on the group's first full day in Israel, after the scheduled stops at the Carmel Winery and Weizmann Institute, Rabbi Gaffney persuaded the driver to head further south along the Mediterranean coast, through Gaza, into Sinai, and finally to the Jewish town of Yamit, epicenter of resistance to the peace treaty with Egypt.

The Camp David accords of 1979 had stipulated that Israel would withdraw from the Sinai Peninsula it had captured in 1967 as a condition for Egyptian president Anwar Sadat signing a separate peace, one that left intact Israel's hold on the West Bank, Gaza, and the Golan. The Israeli civilian presence in Sinai consisted only of a dozen settlements and two towns, Ophira and Yamit, a community of 2,500 founded in 1975. Ophira's residents willingly evacuated in exchange for financial compensation. Yamit, however, became the Masada of the right-wing settlers' movement. Both Gush Emunim, the Bloc of the Faithful, and Meir Kahane's Kach party considered Israeli control of Sinai nothing less than divinely ordained. They also feared the precedent being set in the land-for-peace deal, one that could someday be employed in other occupied territories, especially the West Bank regions they called by the biblical names of Judea and Samaria. "Today Yamit," went one of their chants, "tomorrow Hebron."

In May 1981, nearly a year before the Shapiros' trip, a hundred thousand supporters of the settlement movement had rallied in Yamit to proclaim that Israel would someday stretch "from the Euphrates to the Nile."* That October, Yamit residents blocked government bulldozers that had been sent to dismantle their homes. Two months later, business owners welded shut the town gate and circled the perimeter with barbed wire. As many of Yamit's residents ultimately gave up and departed, they were replaced in almost equal numbers by Gush Emunim loyalists, many of them transplanted Americans. A radical handful, mostly Kahane's followers, went on to fire-bomb government offices, beat up negotiators, and seize a bomb shelter, which they occupied, threatening suicide.

As the Passover deadline for eviction neared and even many diehards departed, Yamit served less as a threat than a symbol. It was, however, an ever more effective symbol. Months earlier, Sadat had been assassinated for making peace, raising widespread doubts that Egypt would honor the Camp David treaty. A million Israelis, roughly one-fifth of the country, no mere fringe of messianic pioneers, signed petitions to protest the Sinai withdrawal.

The prospect of visiting Yamit so divided the Shapiros' tour group that the bus stopped partway there for a vote on

---

* This phrase went back to a speech in 1949 by the Lehi leader Eldad Scheib, who claimed Israel should have continued fighting its war of independence until it controlled all the territory from Iraq to Egypt.

whether to proceed or turn back. They would be bearing witness to history, Rabbi Gaffney argued, they would probably be the last tourists ever to see Yamit. A majority, including Philip and Sandy, agreed. So the Shapiros and their companions rumbled past the Army checkpoints and through the barbed-wire barricade only to find Yamit empty but for a skeleton corps of resisters. The desert wind whistled through stucco homes, now abandoned, and sand drifted across the fields, ruining gardens and orchards. In the town square, hardly a footprint disturbed the coating of dust. Philip lingered at the memorial to soldiers killed in the 1967 war, an eighty-foot tower surrounded by smaller columns, like the charred trunks of a burned forest. Among the villas and synagogues and shops there appeared placards of a little boy standing beside a tree. *Al na ta'achor na tu a*, read the slogan, which quoted from a popular song, Don't uproot what's been planted. Other signs declared, We Will Not Surrender.

The message especially haunted the Shapiros because of a stop they had made on the way to Yamit. Before entering Gaza, their group had visited Yad Mordecai, the kibbutz where 120 Jewish farmers had held off seven Egyptian regiments for nearly a week during the 1948 war. It was to such Zionist heroes that Gush Emunim's legions compared themselves. And the point was not lost on Philip and Sandy Shapiro, even when they returned to the safety of America.

They told their children about Yamit. They showed their snapshots. None of the Shapiro siblings had ever heard their parents so impassioned about Israel. Philip had always been a political conservative, but even Sandy, the liberal partner in the marriage in all respects, bristled with outrage. You had to have seen Yamit, just rising up from the sand dunes, a mirage that was real, all the houses and farms built by Jews with their bare hands. No wonder the Arabs coveted the land, Sandy said, they were too lazy to improve it themselves. That Palestinian laborers had actually done most of the construction was an ironic truth few Americans even realized and most Israelis ignored. As for Harry, he dwelled on a photograph of the war memorial, proof of all he had learned in Rabbi Kentof's class about the price of Jewish survival.

When twenty thousand Israeli troops routed the last holdouts from Yamit in late April and dynamited the town to rubble, Philip Shapiro and Rabbi Gaffney were interviewed by Jacksonville's daily newspaper, the *Florida Times-Union*. It published Philip's photograph of the war monument. The article quoted Rabbi Gaffney as saying, "The peace treaty seems to be a big question mark in Israel today." Shapiro, characteristically blunt, told the reporter, "They feel they're giving it [Sinai] back for a piece of paper."

Sixteen years old and repeating tenth grade, anchored only by his Jewish identity, Harry seized upon Yamit like a Bible story, a Talmudic parable. "It was the first tangible proof for me that Jews were willing to die for what they believed in," he said later. "The wars were different. In a war, you're fighting to stay alive. Here, they were fighting for what is right. They were giving back land that was captured because of an unprovoked attack by the Arabs. It was as if the Arabs had their punishment taken away. As if you can attack Israel and get away scot-free. Israeli soldiers died taking that land. To give it back makes the deaths meaningless. So I totally identified with the settlers. This was the first battle against peace at any cost."

WEARING A KNIT, COLORED YARMULKE of Modern Orthodox style and holding a one-way ticket, Harry Shapiro flew to Israel in February 1984. He had earned his high school diploma and even been offered a two-year scholarship to a junior college. But he had spurned it to make *aliyah*, "to prove to myself," as he later put it, "that I could put my words into action and lay my life on the line."

He would begin Israeli life with a combination of farm labor and Hebrew-language immersion on a kibbutz called Sde Eliyahu, one that he had chosen deliberately. Sde Eliyahu was a religious collective that had been founded by the Mizrachi movement in the late thirties. A half-century later, it remained a place whose pioneering simplicity, Orthodox commitment, and Likud loyalty etched a sharp contrast both to the left-wing, secular kibbutzim of Zionist lore and to modern Israel's evolving suburban bourgeoisie.

Politics, in the case of Sde Eliyahu, very much followed on geography. Even by the standards of Israel, the kibbutz had been founded in an especially vulnerable spot. It was squeezed into the narrow Bet She'an Valley, a finger of land pressed against the Jordanian border on the east and the West Bank on the south, and overseen by the Arab gun placements perched several thousand feet up the Gilead Mountains. Harry's route from Tel Aviv to Sde Eliyahu passed within sight of the pre-1967 border, the minarets of Arab villages easily visible, each one testimony to the insecurity of Israel's original contour. Through the sunflower fields of the Jezreel Valley, between the limestone formations, past the apartment blocks of Afula, the road signs kept counting down the distance to enemy land—Jordan 50 km, Jordan 25 km, Jordan 5 km.

Harry was determined to adopt the Israeli way, going about daily life despite the danger. His routine consisted of wake-up at six, davening *Shacharit*, breakfast, work from eight until one, lunch, language class until dinner. He made it his mission to defy the Israeli stereotype of the rich, soft American; five-foot-ten and nearly two hundred pounds, broad as a full-back in the shoulders and chest, meaty in the forearms, Harry weeded the cotton fields and packed fifty-pound bags of carrots and even volunteered to sweep manure out of the chicken coop. On a rare day off, he would travel to Jerusalem to pray at the Western Wall, and in the Old City he learned how the Jordanians had destroyed every synagogue prior to 1967, yet another proof of how vital it was to hold onto the territory. Harry occasionally called a family friend in Tel Aviv, a food importer named Roni Kol, just to enthuse about the kibbutz, the crops and Hebrew lessons, and the wonderful host couple, Yossi and

Brucha, who treated him like their own son. "He thought," Kol recalled years later, "that he had found his place."

In the process, Harry absorbed the communal memory of Sde Eliyahu. It made the current calm along the Jordanian border, a posting Israeli soldiers much favored over Gaza or Lebanon, seem ephemeral at best. Until Black September of 1970, when King Hussein drove the PLO out of Jordan, terrorists had steadily tried to infiltrate the kibbutz. Several years later, two newly arrived kibbutzniks discovered a land mine while tending crops. It exploded moments later, killing one of them. For all the lushness of Harry's new home—the date groves, the fish ponds, the fields of cotton and carrots, the gardens of oleander—Sde Eliyahu stayed on combat footing. Guard towers and bunkers marked the landscape. Dogs patrolled the perimeter. Every building had a concrete-reinforced room for bomb attacks. Small arms and anti-tank weapons were kept oiled and ready. Sde Eliyahu, like the famous kibbutz of Yad Mordecai that Harry's parents had seen, expected to hold the front until the army arrived.

One night, Harry watched as the kibbutz's soldiers hurriedly armed themselves after footprints had been spotted along the border. Five or six times, he heard the whistle and boom of Katyusha rockets zeroing in from Jordan. After each attack, Israeli F-14s screeched through the sky, sighting targets for retaliation. And these were just the most proximate instances of ongoing, if undeclared, war.

Elsewhere in Israel, a season of staggering violence, even by the standards of a besieged nation, was unfolding. The terror had begun in December 1983, a few months before Harry's arrival, when Palestinian guerrillas bombed a Jerusalem bus, killing six people and wounding forty-one. On February 28, days after Harry landed in Israel, terrorists planted two grenades outside a clothing store in downtown Jerusalem, injuring twenty-one. *March 7:* A bomb explodes on a bus in Ashdod, a city near Tel Aviv, killing three Israelis and wounding nine. *April 2:* Three guerrillas with automatic weapons and hand grenades injure forty-eight civilians as they randomly attack a crowd of Jerusalem shoppers. *April 12:* Arab hijackers seize an Israeli bus, holding thirty-five passengers hostage for ten hours until Israeli troops storm the vehicle. Time and again, Harry went to the Sde Eliyahu synagogue for memorial services. Once he rode on a bus that was evacuated in hysterics because a piece of luggage could not be matched to a passenger.

In this climate of terror, Harry began to think that perhaps stoicism and the Israel Defense Forces weren't enough. Whenever he visited Jerusalem, he sought out the Gush Emunim faithful, recognizable by their large knitted *kippot.* The Gush settlers saw themselves as both the generational and geographical extension of the Mizrachi movement that had built Sde Eliyahu. From them Harry learned that Judea and Samaria were vital to Israel for more than security alone. It was no mere military triumph that had brought Israel the Old City of Jerusalem and the West Bank in the 1967 war; it was God's will, the Torah's word, that Jews abide in all of Eretz Israel.

With understanding and some admiration, Harry read about the Jews who retaliated on their own, opening fire on Arab buses, laying booby-trapped explosives outside mosques, even plotting to bomb the Dome of the Rock. What he couldn't comprehend was that the Israeli police, unable to protect their own citizens, had found the time in the bloody spring of 1984 to arrest fellow Jews. Among those charged were Americans tied to Meir Kahane's Jewish Defense League and Kach party, as well as ultra-Orthodox Israelis. They called their group Terror Against Terror, with the Hebrew initials translating to TNT. When their pictures appeared on the front page of an Israeli newspaper, Harry hung a copy on the wall of his room. "To me," he recalled, "they were heroes."

Harry held these views against the backdrop of an increasingly polarized Israel. Through the spring and early summer of 1984, the Labor and Likud parties, and their respective leaders, Shimon Peres and Yitzhak Shamir, fought a brutal election campaign. Labor had been ousted from power by Menachem Begin in 1977, but now, with Begin retired and in seclusion, with inflation soaring to 400 percent and the Israeli army bogged down in an unpopular occupation of much of Lebanon, the left-wing party stood as a strong favorite. Polls predicted that it would win as many as fifty-five seats, leaving it easily within reach of the sixty-one needed for a governing coalition in the Knesset. Such a coalition would select Peres as prime minister.

For a political leader deeply rooted in the Israeli saga—a man who made *aliyah* from Byelorussia in 1936, recruited soldiers for the Haganah, and developed the aircraft and nuclear arms programs for the Israeli military—Peres remained a divisive figure. He had never served in battle, went one criticism. He fancied himself a European aesthete, dapper and multilingual. He was a utopian dreamer in the globe's nastiest neighborhood.

During the campaign, Peres called for Israeli withdrawal from Lebanon, peace negotiations with King Hussein, and an end to government subsidies for many West Bank settlements. Purportedly, that last plank was part of his plan for reducing inflation. But it excited doubts on the Israeli right that, even though the settlements program had begun under earlier Labor governments, Peres would dismantle Greater Israel. Watching the campaign as it played out in Sde Eliyahu, Harry could see who would vote Labor: the longhairs who spent their evenings under the date palms playing guitar and chewing sunflower seeds. The Likud supporters, it seemed to him, were the realists who saw the world as it was: the foremen, the veterans, the businessmen like his family friend Roni Kol. "Too permissive, too weak," Harry said later, recalling his thoughts on Labor. "You could say my problems with Mr. Peres's ideology began back then."

On election day, July 23, Israeli voters delivered a shocking verdict. Heavily favored, Labor essentially deadlocked with Likud, forty-four seats to forty-one, leaving a society divided down the middle and gathering strength at its extremes. No one was more extreme than Meir Kahane, who won a Knesset seat despite an earlier election board ruling, reversed during the campaign by the Israeli Supreme Court, that his Kach party be banned as racist. The morning after his victory, Kahane led his supporters to the Western Wall and announced, "I am going to, in my first speech in parliament, make the issue of throwing out the Arabs. . . . We will make this country Jewish again."

For the moment, a shaky and improbable center coalesced. Peres and Shamir negotiated a national unity government combining their parties and providing for each man to serve as prime minister for twenty-five months. In the course of striking the deal, Peres tried one last time to curb the Jewish influx to the West Bank by insisting that any new settlements receive a two-thirds majority in a cabinet vote. He ultimately relented and in September took office as prime minister, calling the ruling coalition a "government of disagreement."

Harry Shapiro, meanwhile, was about to return to Jacksonville for practical reasons. Sde Eliyahu crouched in marshy ground six hundred feet below sea level, and in the summer temperatures routinely soared above 110°. Even though he was accustomed to the sultry weather of Florida, Harry had grown weak and ill from intestinal problems. He was hospitalized for three weeks in August, his weight dropping from 186 to 132 pounds. Back in America, Philip had just suffered a ruptured artery during an angioplasty procedure. And he was alone now, divorced from Sandy. So, out of futility and fidelity, Harry bought a one-way ticket home. He arrived haggard, frustrated, but wearing, in an act of both solidarity and self-delusion, the distinctive *kippa* of Gush Emunim.

JUST BEFORE THE FALL SEMESTER of 1988 opened, an unlikely hybrid of a vehicle pulled into the Manhattan campus of Yeshiva University. It was a pickup truck, consummately Southern from its shotgun rack to its Eat More Possum bumper sticker, except that one door bore the Hebrew letters spelling "Yitzhak," Harry Shapiro's Jewish name. Now twenty-three, out of high school for seven years, most recently employed in a frozen-food warehouse, Harry had resolved to acquire not only a college degree but an advanced religious education. And Yeshiva, founded on the philosophy of *Torah Umaddah*, Torah and worldly knowledge, offered the ideal setting for his quest.

Harry had abandoned his dream of moving permanently to Israel after a month-long trip there in 1986. Hoping to work as an auto mechanic, he discovered that Palestinians already glutted the field. That gave him just one more reason to resent them. Low on money, lacking a fallback plan, Harry took the cheapest hotel room he could find, which turned out to be in Tel Aviv's red-light district. Roni Kol whisked him to a youth hostel and soon after put him on a jet home. Back in Jacksonville, having twice failed at *aliyah*, his love for Israel unrequited, Harry looked again to religion as his refuge.

It was oddly appropriate, then, that Yeshiva assigned him a room in Muss Hall, colloquially known as the *smicha* dorm, the ordination dorm, because it housed students advancing toward the rabbinate in the university's seminary. Having already completed their undergraduate courses, they were closer in age to Harry than a bunch of eighteen-year-old freshmen would have been. The affinity seemed at first to end there. In a *frum* domain, among young men with black hats and *tzitzis* out and shirts buttoned to the collar, here lumbered Harry with a Dixie accent, several guns, and a side income repairing cars at curbside for the neighborhood Dominicans. More problematically, Harry realized quickly how deficient was his Hebrew literacy to the demands of religious scholarship. In Israel, he had studied modern, conversational Hebrew, and during his childhood years at Etz Chaim he had learned to read but not understand classical Hebrew. Yeshiva put Harry in its remedial program along with several dozen *ba'alei teshuva*, returnees to the faith, and even among neophytes he foundered.

So when Harry was trying to study one Thursday night that autumn and kept being interrupted by a metallic din from down the hall, he went to investigate, fuming. Amid a sea of aluminum cans waded two aspiring rabbis, Daniel Wolf and Dani Rapp, known in the dorm simply as "the two Dannys." They regarded Harry with trepidation; earlier in the fall, he had put a BB gun to another student's temple, supposedly as a joke. All the noise, the two Dannys hastily explained, came from sorting the cans. They returned the empties for deposit— six and a half cents apiece instead of the usual five if the cans were separated by brand—and used the money to buy and deliver meals to homebound elderly Jews. They called themselves the Yeshiva University Philanthropy Society, and the can-redemption program was their form of charity, *tzedakah*.

The society and its mission instantly appealed to Harry. Bolstered by his energy and muscular back, the two Dannys were harvesting $200 a week from their cans by early 1989. Besides feeding the aged Jews who lingered in Washington Heights, Yeshiva's neighborhood, they began assisting the Soviet Jewish refugees being settled there. They hauled donated furniture to the families, usually with Harry at the wheel of a rented truck, and put on Hanukkah and Purim parties for the children. When Harry encountered a thirteen-year-old Russian boy who had no tefillin, he pulled $400 from his pocket to buy the phylacteries. Another time, he labored all night to fill a twenty-four-foot truck with chairs and desks being given to a yeshiva for Soviet Jews. And the efforts got noticed—by Jewish publications, by a campus stringer for the *New York Times*, and ultimately by the New York state legislature, the United States Information Agency, and even President George Bush, who hailed the society as a prime example of the voluntarism he had famously called "a thousand points of light."

In an indirect way, the *tzedakah* also saved Harry's academic career. When the spring semester of 1989 ended, Harry had flunked out of the remedial program and thus out of Yeshiva. This time the F's hadn't been deliberate. Harry's father had been suffering from cancer during the whole school year, finally dying in May, and Harry regularly drove the 2,000-mile round-trip to Jacksonville as his class assignments piled up. The two Dannys pleaded Harry's case with the program's dean and won a conditional reprieve: Harry could stay if he spent the summer at the Morasha Kollel, a combination camp and religious studies institute, with Dani Rapp serving as his roommate and tutor.

Morasha Kollel came closer than anything in America to approximating the community Harry had known at Sde Eliyahu. Along the shores of Lake Como in the Pocono Mountains, Harry spent his days in prayer and study, reciting kaddish for his father every morning in the woodland quiet, learning the Gemara literally word by word. More than any specific material, he absorbed a way of life. Even at Yeshiva University, so many Orthodox Jews watched television on Sabbath that the administration had ordered a crackdown during Harry's freshman year. The future rabbis in the *smicha* dorm used to crack disdainfully that the Yeshiva philosophy wasn't *Torah Umaddah* but *Torah doesn't matter*. Jews like Dani Rapp, though, davened themselves into the spirit of *Shabbos;* they lived the mitzvot through the Philanthropy Society. "They embodied," Harry said later, "the whole concept of being a Torah-observant Jew." For his part, Harry dazzled the *kollel* with his pickup truck and a bow and arrows set. To most Orthodox Jews, a ram was what Abraham sacrificed in Isaac's stead; Harry Shapiro had hunted rams with his father on a private game preserve.

"Those were the best times for Harry," Dani Rapp said years later, recalling both summer at the *kollel* and the Philanthropy Society's activity. "The best times, for sure."

The best times ended with a surgeon's scalpel. Sandy Shapiro underwent a mastectomy in October 1989. Once more commuting between Manhattan and Jacksonville and inevitably falling behind in his work, Harry realized he would have to drop out of Yeshiva University. The Philanthropy Society, meanwhile, waned when Daniel Wolf was hired to direct a Russian resettlement program in Queens. What could give Harry Shapiro a sense of purpose now? He decided to stay in New York, training to become a kosher butcher—not as prestigious as becoming a rabbi like the two Dannys, true, but a way to remain in the *frum* culture that so nourished him. With a degree or without it, Harry had deepened his Jewish knowledge at Yeshiva. He wore *tzitzis* himself now, and a black fedora. And, thanks to an event Yeshiva University had tried to prevent, he now possessed a political as well as a religious belief system.

In the winter of 1989, as Harry was beginning his second semester at Yeshiva, Meir Kahane had been invited to speak on campus. Pariah though he was in liberal Jewish circles, Kahane enjoyed substantial support among the right-wing Orthodox in America, raising upwards of a half-million dollars annually from U.S. donors. He had made similar appearances at the university every two or three years, delighting in his ability to attract hecklers and inspiring scores of students to enlist in the Kach movement and the Jewish Defense League. This year, however, he was arriving at a pivotal moment in his political career, a fulcrum of forced transformation from provocateur within the system to official outcast.

Only a few months earlier, with the *Intifada* raging in the occupied territories and the Arab birth rate within Israel doubling that of Jews, Kahane's platform of expelling Palestinians was reaching a growing constituency of Sephardic, Russian, and American immigrants. As the November 1988 Knesset election neared, polls had estimated that Kach could win 100,000 votes and four seats in the parliament, quadrupling its 1984 result. The militant rabbi loomed as a potential kingmaker in Israel's coalition politics, with Yitzhak Shamir's Likud and Shimon Peres's Labor again headed for a stalemate. But barely two weeks before the election, Israel's Central Election Committee, composed of Knesset members from both major parties, had barred Kach from competing, calling its policies "racist" and

"Nazilike." The Israeli Supreme Court, which had reversed a similar ruling in 1984, now upheld the ban. Among all but the most radical adherents of Gush Emunim, Kahane was disparaged as a crank, an outsider. Kahane even had to sue in U.S. Federal Court to be admitted to America for a speaking tour over State Department objections. He had taken to saying that Jews had to choose between democracy and Torah.

Now even Yeshiva was distancing itself from Kahane. Although the student council scheduled the rabbi to speak on February 14, the university administration refused use of Belfer Commons, the usual setting for lectures by major visitors because it could accommodate a crowd of several hundred. Then two different student groups, the Israel Affairs Society and the Political Science Society, refused to sponsor the event or even to provide a member to introduce Kahane.

As Harry followed the controversy, he began reading up on Kahane, this Jew so dangerous that other Jews tried to silence him. He pored over books, newspaper columns, transcribed speeches, and Kach publications. Harry had grown aware over the years of the Jewish Defense League, its catchphrase "Never again," the Kach movement to purge Israel of Arabs, but only now did he trace the common ancestry of them all to Meir Kahane. Dani Rapp warned Harry that Kahane, while he had many admirable qualities, was "too radical for the times." But Harry was gripped by the spectacle of a Jewish university disowning a rabbi, a member of the Knesset. For all their putative devotion to Torah and *Klal Yisrael*, the Modern Orthodox of Yeshiva University were just like the timid, cowed, assimilated Jews whom Kahane always branded "nice Irvings."

Finally, the university relented and allowed Kahane to speak in a dormitory chapel less than half the size of the commons. Harry arrived forty-five minutes early to make sure he got a seat, and indeed the standing-room crowd stranded fifty latecomers in a hallway. When Kahane rose to the lectern, he surprised Harry with his topic, "A Perspective on the Halakhic Status of Non-Jews Living in Israel." He wasn't talking about politics but about Torah and Talmud and the Rambam. Most of all, drawing back his shoulders, narrowing his eyes, shaking his forefinger skyward, he spoke of *milchemet* mitzvah, the commandment of mandatory war in national defense. "Why is mandatory war so important?" Kahane demanded. "The answer lies in sanctifying God's name. If we lose, our cities will become theirs and their gods'. Their gods will appear superior, and God will appear weak. The entire issue of *chilul Hashem*, desecration of the Holy Name, exists whenever the Jew is defeated. It was after the epitome of the worst *chilul Hashem*, that of the Nazi Holocaust, that God decided, 'Enough.' Now He has begun to sanctify Himself through us. Now He has returned Israel to us and made her mighty." All through the Bible, Kahane continued, with Abraham and David and Yiftach the Judge, Jews had fought for the land of Israel or been punished by God for compromising. "Only in our days," he said, now fusing past and present, "does the enemy come offering 'peace' and we say, 'Here, take this, take that. Peace now, peace immediately, peace in ten seconds.'"

For Harry, Kahane's oratory summoned one particularly vivid memory of Sde Eliyahu. It was about eleven on a night shortly after he had arrived, and he was walking to the kibbutz telephone to call his mother. Suddenly he heard whistles and booms, sounds that as a newcomer he didn't recognize. Only when he saw men scrambling to the kibbutz armory did he realize that the noise had been rockets. Sde Eliyahu was preparing in its well-trained fashion for terrorist infiltration, and to Harry, the new kibbutznik, it felt like an imminent invasion. Although no onslaught ever came, he remembered that first jolt of vulnerability. On this night four years later in a Yeshiva chapel, Meir Kahane was describing the ultimate security, a Jewish nation for Jews alone.

As the speech ended and Kahane moved toward a waiting car, Harry managed to press close enough to exchange a few words. *I don't want to kill Arabs*, Kahane explained, *they just can't live together with Jews*. A few days later, Harry posted a bumper sticker on his door: Transfer the Arabs. He continued to compile material from Kach—photos, transcribed speeches, Torah passages. When Kahane was assassinated during an appearance at a Manhattan hotel on November 5, 1990, Harry wept and guessed correctly that an Arab had pulled the trigger.* But he also felt a certainty he had never before known both about Kahane and the nice Irvings who had betrayed him.

"The assassination sealed my belief in him," Harry recalled later. "If he wasn't on the right track, if he wasn't a danger to the Arabs, then he wouldn't have been cut down. This was a man who was a learned scholar, who used as his argument the Torah. He was killed for espousing what the Torah says. And the beginning of his death was his censure by the left-wing Jewish parliament. Jews targeted him politically, monetarily, emotionally. I blamed left-wing Jews for making him a pariah, an outcast, a target."

WHEN HARRY SHAPIRO RETURNED to Jacksonville from New York in the spring of 1991, he returned in something like triumph. With $70,000 in capital and the skills acquired during an apprenticeship in the Bronx, he opened a butcher shop called Kosher Kuts. The *Florida Times-Union* spread its story all over the front page, beneath the headline saying, "Prepared Biblical Way." A photograph showed Harry in his *kippa* and apron trimming fat off a roast.

He had learned how to do much more than that. As a kosher butcher, he could expertly *nikkur* meat, remove the veins, and then salt and soak it. He knew how the major blood vessel in a cow's foreleg split like the Hebrew letter *shin* and where to hook the single vein in a tongue so it could be pulled out in a stroke. For nearly twenty years, since Jacksonville's last

---

* El Sayyid Nosair, an Egyptian immigrant who belonged to a fundamentalist Islamic mosque in Jersey City, was arrested and tried for Kahane's murder. Despite the testimony of more than fifty witnesses, a jury acquitted him of murder, though he was found guilty of gun possession and other lesser charges.

kosher butcher shop had closed, the city's ten thousand Jews had had no choice but to order frozen meat by mail from New York or Chicago. Etz Chaim's own rabbi had urged Harry to fill the void.

And he filled it with family. Harry's maternal grandmother, Ann Greenburg, worked the cash register, and his brother Steve ran the deli section. His mother Sandy stopped in to help on breaks from her job selling real estate. Harry had inherited much of the start-up money from his father. Once again, as at Sde Eliyahu and Yeshiva and the Morasha Kollel, he appeared to have found community.

But Harry soon discovered why the last kosher butcher had shut down. Jacksonville's Jewish population, neither large nor especially observant, didn't provide enough business for a profit except at Passover. Many of those who did keep kosher complained to Harry that his fresh meat cost more than the frozen mail-order variety. And Harry remained as soft a touch as ever for *tzedakah*, refusing any profit when catering Sabbath lunches at Etz Chaim and a Soviet Jewish boy's bar mitzvah reception. The deeper he slid into debt, the shorter his temper got, and his abrasiveness drove off his customers. On January 9, 1993, the *Florida Times-Union* again put Harry and Kosher Kuts on its front page, this time to report the shop's demise.

The failure might never have mattered in any political way except that it left Harry available eight months later, when one of his Yeshiva University friends called from New York to say that a kosher butcher in Staten Island was looking for a *mashgiach*, the person who observes all slaughtering to ensure that it conforms to religious law. When Harry arrived to start work in late August 1993, three weeks before Yasir Arafat and Yitzhak Rabin signed the Oslo accords at the White House, he was coincidentally immersing himself in one of the hotbeds of opposition to the peace process.

After a year on Staten Island, Harry took a *mashgiach* job in the Borough Park section of Brooklyn, whose politics were defined by the largest concentration of ultra-Orthodox

Jews outside Israel and an uncommonly large number of Holocaust survivors. A few miles away stood Crown Heights, center of the Lubavitcher Hasidim and site of an August 1991 riot during which one group of blacks stabbed to death a religious scholar named Yankel Rosenbaum while others compared themselves to Palestinians.* Even closer to Borough Park spread Flatbush, East Flatbush, and Midwood, the neighborhoods where Meir Kahane had formed the Jewish Defense League in the late sixties, offering as his remedy for racial turmoil the slogan "Every Jew, a .22." The *Jewish Press*, weekly organ of right-wing Jewry, was published in Brooklyn. The state assemblyman from the area, Dov Hikind, was a product of the Jewish Defense League. Much of the local Orthodox rabbinate, believing that Israel's victory in 1967 anticipated the coming of the Messiah, considered any return of territory a blasphemy. Indeed, the connection to Israel was more than a matter of sentimentality and rhetoric in the Orthodox districts of Brooklyn; they provided, by one estimate, a quarter of all the Americans making *aliyah* in the early nineties. Many of these immigrants were bound for the frontier settlements of Judea and Samaria.

The Oslo agreement struck Harry as worse than betrayal, because it was a betrayal he had been expecting ever since Labor took control of the Knesset in the 1992 elections. Shimon Peres, it was now being revealed, had been secretly meeting with the PLO as far back as 1988—meeting with that murderer at the same time Meir Kahane's party was being outlawed for wanting to keep the Jewish state Jewish. Harry decried the pact in conversations with his boss's son, a veteran of the Israeli army who couched his condemnation in terms of security. Attending various synagogues, Harry heard the theo-

---

* The violence began after a Hasidic driver lost control of his vehicle and swerved onto a sidewalk, striking and killing a black child named Gavin Cato. Prior to the incident, there had been substantial political tension between the Hasidic and Afro-Caribbean populations that live in different parts of Crown Heights.

logical brand of denunciations. The *Jewish Press*, its hyperbole prophetic this time, headlined a front-page story on the pact, "May Lead To Civil War."

On the morning of February 25, 1994, a son of Brooklyn took action against Oslo, unleashing a fusillade from his Glilol assault rifle that slew twenty-nine worshippers in a Hebron mosque before being killed himself. A doctor in the West Bank settlement of Kiryat Arba, Baruch Goldstein had grown up in Bensonhurst, gone to high school at the Yeshiva of Flatbush, and joined the Jewish Defense League in the late seventies. After making *aliyah* in 1983, he worked closely with Kahane's Kach party, managing one of its election campaigns and running on its slate of parliamentary candidates. In an interview he gave a visiting journalist in 1988, he expressed a philosophy very close to Harry Shapiro's:

> In Judaism we have an absolute truth. This is the Torah. This is our law. It's above the decisions of man. The fact that this has to be a Jewish state is not something we decided but which we believe God decided. We have no right to democratically or any other way allow this state to become a non-Jewish Arab state. . . . I'm looking to rid ourselves of that danger, and any way that's possible, I think it should be done.

In Kiryat Arba, perhaps the most radical settlement in the occupied territories, Goldstein received a funeral befitting a hero, and in the years to come his gravesite was treated by Kach partisans as a shrine. In Brooklyn, Harry Shapiro spoke of him with reverence. "Reb Goldstein," he called him, using the term of affectionate respect for someone learned. He was "a martyr who gave his life to save Jewish lives and will get his reward in *Gan Eden*," the Garden of Eden, the Jewish conception of heaven. Chatting by phone with his sister Juli, Harry put his feelings more colloquially. "Good," he said of the Hebron shootings. "Whoopee."

Far from discrediting the anti-Oslo movement, Goldstein's rampage hardened its resolve, especially in Brooklyn. Four days after the Hebron attack, a Lebanese immigrant opened fire on a vanload of Hasidic youngsters crossing the Brooklyn Bridge, killing one and paralyzing another. By one interpretation, the gunman had acted in retaliation for Goldstein. But in the ultra-Orthodox neighborhoods, which prided themselves on their yeshiva *bochurim*, their yeshiva boys, the attack provided yet another reminder of why Jews like Baruch Goldstein needed to strike preemptively.

In the emerging consensus in Brooklyn, the enemies of Israel were not only the Palestinians but the nation's own leaders. Avraham Hecht, who led 2,000 congregants in the borough as rabbi of Shaare Zion synagogue and 540 colleagues as president of the Rabbinical Alliance of America, grew more outspoken than ever in the months after the Hebron massacre. At a June 1995 meeting of the International Rabbinical Coalition for Israel, a 3,000-member group opposed to the Oslo accords, he declared that surrendering any of Eretz Israel violated *halakhah*, and anyone who did so could be killed as a *rodef*—literally, "one who pursues a Jew trying to kill him"; colloquially, a traitor.

Two months later, in an open letter to rabbis published in the *Jewish Press*, Hecht wrote, "The Torah permits the most extreme action against those who harm our fellow Jews." Asked by *New York* magazine in October to clarify what sounded like a religious death sentence against the Israeli prime minister, Yitzhak Rabin, Hecht explained: "All I said was that according to Jewish law, any one person—you can apply it to whoever you want—any one person who willfully, consciously, intentionally hands over human bodies or human property or the human wealth of the Jewish people to an alien people is guilty of the sin for which the penalty is death. And, according to Maimonides—you can quote me—it says very clearly, if a man kills him, he has done a good deed."

Amid such rhetoric, Harry Shapiro went about his life. He held two part-time jobs in addition to being a *mashgiach*, trying to repay his debts from Kosher Kuts, because declaring bankruptcy would have been dishonorable. He moved furniture, painted houses, repaired cars for his old Yeshiva classmates. He often cooked dinner for his landlord's family. As Sukkoth approached, he helped neighbors erect the outdoor booths for which the harvest holiday is named. Meanwhile, Rabbi Hecht's theology completed a circle for Harry. Years ago, Gush Emunim had taught him that God granted Eretz Israel to the Jews; then Meir Kahane demonstrated how one could hate Jewish leaders in the name of loving the Jewish people; and now Harry understood the penalty for disobeying divine commandment. "The Torah is our deed to that land," Harry put it. "Who is man to give it back?"

He certainly professed no loyalty to the man leading Israel. How could this Yitzhak Rabin, forcing his secret agreements down Israel's throat, be the same person who had come to Jacksonville in the year of Harry's bar mitzvah to declare he would never negotiate with the PLO, "that murderous organization"? Philip and Sandy Shapiro themselves had sat in the audience that night at the Beauclerc Country Club to hear Rabin state in his unsentimental soldier's way, "We live in a cruel world. It is a world where it isn't enough to be just."

These days, Harry tracked the perfidy of the Labor government in the pages of the *Jewish Press* and *Yated Ne'eman*, a *haredi* weekly from Monsey. There was that time in March 1994 when Israeli police beat the Women in Green—so named in contrast to a left-wing group called the Women in Black—for reading aloud the names of all the Jews killed by terrorists since Arafat and Rabin had shaken hands on the White House lawn to seal the Oslo accords. Rabbi Hecht was being refused entry to Israel and forced out by his own congregation, both due in the right-wing view to diplomatic pressure from Jerusalem. Then came the waves of Hamas bus bombings—seven soldiers dead in Gaza in April 1995; six civilians dead and thirty-two wounded outside Tel Aviv in July; four dead and a hundred wounded in Jerusalem in August. Here was the same terror Harry had witnessed a decade earlier from Sde Eliyahu, only this time abetted by an Israeli regime foolish enough to talk peace with blood enemies.

Harry was davening on the Sabbath afternoon of November 4, 1995, when he heard of the assassination of Yitzhak Rabin by Yigal Amir. It being *Shabbos*, none of the synagogue's Orthodox Jews would have been watching television or listening to the radio; perhaps someone in the minyan had learned the news from a neighbor or caught a bulletin from the window of a passing car. A few members of the congregation spoke prayers for Rabin during services, but Harry withheld any reaction until sundown, when he could switch on CNN. The first image he saw was of President Clinton weeping. Then he listened to the reports of how Amir had claimed a religious sanction for killing a *rodef.* Harry took immediate satisfaction from "a blow being struck against the side that's wrong."

Several weeks later, Harry visited Jacksonville and shared Sabbath dinner with his relatives. The conversation turned to Amir. This was no table of doves. Harry's brother Steve and his sister Juli both opposed the land-for-peace policy. His aunt and uncle, Michael and Charlotte Greenburg, had witnessed the abandonment of Yamit all those years ago on the same trip with Harry's parents. Still, it fell to Harry alone to defend the assassin.

"There's no justification for this act," Michael Greenburg said, "even if he thought the country was being given away."

"He was carrying out God's will," Harry replied.

Juli listened, mortified. First there had been Harry's crack about Hebron. Then, in a phone call just after Rabin's murder, he'd said that maybe now Israel could make some progress. And now this remark. No longer could she ascribe the rhetoric to Harry being a blowhard, Harry going for shock value. "It was my first inkling," she said in retrospect, "that he had feelings this strong that he couldn't mourn a fellow Jew."

Back in New York, Harry's position gradually changed. There was something horrendous, he now thought, about Jew killing Jew. It couldn't have been a rational man's act. In fact, as Harry came to believe, the shooting really hadn't been Yigal Amir's act at all. Oh, he had pulled the trigger, of course, but he'd been provoked to it, even assisted in it, by the Shin Bet, the Israeli secret service, all as a way of building sympathy for Oslo and demonizing the Orthodox. Week after week, the *Jewish Press* played the story across page one: "Shin Bet Role in Assassination" . . . "Labor Party Uses Rabin Murder to Stifle Dissent." *Yated Ne'eman*, too, trumpeted the proof of conspiracy, the disclosures that Amir had received firearm training from the Shin Bet and that his co-conspirator, Avishai Raviv, was a secret agent.

"The common misperception," Harry said, "is that Orthodox Jews called for Rabin's death. That is totally wrong. What Orthodox Jews said is that the Torah provides the death penalty for one who gives up the Land of Israel. When they were talking about death, they were talking about how heinous the crime of giving back the land was."

Meanwhile, the Knesset installed Shimon Peres as prime minister. He vowed to continue the peace process for which Rabin had sacrificed his life, and which Harry Shapiro among many other Jews considered a *chilul Hashem*, a desecration of God's name.

IN THE SPRING OF 1996, the imminent death of a parent again called Harry Shapiro home to Jacksonville. His mother Sandy, only fifty-five, was in the final stages of breast cancer, and each emergency trip to Florida left Harry torn between a sorrowful family and an infuriated boss back in Brooklyn. Michael Greenburg, Harry's uncle, saw the effect. "Unsettled," he remembered later of Harry's state of mind. "And maybe just angrier."

Much of the anger was of the ontological sort, an anger at the universe for taking away a mother who had been his friend and confidante. But Harry also felt anger of a political kind. In Israel, Shimon Peres was running for a full term as prime minister against Benjamin Netanyahu, and during late February and early March suicide bombers from Hamas had struck Israeli buses four times, killing sixty-two people. After one of the attacks, several hundred protesters gathered outside a cabinet meeting to burn torches and chant, "This is not peace," "Death to the Arabs," and "Peres next!"

Sandy Greenburg died on April 3, a Sabbath on the eve of Passover. Harry delivered the eulogy at her funeral, and even those Jacksonville Jews who had always dismissed him as an oddball and a loser admitted to admiration at the passion and erudition of his words. He drew on Kabbalah, Psalms, Sabbath songs, and rabbinic commentary before ending with a more personal kind of prophecy. "You will be missed," Harry said, addressing his mother instead of the mourners, "and our lives will never be the same. To me, you were the light at the beginning of the day and the pillow at the end. Always there, always to be counted on. The light is now gone. Go on your ascent, knowing that you provided your family and friends with the path through the darkness that will follow."

For Harry, that darkness took both the literal and metaphorical form. He moved back to Jacksonville, living by himself in a rented condo, and working alone pumping gas on an overnight shift. He left the service station at daybreak to pray kaddish for his mother at Etz Chaim. Then he slept into the afternoon, his work schedule compounding the alienation he felt. Unmarried at age thirty, a rarity in *frum* culture, Harry was so lonely that a family friend named Jay Graff urged him to relax his religious standards and date a shiksa, if only "for target practice." Harry instead found solace where he so often had, in the synagogue. The new rabbi at Etz Chaim, Avraham Kelman, had young children whom Harry baby-sat. When the family returned from a vacation, Harry was waiting with a kosher pizza. And it was Harry whom Rabbi Kelman called when the Leibov family's van crashed on the road back from Disney World.

Perhaps nothing would have ever happened to single out Harry Shapiro from the Jews who merely cried "Peres next!"—or the millions in Israel and America who phrased their opposition to Oslo more decorously—had not a telemarketing executive named Doron Nevo approached Rabbi David Gaffney with a brainstorm in early 1997. An Israeli immigrant with a secular Zionist background, Nevo maintained ties to Labor party leaders, and he knew that Shimon Peres was visiting Florida in February to raise money for the Peres Institute for Peace. He proposed that Jacksonville host a speech.

Rabbi Gaffney confessed to mixed emotions. Wary of the land-for-peace formula since his trip to Yamit, he considered Peres a "starry-eyed, naïve" prime minister who had returned territory at a time when the Palestinians "weren't owning up to their obligations." Such pessimism was the majority opinion in Israel, too, where Peres lost to Netanyahu in the May 1996 election. Although the overall margin was minuscule—29,000 votes out of nearly two million cast—only the nearly unanimous support of Arab citizens had spared Peres from a double-digit defeat. The ultra-Orthodox went against him 95 to 5 percent.

Still, Rabbi Gaffney recognized the prestige of having a Nobel laureate in Jacksonville, a city otherwise struggling to prove its stature with a National Football League franchise. His synagogue, the Jacksonville Jewish Center, had the largest capacity of any local Jewish institution. Soon a plan emerged— a fund-raising cocktail party for the peace center, hosted at a private club by a Jewish executive, followed by a speech at the synagogue for donors to the local Jewish Federation.

As soon as Harry heard of the event, in mid-January, he resolved to make some kind of protest. No matter that Peres had already been repudiated at the polls. Even under Netanyahu, Israel was saddled with Oslo, with bus bombings and the dubious partnership of Yasir Arafat. Harry recalled a Talmudic concept he had learned at Yeshiva University, *pikuach nefesh*. It meant protecting a life, including your own, by any means possible. During his college years in Washington Heights, *pikuach nefesh* was a reason not to ride the subway at one in the morning. Now, it was a reason for Israel not to, as Harry put it, "invite your enemy to live in your house after he's sworn to kill you and tried to kill you for many years."

What was Shimon Peres seeking in Jacksonville, after all, except money and support for extending the PLO just such an invitation? Something had to be done. Never able to join the battle against Arabs in Eretz Israel, Harry decided to carry it against a Jew on American ground.

"You want to make a protest?" Jay Graff advised Harry. "I want to protest, too. My protest is going to be not going. The best protest is a no-show. Peres can't talk to an empty house."

An empty house hardly seemed likely. Harry's uncle and aunt, the Greenburgs, were planning to attend. His sister Juli called up one afternoon all excited about her ticket. Harry interrupted her enthusiasm by simply asking, "And?"

"And what?" Juli replied. "What do you mean?"

"I can't believe you support him."

"I don't support him, either," Juli said. "But he's a part of history. And there's the honor of hearing him speak."

"You couldn't pay me," Harry muttered.

Alone with his indignation, Harry decided his best hope was to wreck the speech. Carrying a picket sign wouldn't stop it. Calling in a bomb threat wouldn't work; in half an hour, the police would sweep through the synagogue, pronounce it a hoax, and invite everybody back to their seats. But Harry figured that an imitation bomb—built to resemble the real thing but not to explode, hidden just well enough to avoid casual detection—would empty the hall for the night. It might not silence Shimon Peres forever, but at least it would stop him from spewing propaganda in Harry's hometown.

At eight o'clock in the morning on Monday, February 10, three days before the Peres speech, Harry finished his shift at the gas station. He stopped at a red light on San Jose Boulevard, the main road through the Jewish section of Mandarin, the route to Etz Chaim and the Jacksonville Jewish Center and the former Kosher Kuts and his garden apartment. A spasm of doubt passed through him. If he was going to do this, he had to decide now. Drive straight and go home to bed; turn right for the sporting goods store. The traffic light changed to green. Harry made the right turn.

In the sporting goods store, he bought a twelve-ounce can of black gunpowder. The owner, perhaps suspicious, asked Harry what he was shooting. A forty-five–caliber ball-and-powder pistol, Harry replied calmly. He owned one, in fact, having inherited it as part of his father's gun collection. Harry then drove to a hardware store, where he bought a length of threaded pipe and two end-caps. His errands completed, he went home to sleep.

When Harry awakened in the late afternoon, he set about assembling the bomb in his kitchen. Wearing gloves to avoid leaving fingerprints, he drilled holes in one end-cap, then poured about half the gunpowder into the pipe. He screwed on both end-caps, being careful that the friction in the threading did not ignite the powder. Then he set about ensuring that the bomb could not explode. For the timing device, he used a broken watch. For the power source, he fished a leaky nine-volt battery out of his tool kit. He ran wires from them into the packed powder, then wrapped the whole contraption in duct tape and masking tape. Concerned not to leave any evidence behind, he scrubbed down the kitchen floor and counters, flushed the remaining powder down the toilet, and threw his gloves, shopping bags, purchase receipts into a dumpster. The whole process had taken just twenty minutes.

On Tuesday afternoon, two days before the speech, Harry put on his overcoat, tucked the bomb in one pocket, and went to the Jacksonville Jewish Center. He paced the halls for perhaps ten minutes, looking for a place where the device "could be easily found but not easily seen." Finding just the right niche, he knelt alongside the memorial panels, slipping the bomb in the several-inch space between the metal slabs and the wall. By his own thinking, he had inserted enough powder for a bomb-sniffing dog to find the device, and had rigged the electric charge not to work. The task completed, he walked over to the Jewish Center's preschool, which his nephew attended, "to see if Seth was having a good day."

The next day, with barely twenty-four hours remaining until the speech, Harry paid a visit to Rabbi Kelman at Etz Chaim. "Do you believe in clergy privilege?" he asked Avi Kelman, and the rabbi answered that he did. Harry pulled him into the synagogue kitchen, deserted at this hour, and confided his plan. In Harry's recollection, Rabbi Kelman told him, "You need to take it out. Just call in the threat." Rabbi Kelman, later interrogated by an agent from the Bureau of Alcohol, Tobacco, and Firearms, recalled having said, "You're not serious, you're joking," and "Harry, tell me you're not going to do it."

That night, Harry later said in an interview, he was driving through the Mandarin section when his car passed Rabbi Kelman's. The rabbi honked and motioned Harry into a nearby parking lot.

"Tell me you didn't put anything there," Kelman said.

"But you know that I did," Harry replied.

"I just want you to tell me you didn't put anything there."

So Harry, not wanting to lie to his rabbi, envisioned a part of the Jewish Center other than the memorial wall, and said, "I didn't put anything *there.*"

At five o'clock on the afternoon of Thursday, February 13, three hours before Shimon Peres was to address the Jewish Center audience, Harry drove to a pay phone across town from his apartment. Again wearing gloves, he dialed 911 and called in the threat. He threw in the word *Yahudi,* the Arabic word for "Jewish," as a bit of Middle Eastern verisimilitude; he remembered it from three Arab brothers he'd known during childhood. They were Palestinians, actually, originally from Ramallah on the West Bank, and in Harry's estimation "honest, hardworking, fine people." In other words, so unlike the ones blowing apart buses in Israel.

Then Harry drove over to his gas station, expecting to see police cars and firetrucks streaking down San Jose toward the synagogue. None ever appeared. As it turned out, the bomb squad came and went discreetly, finding nothing more incendiary than the braided candle and box of matches kept behind the Ark for *havdalah*, the ceremony marking Sabbath's end. The speech went ahead without the slightest wrinkle, at least so far as the audience knew. All 1,300 listeners gave Peres a standing ovation as he declared, "It is time for peace."

The only crime at a synagogue that night took place at Etz Chaim, where three Russian Jews and an Israeli had shown up begging for charity. They had pulled the same stunt a few days earlier in Savannah, Georgia, and walked off with $250 in *tzedakah*—and $10,000 worth of silver Torah pointers, tallit clips, and other ritual items that they had pilfered. Alerted to the scheme by the Savannah rabbi, several Etz Chaim congregants called the police to arrest the thieves. The Jacksonville cops in turn informed federal agents, who, thinking they had their bombers, staked out the home of the local Hasidic rabbi, the latest stop for the con men and their spiel.

Nine days passed before the group of children discovered the bomb during Aliza Morris's bat mitzvah. Cutting through the Jewish Center's property on his walk home from Sabbath services at Etz Chaim, Harry saw the parking lot filled with police cars, and assumed the rest. All that afternoon in his apartment, he literally shook with fear. But he kept reassuring himself that he'd covered his tracks. No fingerprint, no evidence, no proof. Then, davening the *Mincha* service at Etz Chaim that night, he noticed Rabbi Kelman staring at him. Harry sensed right then he was about to be turned in.

The next morning, he phoned his brother and sister to tell them what he had done. That night, they talked him into surrendering himself through Barry Zisser. Harry kept insisting that the bomb had been a dud. It never could've gone off. He'd never have set out to hurt anyone. But he also realized the utter failure of his protest. He had imagined that by muzzling Shimon Peres, however briefly, he would be protecting *Klal Yisrael*. Instead, he had driven a wedge into it. His sister had attended the speech. His uncle and aunt would have been there, had not Michael Greenburg left the tickets at his dental office. A Christian church up the street from the Jewish Center had enlisted a hundred volunteers to guard the synagogue around the clock, assuming like everyone else did that the culprit was an Arab or a skinhead or a neo-Nazi militiaman, and now the world knew a Jew had planted a bomb among fellow Jews.

Arrested, arraigned, and jailed on million-dollar bail, Harry Shapiro tried to commit suicide, swallowing the pills he had brought with him when he surrendered. As the state charges were pending, a federal grand jury convened. Barry Zisser thought it likely Harry would face three federal counts—for placing the bomb, threatening a head of state, and attacking a house of worship—that together carried a prison sentence of forty-five years. He negotiated with federal prosecutors for Harry to plead guilty to a single charge of using an explosive to commit a felony, a charge that carried a mandatory penalty of ten years.

Bound with handcuffs and leg irons, Harry appeared before U.S. Magistrate John E. Steele on March 19, 1997, to admit his guilt. "I placed gunpowder in a pipe," he told the court. "I placed it in a house of worship. I threatened the life of a human being with it. I called 911 and issued a threat to keep Mr. Peres from speaking."

The plea bargain left several matters forever unresolved. Federal authorities maintained that the pipe bomb had been viable, a genuine threat. Harry insisted he had carefully built a device incapable of exploding, despite his own fear of igniting it by accident when he had assembled it. Because the bomb squad blew up the evidence on that Sabbath morning outside the Jacksonville Jewish Center, there will never be any way of knowing. Nor is it clear exactly how Harry had learned to assemble a bomb. Federal investigators theorize that he downloaded plans while visiting Web sites devoted to the World Trade Center bombing, the FBI assault on the Branch Davidian compound in Waco, and the retaliatory bombing of a federal office building in Oklahoma City. Harry denied this during several interrogations. All he has ever said of the pipe bomb's design is: "It's common knowledge."

On June 25, 1997, Harry stood again shackled in federal court to accept his sentence. His brother and sister and grandmother looked on. Rabbi Gaffney, feeling more pity than rage, attended. None had seen Harry as gaunt since he returned ill and despondent from Israel in 1984. He had been on a hunger strike because he was not permitted to wear a *kippa* in jail, and the dress suit his siblings had brought for him, the last civilian clothes he would wear for a decade, hung limply on his frame, the pants legs puddling at his feet. But apparently he had prevailed, because now, as Harry stood shoulder to shoulder with Barry Zisser several feet in front of Judge Ralph W. Nimmons, a black *kippa*, the *frum* kind, rested on his bristly hair.

In somber, deliberate tones, Harry apologized to his family, the Jewish community, even the Muslims he had tried to implicate. He talked with regret of having ruined the *simcha*, the celebration, of Aliza Morris's bat mitzvah, and having dishonored a house of God. But he spoke, too, of his cause, the sum total of Yamit and Sde Eliyahu, Gush Emunim and Meir Kahane, *rodef* and *pikuach nefesh* and *milchemet* mitzvah, the murder of 250 innocent Jews by terrorists since the Oslo accords had been signed. Apologizing for his crime, he made no apology for his cause.

"As to why," Harry told the courtroom, "that seems to be the question so many people want answered. Why a bomb? Why this event? What could ever induce me to do something so crazy? I owe it to them to face up to the questions and answer them the only way I know how: honestly."

Barry Zisser took several steps back and away from Harry. When he had seen Harry's original draft of this statement, he had advised, insisted, pleaded with him not to talk about Israel. But here was Harry, doing it, right in front of a judge who'd been Zisser's law school classmate and fraternity brother.

"I feel that Mr. Peres," Harry continued, "more than any other Israeli official or leader, is responsible for the death and injuries that have occurred as a result of the Oslo I and Oslo II accords that he secretly negotiated and then forced upon the Israeli people. Against the wishes, as the last year has shown, of the majority of the population, by a wide margin, and to the furtherance of his own ambitions and ego. When I heard that he was coming to speak, I wrongly assumed that I had the moral obligation of trying to stop that speech by any means possible, short of harming someone. My passions overrode my logic, and I did a very stupid, very idiotic thing."

Zisser himself had been in Shimon Peres's audience that night. He had fired clients for less insubordination than this. But you couldn't fire a family friend you were representing pro bono. And you couldn't talk a zealot out of his zeal.

"To Mr. Peres, I apologize, for I was wrong in thinking that I should be part of your punishment," Harry went on. "Your punishment will come from heaven."

As HARRY SHAPIRO began serving ten years in federal prison, the consequences of his action continued to ripple through two nations. Assistant U.S. attorney Mark E. Devereaux, who prosecuted the case, received an award for "superior performance" from Attorney General Janet Reno. Federal authorities decided not to seek the indictment of Avraham Kelman, despite the rabbi's failure to inform police of Harry Shapiro's threat until after the bomb was discovered. Kelman left his pulpit at Etz Chaim for a synagogue in Massachusetts. The Israeli secret service conducted an internal investigation to determine how its agents could have failed to discover the bomb on the night of Peres's speech. Far from considering Shapiro's bomb an aberration, the Israeli consul in Miami told the *Florida Times-Union*, it demonstrated the depth and persistence of violent opposition to the peace process. "We saw the assassination of Prime Minister Rabin and we thought it was an exception," said the diplomat, Danny Haezrachy. "Such activity shows that things can happen again."

Meanwhile, federal inmate number 19669–018, Harry Shapiro, occupies a cell in a medium-security prison in Jesup, Georgia, several hours from Jacksonville. He wears a *kippa*, observes kashrut as closely as possible, and studies periodically with a visiting Lubavitcher rabbi. He follows events in Israel through a variety of publications—*Yated Ne'eman*, the *Forward*, the *Jerusalem Post*, *U.S. News & World Report*. The *Jewish Press*, he has decided, is "a little loud for my taste," although he appreciates the printouts his brother sends him from a Web site honoring Meir Kahane. Among his belongings, Harry keeps a folding map of Israel. He studies it every time he reads about the government returning territory, building bypass roads, or suggesting a Jerusalem suburb as the capital of a Palestinian state.

Who Owns Orthodoxy?

THE INFLUENCE that America's Orthodox Jews exerted on Israel, whether by legitimate or violent means, could hardly have been foreseen. While the United States was a stronghold of religious Zionism, the Orthodox world as a whole rejected it before and even beyond statehood. And, more to the point in America, Orthodoxy gave every indication early in the twentieth century of withering to a vestige. As late as 1955, the noted sociologist Marshall Sklare dismissed the Orthodox experience in the United States as "a case study of institutional decay."

The Orthodox renaissance, then, stands as the most striking and unexpected phenomenon in modern American Jewish history. With less than 10 percent of the Jewish population, the Orthodox disproportionately affect the larger community, and on many issues besides the peace process. Orthodox hands, as we have seen in previous chapters, hold the levers of halakhic power on conversion standards and women's participation in worship. Orthodox educators often staff the day schools and Hebrew schools of the Conservative and 217

Reform movements, which cannot produce enough skilled teachers of their own. The Lubavitcher Hasidim dispatch emissaries to the tiniest Jewish enclaves in America as well as outside it. Shlomo Carlebach's songs and Adin Steinsaltz's English translation of the Talmud are integral parts of religious life in all Judaism's branches. Some of the most important literature of recent years has emerged from writers steeped in, if not always still part of, Orthodoxy—Cynthia Ozick, Allegra Goodman, Leon Wieseltier, Nathan Englander, Rebecca Goldstein, Blu Greenberg, Arthur Hertzberg. Defying the gravitational pull of assimilation, thousands of relatively secular Jews have adopted Orthodoxy as *ba'alei teshuva*, returners to the faith. And in an inchoate way that less observant Jews rarely acknowledge, much less articulate, many of them look to the Orthodox for acceptance, approval, and legitimacy. That is precisely why the condemnation of the Reform and Conservative branches by even marginal Orthodox groups like the Agudath Harabonim provokes such anguish and outcry.

So it matters immensely to American Jewry as a whole who speaks for Orthodoxy, and that role has been strenuously contested over the past several decades. The Orthodox renaissance is really two competing renaissances, one begun by the Modern Orthodox movement in the early 1900s, the other by the ultra-Orthodox *haredim* at the end of World War II. The rift extends even to the type of head covering one wears—a small *kippa seruga*, or knitted yarmulke, for the Modern; a larger *kippa seruga* for militant religious Zionists; a black velvet *kippa* for non-Hasidic *haredim*; a black fedora or fur *shtriemel* for Hasidim. And in the struggle for supremacy, American Orthodoxy has swung decisively to the right on theological, cultural, and political issues. This process of "haredization," to use sociologist Chaim Waxman's phrase, has contributed greatly to the acrimony among American Jews.

The intra-Orthodox struggle originated in nineteenth-century Europe as Jews were finally being emancipated. In Germany, the rabbi Samson Raphael Hirsch (1808–88) led the so-called Neo-Orthodox movement with its ideal of *Torah im derekh eretz*—literally, "Torah and the way of the land," but colloquially the coexistence of religious and secular studies. "I bless the Emancipation," Hirsch once declared, and he himself wrote in German, was influenced by Schiller, and for a time as a young rabbi went beardless. To Hirsch's engagement with modernism, his colleagues and disciples added two other core principles, support for Zionism and the willingness to collaborate with non-Orthodox Jews.

Outside the sort of cosmopolitan environment Hirsch and his followers occupied, the specter of modernity threatened two groups of Orthodox Jews who normally fought each other—the shtetl Hasidim and the Talmudic scholars of the Lithuanian yeshivot. Their motto came from Rabbi Moses Sofer (1762–1839), who proclaimed, *"He chodosh osur min ha torah,"* the new is prohibited by the Torah. Liberation into secular society, these Orthodox believed, would endanger Jews and Judaism more than persecution as a religious minority ever had. And America, because it offered the greatest acceptance, posed the greatest danger.

So as the *haredi* rabbis instructed their faithful to spurn the *Treif Medinah*, the Unkosher Land, the Modern Orthodox movement took its agenda across the ocean during the great wave of Jewish immigration. What it encountered in America early in the twentieth century was less Orthodoxy as a belief system than "Orthopraxis" as a set of customs and gestures. And even these practices were dying off with the older generation. Barely one-sixth of Jewish children received any religious education, and only a handful of day schools existed. Even the Jewish Theological Seminary, founded in 1886 to produce an English-speaking rabbinate for American Orthodox congregations, forsook its origins to help create the Conservative movement in 1913.

Over nearly half a century, though, a kind of infrastructure took hold, bound by a belief, as the prominent rabbi Leo Jung put it, that "Orthodox Judaism is not to be identified with ghetto conditions." The key institutions ranged from the Young Israel association of synagogues (founded in 1912) to the Hebrew Theological College seminary outside Chicago (1921) and the Rabbinical Council of America (1935), all of them clean-shaven, unaccented challenges to the immigrant rabbinate, with its severe attire and Yiddish speech. One of the early day schools, Yeshiva Etz Chaim in Manhattan, gave rise in 1928 to Yeshiva University, the intellectual capital of Modern Orthodoxy, and the university's first president, Bernard Revel, coined a slogan not only for the academy but for the movement—*Torah Umaddah*, Torah and worldly studies.

Four years after Yeshiva's founding, the personification of its precepts arrived in America. Born in 1903 in what is now Belarus, the son and grandson of Talmudic masters, Joseph Dov Soloveitchik at age twenty-two entered the University of Berlin to study philosophy, ultimately writing his doctoral dissertation on epistemology and metaphysics. Soon after immigrating, Soloveitchik founded the Maimonides School in Brookline, Massachusetts, which daringly provided Orthodox girls with Torah and Talmud studies. In 1941, he began forty-three years of teaching at Yeshiva, devoting himself not only to the Talmudic lectures called *shiurim* but courses in philosophy and the publication of essays that explored Western thought from Plato and Aristotle to Hegel and Kant. He sent his own son to Harvard. Soloveitchik's moderating influence pervaded American Orthodoxy, both as a decisor of *halakhah* for the Rabbinical Council and the mentor to thousands of young rabbis. They called him the *gadol*, the great rabbi, or the *Rav*, the master teacher.

As Yeshiva trained and ordained rabbis from its own seminary, it dispatched them to pulpits across America. By necessity as much as idealism, these young men created day schools so their own children could be educated. Where there had been 5 day schools in 1917, 55 were operating by 1944, and 425 by 1975, with at least one in every community of more than

7,500 Jews. Political and cultural events—the Six-Day War, the Save Soviet Jewry campaign, the replacement of the melting-pot ideal by the model of an ethnic mosaic—all contributed to a surge in Jewish pride that made Modern Orthodox Jews more visible than ever in their *kippot serugot*.

Nowhere was the seeming triumph of Modern Ortho-doxy, this sense of inevitability, rendered more vividly than in Chaim Potok's popular novel *The Chosen*. Set in the forties but written in the sixties, *The Chosen* traces the unlikely and turbu-lent friendship between two Jewish teenagers, both of them observant and Orthodox, but one the son of a Zionist organizer and the other of a Hasidic rabbi. By the book's end, it is the *haredi* boy, Danny Saunders, who not only attends a thinly veiled version of Yeshiva University, rare enough in Hasidic circles, but shaves his beard and cuts off his *peyes* to start gradu-ate school in psychology at Columbia.

Truth, in this case, was indeed stranger than fiction. In-stead of shrinking into a remnant worthy only of pity and nos-talgia, the *haredi* Jews who staggered into America after escaping a Europe dominated by Hitler or outliving his Final Solution, fewer than a hundred thousand in all, rose to vie for control of the Orthodox movement. The years from 1934 to 1950 saw the arrival of such major rabbis as Aaron Kotler, Joel Teitelbaum, Yitzhak Hutner, Moshe Feinstein, Chaim Mordechai Katz, Elijah Meir Bloch, and Abraham Kalman-owitz and the establishment of such yeshivot as Mirrer and Chaim Berlin in Brooklyn, Telshe in Cleveland, and Beit Medrash Gevoha in Lakewood, New Jersey. Indirectly, the refugees revived older yeshivas like Torah Vodaat in Brooklyn and Mesifta Tifereth Jerusalem on Manhattan's Lower East Side. Agudath Israel, a coalition of *haredi* groups that had been derided as a "sick weed" when it opened an American office in 1939, grew into one of the most powerful bodies in domestic Orthodoxy. Like a right-wing mirror image of Joseph Soloveitchik, Aaron Kotler spread his influence both through protégés and institutions, particularly the national organization of the day school movement, *Torah Umesorah*, Torah and Tradition.

More than brick and mortar, the *haredi* rabbinate brought a version of Orthodoxy drastically divergent from the Modern variety. *Erlicher Yidn*, they called themselves, virtuous Jews. They disdained secular education except for the necessity of getting a job, refused cooperation with the non-Orthodox branches, and renounced Zionism as blasphemy, at least until the Six-Day War was interpreted as proof of a divine plan. The greatest number of the postwar *haredim* were among the most uncompromising of all—Hungarians who had legally segregated themselves from that nation's Jewish community after emancipation. Now, with their former world destroyed, the *haredi* survivors held the responsibility for its rebirth. Their mission in America, as the sociologist Samuel Heilman has written, was to "maintain tradition when all about you others do not, to define a world of sacred order when the profane is the order of the day, to assert that change need not occur when all around you has undeniably changed."

Despite all their difference from the *haredim*, the Modern Orthodox in many ways benefited from the influx. Figures such as Rabbi Kotler were respected throughout Orthodox circles as world-class scholars. Orthodox Jews from far outside the Hasidic orbit danced in the streets of Crown Heights with Lubavitchers, celebrating Simhat Torah with an infectious joy. The word *lernen*, Yiddish for learning, moved from the *haredi* subculture into broad Orthodox circulation as the preferred term for studying Talmud. Along with it, the *haredi* regimen of studying Talmud *daf yomi*, a page a day, seeped into Modern Orthodox communities, too, and by 1990 Agudath Israel could draw twenty thousand Jews to Madison Square Garden for a ceremony culminating the seven-year cycle of reading the entire text.

For the first time since the great wave of East European immigration, there existed a critical mass of Orthodox Jews capable of supporting an entire commercial structure that obeyed *halakhah*. The journalist Michael Shapiro revisited his childhood neighborhood of Flatbush in Brooklyn in 1985 to find it transformed from a mélange of Italian Catholics and diverse Jews into an Orthodox metropolis replete with wig shop, religious scribe, delicatessens, van service to the Catskills, a dry cleaner closed on Saturday but open on Sunday, and a fast-food restaurant called Kosher Country "that has the prayer for ritual washing posted above the washstand." By the late nineties, one could eat kosher Tuscan cuisine on Manhattan's Upper East Side, visit a kosher concession stand at the Cleveland Indians ballpark, take a kosher Passover tour to the French Riviera, and sweat off the pounds in a Long Island aerobics class that separated the sexes and required modest attire.

But the same *haredi* zeal that revived neighborhoods and spread Talmud study could also be put to divisive purposes. As if emboldened by the first trickles of *haredim* arriving from Europe, the Agudath Harabonim at its 1945 convention formally excommunicated the Conservative leader Mordecai Kaplan for "atheism, heresy, and disbelief in the basic tenets of Judaism" and burned a copy of the *Sabbath Prayer Book* he had edited. In 1956, ten prominent religious scholars, including Aaron Kotler, issued an *issur*, a prohibition, against Orthodox participation in any joint rabbinical organizations, a direct blow against such umbrella organizations as the New York Board of Rabbis and the Synagogue Council of America. In 1979, a vigilante group calling itself TORAH—Tough Orthodox Rabbis And Hasidim—spray-painted swastikas and anti-Semitic slurs on the only Conservative synagogue left in the *haredi* stronghold of Borough Park in Brooklyn. In 1984, the Agudath Harabonim ran advertisements just before the High Holy Day urging Jews "not to pray in a Reform or Conservative Temple . . . whose Clergy have long rebelled against numerous sacred laws of the Torah and mislead thousands of innocent souls." In 1994, the Synagogue Council of America disbanded. It had taken nearly forty years, but the *issur* had triumphed in its goal of depriving Reform, Conservative, and Reconstructionist rabbis of any national organization where they would be recognized by the Orthodox clergy as equals. One Orthodox leader recited the *Sheheheyanu*, a prayer for any new event or experience, in thanksgiving.

Within Orthodoxy, the rise of the *haredim* dramatically altered the balance of power. The yeshiva superseded the family or the synagogue as the epicenter of Orthodox life, and the *rosh* yeshiva, the head of yeshiva, reigned as the arbiter of Orthodox authenticity. As a result of this "text culture," the historian Haym Soloveitchik (Joseph's son) has written, "Behavior, once governed by habit, is now governed by rule. . . . For in the realm of religious practice, custom, no matter how longstanding and vividly remembered, has little standing over and against the normative written word."

Rabbis produced by such *haredi* yeshivot as Torah Vodaat, Chaim Berlin, and Rabbi Jacob Joseph increasingly took pulpits that had been the province of Modern Orthodox clergy minted by Yeshiva University. As early as the mid-sixties, *haredi* rabbis led more than half the Young Israel synagogues, once strongholds of Modern Orthodoxy. While Modern Orthodox Jews engaged the contemporary world by working as doctors, lawyers, and academics, snubbing the occupation of day school teacher as one of low pay and low prestige, *haredi* men and women, dissuaded from attending college and thus limited in their career options, eagerly filled those positions. By the eighties, the day schools that had been Modern Orthodoxy's proudest achievement began in many cases to bear the *haredi* imprint—teaching boys and girls in separate classrooms, celebrating Israel Independence Day in a perfunctory way if at all. Similarly, the Modern Orthodox parents who sent their children to learn in Israeli yeshivot before college often saw them return home as *haredim* full of censure at any perceived compromise. The process was colloquially known as "flipping."

Orthodox life by the eighties was governed more and more by *chumrot*, stringent religious rulings issued so frequently by halakhic authorities that a bitter joke referred to the "*chumra*-of-the-month club." Milk had to be *cholov Yisrael*, handled only by Jews on its route from cow to cup. It was not enough to avoid spelling God's name by using the term *Hashem*, which literally meant "The Name"; now even that word had to be rendered as *Hash-m*. In a direct affront to Joseph Soloveitchik, then ailing and near retirement, five Talmudic scholars at Yeshiva University in 1985 ruled that *halakhah* forbade women from participating in the prayer groups then emerging in Modern Orthodox circles.

Most visibly of all, *glatt* became what might be called the industry standard for kosher meat. There was no such designation as *glatt* when the Orthodox Union formalized the certification of kosher meat in the thirties; the concept came out of the Hasidic community in the postwar years. Under the traditional rule of kosher slaughtering, if an animal had any growth in its lung, that tissue had to be removed before the meat was considered kosher. Under the rule of *glatt*, a Yiddish word meaning smooth, only an animal with an unmarred lung sufficed. By living in densely populated neighborhoods and buying only kosher food when few Jews did, Hasidic customers held a decisive market share, and kosher butchers complied with *glatt* less out of religious solidarity than business savvy. But once established, *glatt* became accepted by virtually all Orthodox Jews as the benchmark, and yet another example of what the sociologist Charles Liebman has termed "extremism as the religious norm."

Since Joseph Soloveitchik's death in 1993, which itself was preceded by almost a decade of incapacitating illness, Modern Orthodoxy has lacked a comparable leader. Much of Soloveitchik's intellectual legacy has been lost with the unexplained disappearance of the tapes of 1,800 Talmud lectures. The very term "Modern Orthodox" has become so disreputable—it is to observant Jews what "liberal" is to Democrats—that even many practitioners prefer to call themselves "centrist" or "traditional." The *haredi* faction, meanwhile, had developed such leaders as Moshe Sherer and Moshe Feinstein well before Aaron Kotler died in 1962. And its birth rate, roughly double the Modern Orthodox average and quadruple the figure for American Jews as a whole, ensures it of impact for decades to come.

One Sunday in February 1999, however, the Modern Orthodox movement climbed back up from its knees for the inaugural conference of a group called Edah, or Community. Where five hundred attendees had been expected, fifteen hundred appeared, a groundswell responding to the slogan "The Courage to be Modern and Orthodox." Courage plainly was needed, for in the weeks before the conference two of Yeshiva University's most respected religious scholars had attacked Edah, with Moshe Tendler placing it "outside the pale of Judaism" and Herschel Schacter calling it "a sort of internal Amalek."

Entering the next century, America's 400,000 Orthodox Jews are divided almost equally between the *haredi* and Modern camps, and the line separating the factions is porous rather than impermeable. A balance of power shifts when enough individuals change their minds and their loyalties. One of those who did so in the realignment of Orthodox Judaism in America was a lawyer turned rabbi named Daniel Greer.

CHAPTER FIVE

New Haven, Connecticut, 1995–1999

O<small>N A CHILL, DRIZZLY AFTERNOON</small> in January 1998, Rabbi Daniel Greer settled down at his desk in the Yeshiva of New Haven, across the room from a portrait of his former self and prior life. It was a framed enlargement of a black-and-white photograph, showing a clean-shaven young man in an oxford shirt and paisley tie, speaking with some urgency to his boss. Although the photo is undated, Daniel Greer could trace it to September 1969, his most exhilarating time in the service of Mayor John V. Lindsay of New York.

Officially, Greer then held the title of First Deputy Commissioner of Ports and Terminals, but Lindsay preferred to think of him as "Mr. Jew," one of his unofficial liaisons to New York's largest bloc of voters. In the final weeks of a brutal reelection campaign, with Lindsay forced to run on a third-party line, the Israeli Prime Minister Golda Meir had arrived on a state visit. Greer put together a uniquely Jewish way of welcoming her, a black-tie banquet for 1,400 served in a vast sukkah in recognition of the harvest festival of Sukkoth. There were "Shalom, Golda" buttons and meals of kosher game hen. A picture in the next morning's *Times* showed Meir being escorted to her table by Mayor Lindsay, her Zionist heroism rubbing onto the embattled Wasp liberal. Five weeks later, Lindsay won, and soon there was talk of a race for the presidency.

Now the beard that Rabbi Greer had begun growing a decade after that magical night, during the ritual mourning period leading up to Tisha b'Av in 1979, reached his chest in graying fullness. He wore dark, subdued suits and crowned his head with a black velvet *kippa*. Over the years, he had abandoned careers in the lofty reaches of politics and law, moving instead with his wife to this beleaguered city to launch several Jewish schools and pioneer an Orthodox neighborhood amid the slums beyond Yale's campus. His sons wore *peyes* and tzitzis, his daughters skirts to mid-calf and sleeves to the wrist. Next to the photo of himself and Mayor Lindsay he had tacked up a note from a local parent, wishing him in Hebrew 120 years of life.

In the fifty-seven years he had managed so far, Daniel Greer had rebelled in a quiet, gradual, and yet inexorable way against his origins. He described himself these days as a "political *ba'al teshuva*," colloquially a returnee to the faith, but literally, and perhaps more aptly in his case, a "master of repentance." Rejecting the liberalism personified by John Lindsay, he subscribed to the conservative gospel of smaller government and family values. And he had made a similar journey rightward in his religious life. The usual revolt against Orthodoxy took the form of dating a shiksa, daring a shrimp cocktail, sleeping in on Sabbath. Daniel Greer instead had questioned and finally abandoned the Modern Orthodox world for a version of Judaism he described as "richer" and "fuller." Once he had embodied the ideal of engagement with secular society, the Modern Orthodox concept of *Torah Umaddah*, attending Princeton, earning his Juris Doctor from Yale Law, working in a Wall Street firm and on a mayoral staff, all without sacrificing his observance. Now he viewed much of American culture as a "secular orthodoxy" determined to undermine morality; the wider world had to be handled cautiously instead of embraced. He intended to provide his own children, and the students he educated, a Judaism that looked not to contemporary America but to pre-Holocaust Europe for its models.

For most of his years in New Haven, Rabbi Greer's efforts had proceeded in relative obscurity. Outside the metropolitan centers of American Jewish life, he transformed a decrepit old public school building into a religious academy and created a nonprofit agency to buy and overhaul the frame houses ravaged by landlords and tenants alike. He sent his four eldest children from his own school into Israeli yeshivas and seminaries and, thus grounded and girded by Torah, finally on to Yale. Hardly anyone outside New Haven noticed the accomplishments.

Then, in October 1997, Daniel Greer's daughter Batsheva, six weeks into her freshman year at Yale, filed a federal lawsuit against the university along with three Orthodox classmates. One of Daniel Greer's old friends, an Orthodox Jew and constitutional lawyer named Nathan Lewin, represented them. The students, dubbed the Yale Five to include a sympathetic classmate,* challenged the university's rule that they reside on the campus as freshmen and sophomores, arguing that it violated their religious freedom. The Torah demanded of a pious Jew *tznius*, modesty, and life in a coed dormitory with shared bathrooms and condom distribution and mandatory lectures on safe sex destroyed it.

In Daniel Greer's revulsion at Yale's regimen, his political and theological conservatism were fused. What had been his private and personal migration from one type of Orthodoxy to another now informed a controversial lawsuit being covered

---

* That student, Rachel Wohlgelernter, was not a plaintiff because by the time the suit was filed she had gotten married and was therefore exempt from the on-campus housing regulation.

avidly both in the United States and Israel. The Yale Five's stance predictably inflamed less observant Jews, among them Yale's dean and president. More important, it carved a divide within Orthodoxy, separating the Modern faction from the rest. The Orthodox students already living in Yale's residential colleges fumed that the Yale Five were impugning their Jewish identity. The Orthodox rabbi affiliated with the university decried the suit. From the network of Orthodox day schools sounded the protests of educators and pupils alike: Yale won't admit us now. You're making Yale hate the Orthodox.

What was the whole point of Modern Orthodoxy if not to bear the yoke of the mitzvot alongside the worldly challenges of Yale, finding your *tznius* strengthened by the encounter with a coed dorm? What had Daniel Greer as a younger man done but prove that there was a place for Orthodox Jews in the Ivy League? He'd already won the battle. Look at the *kippot* the students unashamedly wear. Look at the kosher kitchen on campus. Look at the glistening new Slifka Center for Jewish Life. What did the Yale Five want?

On this dismal January afternoon, Daniel Greer, the white-shoe lawyer turned *minahel*, religious-school dean, wanted to check on the repairs at a house around the corner, the latest of his rehab projects. There was nothing he could do today about the Yale Five case. Nathan Lewin had filed the complaint; the university had responded by seeking dismissal; the Federal District Court judge would rule whenever he felt like ruling. Meanwhile, to protect Batsheva from expulsion, Rabbi Greer was paying $6,800 in fees for the dormitory room she would never occupy.

Rabbi Greer resisted the labels others sought to hang on him—*haredi*, ultra-Orthodox, right-wing, words often spoken with a pejorative undertone. He saw his own life not as a reversal but as a continuum, and Batsheva's life as part of the same "golden thread." All he could say was that as much as he loved elements of America, New Haven, and Yale, he wanted to remake his part of the world more in the image of Vilna, lost

Vilna, the capital of Jewish learning for five centuries before the Holocaust, the "heavenly city."

"We'd like to restore the crown to its former glory," he put it. "So many American Jews were first-generation and so concerned with fitting in. 'Let's not make waves. Don't look different. Don't take a chance. It'll make us look bad.' We want to recall the world we've been cut off from by the Enlightenment and the world wars. We want to restore a more demonstrative, open, all-encompassing experience. Jews who've been Americanized want to return to a world that's richer than even the Orthodox Judaism we were expressing in the forties and fifties. An Orthodox kid then just went through the motions."

DANIEL GREER, the child of cosmopolitans, spoke French before English. His mother Angéle was a Sephardic Jew who had grown up in Egypt, been educated at the Sorbonne, and come to America in 1939 for the World's Fair. There she met Moses Greer, a businessman's son who had graduated from City College in the twenties, when immigrant Jews were fortunate to complete high school. Moses made his living in a prosaic way, wholesaling reprocessed wool, but he dreamed of directing the Judaica section of the New York Public Library. He read John Dewey, quoted *The Way of All Flesh*, and laced his conversation with wisdom from the Talmud. The family's apartment welcomed a spectrum of guests; decades later, the Greek ambassador to NATO would recognize Daniel Greer from a dinner there.

Pious and worldly at once, the Greers meshed easily into the Upper West Side of the interwar and immediate postwar decades, the epicenter of Modern Orthodoxy. Already home to fifty thousand Jews in the twenties, the neighborhood absorbed nearly twenty thousand more in the thirties, as Hitler's mounting power sent refugees fleeing from Germany, Belgium, and Holland. Many landed initially in residential hotels like the Millburn and Marseilles, thanks to resettlement agencies, and gradually found their own sprawling apartments in rent-controlled buildings. The old German Jewish Reform elite, "Our Crowd" in the popular historian Stephen Birmingham's phrase, might luxuriate on Fifth Avenue, but for Jews like the Greers and their refugee neighbors intellectualism rather than income defined status. As a boy, Daniel Greer saw none other than Alexander Kerensky, the prime minister of Russia's shortlived democracy, resting on a bench along Broadway.

Beyond Judaism or Jewish culture in general, Modern Orthodoxy in particular permeated the Upper West Side. Within a dozen blocks stood the reigning kosher bakery, Lichtman's, the Bretton Hall meat restaurant, and its dairy peer, Steinberg's, where a Yiddish-language novelist named Isaac Bashevis Singer could often be seen pushing his tray down the serving line. Saturday afternoon meant promenading up Riverside Drive after shul, and Rosh Hashanah brought families to the Seventy-ninth Street Boat Basin for *tashlich*, casting their bread upon the waters of the Hudson.

Most of all, the Upper West Side abounded in synagogues, twenty of them in a thirty-block area, including such hubs of Modern Orthodoxy as the Jewish Center, West Side Institutional, and Young Israel. These congregations and their rabbis epitomized what the historian Jenna Weissman Joselit has called "an ongoing romance with modernity." The Jewish Center, for instance, placed its *mechitzah* only waist-high and allowed women to sing; Young Israel held socials with mixed dancing for its teenagers.

The Greers reared young Daniel accordingly. He went to the elementary grades at Manhattan Day School, a Modern Orthodox institution, and then on to the Manhattan Talmudical Academy, the first Modern Orthodox high school in New York. He learned to honor the mitzvot without sticking out by wearing a *kippa* inside school and a baseball cap on the street. As Joseph Lookstein, the principal of the Ramaz School on the East Side, often put it, the yarmulke was "an indoor garment," to be removed even when students stepped outside for a fire drill. Within schools like Ramaz, the favored style was the "Ivy League yarmulke," made of plaid fabric with a tiny buckle in the back.

Politically, Daniel Greer adopted liberalism as a kind of secular faith. His parents admired not only Franklin Delano Roosevelt, nearly a deity for many Jews, but Woodrow Wilson, believing that had his League of Nations lasted it would have prevented World War II and the Holocaust. Republicans did not even figure into the Greer household's electoral calculations. The only question was whether to pull the Democratic or Liberal party lever; the same approvably progressive slate usually ran on both ballot lines.

The passion that Moses and Angéle Greer held for the wider world became most clear when the question of college impended. Manhattan Day and Talmudical Academy formed the first two links in a system feeding Yeshiva University, the academic capital of Modern Orthodoxy. Ever since Daniel's years in grade school, however, his mother had planted in him the goal of Princeton. Princeton was where Woodrow Wilson had been president, where Einstein whet his brilliance at the Institute for Advanced Study. A friend of the Greers, as it happened, had gotten to know the physicist years earlier while delivering him butter and eggs, and he took Angéle and Daniel to meet the great man. Einstein wasn't home that day, but his sister was, and after the brush with genius-once-removed Angéle walked Daniel to the main gate of the campus and announced, "This is where you're going to college."

Sure enough, in the fall of 1956, Daniel Greer did. He was the first product of the Manhattan Talmudical Academy ever to enter Princeton and part of a wave of Jews reshaping the leafy realm of inherited privilege. As recently as 1936, Jews had comprised only 2 percent of Princeton's student body. In 1941, with admission still a function primarily of prep school credentials and family tradition, only 795 young men applied for the

740 places in the freshman class. By the time Daniel Greer arrived, the number of applicants had soared above 3,000, and about 15 percent of the students were Jews.

Being in a vanguard, though, had its price. And Daniel Greer was in a vanguard twice over, once as a Jew and again for being Orthodox.

FROM HIS ROOM on the second floor of 1915 Hall, Daniel Greer could hear the same clamor three times every day of his freshman year. The dormitory stairs passed just outside his door, and down those stairs bounded all the other residents, heading for breakfast, lunch, and dinner at the commons. In the silence they left behind, Daniel might gaze out his windows onto cornfields and beyond them the woods lining Carnegie Lake. Then he would turn his attention to the hot plate and half-size refrigerator that sat in the corner of his room and set about cooking and eating alone.

It was hard enough for Daniel starting Princeton at sixteen, his face more peach fuzz than bristle, his frame so slight he met the physical education requirement as a crew's coxswain. His classmates wore a uniform of chino trousers and oxford shirts with an ease that eluded Daniel; in this election season, they touted Eisenhower, the hero of D-Day, while he quietly rooted for Adlai Stevenson, an egghead for an egghead. While Daniel's forebears had been toiling in the Pale and the Levant, the Continental Congress was meeting in Nassau Hall.

To be set apart in so many ways already and trying to observe the mitzvot besides—well, that meant enduring isolation even among four hundred Jewish students. Daniel's rabbi from home, Emanuel Gettinger, advised him to form a minyan on campus. The Hillel center held a service only on Saturday, and the nearest Orthodox shul was in Trenton, ten miles away. So Daniel wandered from carrel to carrel in the Firestone Library, asking anyone who looked even faintly Semitic, "Are you Jewish?" "I'm Hebrew," some answered, choosing the term

German Jews often used to distance themselves from the Eastern European rabble. Others replied evasively, "My ancestors were."

Had Daniel not ridden the train home for Shabbat, he could not have survived even this long. He returned on Sunday with home-cooked kosher meals to last until the next Friday, and week after week, he ate them alone. Far from the garrulity of the Greer family table, the soup-to-nuts schmoozing, he read the newspaper or listened to the radio reports on the Suez invasion, Israel's military campaign. His own mother's family was expelled from Egypt halfway through his freshman year, banished with twenty English pounds, and there was nobody at Princeton to tell. "I was marooned," he later recalled. "I was not part of a community that cared what was going on."

Then, on Sukkoth, Daniel was scrambling through campus in a panic, searching for a *lulav* and *etrog*, the harvest holiday's traditional branch and fruit, when outside '01 Hall he caught sight of a wraith in a black *kippa*, clasping both items in his hands. The fellow's name was Harry Furstenberg, and he had earned his bachelor's degree at Yeshiva University before embarking on graduate studies in math at Princeton. From that day on, Furstenberg sometimes joined Daniel for hot-plate meals in the dorm room, and occasionally brought along another Orthodox mathematician named Leon Ehrenpreis. Most importantly, he told Daniel about Helen Feddy on Witherspoon Street. A widow who raised money for Deborah Hospital in Israel, Mrs. Feddy was perhaps the one Jew in Princeton who kept kosher. And it was her mitzvah to occasionally invite this handful of observant students for hot meals.

In his academic life, too, Daniel struggled to reconcile Princeton with his religious beliefs. On one of the shortest days of winter in his freshman year, when night was falling by four o'clock, Daniel faced a three-hour French exam that would end a half-hour into *Shabbos*. He presented himself to the dean, an austere and balding man with wire-rimmed glasses who bore the Hawthornian name Jeremiah Finch, and asked special dispensation to begin the test one hour early. Finch refused. How could he be assured Greer wouldn't give the answers to others? Daniel answered that by the time he finished, everyone else would be more than two hours into the exam. Unmoved, Finch ushered out Daniel. But on the Friday morning of the test, he issued permission.

The next battle was more public. For nine days in late January and early February of 1958, halfway through Daniel's sophomore year, Princeton enacted its annual rite of social hierarchy, the Bicker. Seventeen private clubs provided meals, companionship, and future connections for the university's upperclassmen, and during Bicker current members interviewed and then extended invitations to desirable sophomores. Although the clubs had been created to replace a system of exclusionary fraternities, and collectively accepted nearly every student, they operated on a caste system of their own. And in the almost total absence of blacks—there was exactly one in Daniel Greer's sophomore class—the lowest caste of all consisted of Jews. Five of the clubs maintained formal quotas against Jews. As for the rest, the higher a club stood on the social ladder, the fewer Jews it contained. And far from denying the pattern, Princeton's leading students defended it.

"The so-called prejudice against Jews," a Bicker chairman put it, "was not so much an opposition to them as such, as to the fact that most of them . . . were simply poor mixers and did not fit well into a purely social organization." One club's president maintained that the quotas actually did Jews a favor. "As soon as quotas were [to be] abolished," he wrote, "one, two, possibly three clubs would become predominantly Jewish, and the ensuing social stigma would keep them that way. . . . Quotas, then, are practical means to avoid such a monstrosity."

The 1958 Bicker ended, however, with only 23 sophomores from a class of 718 spurned by every club, and most of those rejects were Jews. Fifteen Jewish students signed a statement charging, "I feel I have been discriminated against because of race or religion." One alerted the *New York Post*, the daily newspaper of choice in Manhattan's liberal Jewish circles, and it covered the story under a banner headline that read in part, "How It Feels to Be an 'Outcast' at Princeton." The *New York Times* ran its own series of articles on the controversy. The Princeton elite, meanwhile, compounded the damage with every attempt at justification. Nelson Rockefeller's son Steven, the president of the most selective club, blamed the conflict on Jewish "troublemakers" with "exaggerated ideas." The university president, Robert F. Goheen, claimed he had found "no positive proof of religious discrimination." Even Princeton's Jewish chaplain, Rabbi Maurice Levey, described the charge of bias as "unjust" and "unnecessary."

 Daniel Greer observed the imbroglio with a mixture of fascination and detachment. He hadn't been one of the Jewish sophomores waiting eagerly each night in hopes that a Bicker team from one of the better clubs would knock on the door; he hadn't been one of the pariahs gathered outside Bicker headquarters after the last invitations had been made, screaming and weeping and shivering in the February night. He couldn't imagine why any Jew even wanted a piece of the old, smug Princeton, the residue of F. Scott Fitzgerald. He was planning to spend his junior year abroad at Hebrew University in Jerusalem.

 Without any personal stake in its outcome, Daniel evaluated the Bicker scandal in an almost clinical way. In a nation alerted to the price of bigotry—by the Holocaust, by the recent civil rights battles in Montgomery and Little Rock, even by the movie *Gentleman's Agreement*, an Oscar winner as well as a box-office smash—the club system represented something worse than snobbery. "It was classical Princeton," Daniel put it later, "against the change in America." But he also relished the shock that the scandal administered to Princeton's Jews. He thought of all those self-proclaimed "Hebrews" who couldn't be bothered joining his minyan. He thought of Rabbi Levey, who posted his mezuzah discreetly inside his office door. Daniel knew the Yiddish snub for such a man, a *Golus Yid*. It literally meant a Jew of the Diaspora, but the Zionist movement had freighted it with contempt for the timid, prideless Jew, tiptoeing through his adopted land. "The Bicker was their defining moment," Daniel said in retrospect. "There may've been 10 or 15 percent Jews at Princeton. But it was a closet experience. A Marrano existence."

Daniel Greer was nobody's *Golus Yid*, nobody's Marrano, practicing his faith only behind a Christian facade. In the summer of 1958, he sailed to Israel on the SS *Zion*—two weeks at sea, eight to a cabin—and then enrolled as one of about twenty Americans in Hebrew University. He had grown up with an Israel more mythical than real, listening riveted to the radio broadcast in May 1948 of President Truman extending American recognition to the newly founded Jewish state, hearing his first-grade teacher tell of her soldier brother, slain when the Arabs overran Gush Etzion in the 1948 war. A decade later, much of actual Israel enthralled Daniel—the Sephardic elders draped in white to greet the Sabbath, the desert twilight casting pastel colors on the Jerusalem limestone, the unattainable nearness of the Old City, still in Jordanian hands. He had not reckoned, however, on the intensity of secularism in the Jewish state. Hebrew University placed Daniel initially in a coed dorm, and he and two other Orthodox students moved to a religious residence across the city. The cinemas opened on Saturday afternoon, and once Daniel saw the police take truncheons to a group of Orthodox protesting the desecration of Shabbat. When he returned to Manhattan at year's end, he could hardly explain Israel's contradictions to his parents.

Still, Zion had refined Daniel's direction. He switched his major from biology to Near Eastern studies. He resolved to study Talmud and Torah more deeply after graduation. And he felt an ineffable confidence, tribal as much as personal, which would matter enormously decades later at Yale. "You came back emboldened," Daniel said. "Israel gave you a sense of pride and identity and security that you could assert yourself as a Jew, that you had the right to do what you wanted."

Back at Princeton for his senior year, he pored over the roster of incoming freshmen to identify every one who had graduated from a Jewish day school. Then he invited each of them to join him in a kosher kitchen—that is, a hot plate and refrigerator in his new room, 36S Edwards Hall. He wound up with four takers. Before leaving Princeton in 1960, he moved his kosher kitchen to an off-campus apartment and enlisted a dozen students to participate. The next year, Daniel's younger brother Jonathan, an incoming freshman, joined them. Decades later, when Daniel spoke of his accomplishments at Princeton, he neglected to mention his Phi Beta Kappa ring and magna cum laude diploma and Woodrow Wilson fellowship. He talked instead of the kosher kitchen.

"I didn't want my brother to go through the things I had gone through," he recalled. "I didn't want him to have the loneliness of not having a place to eat. I wanted to spare him the situation of eating alone in his room that I had for two years. I knew I was lonely when it was happening to me, but I don't think I realized how cosmically lonely I was. Or else I couldn't have done some of the things I did."

With Princeton behind him, Daniel used his Wilson fellowship not for research in his academic field of Near Eastern studies but rather for religious scholarship under Rabbi Joseph Soloveitchik of Yeshiva University, the totemic figure of Modern Orthodoxy. Three times each week, Soloveitchik delivered *shiurim*, lectures on Talmud, to about thirty advanced students, discoursing in Yiddish for two or three hours at a stretch. He could see Daniel struggling and in front of the entire class asked why. Daniel had to admit he wasn't fluent enough to understand the *shiur*. After class that day, the gray-bearded, dark-browed rabbi paced the hallways with Daniel, three times up and back, asking more about his background. "Come back tomorrow," Soloveitchik finally said. "There will be no problem."

Indeed at the next *shiur*, and for the remaining years of his public teaching, Soloveitchik orated in English. Privately, he took a special interest in his Princeton acolyte. Himself a Ph.D. graduate of the University of Berlin steeped in Enlightenment philosophy, Soloveitchik so admired the Ivy League that he sent his only son to Harvard. Now that son, Haym, was rooming with Daniel in New York; in time, Daniel would be a guest at the Soloveitchik family's Sabbath table. Midway through his year at Yeshiva, Daniel was admitted to Yale Law School for the next fall. And Rabbi Soloveitchik, however proud he may have been of such worldly achievement, urged Daniel to forgo the law, to stay with him and learn. This was the *Rav;* this was the *gadol.* Yet even in that moment, suffused with an inexpressible wanting, Daniel Greer bowed instead to obligation and expectation and conventional definitions of status, from his parents and from America itself. He said he ought to go to law school.

IN THE FALL OF 1961, less than one year into the presidency of John F. Kennedy, Daniel Greer entered Yale Law School, part of a class that shone even against the institution's usual standard of luster. The Class of 1964 included Gary Hart, the future senator; Jerry Brown, later to be California's governor; Robert Rubin, who would serve as Treasury Secretary in the Clinton administration; Eleanor Holmes Norton, the civil rights leader; Charles Halpern, an innovator in public-interest law; and Michael Horowitz, the architect of an international human-rights campaign against the persecution of Christians. Not surprisingly, perhaps, Daniel Greer, short and brown-haired in thin dark ties, qualified as one of the quieter types.

Like the rest, though, he received an education less in law itself than law's role in achieving social change. The class of 1964 moved through Yale against the backdrop of Kennedy's charmed reign and early death, Martin Luther King's "I Have a Dream" speech at the March on Washington, Freedom Rides, the Peace Corps, Lyndon Johnson's passage of landmark civil rights bills. It was Jerry Brown's own father who, during the class's second fall at Yale, dispatched Richard Nixon to political oblivion, or so it seemed, with defeat in California's gubernatorial race. Faculty members wrote briefs for civil rights, civil liberties, and welfare rights. Even the dean, a few years away from being a Vietnam hawk, was named Eugene V. Debs Rostow after the American Socialist leader.

"Conventional liberalism was the order of the day," Michael Horowitz later remembered. "There was a notion all it took to solve social problems was the application of goodwill." And it was up to Yale lawyers to apply it. "We were given a sense of capacity to build institutions and move institutions," Charles Halpern recalled. "The message was that we were the leadership-to-be, and we should have the confidence to pursue and set up our own ideas and present them on a large stage. There was little humility in the message."

Such political faith eclipsed the religious sort. "There was neither Jewish nor Protestant at Yale Law," said Horowitz, himself then the wavering product of a yeshiva education. "We were the New Establishment. This was a New Enlightenment. Any ambivalence you had about your own ethnicity, your own religion—this allowed you the illusion of escape from it."

In the apartment that Daniel Greer shared for two years with Jerry Brown, however, faith persisted. Brown himself had studied for the priesthood with the Jesuits, and he watched with respect as Daniel wound tefillin round his forearm for morning prayers. The roommates shared kosher dairy meals and talked about the Jewish theologian Martin Buber. On the surface, Brown noticed, Daniel clad himself in the proper Yale uniform, complete with a J. Press blue oxford shirt "with the proper amount of fraying in the collar." But as one who had heard God's call in his own life, Brown knew the surface was just that. "Danny had the idea that once the covenant is agreed to," he recalled later, "it doesn't get changed."

John Vliet Lindsay was a leader made to measure for the Yale Law class of 1964. Blond and dashing at six-foot-four, he had prepped at St. Paul's before earning both bachelor's and law degrees from Yale. Representing the Silk Stocking district of Manhattan's Upper East Side in Congress, he stood up to the House Un-American Activities Committee and helped draft and floor-manage the Civil Rights Act of 1964. Then, in 1965, he entered the New York mayor's race as the candidate of both the Republican and Liberal parties, just as the legendary Fiorello LaGuardia had been. Even against a Jewish Democratic opponent, Abe Beame, Lindsay won the support of the *New York Post*, the liberal daily owned by Jewish Dorothy Schiff, and of David Dubinsky's International Ladies Garment Workers Union, the very soul of Jewish social activism. "New York City cries out for a new era," wrote James Wechsler, the *Post*'s influential editor. "And that is what this battle is all about."

Lindsay won on the slogan "Proud City" and the promise of Kennedyesque vigor. In his inaugural address on January 1, 1966, he called for "men of conscience and conviction" to "enlist in the fight for a better New York—the fight to revive the hopes of the downtrodden, the sick, the exploited; the fight for new and better employment; the fight against wretched slums, poisoned air . . . ; the fight for excellence and equality in our education."

Daniel Greer heard and answered the summons. A junior associate at the Wall Street firm of Simpson Thacher & Bartlett, he grated under its hierarchy, which allowed him discretion over little more than the color of stripes on his rep tie. And it required no brilliance to feel the winds of political change. One day on Wall Street, Daniel spotted Richard Nixon, now reduced to private legal practice, and cracked to a fellow associate, "There goes a has-been."

The bright young men drawn to Mayor Lindsay included Thomas Hoving, later to direct the Metropolitan Museum of Art, the future media consultant David Garth, and even a young gofer named Jeffrey Katzenberg, who would ultimately become a Hollywood mogul with Disney and DreamWorks. Daniel Greer started in Lindsay's administration in 1966 as an examining attorney for the Commissioner of Investigations, surrounded by other young, idealistic expatriates from white-shoe firms. He rose by mid-1967 to general counsel, and early the next year, Lindsay appointed him Deputy Commissioner for Ports and Terminals. Later, Daniel directed the city Firearms Control Board.

While the night of the sukkah for Golda Meir may have been Daniel's most intoxicating one in the Lindsay administration, he contributed in concrete ways to realizing its vision of the Proud City—creating parkland on what had been a tumbledown stretch of Hudson River waterfront, constructing a wholesale produce market in the Bronx. He worked eighteen hours every day but *Shabbos,* driven by "the belief we were going to save the city." A vacation consisted of taking a city car to the Rockaways for a late afternoon swim.

An activist in the campaign to rescue Soviet Jewry before joining the Lindsay administration, Daniel traveled to the Soviet Union in the summer of 1970 to investigate conditions. There he encountered a thin, goateed physicist named Leonid Rigerman, whose cause became his own. The son of American radicals who had moved to Russia in 1931 but never renounced their U.S. citizenship, Rigerman insisted he was free to emigrate. But when he tried to enter the American embassy in Moscow in November 1970, Soviet guards arrested him. The very next day, Daniel brought Rigerman's case to the State Department. Three months later, Soviet authorities allowed the physicist and his mother to leave, and Daniel helped arrange the raucous midnight welcome for them at Kennedy Airport.

The Rigermans' exodus confirmed for Daniel the virtues of the confrontational style of the Save Soviet Jewry movement, the willingness of its young troops to strike more boldly than the Jewish establishment, both present and past. The older generation, to their way of thinking, had let the Holocaust happen by not daring to pressure Franklin Roosevelt. They would stop the next Holocaust by shouting, marching, harassing diplomats, even at the extreme threatening violence, Nixon's détente with the Russians be damned.

Daniel entered electoral politics, running for the Democratic nomination for State Assembly in 1972. The Upper West Side being the Upper West Side, this battle pit one young liberal Jew (Greer) against another (Richard Gottfried, the incumbent). Both candidates favored abortion rights and opposed the Vietnam War. After Gottfried's campaign papered the assembly district with a flyer featuring photos of their man and the antiwar presidential candidate George McGovern under the headline, "The McGovern Team," Daniel's crew answered with an almost identical handout for "The Peace Team, McGovern-Greer." It was also, to a large extent, the Modern Orthodox team. A recent Yeshiva University graduate named Ari Goldman, later to become the first *shomer Shabbos* reporter on the *New York Times*, helped manage Daniel's campaign. His troops spent as much time at Lincoln Square Synagogue, Steven Riskin's popular shul, as they did at their official headquarters above the Fine and Shapiro delicatessen. They had jeans, beards, and mounds of frizzy hair, invariably topped by a *kippa*. It was Daniel who wore a hat in public, still treating his yarmulke as an "indoor garment."

Daniel wound up losing to Gottfried, though not without giving the incumbent a scare, and even in defeat elevated his image as a Modern Orthodox role model. "He was the perfect synthesis of both worlds," Ari Goldman later reflected. "The best of being Orthodox and serious about it and the best of the secular world. He had achieved the best America had to offer. He was *Torah Umaddah* incarnate."

Amid all the public accomplishments, however, Daniel Greer was enduring a private crisis of political faith. During Lindsay's first term as mayor, he had infuriated much of New York Jewry with his support for community control of ghetto schools. The plan formalized an alliance between white elites and the black poor against the ethnic middle class, the meritocracy created by civil service. And when the black community board in the trial school district of Ocean Hill–Brownsville in Brooklyn fired a dozen Jewish educators in 1967, branding them racists and outsiders, the heavily Jewish teachers' union retaliated with a series of strikes.

Against that backdrop, Daniel Greer built his own bill of indictment against John Lindsay and liberalism itself. As an attorney with the Commissioner of Investigations, he had probed a series of scandals—kickbacks in construction of Mitchell-Lama middle-income housing; the theft of millions of dollars in coins by parking meter attendants; fraudulent bills from moving companies hired by the city to relocate welfare families. The most disturbing episode of all occurred after Daniel had moved onto Ports and Terminals, but his former colleagues in Investigations kept him informed of all the tawdry details. The Human Resources Administration, the city's major antipoverty agency, was being pillaged. As a Lindsay appointee named Charles Morris later summarized the events: "A million dollars in HRA checks turned up in a numbered Swiss bank account. A man attempted to use a $52,000 HRA check to buy a house in Los Angeles. Four enterprising young men from Durham, North Carolina—the 'Durham mob'—quietly looted $1.75 million from the summer work projects by programming a computer to produce checks for phantom employees. The scheme was uncovered only when a patrolman noticed a case of HRA checks in the back of an illegally parked car."

Municipal corruption was a venerable tradition in New York, dating back at least to William Marcy "Boss" Tweed more than a century before Lindsay. Still, to Daniel Greer the welfare scandals attested to a certain willful naïveté, a misguided pity that absolved the poor of adult responsibility. Welfare rolls as a whole rose more than 25 percent a year throughout much of the Lindsay mayoralty. The welfare commissioner, a former Columbia professor named Mitchell Ginsberg, had helped devise the welfare-rights strategy of giving clients more money with less oversight by caseworkers. Supposedly he said, after being confronted with evidence of the Durham mob's thievery, "How else are we going to create a black middle class?" Whether true or apocryphal, the comment lodged in Daniel's consciousness.

"The Lindsay years taught me how failed a god liberalism is," Daniel said. "Government can't do. It can only assist. And where it arrogates to itself the idea of running families, schools, cities, it makes them worse. It destroys more than it builds." Daniel's movement to the right, as his choice of imagery suggested, reflected religion as much as politics. As an Orthodox Jew who revered tradition and the past, he was by temperament a conservative beneath his Manhattan-liberal veneer. The giveaway ethos of the welfare state contradicted his Jewish belief that God invested humans with free will. It devalued the selflessness of *tzedakah*, the charity that Jews are divinely commanded to give. "One has to be careful," Daniel put it later, "not to have the state take over for the Almighty."

In one regard, though, Daniel Greer emerged from the era with admiration for its mavericks. Like the Young Republicans and Young Americans for Freedom, who abhorred the New Left's positions even as they appropriated its style of political theater, Daniel found affirmation for his religious observance in the way the civil rights movement and the counterculture celebrated dissent. "The sixties imparted a do-your-own-thing feeling," he said. "And unfortunately in American society that became the cause for a lack of structure, an emptiness. But it also gave people with strong feelings more security about expressing them, about indulging them and living them more fully than they did in the fifties. Out of 650 kids in my class at Princeton, there was not one with hair on his face. They all combed their hair the same way, wore the same clothes. In the aftermath of the sixties and early seventies, there was no longer the pressure to conform. It wasn't just a 'me' thing. I was part of a group who wanted a fuller expression of our Judaism."

• •

IN MAY 1973, several months after resigning from the Lindsay administration, Daniel Greer flew to Israel with his wife of two years, Sarah Bergman. They held tourist visas and owned a co-op apartment on Riverside Drive. But, still, both understood this trip as a try-out for *aliyah*. Orthodox Judaism had brought Daniel and Sarah together. Or, more precisely, Steven Riskin had, playing the matchmaking role of *shadchen* for the lawyer and the day school educator, both of them active in the Soviet Jewry movement and Lincoln Square Synagogue. Daniel had even bought the potted plants that made up its first *mechitzah*.

Daniel had often regretted passing up an offer to visit Israel in the heady days after the Six-Day War. A month-long vacation there with Sarah in 1972 only reawakened his longing for the place. They meandered through the crooked alleys of the Old City, explored Hebron, worshipped in Gush Etzion, where Jewish settlers were reclaiming the land overrun by Arabs in 1948, the land his day school teacher's brother had died trying to defend. Now, equipped with working papers and a client interested in acquiring a chain of hotels, Daniel exulted in the continuing glow of Israeli invulnerability.

So Daniel was mystified on the early afternoon of Yom Kippur, when he heard from inside a Gush Etzion yeshiva the roar of jets overhead. Egyptian forces, he soon learned, had crossed the Suez Canal. A few hours later, army trucks rolled up to the yeshiva to collect its soldiers, who assured Daniel and the rest that this new war would be over fast, just like 1967. After breaking the fast, their spirits festive enough for dancing, Daniel and Sarah drove back into Jerusalem to find the Old City walls floodlit as if for *Son et Lumière*, as if the war didn't even merit the precautions of a blackout.

Within several days, the Greers harbored no such illusions. One of the Gush Etzion soldiers, newly married, was killed. Neighbors across the street from the Greers in Jerusalem lost their son. The son of an Israeli friend disappeared while fighting in the Golan. Even after the combat ended, with Israel staggered but intact, the wounded trickled back home, missing limbs, mute with shell-shock. "Sometimes in life, you lose everything in an instant," Daniel said decades later. "It was that way with Israel after Yom Kippur. The glass was cracked and could never be put together."

At a more practical level, Daniel's own plans changed drastically. Tourism from America shriveled in the aftermath of the war. Then the 1974 Arab oil embargo further isolated Israel from the world. Daniel found himself representing a hotel developer in a country suddenly awash in empty hotel rooms. The entire plan fell through, dimming any prospects he and Sarah had of immigrating. Still, if there were a symbol of continuing possibility, it arrived on the eleventh of Tishri, 5735, a year and a day after the outbreak of the Yom Kippur war, when Sarah Greer gave birth to a son named Dov.

Daniel pursued admission to the Israeli bar, and he spent his required six-month apprenticeship with an attorney named Eliyahu Lenkin, who taught him about much more than the law. Lenkin had commanded the *Altalena*, the ship carrying weapons and volunteers for the Irgun militia that was blasted and sunk in April 1948 by the Israeli army on David Ben-Gurion's orders. In related fighting onshore, Yitzhak Rabin, then an army colonel, led a grenade assault against Irgun attackers. After the violence subsided, Lenkin had been arrested, beaten, and interrogated by his own nation's soldiers. A quarter-century later, the episode still underlay the contempt of Revisionist Zionists like Menachem Begin for the Labor regime, and it was also increasingly part of the *haredi* view of Israel's secular leadership as illegitimate.

In daily life, the saga of the *Altalena* confirmed Daniel's firsthand critique of Israeli socialism. He and Sarah wearied of lines to obtain permissions, red tape to transfer funds, delays for mail from America to be released, arguments with apartment neighbors over how to divide a communal supply of heating coal. From an Israeli bureaucrat, "yes" meant "maybe" and "maybe" meant "never." Here was John Lindsay's New York with its welter of departments and agencies grown to cancerous proportions.

More profoundly, Daniel lost his admiration for that generation of Zionist founders he had feted when Golda Meir visited New York. Eliyahu Lenkin's ordeal, he said later, "was living proof of the seamier side of what happened in Israel, the side that is glossed over and papered over." He never forgot the unspoken wryness Lenkin exuded on the day in December 1973 when David Ben-Gurion died, Ben-Gurion who had said the gun used against the *Altalena* was "blessed." Decades later, after Yitzhak Rabin had been assassinated and lifted to martyrdom in liberal Jewish circles, Daniel would dismiss him as a man who killed fellow Jews.

Even as he mastered Israeli law and Revisionist Zionist history, Daniel pursued *smicha*, the rabbinic ordination he had forgone when he went to Yale Law instead of remaining a student of Rabbi Soloveitchik. He studied partly with Rabbi Yehoshua Neuwirth, the author of a seminal work on the laws of the Sabbath, *Shemirat Shabbat Kehilkhata*, and a man sought out by Orthodox Jews worldwide as a *posek*, a decisor of *halakhah*. Sometimes Daniel learned in the time-honored way, with a study partner, a *chavruta*, in the study house, the *beit midrash*; sometimes he lugged his volumes of commentaries to an unsurprisingly deserted place—the Museum of Islam in the thoroughly Jewish New City. After two years of preparation, he presented himself at Rabbi Neuwirth's living room table for his *bechinah*, his test.

Newly ordained, Rabbi Greer realized he no longer had to be a lawyer; he no longer had to settle for lay leadership, buying plants for the *mechitzah* in somebody else's shul. He vowed to give his own children the finest Jewish education possible, and now he possessed the credential to provide it. Sarah, too, had been deepening her religious knowledge, studying with the renowned Bible scholar Nehama Leibowitz. There were times when the Greers watched Dov toddle across the room to flip the pages of a Talmud tractate, and saw in his antics the design of their future.

"To truly learn, to know—that's what a Jew is," Rabbi Greer said. "It's inconceivable that anything else is important. A life of real learning knows nothing else. Other external things are only disturbances. No one who studies—even world history—thinks it's of ultimate importance. When you're studying Torah, it's not only intellectually challenging, it's divining God's plan."

Rabbi Greer divined his own plan with a road atlas and a geometry compass. He visited New York in 1975 with Sarah, baby Dov, and a map showing a hundred-mile radius around the city. Within that border, he searched for a community equipped for Orthodox life—not just the shul and butcher and kosher pizzeria, but day schools and a *mikvah* and Torah study groups. Most of the likely candidates, places like Teaneck and Monsey and Lakewood, struck the Greers as too suburban, too bland. But a yeshiva was just opening in New Haven. Yale supplied intellectual and cultural life. And Rabbi Greer had contacts enough in the city to resume his law practice, not an affair of the heart for him, but a necessity as the father of a growing family.

In the summer of 1976, just before moving to New Haven, Rabbi Greer hosted a final gathering in his Upper West Side apartment. His law school roommate, Jerry Brown, was heading into the Democratic party convention as a surprisingly strong contender for the presidential nomination. Rabbi Greer had already driven Brown to Charlotte Street in the Bronx, introducing him to the desolate, abandoned block that Jimmy Carter and Ronald Reagan would ultimately make the national symbol of urban ruin. Now the rabbi would preside over a fund-raiser. It was a favor to a friend, a farewell to a city, and the punctuation, perhaps, on a certain kind of life.

•   •

A YEAR AFTER Daniel and Sarah Greer arrived in New Haven, renting a home alongside a park, they went looking for an Orthodox preschool for three-year-old Dov. The only one in the area didn't strike them as religious enough. The Greers' second child, Esther, was nearing her second birthday and would soon need to start nursery school, too. So the Greers founded their own preschool, renting a basement, posting handmade flyers, and eventually enrolling six other Jewish children. From that beginning, the Gan School expanded over the next five years to thirty students through third grade. The Greers themselves had three more children—two daughters, Hannah and Batsheva, and a son, Eliezer Shalom.

As Sarah oversaw Gan day-to-day, Rabbi Greer supported the family by practicing law in partnership with two other Yale graduates. He served as well on the city's police commission and chaired its redevelopment agency, developing contacts with the blacks and white ethnics who tended to dominate politics in New Haven. And he located and befriended other Orthodox Jews with young families, including a lawyer and alderman named Ed Zelinsky and a Yale lecturer in Greek history named Harold Hack. In time, both families sent their children to the Gan School.

So when Rabbi Greer learned in 1982 that New Haven was selling a vacant elementary school near his home, he acted. For $30,000 he got 29,000 square feet, but also a decade's worth of deterioration. Rain flooded the top floor through holes in the roof. Water wormed inside the walls. Asphalt tiles lay scattered like playing cards across the floor, and eighty windows were cracked or broken. The $250,000 that Rabbi Greer had budgeted for renovation and restoration ballooned to $1.5 million, and by necessity the lawyer became both a fund-raiser and a nonprofit developer. When the work was completed, however, the school gleamed from its hardwood floors to its brass doorknobs. By the late nineties, the building would contain two schools—Yeshiva Elementary, as Gan was renamed, for boys and girls in grades K through eight; Tikvah High

School for girls—while the Mesiftah of New Haven for boys would occupy a former mansion nearby. Under the collective rubric of the Yeshiva of New Haven, Rabbi Greer's schools taught 130 students, some coming from as far as Hungary, Israel, and Colombia.

Rabbi Greer withdrew from his law firm in 1990 to concentrate on overseeing the schools and reviving the surrounding area. Impressive as it was, the elementary school building sat in a troubled, unstable neighborhood. The district took its name from Edgewood Park, which Frederick Law Olmsted had designed near New Haven's western border, and in the past its late-Victorian homes had housed Irish, Italian, and Jewish families. But contemporary New Haven was a city of closed factories and failed urban renewal schemes—a downtown mall and arena both struggling against bankruptcy, a six-lane highway that gouged through the breadth of the city. The ethnic middle class had fled for Hamden or West Haven, leaving virtually no buffer, demographically or geographically, between Yale's neo-Gothic glory and the black slums.

The block of Elm Street just south of Rabbi Greer's school rated as one of New Haven's worst. Absentee landlords had partitioned single-family homes and roomy flats into warrens of apartments for the poor, pocketing rent from welfare subsidies or the federal Section 8 program. Doors swung loose from broken locks, abandoned cars rusted in front yards, beer bottles collected under porches. When New Haven police shut down the city's red-light district downtown, prostitution moved into Edgewood Park. One neighborhood lawyer, disgusted at seeing solicitations outside his window as he ate breakfast, joined Rabbi Greer in a campaign of public humiliation. The men drove through Edgewood Park taking pictures of the hookers' customers, prodding the cops to make arrests, and hanging posters with the name and address of what they called the "John of the Week."

Rabbi Greer also formed three nonprofit corporations to buy back the neighborhood, at least chunks of it, from distant owners and banks. The rehabilitation was slow and hideous work. Hundreds of cockroaches fell onto a yeshiva alumnus who was probing a weak ceiling in one house. Creeping up the rotted stairs of another building, Rabbi Greer roared, "The one good thing Stalin did was shoot people for economic crimes. Slumlords should be shot." Ultimately, the nonprofit corporations restored nearly thirty homes in an eight-block area around the school, renting them to a variety of families, including a contingent of Orthodox Jews. Compared to the eyesores that preceded them, the Greer houses with their picket fences and porch swings and bright hues shone like transplants from Martha's Vineyard. Among them, Daniel and Sarah Greer raised their own family.

In a nation and a generation that spouted clichés about diversity, the Greer children belonged to a neighborhood of demonstrable racial and economic range. Their census tract was 40 percent nonwhite and 90 percent renters; more than one-quarter of children and one-half of senior citizens lived below the poverty line. In their spare time, the young Greers delivered meals to elderly Jews, volunteered in a soup kitchen, organized a summer day camp for local kids. Rabbi Greer brought them to hear the cellist Mstislav Rostropovich play at Yale's Woolsey Hall. Nine or ten times, the family vacationed in Europe, traveling on off-peak tickets with a cache of kosher cheese.

Rabbi Greer at the same time projected a model of unstinting Orthodoxy. He grew his beard and began wearing tzitzis out, manifesting what he called "not so much an increase in observance as an increase in confidence." Reared as a conventionally Zionistic American Jew, Rabbi Greer now viewed Israel more like the non-Zionist factions of *haredim*. Of course, he valued the Land of Israel and its five million Jews; but he thought the secular state was "of minimal importance to religious Judaism" and "not relevant to Jewish survival." When Greer's former campaign manager and longtime admirer Ari Goldman sent an inscribed copy of his memoir, *The Search for*

God at Harvard, the rabbi read with disdain Goldman's account of trying to observe Orthodoxy while undertaking newspaper assignments on Sabbath. Ari was a "lovely person," Rabbi Greer thought, but he was "worshipping the Golden Calf." He threw away the book.

In the fall of 1991, Dov Greer reached his final year of high school and a decision about where to attend college. Rabbi Greer, naturally enough, recommended Princeton, his own alma mater. He and Dov happened to visit the campus several days after an annual event for sophomores held to mark each winter's first snowfall: the Nude Olympics. The Princeton that Daniel Greer had attended a generation earlier, for all of its discomfort with Jews, had at least espoused some moral values in which he could believe; he remembered students being expelled for sneaking girls into their dorm rooms for the night. Now, he discovered, you had hundreds of kids running stark naked through campus, drinking themselves insensate, fornicating for all to see. Right then, he decided Dov would never attend Princeton. A few years later, he stopped sending his own annual donation of $15.

Instead, Dov chose his father's other alma mater, Yale. He immediately deferred enrollment for two years, until September 1994, to permit him to study a year apiece at yeshivot in Monsey and Jerusalem. In his own young adulthood, of course, Daniel Greer also had studied in Israel—but at Hebrew University, a secular institution, on a junior-year-abroad program that was part of his collegiate experience. Dov, in the manner of a new generation of American Orthodox Jews, concentrated solely on religious subjects. And in the abstemious culture of the yeshivot, where the rabbis and teachers were largely *haredim,* where davening and learning stretched from dawn until midnight, he also donned a kind of moral armor. Only equipped with it did he return to Yale and secular society.

His younger sister Esther joined him in starting freshman year. She had learned for a year in Jerusalem between high school and Yale. Avi Hack, a son of Daniel Greer's friend

Harold Hack, was a classmate as well, entering Yale after two years of Jewish scholarship. A year later, in September 1995, Hannah Greer entered Yale after a year split between studying in Israel and teaching religious subjects to Jews in the former Soviet Union.

Rabbi Greer had reared his children on the parable of keeping kosher at Princeton. Nearly forty years later, he still kept the half-size refrigerator from his dorm room for them to see. The children might be entering in Yale a university that offered kosher meals and barely blinked at a student with a *kippa*, but the Nude Olympics episode had already served notice to their father that college life, if more open now to Orthodox Jews, presented them with challenges unimagined in his era.

"We were brought up at home to believe that one goes out into the world," Dov Greer put it, "but one doesn't accommodate one's religion for one's college. All Orthodox Jews know they live in a society that has some values that aren't ours. My father's main point is that the most important thing is that you are an Orthodox Jew."

ONE SNOWY FRIDAY AFTERNOON in early 1996, Daniel Greer welcomed a Yale couple named Betty and Alan Trachtenberg for the Sabbath. She was the dean of students and he a professor of American studies who was Hannah Greer's freshman adviser. They made the mile-long trip from campus to the yeshiva in time for *kabbalat* Shabbat service, Alan joining the men and Betty among the women behind the *mechitzah*. Then they walked the downy streets to the Greer home, where Sarah Greer had laid the table with homemade challah and her mother's candlesticks. Over the hours, they ate roasted chicken and discussed the week's Torah portion and lifted voices in the Sabbath songs.

The evening suffused Betty Trachtenberg with a sense-memory of childhood, and most especially of her Orthodox grandparents. She remembered sitting with her *bubbe* Sophie in the synagogue balcony on Yom Kippur. She remembered catching sight of her *zayde* Velvel at home laying tefillin, his coarse longshoreman's hands so deft with the leather straps. She remembered Sabbath dinners, not unlike this one, when Sophie covered her head with an ivory shawl and brought flame to wick with the words of a *brucha.*

More than nostalgia warmed the occasion; there was an undercurrent of triumph about it. Such a Sabbath would have been inconceivable in the Yale of the past, the Yale founded by the Congregational Church, presided over by ministers until 1899, and officially biased against Jews in admissions. By now, thirty-five years has passed since Yale renounced its quota system, and in the Greer home sat a Jewish Yale dean married to a Jewish Yale professor who both served a Jewish Yale president on behalf of a student body that was one-quarter Jewish. Daniel Greer, a Yale Law alumnus, had fathered three of those current students, Dov, Esther, and Hannah.

These days, Betty Trachtenberg considered herself "culturally Jewish." She no longer observed the religion; none of her children had celebrated a bar or bat mitzvah; two of them had married gentiles. Still, as both a dean and a Jew, Trachtenberg took pride in Yale's commitment to accommodating the needs of Orthodox students. Yale recruited at the leading day schools. It had donated land for a privately funded Jewish center where students could use their meal plan in the kosher cafeteria. It even provided old-fashioned keys to observant students so they would not violate the Sabbath by using electronic key cards to enter their dorms.

The Greer children experienced Yale's flexibility firsthand. The university supplied Hannah with a private female tutor for a music course so she would not breach *halakhah* by letting a man hear her sing. Dov made friends and study partners in his classes from as far afield as Nigeria. For their part, the young Greers did not take academic shelter in the majors like Hebrew or Judaic studies that would have drawn most readily on their religious educations, but instead ventured widely—Dov majoring in military history, Esther in linguistics, Hannah in architectural theory.

Entering the 1995–96 academic year, Yale revised its housing policy. All unmarried freshmen and sophomores, including those from New Haven, would be required to live on campus. Yale depicted the change as consistent with its educational mission. For decades, the university had structured undergraduate life around its residential colleges, each consisting of a dormitory, commons, classrooms, and faculty apartments. These colleges, Yale held, were the building blocks of community, a microcosm of the real world with all its variety and challenges. From the turmoil of the sixties through the identity politics of the nineties, Yale had resisted the pressure to create separate housing for racial minorities, as had colleges such as Cornell and Dartmouth. Yale stubbornly threw together Muslim and Mormon, straight and gay, preppie and scholarship kid in what the university president, Richard Levin, extolled as an "encounter with difference."

What Yale also did, however, was make every one of its dormitories coed, whether room by room or floor by floor. Hallway bathrooms were open to both genders. Incoming freshmen were required to hear a lecture on safe sex. Dormitory advisers sometimes made available free condoms. Barely enforcing its own rule forbidding overnight guests in the dorms, Yale portrayed itself as acknowledging reality—the reality that students are sexually active, the reality of the AIDS epidemic.

But for Rabbi Greer, this program of forced cohabitation, this acceptance if not encouragement of premarital sex, all this at a university that had not even admitted women until 1969, violated *tznius*, the Talmudic ideal of modesty, just as brazenly as had the Nude Olympics. "The ethos of today—everything goes—is incompatible with a religious lifestyle," he would write in a letter somewhat later. "I cannot imagine any truly devout person, whether Christian, Muslim, or Jew, living in a mixed-sex environment."

Until now, he had managed to safeguard his own children from such blasphemy. Dov and Esther had been admitted to Yale under the previous housing policy, which only required freshmen to live on campus and exempted students like them who resided with their own families in New Haven. Hannah, starting college the fall the new rule took effect, pursued and won a waiver on religious grounds partly through the efforts of Yale's Jewish chaplain, a Conservative rabbi named James Ponet.* Rabbi Greer wrote him in August 1995 to express appreciation for "what you have done for Hannah and for all those—may their numbers increase—who in future years will benefit from your efforts."

The numbers indeed were about to increase, and with them the friction. In April 1995, Yale admitted Harold Hack's son Elisha and two seniors from an Orthodox day school on Long Island, Lisa Friedman and Jeremy Hershman. Friedman and Hershman each deferred enrolling for one year and Hack for two, to allow for advanced religious study. Before going off, the three met through Rabbi Greer, who had been recommended to Friedman and Hershman as the hub of New Haven's Orthodox community, and while they were studying in Israel they heard of Hannah Greer's apparent exemption from the housing rule on religious grounds.

With that in mind, Hershman wrote to Betty Trachtenberg in March 1996 to request a similar waiver, contending, "I have been so advised by my Rabbis, that it would be impossible for me to adhere to my religious restrictions and obligations while living in university dormitories." As for those Orthodox Jews already doing so, he added, "Their level of adherence to the precepts of Orthodox Judaism may be different from mine."

Four weeks later, on April 15, 1996, Dean Trachtenberg replied. Yale would be "sensitive to all our students'

---

* Yale subsequently claimed that Hannah had been "grandfathered" in under the old policy, although the existing correspondence does not indicate this.

needs." Yale would "accommodate their religious practices." But living in a residential college was "at the very center of a Yale education." Therefore, she concluded, "I must deny your request."

That same month, Batsheva Greer earned admission to Yale. Like her siblings and her future classmates, she would first learn for a year in Israel. During the spring and summer of 1996, just before she departed, her parents met with Rabbi Ponet and the university chaplain, Reverend Frederick Streets, seeking the kind of influence with Yale that had helped to gain a waiver for Hannah. The Greers got encouragement, but no more. As Batsheva studied thousands of miles away, Lisa Friedman and Dov Greer presented the students' concerns to Yale professors with expertise in constitutional law and religion in American civic life, again winning nothing more than sympathy.

Batsheva flew back from Israel for Passover in late April 1997. During the visit, she joined Dov, Friedman, Hershman, and Elisha Hack for a meeting with Yale officials including Betty Trachtenberg, who had joined the Greers for Shabbat barely one year before. As the students later recounted the events, the dean told them, "This may sound a little bit harsh, but you knew about the housing rules before you applied to Yale. If our rules are not suitable, you should not have come." She concluded the meeting by remarking, "How do you ever expect Orthodox Jews to integrate into the real world?"

By her own recollection, Trachtenberg suggested to the students that, knowing of Yale's policy, they could have found single-sex dorms at Harvard or MIT or other excellent universities. Unspoken but understood were the options of Yeshiva University and its women's division, Stern College—not Yale's equals academically, of course, but institutions created to conform with Orthodox observance. Trachtenberg tried to convince the students that even in a coed dorm their religious obligations could be respected. As freshmen, they could live on a single-sex floor; as sophomores, they could choose roommates who shared their beliefs. Seventy-five times out of seventy-six times they went to use a coed bathroom, Trachtenberg tried to assure them, it would be empty.

The meeting ended with Yale and the students more estranged, more hardened in their positions. The students took to referring to the encounter as the "back-of-the-bus meeting," likening their plight to that of blacks in the Jim Crow South. In a subsequent letter to Reverend Streets, the university chaplain, Rabbi Greer wrote of Yale's officials, "No doubt, the learned of Sodom and Gomorrah also believed themselves similarly cultured and well-intentioned." Such language hardly encouraged mediation; it was a language of moral absolutes. Batsheva Greer, in fact, thought the "worst possible outcome" would be to get an individual waiver while the housing policy remained unchanged. She wanted to win on the principle.

OF ALL HIS CHILDREN, Rabbi Daniel Greer liked to say, Batsheva was "the least likely revolutionary." She had delicate features and wire-rimmed glasses and a presence so gentle she didn't seem to displace any air when entering a room. Amid the bustle of family dinners, she listened or cleared the dishes or tugged on a loose stitch of her sweater. She winced at gossip, even the favorable kind.

Beneath it all lay an iron resolve. Batsheva had never known the insecurity of her father's generation of Orthodox Jews, the concept of a *kippa* as an "indoor garment." Nor had she known an America that prided itself on the melting-pot myth of assimilation. The ideals of the nineties—cultural pluralism, diversity, group rights, identity politics—told Orthodox Jews that like other minorities their very refusal to melt gave them integrity. With the adoring eyes of a little sister, Batsheva had watched Dov march off to Yale, tzitzis out, *peyes* dangling to his jawline, flagrantly, unashamedly *frum*. "My brother walks around campus looking like a yeshiva *bochur,*" she said, using the term of endearment and admiration for a yeshiva student. "My brother doesn't compromise on anything."

Neither would she. Of all the Greer children, Batsheva had attended the most insular, *haredi* seminary, Bais Ya'akov Yerushalayim. When her freshman year at Yale began in September 1997, she never set foot in her assigned room in Saybrook College. Her mother did inspect it and returned saying she could not even describe the wantonness within. Her father paid the fee for it as a kind of ransom. Like all beginning students, Batsheva was invited to attend orientation sessions on topics ranging from safe sex to diversity. She boycotted every one. "They weren't places for a nice religious Jewish girl," she explained. Her absence from the safe-sex lecture in particular drew the notice of her student adviser, who, she said, called her repeatedly, warning that as punishment she wouldn't be officially registered for classes. Batsheva threatened to call a lawyer. Only then did the adviser desist.

As first semester proceeded, Batsheva picked her way through Yale as if she were navigating a minefield. She lived at home. She consulted a rabbi in choosing her courses. When the required freshman composition class discussed an essay on abortion, she took refuge in silence. "I figured," she said, "I can always talk next week." One of the other Orthodox students, Jeremy Hershman, adopted a similar strategy. A biology major, he "tried not to think" about whether evolutionary theory squared with the Torah's account of creation.

And Batsheva considered classes the least of her obstacles. "When something is said in a classroom, you can listen and write notes and it doesn't make an impression on you," she explained. "But when you're in an immoral environment, it has a detrimental effect. Actions are just more detrimental than words. They aren't good for one's soul."

A teaching assistant in one of Batsheva's classes asked all the students to drop off an assignment at her apartment in one of the residential colleges. Determined not to step inside, Batsheva instead left her paper with the college master, a faculty member whose apartment opened directly onto the street. Another time, Batsheva mentioned to a classmate that she needed to make a telephone call. The student offered to let Batsheva use the phone in her dorm room. Distressed by a show of kindness she dare not accept, Batsheva said, "That's all right. I've got to be going now." She had grown accustomed to giving such polite, if abrupt, demurrals. Only rarely, with a classmate who recognized the depth of her Orthodoxy, would Batsheva answer candidly, "I can't go up and you'll understand."

Batsheva and her Orthodox peers—Friedman, Hershman, Elisha Hack, and another freshman named Rachel Wohlgelernter, whose father had helped Daniel Greer establish the kosher kitchen at Princeton—devised a double-edged campaign against Yale. The students called on Nathan Lewin, Rabbi Greer's longtime friend and an attorney specializing in cases involving religious freedom, to bring suit against the university on the grounds of religious discrimination. And they designated Elisha Hack to lead a public-relations assault designed to cast Yale, in Rabbi Greer's phrase, as "Sodom and Gomorrah." An article about the Yale Five case in the *New York Times* on September 7, 1997, projected the controversy onto the national stage. Two days later, in an op-ed essay for the *Times*, Hack wrote:

> Bingham Hall, on the Yale quadrangle known as the Old Campus, is one of the dorms for incoming students. When I entered it two weeks ago during an orientation tour, I literally saw the handwriting on the wall. A sign titled "Safe Sex" told me where to pick up condoms on campus. Another sign touted 100 ways to make love without having sex, like "take a nap together" and "take a steamy shower together."
>
> That, I am told, is real life in the dorms. The "freshperson" issue of The Yale Daily News sent to entering students contained a "Yale lexicon" defining "sexile" as "banishment from your dorm room because your roommate is having more fun than you." If you live in the

dorms, you're expected to be part of the crowd, to accept these standards as the framework of your life. . . .

Yale is proud of the fact that it has no "parietal rules" and that sexual morality is a student's own business. Maybe this is what Dean Richard H. Brodhead meant when he said that "Yale's residential colleges carry . . . a moral meaning." That moral meaning is, basically, "Anything goes." This morality is Yale's own residential religion, which it is proselytizing by force of its regulations.

Nearly three months later, on December 4, 1997, Nathan Lewin filed suit in U.S. District Court in Hartford charging that Yale had violated the "religious freedom and constitutional rights" of Batsheva Greer, Elisha Hack, Lisa Friedman, and Jeremy Hershman. (Rachel Wohlgelernter had made a civil marriage during first semester, three months before the date of her Jewish ceremony, in order to gain an exemption from the housing policy.) Lewin's suit, in certain ways, had little to do with the essence of the case. It argued that Yale's residential-college rule amounted to an unfair monopoly on housing. It argued that Yale, because it accepted federal grants and had Connecticut's governor and lieutenant governor on its board, was in fact a "state actor," a public institution subject to federal antidiscrimination laws. Yale, predictably, submitted a motion for dismissal on grounds that the lawsuit was an "imaginative but wholly wrongheaded attempt to challenge . . . a private college's prerogative to maintain . . . a rule important to its educational philosophy."

But the Yale Five case, as it was known even without Wohlgelernter, by then had achieved a flourishing life of its own outside court. Close to a hundred articles and broadcasts were devoted to it during the last four months of 1997, from National Public Radio to "ABC World News Tonight," the *Des Moines Register*, the *Jerusalem Post*, the *Washington Post*, the *Fresno Bee*, *American Lawyer*, and the *Chronicle of Higher Education*. Even the student newspaper at DePauw University in

Greencastle, Indiana, weighed in. With its starkly defined antagonists, the case proved irresistible to pundits of all bents. Wendy Shalit wrote in the conservative monthly *City Journal*, "Diversity, it seems, ends where traditional morality begins." In the *New Yorker*, a bastion of urbane liberalism, David Denby maintained, "The students' grievance appears to be produced by a combination of harsh medieval ardor and culture-of-complaint sensitivity."

Meanwhile, all but unnoticed, the case had acquired a different, more disturbing meaning within American Jewry. It called into question, into doubt, the essence of the Jewish compact with America, the terms of engagement with the Golden Land. By one measure, nothing bespoke Orthodox security in America as a nation more than the Yale Five's willingness to fight their battle in federal court; by another, nothing bespoke Orthodox antipathy for America as a culture more than their insistence on participating in a great university only on the selective, separatist terms they alone would dictate. The hidden issue in the Yale Five case, to be found nowhere in all the legal documents, was who established the definition of Jewish, and more specifically Orthodox, authenticity.

"I don't like to think of myself as an enemy," Betty Trachtenberg said a few months after the case went to court. "Here I am, a person who identified as a Jew, raised my kids as Jews, and now has my little grandchild to our seder—I didn't want anyone to call into question who I was. When they filed this suit, it wasn't against 'Betty Trachtenberg, granddaughter of Velvel and Sophie,' but that's part of who I am. I honor the memory of my grandparents, and I feel that my memory has been compromised."

Eight blocks from the Yale campus, in the Orthodox enclave he had created, Rabbi Daniel Greer maintained that it was his version of Judaism that was being undermined. "You have a group of people who have arrogated to themselves the determination of what is or is not properly Jewish," he said. "And they have a certain resentment against people who are

Jewish in a more, quote, Orthodox way, and do not want to buy
into the politically correct agenda. Jews have still not gotten
over the ghetto mentality." As for those, including the Orthodox, who pointed to the room keys, the kosher meals, the Slifka
Center as proof of Yale's goodwill, Rabbi Greer responded with
a verse from Torah: "Favors will blind even the wise and distort
the words of the righteous."

ON A RAINY AFTERNOON in April 1998, five months after the
Yale Five filed their lawsuit, a twenty-year-old junior named
Evan Farber unlocked the door to his room in Branford College, pausing by habit and obligation alike to kiss his fingers
and touch them to the mezuzah nailed on the portal. He wore
faded jeans, a flannel shirt, high-top sneakers and, atop his
dirty-blond hair, a knit green *kippa* of the Modern Orthodox
sort. Inside the room, his tefillin bag lay beside a Mets cap on a
bookshelf and his *siddur* stood between a dictionary and the-
saurus. "Sodom and Gomorrah," he muttered.

Farber was one of sixty Orthodox Jews enrolled at Yale
at the time, and like the vast majority of them he had attended
day school, Ramaz in Manhattan in his case. Three springs earlier, given the college choices that his 1450 SAT score had provided, he had chosen Yale largely on the strength of its
Orthodox life—the number of students, the kosher meal plan,
the *beit midrash* and daily minyanim at Hillel. Now, as an up-
perclassman, he helped lead the Young Israel chapter on campus and gave tours of Yale to prospective Jewish students.

There were times, he had to admit, when his *tznius* was
sorely tested. During freshman year, one of his roommates in a
five-person suite regularly invited his fiancée down from MIT
for the weekend. Out of deference to Farber, the couple slept in
the living room and "didn't do anything," or at least kept it too
discreet for Farber to notice. "The deal I had with my roommate," he recalled, "was that I wouldn't object to his girlfriend
being there, and he wouldn't object to my getting up at seven in

the morning to go to services." As a sophomore, Farber shared a hallway bathroom with seven classmates, two of them young women. "People wore bathrobes," he said. "It wasn't an issue."

It only became an issue, as far as Farber was concerned, when the Yale Five and their supporters decided that no observant Jew could possibly live in a coed dorm. He felt judged. And the guilty verdict was not only personal but communal. As his Jewish legitimacy was being questioned, so was that of the Modern Orthodox community from which he had come. He remembered a speech that Ramaz's principal, Rabbi Haskel Lookstein, had given after the death of Joseph Soloveitchik, in which he recalled the *Rav* warning, "Don't let them move you to the right."

"Confronting and solving an issue is a strengthening process," Farber maintained. "But I know the arrangement I had freshman year wouldn't have been acceptable to those who sued. I assume they'd also be unhappy about taking an art history class with paintings of nudes. And probably they'd also have a problem walking across campus on a hot spring day when people are sunbathing. Part of the difference is a strictness in interpreting *halakhah,* and part of it is the willingness to compromise. The question is whether Jewish values and activities should be fused with those of the secular world or set apart from it. Modern Orthodox feel we should take the best of it. *Haredim* think we should not."

Indignation such as Farber's could be heard from much of Yale's Orthodox community. Shortly after Elisha Hack's op-ed essay appeared in the *Times*, the Orthodox student who would have been his dormitory roommate fired back in a letter to the editor, portraying a campus life that included Talmud study, daily prayer, and observant roommates. "Thanks to Yale," Saul Nadata concluded, "for giving us the opportunity to grow without sacrificing our beliefs." The Orthodox rabbi affiliated with the Slifka Center, Michael Whitman, acknowledged the challenge posed by coed dorms even as he, too, assailed the Yale Five's tactics. "The problem I have is how their argument has been made," he said. "You can say, 'I know there are Orthodox students in the dorms but I just can't live that way.' I can respect that. But to say that the students in the dorms are not as Orthodox or not as observant of the laws— that is just not factually accurate."

On Long Island, the principal of the Orthodox day school that had educated Jeremy Hershman and Lisa Friedman discovered the case, quite to his shock, through a front-page article in the *New York Jewish Week*. "I thought I was going to drop dead," Daniel J. Vitow of the Hebrew Academy of the Five Towns and Rockaway later told the Jewish Student Press Service. He went on: "This is not a moral issue. This is an issue about money [in housing fees]. No one was holding a gun to these kids' heads telling them they had to go to Yale."

It is possible, of course, to view Farber, Nadata, and Whitman as biased by self-interest. Naturally, they would want to defend the validity of their Jewish lives at Yale. And Vitow could be dismissed as a principal eager to ingratiate himself to Yale lest he damage the chances of his students applying there. All that could be said, except for one thing: the same kind of outrage arose from Modern Orthodox Jews with no ties to Yale. When the *New York Times Magazine* published an article about the lawsuit in May 1998, dozens of letters poured in from Orthodox readers. A great many of them, while evincing no particular support for Yale's housing policy, expressed contempt for the Yale Five.

"My Modern Orthodox yeshiva of the 60s was part of a broad Jewish movement to engage with the non-Jewish world as equals," wrote a Maryland doctor. "As my yeshiva has been taken over by fundamentalists, so has the Modern Orthodox movement, and it now has more in common with other religious fundamentalists than it does with centrist Orthodox and the majority of world Jewry."

"I feel sorry for Yale dean of students Trachtenberg," a physician from Houston said in an E-mail to the *Times*, "because I too just don't understand. I went to yeshiva high school, spent a year at an Israeli yeshiva, and went on to four years at Columbia University. I lived in both single-sex and mixed suites without incident. It was the real world."

A yeshiva graduate descended from several generations of Orthodox rabbis contrasted the Yale Five to the biblical Daniel. "Unlike Yale, Babylon forced Jews to change their names, language, and customs," she wrote. "Daniel's faith withstood this test as he continued in his observance. Even when thrust into the lions' den . . . Daniel's unwavering faith allowed him to emerge intact in both spirit and flesh. Daniel's message is one of strength in adversity. How fragile is the faith of these young people! They flee from the merest whisper of the challenge."

If a single exchange conveyed just how deep a fissure the Yale Five case had opened among Orthodox Jews in America, it came when the Jewish Telegraphic Agency polled leaders of the Orthodox Union, the umbrella group for congregations nationwide. The union's president, Mandell Ganchrow, hailed the students for fighting to "lead a moral life that's prescribed by their Bible, that was accepted before MTV came along." The chairman of the union's Institute for Public Affairs, Richard Stone, called the lawsuit a "serious mistake." A university like Yale, he suggested, is not "for everybody."

The Yale Five, of course, enjoyed support of their own, but what was most striking were its sources. The Catholic League for Religious and Civil Rights submitted an amicus brief on behalf of the students, as did several conservative foundations that advocate school vouchers and school prayer. The Christian news magazine *Insight* published perhaps the most sympathetic article about the students and their cause. Elisha Hack received an unsolicited E-mail of support from a Protestant minister. Batsheva Greer heard on-line from observant Christians and Muslims. "I would like to commend you on your bravery and tenacity in this matter," went one message, from a Muslim student at UCLA. "I just want to say don't give up. . . . Good things come to those with patience. Think of Joseph in the Bible for inspiration."

Only two mainstream Jewish organizations—the American Jewish Congress and the Anti-Defamation League—filed amicus briefs. Lewin and Rabbi Greer were convinced that Jews would have eagerly supported blacks or Hispanics or gays seeking a similar concession from Yale. Jonathan Rosenblum, the self-described *haredi* columnist for the *Jerusalem Post*, likened Jewish officialdom inside and outside Yale to "assimilated suburbanites" horrified by "the appearance of a *hassid* in town." Indeed, the most vociferous advocacy for the Yale Five in the Jewish institutional world came from Agudath Israel of America, an umbrella organization of ultra-Orthodox groups. And it presented the case less as a battle for Orthodox Jews' rights than as a cautionary tale of the secular world's menace. As Chaim Dovid Zwiebel, the organization's general counsel, wrote:

> Virtually all of us do find it necessary, in one form or another, to confront the outside world—in jobs, dealing with neighbors, or even walking the streets. Virtually all of us find it necessary to strike some balance between isolation and interaction, between insularity and exposure. Virtually all of us must therefore learn how to recognize the danger of outside infection and resist it. So long as we are in this imperfect world, awaiting the redemptive power of *Moshiach*, the Yale dormitory is all around us.

There was a certain irony to such praise for Daniel Greer's cause. He had not lived his own life—from the Upper West Side to Princeton to the Lindsay administration to Edgewood Park—fearful of "infection." He had chosen to send his children to college, as few *haredi* parents do, particularly when the child is a daughter, and he had sent them to the Ivy League rather than Yeshiva or Stern at that. He had urged on them his example of "being on a wide screen." Ed Zelinsky, a neighbor and colleague in New Haven, considered Rabbi Greer the closet moderate of the Yale Five case and his young plaintiffs the unbending purists. "Thunder from the right," Rabbi Greer himself joked of his children.

Yet the confrontation bore Daniel Greer's imprint more than anyone's. The lawsuit included one of his children and one of his alumni among its complainants and a lifelong friend as the lead attorney. Its moral premise rested on Rabbi Greer's interpretation of Torah and his renunciation of liberalism. His flights of rhetoric—Yale as "Sodom and Gomorrah," threatening to any "truly devout person"—polarized fellow Jews. How had Daniel Greer, *"Torah Umaddah* incarnate," become a hero of the *haredim*? Or, to put it another way, which had changed more over the decades: America or him?

SEVERAL BLOCKS NORTH of the municipal office building where he had worked for John Lindsay a generation earlier, Daniel Greer entered the U.S. Court of Appeals for the Second Circuit on the balmy morning of March 29, 1999. The chief judge, Pierre Leval, had called for oral arguments in *Hack* v. *Yale* by the time the rabbi reached the seventeenth floor, and as he stepped into the courtroom wearing a charcoal pinstripe suit and a *kippa*, Nathan Lewin was standing before the three-judge panel in the midst of a sentence about "sifting facts and weighing circumstances."

Rabbi Greer took a seat in the gallery. His wife and children had already arrived, as had Elisha Hack, Lisa Friedman, and several of Jeremy Hershman's relatives. Some held religious texts in Hebrew that they had been reading while the court was hearing several earlier cases. The men wore *kippot* and tzitzis and *peyes;* the women, ankle-length skirts and chenille hats with large bows, shul hats. Before them played the drama of jurisprudence, with Lewin fielding questions from the judges, who were framed by a stained-glass rendering of justice's scales.

Lewin had brought the case here after the U.S. District Court in Hartford dismissed the Yale Five's complaint in July 1998. Judge Alfredo Covello had refuted Lewin on the central point that Yale was a "state actor," an institution thus subject to the constitutional guarantee of religious freedom and federal laws on fair housing. In words that echoed Betty Trachtenberg's, the judge wrote in his decision, "The plaintiffs could have opted to attend a different college or university if they were not satisfied with Yale's housing policy."

So now, beneath the gleaming brass lamps of Courtroom 1705, Lewin carried his arguments to the appellate panel, seeking to have it reinstate the case in District Court for trial. "This case offers a flat-out potential for religious discrimination," he insisted to the judges. "They say, 'We'll take your money and you can live anywhere.' That could lead them to ask, 'Will you live in the dorms? If no, we won't admit you.' And this will bar Orthodox Jews from Yale."

"Does that necessarily follow?" Judge Rosemary Pooler asked.

"The problem I have with your argument," Judge Leval added, "is that the number of injunctions that religious groups can impose on their adherents is innumerable. [It's] hard to conceive of any set of rules that wouldn't infringe on someone's religious beliefs."

When Felix Springer rose to represent Yale, the judges asked just a few questions. The attorney ended his brief appearance by saying, "We rest on the briefs."

Then Lewin stood for rebuttal and his last chance at persuasion. The Yale Five were more than clients to him. As much as Rabbi Greer, he saw this as a case not just against one university but against the timidity of the Modern Orthodoxy he recalled from boyhood. He cited several federal cases as precedents for Yale being viewed as a state actor; he pressed to be allowed more discovery to prove that Yale granted exemptions to other students while denying them to Orthodox Jews. And then, oddly desperate, he raised the specter of a university more bigoted than any Ivy League institution had ever been at its anti-Semitic worst. "If Yale is a private actor," Lewin contended, "then it could say that we will not admit Jews."

Less than an hour after the hearing began, Judge Leval adjourned the court. The plaintiffs and their families gathered around Lewin and Rabbi Greer, exchanging handshakes, attempting optimism. Lewin worried aloud about the relative silence of the third judge, James Moran, who was new to the court. Rabbi Greer didn't dare to speculate how the ruling would go.

Under the rules of law, the court had not been permitted to hear perhaps the most damaging evidence of all. In November 1998, Antonio Lasaga, the faculty master of Saybrook College, where Batsheva, Friedman, and Hershman had been assigned as freshmen, had resigned while being investigated by the FBI for possession of child pornography. A month after that scandal, a Yale senior named Suzanne Jovin was stabbed to death several miles from campus. The police later named as a suspect James Van de Velde, the academic dean of Saybrook College, and one of the Yale officials who had clashed with the Orthodox Jewish students at the "back-of-the-bus meeting."

Twelve months after the court of appeals heard the Yale case, nearly four times as long as the judges generally take to hand down a decision, Rabbi Greer and everyone else was still waiting for a ruling. He interpreted the delay as a favorable omen; it would have been easy, quick work to merely uphold the lower court.

And maybe Rabbi Greer had won already. During his childhood, and for much of Jewish history in America, the observant had been on the defensive, reeling from a wave of assimilation, clutching the old ways in *shtibel* and *cheder*. Jewish immigrants, very much unlike Irish Catholics, for instance, had deliberately chosen to send their children to public schools rather than building a parochial system as their bulwark. Now, due in part to the Yale Five case and the rightward movement within Orthodoxy that underlay it, the positions had reversed. "We're the wave of the future," Rabbi Greer put it, "not holding on by our fingernails to what might not survive." No longer was the question within Jewry, "Why aren't you being modern?" It was, "Why aren't you being *frum*?" Or, to use a term Elisha Hack coined, "Yeshivish." And no Jews were stung more by that question than the Modern Orthodox, who considered themselves obedient to Torah.

"People ask, 'Why do you insist on putting religion in everything?' " said Harold Hack, Elisha's father and Rabbi Greer's friend. "And we say, 'Why do you insist on taking it out?' We do not want to have our children compartmentalizing what they do into what they do Jewishly and what they do elsewise. What we lost in the Great Migration and the Great Destruction is that sense you're a Jew, no matter what you are doing. Whatever decisions you make are made with *halakhah* in mind. Nothing in the world can be separate from davening in the morning."

As for those children, Jeremy Hershman and Lisa Friedman, two of the original plaintiffs, married each other. Like Rachel Wohlgelernter, they were thus exempted from Yale's housing policy. Elisha Hack and Batsheva Greer finished their sophomore year in May 1999, and were allowed to live off-campus. Dov, Esther, and Hannah Greer all graduated from Yale. Dov went on to study at a Brisk yeshiva in Jerusalem, Esther and Hannah to teach in women's seminaries in Israel. Rabbi Greer ensured that his last child, Eliezer Shalom, was safe from Yale. During *Pesach* of 1999, two months shy of graduating from his father's yeshiva high school, Eliezer Shalom got engaged to Rena Hack, Harold's daughter. And he won admission to Brown.

"The world is so different," said Rabbi Daniel Greer, surveying his empty nest with wistful pride. "In my time, one was supposed to be a professional. One ought to go to law school. Today it's transformed. Jewish life is so much more vital. Dov is excited because he's learning with a first cousin of the *Rav*. One way or another, all my kids are going to spend their lives in the Torah world."

Unity versus Pluralism: Visions of Jewish Community

WHEN THE YALE FIVE took their case into federal court, they were not only seeking legal redress as American citizens but raising an essential question for Jews over two millennia of exile. What is the nature of Jewish community in the Diaspora? What is it that binds together Jews in nations where they live as a minority? The famous slogan of the United Jewish Appeal proclaimed, "We Are One," as if intoning a biblical injunction. Yet nowhere more than in the United States, with its unparalleled climate of tolerance and modernity, have Jews struggled to unite their competing and often contradictory strains.

The dilemma can be traced back to the last days of the Second Temple. When the Romans sacked Jerusalem and cast out its inhabitants, they deprived the Jewish people of nearly everything that had made them a people—a homeland, the temple cult, a royal line. Nearly five centuries after that forced dispersal, the scholars of Babylon, themselves descendants of an earlier exile, assembled the Talmud. Whatever else it may have been, it was a manual for Jewish survival in exile. A thou- 275 sand years later, another diasporic Jew, Joseph Caro of Italy, distilled Talmudic teaching into the legal code called the *Shulchan Aruch*, the Arranged Table. As if addressing all the world's displaced Jews, a compact edition of the code promised on the title page that "it can be carried in one's bosom and may be referred to at any time, while resting or traveling."

Practically speaking, from the Roman era to the Enlightenment, from the Moorish empire to the Baltic kingdoms, Jews functioned as a kind of internal state wherever they gathered and settled. The precise versions, of course, differed—the princely exilarch who led the Jewish community in ancient Babylon; the elected Council of the Four Lands in medieval Poland and Lithuania; the "court Jew" or unofficial diplomat known as a *shtadtlan* who made himself useful enough to the crown as a financier or the military as a supplier that he could intercede when necessary on his people's behalf. In nearly every variation, however, Jews retained the right to tax, educate, and discipline their own. The historian Salo Baron has written of Diaspora Jewry's "almost 'extraterritorial' status and 'sovereign' political powers and . . . overwhelming control of its members."

In so doing, Jews were not only reacting to specific conditions but following the teachings of their sacred texts, which counseled both docility and separation. The prophet Jeremiah, addressing the Babylonian exiles, urged them against insurrection, saying, "Seek the welfare of the community in which you live, and pray for it, for in its welfare will be your peace." Jewish survival in alien lands depended only on fidelity to the faith. God warned in Leviticus that those "who disobey Me and remain hostile to Me . . . shall perish among the nations." The Bible extolled community perhaps most memorably in Psalm 133: "How good and how pleasant it is that brothers dwell together."

Religious authorities either led the established exilic communities or were incorporated into ruling structures headed by political or commercial figures. Rabbinic Judaism

did not even need to be designated as Orthodox until competing denominations began to arise in the early nineteenth century. Tragedy, too, reinforced religious power, because until
the Holocaust every massacre, expulsion, pogrom, or atrocity
was interpreted at least partially as divine punishment for sin.
The solution, then, consisted of more observance, not less.

The coming of modernism to Europe shook the existing models of community. Liberated politically by emancipation and intellectually by the Enlightenment, Jews no longer
clung together by historical instinct. In both Hungary and
Germany in the 1800s, Orthodox Jews formally severed themselves from nationwide Jewish councils rather than share
power with less observant or secular brethren. The rabbinical
leaders had gone in a relative instant from being the guarantors
of unity to the advocates of fragmentation, the pluralists of
their era.

America shattered what was left of the traditional communal structure. There was no such thing in the United States
as the concept of a national minority with the right to levy its
own taxes. Religious rites like circumcision and institutions
such as the ritual bath fell under the oversight of municipal
health departments. And the Jews who streamed out of Europe,
as we have already seen, were largely those inclined to replace
the old creed with Zionism or socialism or Reform Judaism or
just plain individualism. On American shores, mutual contempt separated German Jews from Eastern Europeans. In the
garment industry, the economic lifeblood of immigrants, Jews
manned both sides of the barricade dividing labor from management. The Conservative movement, an American inven-
tion, inserted itself into the rivalry between Reform and
Orthodoxy that had been transplanted from Europe.

For all that contentiousness, there persisted in American Jewry an undiminished impulse toward community. The
question was what could provide the sense of common purpose
and shared destiny. There was no lack of Jewish organizations;
New York alone counted 3,500 in 1909. On a national level, an

alphabet soup of committees and congresses and agencies were vying for primacy by 1920. B'nai B'rith aspired to combine the fellowship of a fraternal lodge with the substance of Jewish heritage, having members welcome one another with a secret handshake and the Yiddish greeting *Shalom aleichem*. But the mere fact that each chapter selected its members, all of them male at that, meant B'nai B'rith could never encompass the full breadth of American Jewry.

The apparent solution was inspired in 1908, when New York's police commissioner, one Theodore Bingham, claimed in a magazine article that half the city's criminals were Jews. Both the bigotry of the charge and the failure of a fractious Jewish populace to forcefully respond to it struck a rabbi named Judah Magnes. Starting with his own uncommonly wide network of acquaintances, which ranged from the German Jewish gentry in his congregation at Temple Emanuel to Zionists, Yiddishists, and Hasidim, he began to assemble a New World version of the traditional community structure known as a *kehillah*. It very closely followed the European model—an elected board of elders, a stratum of paid administrators, and a base of voluntary associations—even as it adopted the American belief in the "scientific" delivery of social welfare services. During its eleven years of operation, the New York *kehillah* mediated labor strife, operated synagogues, provided relief and education. By 1920, however, even Magnes found it impossible to hold together a coalition that stretched from rabbis to magnates to rabble-rousers, and the *kehillah* disbanded.

One of its alumni, Mordecai Kaplan, then assumed the task of defining an American version of Jewish community. Like Magnes, Kaplan touched multiple bases—as the product of a family of Lithuanian Talmudists, as a Zionist, as an Orthodox rabbi who broke with the movement to adopt Conservatism. He expressed his overarching idea in the title of his 1934 manifesto: *Judaism as a Civilization*. In practice, this meant orienting Jewish life around "synagogue-centers" like his own Society for the Advancement of Judaism, which placed under one roof worship, recreation, cultural programs, and so-cial service, anything that might attract a Jew. "Some basis for creative unity among Jews has to be found," Kaplan wrote, "that will not require anyone to surrender his convictions, or do violence to his conscience."

Kaplan never envisioned that American Jews would co-alesce more often in distress than in celebration. The binding force in their lives would be the danger to Jews abroad. And the dominant way of aiding them would be by donating money. What might be called the "crisis model" of community let American Jews act on some of their faith's imperatives—to be thy brother's keeper, to engage in the communal charity known as *tzedakah*—and simultaneously to show their gratitude for the safety and freedom of the United States. It reconciled Jew-ish loyalty to those potential opposites, tribe and nation. And it effaced the usual barriers between denomination and denomi-nation, between secularist and pietist.

The crisis model had its origin on the day in August 1914 when the American Jewish philanthropist Jacob Schiff re-ceived a cable from the U.S. ambassador in Turkey, Henry Morgenthau, asking him to raise $50,000 in relief for Jews being persecuted by a hostile Ottoman regime in Palestine. As World War I engulfed Europe, cries from the Jewish commu-nities in Russia and Poland reached the United States, too, and before long money was being raised separately by three differ-ent segments of American Jewry—the German Jewish grandees, the socialists, and the Orthodox. Despite their divi-sions, the factions agreed to a plan to funnel all their philan-thropy into a single new agency. It was entitled the American Jewish Joint Distribution Committee, and its unifying role was best expressed by the shorthand with which millions of Ameri-can Jews would refer to it: The Joint.

By the end of World War I, the Joint had spent $16 mil-lion on soup kitchens, hospitals, orphan care, family reunifica-tion, and refugee resettlement, among other programs. The famine and political turbulence in Eastern Europe over the next decade kept the Joint operating, and in 1929 it officially changed from being an emergency organization to a permanent one with an annual fund-raising campaign. The Joint made Jewish consensus as possible as could be. It offered material help to Jews abroad, rather than promoting any potentially divisive political agenda. It did not insist, like the Zionist movement, that American Jews give up their comforts for pioneer life in Palestine. And it asked only for money, not belief in a doctrine.

Within a handful of years in the forties, communal charity took on the status of a moral imperative. The Holocaust and the establishment of Israel, as the scholar Jacob Neusner has written, together formed an epic of destruction and redemption that explained to American Jews "why, in a free society, a person should be part of the Jewish people." Between 1939 and 1943, before the full dimensions of the Nazi genocide were widely known, American Jews donated about $8 million a year to the Joint. Between 1945 and 1948, a period spanning war's end and Israeli statehood, the figure soared to $50 million a year.

By then, the Joint was being supplanted and subsumed by the United Jewish Appeal and its network of local federations. To the ancient practice of *tzedakah* the UJA brought the sophisticated elements of modern fund-raising—advertising, phone banks, direct-mail. But nothing worked as well as trouble abroad. Donations to the UJA rose dramatically in the wake of Israel's 1967 and 1973 wars. The campaign to rescue Soviet Jewry, launched by a small cadre of Jewish students, was adopted (or coopted) by the philanthropic establishment. By the late nineties, the UJA was raising close to $1 billion a year. Asked the secret of the charity's success, one senior official explained, "First you need two thousand years of Jewish suffering."

Nowhere was the importance of tragedy to Jewish community more evident than in attitudes about the Holocaust. Throughout the fifties, when memories of the Final Solution were fresh, American Jews rarely discussed it; they shared in the American understanding of World War II as a triumph over tyranny. Only with two events in Israel—the 1961 trial of the captured Nazi official Adolf Eichmann and the Six-Day War—did American Jewish attention turn belatedly to the slain six million. Once it did, though, it turned with a passion. From Dallas to Boston, from Tucson to Washington, Jewish philanthropy endowed memorials, museums, libraries, and professorships devoted to the Holocaust. Jewish consumers helped to make commercial blockbusters out of such unlikely candidates as Steven Spielberg's film *Schindler's List*, Daniel Goldhagen's book *Hitler's Willing Executioners*, Art Spiegelman's illustrated memoir *Maus*. As membership waned in Hadassah and B'nai B'rith, for decades mainstays of communal life, the Simon Wiesenthal Center in Los Angeles, founded by and named for the Nazi-hunter, grew into the largest organization in American Jewry. Poll after poll of American Jews in the 1990s found that the Holocaust surpassed Israel, Judaism, or any other factor as the basis of Jewish identity.

For all its success, however, the crisis model left American Jewry with a deeply flawed style of community. It defined leadership less by Jewish knowledge or political skill than the biggest checkbook. "Wealth has replaced wisdom as a symbol of leadership," the journalist Gary Rosenblatt observed. "In the early twentieth century, men of affluence in a community lined up to see the rabbi; now rabbis line up to see the philanthropist."

And the crisis model did not foresee the day when crises lost their hold. It did not ask what else made a community of American Jews. What happened when the attachment to Israel dissipated? What happened when the generation that had lived through the Holocaust died off? What happened when the Reform and Conservative branches irreconcilably parted from Orthodoxy in their treatment of converts and women? What happened when America was America, equally tolerant of any mode of Jewish behavior from assimilation to separation?

•   •

ON THE SABBATH MORNING of September 6, 1986, two young strangers entered the Neve Shalom Synagogue in Istanbul just behind most of its modest congregation. Securing the doors with iron bars, they turned submachine guns and hand grenades on Jews whose ancestors had come to Turkey in flight from the Spanish Inquisition. Twenty-one worshippers died, four rabbis among them, in a synagogue whose Hebrew name meant "Place of Peace."

Nearly halfway around the world, in the suburb of Great Neck on Long Island, a Conservative rabbi named Mordecai Waxman began assembling a memorial service. He invited the clergy and laity of every Jewish congregation in town to join him in protest and mourning, as they had after similar terrorist attacks in the past. This time, however, two Orthodox synagogues refused to participate. The memorial service was to include the funeral prayer—*El Moleh Rachamim*, God, Full of Mercy—and Orthodox Jews would not pray in a congregation like Rabbi Waxman's that seated men and women together. Only by removing worship from the memorial service was the rabbi finally able to persuade the Orthodox to attend.

What happened in Great Neck was a harbinger of things to come. In place of the ideal of a single American Jewish community, bound however tenuously by tragedy, there emerged two competing visions of community. One extolled Jewish peoplehood in all its variety; the other extolled religious tradition in all its certitude. One went by the slogan "pluralism," and the other by "unity." To its advocates, "pluralism" meant diversity and tolerance; to its critics, it meant relativism and disorder. To its advocates, "unity" meant unanimity under the banner of Torah; to its critics, it meant fundamentalists calling the shots. Underlying the struggle was a single question: What is it that makes the Jewish people a people?

"There are few places left in the religious Jewish world

where one can find mutual respect and love on the part of one Jew for another despite religious disagreement," the Modern Orthodox rabbi Haskel Lookstein has said. "Indeed, looking at the Jewish community in America these days, I understand as never before the frightening words we recite on the eve of Rosh Hashanah: *'Paninu l'yemin v'ein ozer; l'smol v'ein somech'*—'I turn to the right and there is no support; to the left and there is no encouragement.' "

Great Neck embarked on the debate between unity and pluralism earlier than most places, but the evidence of it spread across the landscape of Jewish America. It could be found in Teaneck, New Jersey, and New Rochelle, New York, in battles over synagogue expansion. It could be found in Willamette, Oregon, whose single shul for a half-century broke into feuding congregations of Orthodox and Reconstructionists. It could be found in the 1997 campaign for seats in the World Zionist Congress, a kind of parliament for Diaspora Jewry, when Reform and Conservative organizations put hundreds of thousands of dollars into electing delegates pledged to pluralism. It could be found when an Orthodox coalition called Am Echad, One People, responded with full-page advertisements declaring, "Pluralism = Disunity."

Most of all, perhaps, it could be found in a suburb of Cleveland and in the lives there of two Jews.

A

CHAPTER SIX

Beachwood, Ohio, 1997–1999

DIVIDED BY ALLEGIANCE and an aisle, David Gottesman and Si Wachsberger awaited the vote of the Beachwood Planning and Zoning Commission on agenda item 96-63. Normally, a half-dozen spectators might sit through the commission's business of density, setbacks, and demolition permits. Tonight four hundred packed the recreation room of City Hall, scrambling to grab the last empty seats, milling three-deep along the rear windows. Television crews assembled along one wall, their satellite trucks idling in the parking lot.

Fifteen years of history led to the evening of March 27, 1997, when a Cleveland suburb that was 83 percent Jewish would decide whether to allow its Orthodox residents to construct several religious buildings. In the language of municipal land use, it required a shift in zoning from U-1, A-2 to U-5, from residential to institutional, from four unkempt houses and a stretch of brambly woods to a landscaped campus of two synagogues, two ritual baths, and a girls' day school. Nearly two hours into the meeting, the chairman polled his members.

Carlin, nay ... Davis, nay ... Gorden, nay ... Seconds later, when the roll call was over, all six members, every one a Jew, had voted against the Orthodox project.

Then, as David and Si watched in amazement from their separate stations, a man named Bob Stark catapulted out of his seat and rushed toward the dais. "This is Purim," he cried. "This is Purim all over again." He waved a foot-long *grogger*, the holiday noisemaker, and over its clack and rattle he shouted, "Haman! Haman!" Stark plopped himself in front of the commission as the crowd rose to its feet. "Shut up!" some hollered. "Go home!" A rabbi and the police chief descended on Stark, one offering solidarity, the other threatening arrest. And still he howled and twirled the *grogger*, a bar mitzvah present for his son, and played out his version of Mordecai in sackcloth and ashes outside the gates of Shushan, bewailing the threatened annihilation of the Jews.

David Gottesman and Si Wachsberger both knew the man and understood the reference to Purim. Stark had grown up with Si's kids, a playmate across the street long before he became a real estate developer and an observant Orthodox Jew. Now he served as vice president to David's president of the local Young Israel congregation. Stark had even tipped off David about tonight's plan, in hopes that he might want to join in a little civil disobedience.

Guerrilla theater wasn't David's style. He spoke with the calm, grainy tones that so comforted the patients in his medical practice. His lanky limbs moved with an athlete's unhurried grace. Behind his oval glasses, though, beneath his well-groomed dark-blond hair, he burned with a rage that made him root for Bob Stark. He'd devoted seven years of his own life to the campus project, seen the land bought, the architects hired, the papers filed and refiled to address every civic concern. Not once did he imagine that after all that Beachwood would say no. Now he knew why two of the zoning commissioners, both patients of his, had averted their eyes from his tonight.

Maybe it was a little hyperbolic, David had to admit, comparing them to Haman, the evil courtier who was Purim's villain. But hadn't it been hyperbolic, too, last week when one of the local foes of the campus, Jewish of course, had claimed it would turn Beachwood into "a little Jerusalem"? Here was David, who didn't wear a *kippa* on the job, whose wife didn't cover her hair, whose boys played in the local softball league, and his own neighbors were treating him like some black-hat in Mea Shearim, throwing rocks at Sabbath drivers.

Si Wachsberger strained his five-foot-six frame to take in the chaos. Never in thirty-seven years of public life in Beachwood, in hundreds of meetings as a member of the City Council and the Board of Education, had he seen anybody pull a stunt like Stark's, not even that ecology nut who ranted about saving the wetlands. Now Si could hear Stark wailing "We Shall Overcome." It was embarrassing to see a bright man, a professional, making a schmuck of himself. Besides, Si believed, it was bad politics.

Even at seventy-nine, his bald dome dotted with age spots, Si bubbled with the pep that had made him a high school cheerleader, then a college leader nicknamed the "Little Corporal." He had put much of his energy lately into assembling opposition to the Orthodox campus, and in a town where he was on a first-name basis with literally thousands of people he made a formidable persuader. He cast the issue as one of preserving Beachwood's residential character, similar to the battle a few years earlier against a shopping center. But the religious aspects were undeniable, and they galled Si. Just a few days before this meeting, a national association of Orthodox rabbis had denounced the Conservative and Reform movements as "not Judaism at all." Closer to home, the Orthodox rabbinate had barred Reform and Conservative clergy from performing conversions in every single *mikvah* in greater Cleveland, forcing them to drive sixty miles to Youngstown for immersion.

The last thing Si needed was a plunge in the *mikvah*. It was the principle that mattered. He'd won a community service award from Israel Bonds, served as executive director of his Reform temple for a decade, taught in its religious school for eight years. Who was anybody to tell him he wasn't Jewish enough? Or that he was some kind of Nazi? Yet the Young Israel rabbi had said exactly that tonight, telling a reporter from the *Plain Dealer,* "We were treated today like the Nazis of Germany treated us."

Toward ten o'clock, Si Wachsberger and David Gottesman reached their homes. Si had a ranch house with spacious yards for his gardening only a short drive from both City Hall and his temple. A mile away, in the Orthodox enclave that had sprung up within walking distance of Young Israel, David owned a 5,600-square-foot battleship of a place, expanded over the years to suit both his growing family and his prospering practice. A neighbor, one of the few who wasn't Orthodox, approached David on the driveway to apologize for the whole tone of the debate. That was cold comfort; the man had already signed a petition against the campus. Meanwhile, Si flipped on the television in his living room and saw Bob Stark's protest replayed on the news. The vote against the campus may have been unanimous, but Si had no illusions that the issue was done with.

Si's political instincts, as usual, would prove correct. The years ahead held lawsuits, lawn signs, more petitions, more clamor at meetings of the zoning commission and City Council, albeit never again with a *grogger.* Beachwood would even hold a municipal plebiscite to try to settle the land-use dispute. It resisted resolution by all of those means because the issue wasn't truly about land use at all. Agenda item 96-63, the Orthodox campus, was about a clash of lives and causes and visions of Judaism, the archetypes of pluralism and unity personified by Si Wachsberger and David Gottesman.

NEARING HIS NINTH DECADE, a grandfather of three, Si Wachsberger lived within ten miles of his birthplace. The proximity of past and present belied the true distance he had traveled, and in his own social mobility he found confirmation of the American promise.

Si was born in 1918 to parents scaling their way out of immigrant poverty. His mother, Ida, had come to Cleveland from Minsk at the turn of the century to join a father peddling fish from a horse-drawn cart; his, father, Adolph, arriving as a child from Austro-Hungary, dropped out of school in Cleveland after fourth grade to start working as a delivery boy for National Biscuit. By the time Si himself was five, though, Adolph Wachsberger had saved enough money to open a shoe store, and a year later he moved his family out of the city to the industrial suburb of East Cleveland. Growing up amid Italians and Poles, Irish and Bohemians, Si never knew the Jewish ghetto as anything but a place to visit.

He returned to the Jewish neighborhood of Glenville for Sabbath dinners with his maternal grandparents in their crowded frame house across the street from a bathhouse, a *schvitz*. His grandmother Gittel fussed over him, giving him first crack at *grivetz*, the chicken skin fried crisp in chicken fat, and ending his meal with cherry preserves swirled into a glass of tea. Sated and drowsy, Si would nap on a bed of pillows spread across several chairs. And when his parents woke Si for the trip home, Gittel would send him off with a kiss, a prayer for his safe return next week, and some advice. "Don't be a horse-and-buggy peddler," she told him. "Be a rabbi."

Precocious though Si was in Hebrew school, Gittel was wishing against the tide of history. The Wachsberger family belonged to a Conservative synagogue in Cleveland Heights, while Gittel remained tied to a tiny Orthodox *shtibel*. Because Ida didn't keep kosher, Gittel refused to eat in her daughter's home. Adolph opened his shoe store every Saturday, his best day for business, and from age ten Si was working there— sweeping the floor, waiting on customers, reorganizing stray shoes, counting down the minutes till eight o'clock closing and the reward of a corned beef sandwich at Benkovitz's. In later years, Adolph opened a second store on Cleveland's eastern fringe, where his regulars included farmers who bartered apples or potatoes for footwear. "I don't care if you lose a sale," Si's father often instructed him. "But never lose a customer."

In East Cleveland, a town generally inhospitable to Jewish home buyers, Si found only acceptance. For solidarity's sake, he concocted an imitation fraternity with a handful of Jewish friends at Shaw High School; the boys even ordered their own rings. But he also joined the tennis team, the cheerleading squad, the school newspaper, even the Esperanto Club. To his knowledge, he was the first Jewish student ever admitted to Hi-Y, a service club associated with the YMCA. The star of Shaw's football team, Tony Guadio, brought Si home to be stuffed with pasta by his mother. "I knew I was different," Si recalled years later, "but I never felt a finger pointing at me."

Graduating from Shaw in 1936, Si chose a college where, once more, he would form part of a tiny Jewish minority. Yet at Miami University in the small southern Ohio town of Oxford, ten miles from the nearest synagogue, yearning for salamis shipped from home, Si again flourished. His immediate circle consisted of Jewish classmates in the Zeta Beta Tau frat, scrappy city kids who made the intramural finals in basketball. Campus life, though, only started there for Si. Delivering student laundry, setting up bleachers in the gym, serving food in the commissary, editing the college paper in tweed coat and pocket square, Si made himself ubiquitous. When his classmates named him chairman of the junior prom, he delivered a battle of the bands pitting Dick Stabile's against Count Basie's. (It ended in a draw.) Si left Miami as the first Jew nominated by the university for the Omicron Delta Kappa honor society, the crowning achievement of what he called "the happiest time of my life."

It was a charmed life for its era, a life without much whiff of anti-Semitism, not even that Jewish rite of passage of being chased home from school by some roughneck calling you a Christ-killer. Si's spunk and athleticism and the salesman's charm he had learned from his father had granted him safe passage through a gentile world. And if his trip into the mainstream proceeded with particular dispatch, it nonetheless typified the kind of acceptance that most of Cleveland's Jews would ultimately achieve.

In a city where topography dictated status, Jewish immigrants started out on the lowlands between the Cuyahoga River's banks and the Lake Erie shoreline. There two Jewish grocers from Breslau settled in 1836, when Cleveland was barely forty years old and still part of the Western Reserve. For nearly a half-century thereafter, Germans comprised the bulk of the Jewish community, some peddling dry goods, some trading with Indians for pelts, the most successful opening garment factories that sewed Union uniforms in the Civil War.

The Jewish community numbered just 3,500 of Cleveland's 160,000 residents in 1880, and yet it was substantial enough to lay claim to the Lower Woodland district, well suited to Jewish merchants because of its nearness to the Central Market, and able to establish a distinct religious identity. Between the German roots of Reform Judaism and Cleveland's nearness to Cincinnati, the "Jerusalem of the West" where the Reform movement had its American seminary, Lower Woodland offered fertile ground for Reform temples. Two of the most enduring in the city had opened by 1850, and it sometimes seemed that Anshe Chesed and Tifereth Israel were competing to see which could throw off more of the old ways faster—banning *kippot*, sermonizing in English, retaining organists and choirs, installing stained-glass windows by Tiffany, celebrating the Sabbath on Sunday.

As the German Jews moved outward and upward into Cleveland Heights, immigrants from Russia, Poland, and Hungary teemed into the old neighborhoods and formed new ones all through Cleveland's East Side, raising the city's Jewish population to 71,000 by 1926. Cigar makers and garment workers rented flats on the maple-lined streets of Mount Pleasant, building in the Socialist Hall and the Workmen's Circle the institutions of their left-wing *Yiddishkeit*. Small shopkeepers favored Glenville, originally a streetcar suburb but by the twenties a cacophonous jumble of tailor shops, rag peddlers, bakeries, fruit vendors, kids chasing ice wagons, and barbershops fronting for card games. The Eastern Europeans brought with them an infusion of Orthodoxy, establishing two dozen Orthodox synagogues by 1920 and sixty-seven kosher butchers by 1945. And the tension between Germans and Eastern Europeans, a staple of the American Jewish experience, ensued. A German Jewish teacher in 1895 disparaged Cleveland's Eastern European immigrants as "bigoted followers of the orthodox rabbinical law [and] uneducated paupers ... whose minds are stunted [and] whose characters are warped."

In fundamental ways, though, the Eastern Europeans followed the German Jewish formula of affluence and assimilation. Cleveland's leading rabbis were Reform and Conservative figures like Barnett Brickner and Solomon Goldman, who preached Americanization as much as Torah. The most influential pulpit of all lay within the ivied edifice of Glenville High School, where a Maine Yankee called Harry M. Towne and the minister's daughter Elsie Davies presided as administrators over the ambitions of a student body that was 90 percent Jewish. This generation, the American-born children of shtetl immigrants, traced the German Jewish route from Lower Woodland eastward to Glenville and Mount Pleasant and finally into Cleveland Heights. And they did so with a haste and completeness striking even by the standards of postwar America. Of the 85,000 Jews in the Cleveland area in 1960, the sixth-largest Jewish community in the nation, only 10 percent remained in the city. The rest, Si Wachsberger among them, had already climbed the hill into suburbia.

Not even World War II had changed Si's fundamental optimism. He enlisted in late 1940, two years before the first authoritative reports about the Nazis' mass murder of Jews reached America, and he spent the war far from any atrocities, initially as a staff sergeant with a hospital unit in New Guinea and then as a bombardier trainer in California. The only injury he suffered was a sprained leg from tripping into a foxhole. In March 1943, while American B-17s were bombing arms factories in Germany, Si married a builder's daughter named Shirley Pollack at Cleveland's Statler Hotel. By V-J Day in August 1945, they had an infant son, Donald.

The new family lived with Shirley's parents in Cleveland Heights from 1945 until 1948, while Si managed classified ads for a weekly newspaper. Next came three years in Detroit, as he worked Michigan as a traveling neckwear salesman. Packing his Nash with a samples case and filling a notebook with details about his customers—who was bald, who wore glasses, who had a mustache—Si reveled in his ability to win business across the lines of religion and ethnicity. Business was trust, and trust was friendship. Still, with two more sons, Ken and Jeffrey, born by 1951, Si longed to get off the road and return home to Cleveland. He borrowed money to launch his own clothing store, naming it the Oxford Shop after his college town, not the British university. And he decided to move into a suburb called Beachwood.

It was not the most obvious choice for a Jew. The established Jewish destinations, Cleveland Heights and University Heights, had the temples, the delis, the fine public schools. Beachwood remained a scattering of farmsteads and subdivisions separated by woods thick with deer and fox. With just 1,800 residents spread over nearly five square miles, it lacked a high school, a first-aid squad, a commuter railroad stop. And Beachwood was known to steer Jewish home buyers north of Fairmount Boulevard, the road that bisected town, because the southern part bordered on Shaker Heights, a garden suburb whose meticulous planning included restrictive covenants against selling property to Jews.

But Si had a friend from Miami University, Robert Goulder, who had just moved into Beachwood. There was plenty of undeveloped land in town, and Si preferred buying a bare lot to an existing house, since Shirley's father could build a custom home for them. He was not unaware of the reality of anti-Semitism. He knew the places that would not have his kind—the country club in Pepper Pike, the City Club downtown. Several of Shirley's relatives in Hungary, Si learned after World War II, had perished in the concentration camps. He belonged to a Conservative synagogue and sent his older boys to its Hebrew school. But his Jewish identity was not defined by Christian enemies. Beachwood touched his memories of crossing borders, of pasta with Tony Guadio's family, of farmers trading fruit for shoes, of Hi-Y and Omicron Delta Kappa, of hitchhiking together on army leave with an Arkansas country boy named Bill Cherry. Where other Jews feared resistance and hostility in Beachwood, Si anticipated America in its polyglot glory. "I didn't want to move into a totally Jewish neighborhood," he said years later. "I didn't want my kids to think that all of life was like that. I wanted them to go out into the world and mix with people of all cultures. Because if you're exposed to them, you're enriched by them."

So Si paid about $30,000 to have his father-in-law build a four-bedroom Colonial with fieldstone facing, hardwood cabinets, and a fireplace. He planted oaks in front and pines in back and kept both yards unfenced. The Wachsberger home, 2574 Edgewood, became the neighborhood hub for barbecues and baseball games and Ping-Pong. As it happened, two of the next families to move onto the block were Jewish, too, Weinstein the furrier and the Freibergs, who ran a hardware store. But Si didn't particularly notice Beachwood becoming more Jewish. And nothing in his own experience led him to believe the gentiles noticed, either. Then Anshe Chesed, the oldest Reform temple in greater Cleveland, decided to move into town.

In the late forties, as its members migrated east and its Cleveland neighborhood corroded, Anshe Chesed purchased thirty-one acres of land along Fairmount Boulevard. Three years later, the congregation applied to have the parcel changed from residential zoning to institutional so it could build a temple. Living a few blocks away from the site, Si attended a few neighborhood meetings to voice concerns about traffic. The proposed temple, after all, would spread over 160,000 square feet, with seating for almost 3,000 worshippers and a parking lot for 300 cars. Si envisioned his block of Edgewood as a honking, idling mess every Saturday. But when temple officials agreed to route the cars from their parking lot onto Fairmount rather than the residential streets, Si counted himself satisfied and assumed the issue was settled.

Instead, the Beachwood council, none of its members Jewish, rejected the temple's application in early 1952. Officially, it claimed Anshe Chesed "would be detrimental to the public safety, welfare, and convenience of the village." Beneath such formality lay the fear of an alien influx. Only twenty of Anshe Chesed's member families lived in Beachwood; many of the other 1,800 were bound to move into town if the temple did. In May 1952, shortly after Anshe Chesed announced its intention to sue Beachwood, residents opened their mailboxes to find a white-supremacist newspaper called *The Plain Truth*. "The battle is on," read a card accompanying the paper. "No longer should we sit idly by and watch our country being taken from us. Act now. Let not the Jew plan succeed."

Confronted for the first time in his life by organized anti-Semitism, Si felt revulsion but not fear. There was a difference between discomfort and persecution, and he put anonymous hate mail, however odious, in the category of an aberration. When a Jewish neighbor worried aloud about the Reform temple being defeated, Si assured him, "Not in America."

Try as Beachwood's leaders might, they could never push the debate back to traffic congestion and square footage, and the association of their stance with anti-Semitism, no longer a respectable belief, sealed their defeat. The Cuyahoga County Court of Common Pleas ordered Beachwood to issue a building permit in late 1952. When the village council sought a reversal, the county Court of Appeals upheld the lower court in a scathing decision. "How is it possible to hold that a religious institution which has been for 100 years one of the outstanding centers of religious education in Cleveland . . . does not serve the public welfare," the three-judge panel stated in a unanimous decision. "Every religious institution contributes to the common good or general welfare of the whole community, even though it be attended by a particular group or is denominational in character. A democratic society . . . cannot succeed without the moral and spiritual influence of the church."

Encouraged by the ruling—by a court that, as Si predicted, had declared, "Not in America"—Jews flocked to Beachwood. Suburban Temple, a Reform congregation, opened in 1954. Anshe Chesed broke ground in April 1955. Just across the street from Beachwood in University Heights, another Reform temple, Emanu El, was dedicated in the mid-fifties. Tifreth Israel, which had begun more than a century earlier as an offshoot from Anshe Chesed, followed it to Beachwood in 1969. Conservative and Orthodox synagogues came in later years, along with a Jewish community center, two Jewish retirement homes, a Jewish adult-education center, and a nondenominational Jewish day school. The open fields that had enticed Si Wachsberger yielded to bulldozers' jaws, and ranches and Colonials filled the town from border to border. The population reached 4,900 in 1958 and 10,700 in 1990, and by 1996 the proportion of Jews had risen to 83 percent.

In booming Beachwood, Reform temples set the tone. Once the province of German elites, they now appealed to Si's generation of Eastern European stock, culturally Jewish but willingly liberated from the strictures of Orthodoxy. The Reform temples, like the malls springing up in Cleveland's suburbs, offered a kind of one-stop shopping—Hebrew school for the children, a social hall for wedding and bar mitzvah receptions, the Sisterhood Gift Shop, the Men's Club with its softball team and fishing outing. Worship was in some ways the least significant aspect of the temples' appeal. Fairmount Temple, as Anshe Chesed renamed itself, counted 5,400 members, yet fewer than 400 attended Sabbath services. For the Jews of postwar Beachwood, Saturday meant sandlot football or matinees at the Cedar-Lee Theater.

Si himself joined Fairmount in the late fifties out of both commitment and convenience. It made more sense to have Shirley walk their older boys, Donald and Ken, there for Hebrew school than drive them forty minutes round-trip to Cleveland Heights with the younger kids, Jeffrey and Bob, whining the whole way from the back seat. Si began teaching Jewish history and literature in Fairmount's Hebrew school, taking the assignment so seriously that he wrote two different scripts for each lesson "in case the first one bombed." He had his pupils trace Jewish immigration through their own family tree; he held a mock trial of a Nazi war criminal. Truthfully, though, he belonged to temple as much for the children as for himself or Shirley. They expressed their Jewishness through B'nai B'rith, Israel Bonds, and Hadassah, rarely going to services except on the High Holy Days. Si disdained pork, but it was getting harder to resist the shrimp at Bamboo Gardens. At least the Reform movement had dropped kashrut ages ago.

If the Reform temples lacked a certain spiritual intensity, they imbued Beachwood with a set of social values that conformed precisely to Si's own, emphasizing community service and political liberalism and frowning on any expression of clannishness. In the early fifties, Si successfully campaigned for Beachwood to construct its own middle and high schools and helped defeat an attempt by the southern part of town, still largely gentile, to secede from the school system. Beachwood elected its first three Jewish members to the village council in 1956, and the next year Si was appointed to a vacant seat on the Board of Education. So began a career of community service that would include fourteen years on the school board, twenty-four on the City Council, membership in the Beachwood Arts Council, and the sponsorship of innumerable Little League teams. Si not only welcomed a foreign-exchange student, a Dutch Christian, into his home for a year, but grew so active in the American Field Service that he and Shirley wound up leading the local chapter. He was, in adult form, still the indefatigable "Little Corporal" of Miami University, and his life aptly represented his hometown. As sectarian as Beachwood could be—a place where even the volunteer firemen were Jewish, where people ended anecdotes by saying, "It was just my *mazel*"—the suburb prided itself on public services: the school system, cultural center, day camp, municipal pool. The most revered rabbi in the community, Arthur Lelyveld of Fairmount Temple, earned national renown for his involvement in the civil rights movement.

Si had first heard Lelyveld preach back in the thirties as a rabbinical student leading High Holy Day services in Hamilton, Ohio, the closest town to Miami with a synagogue. A quarter-century later, Si retained an acolyte's awe every time Lelyveld opened a sermon with his trademark words, "My dear ones." The rabbi represented erudition and integrity to Si, but also just plain guts. When Lelyveld returned from registering black voters in Mississippi in 1964, bloodied from a beating with tire irons, Si was filled with pride that "someone I knew had the nerve to do what he did."

That same year, though, Si and the rabbi had a revealing public flap. Si and Shirley were attending a dinner honoring Fairmount's confirmation class, which included his son Ken, and Si took the occasion to encourage the teenagers to continue their religious education. Realistically, he knew how many Fairmount kids stopped after their bar or bat mitzvah, much less their confirmation. At least give Hebrew high school a try, he told them, before making any final decisions.

Rabbi Lelyveld, following Si at the podium, informed the students, "I only want you to come back next year if you're willing to commit to the following." Then he ran down a list of religious texts and obligations. Too many demands, Si feared as he listened; he could just sense the teenagers thinking, No way. After the dinner ended and the families moved toward the parking lot, he told Rabbi Lelyveld, "You sabotaged me."

Or perhaps Lelyveld had challenged him. The rabbi was placing religion at the center of Jewish identity, while Si considered it one optional element. Reaching middle age in the early sixties, decades removed from his grandmother Gittel's prayers, he didn't even know if he believed in God anymore. But he did believe in being Jewish, and he thought of being Jewish as something apart from piety. "It's a common culture," he later said. "My whole life, I was surrounded by friends and relatives who are Jewish. Having Passover dinner together, going to synagogue on the High Holy Days—enjoyable things you did with people you loved. Being Jewish is the experiences and beliefs you share without even thinking about it."

DAVID GOTTESMAN grew up with the proof of Jewish vulnerability tattooed on his mother's forearm. The Nazis had sent her from Czechoslovakia to Auschwitz as a sixteen-year-old girl, and by the time of liberation two years later she had lost her father, her brother, and her faith in humanity. She made her way back to Prague after the war, reuniting with her mother and sister, who also survived the camps, and several years later met an American butcher named Milton Gottesman who was visiting his Czech relatives. Her relocation to America, though, proved an equivocal kind of deliverance.

Erna and Milton had just one child, David, and they raised him in what might have seemed the idyllic setting of Fairfield, Connecticut. From its salt marshes to its pine-topped hills, Fairfield exuded Yankee spirit. The American Legion post decorated a billboard with the Pledge of Allegiance in foot-high letters. Allington's served hot fudge sundaes with homemade ice cream. At the northern end of town, in the Stratfield neighborhood, Jewish families like the Gottesmans were crossing over from crumbling Bridgeport, planting their flag in suburbia. Most of David's friends belonged to Reform or Conservative congregations. Even though the Gottesmans observed kashrut at home, Milton owned a nonkosher shop with a suitably New England name, Boston Beef. At the Orthodox synagogue the family attended, Ahavath Achim, the rabbi used a microphone, let his flock drive to Sabbath services, and paused in davening to smile at women across the *mechitzah.*

No amount of Americanization, though, could strip the numbers off Erna Gottesman's arm. And her mother, similarly branded, lived for long periods with the family. David had a few friends at synagogue, like him the children of survivors, whose parents warned, "Make sure you have a passport in the house. Make sure you have money in gold." Erna did not issue alarms quite so dramatic, if only because her depression precluded such defiant paranoia. Outside the house, she could attract admiring stares as a comely brunette; when David brought classmates over, she could delight them with homemade cake. After she packed the leftovers and bade the kids good-bye, however, after the world shrank back to her and Milton and David, the curtain descended. She spoke to her husband in Yiddish, to her mother in Hungarian, and to her son in evasions. David never heard from her about Auschwitz or life before it. He did not know enough even to ask the right questions.

Erna's silence echoed a larger one. During David's early childhood, the years before the Adolf Eichmann trial in Israel thrust the Holocaust onto the world stage, American Jews consigned it to the past. Elie Wiesel's memoir *Night* sold barely a thousand copies in the first eighteen months after its 1959 publication. Survivors like Erna Gottesman lived with the conviction that, as a character in one of Wiesel's novels said, "You'll speak, but your words will fall onto deaf ears. You'll try to incite people to learn from the past. . . . They will refuse to believe you." So, lacking his mother's words, David read her face, and from its dour creases he interpreted the lesson of her life. "The whole world is anti-Semitic," as he put it later, "and Jews have to look out for each other."

His closest friends were Jewish kids, and so were most of his classmates in the college-prep track. When Erna's mother died in 1961 and she returned in grief to *shomer Shabbos* observance, he followed her example. At age twelve, still too young to count in a minyan, he knocked on doors around the neighborhood every Sabbath morning to ensure that Ahavath Achim would have a prayer quorum. He forsook school dances on Friday night, football games on Saturday afternoons, television and driving from sundown Friday until *havdalah*. For years, he had been carrying a bag lunch to school every day, not because the cafeteria food was lousy but because it was *treif.*

All those duties left David both prideful and alone. He had been reared with the concept of *za'shtil*. Literally it meant "be quiet," and by inference those words spoke to Jewish existence in America: *We're only guests here. It's a wonderful country, but don't make waves.* And yet, by following the mitzvot, David was sticking out, separating himself from the teenage mainstream of cheeseburgers and joyrides. At his lowest point, he felt himself "an oddball, a freak." He never seriously considered relaxing his observance, though, merely to fit in. His obligations went to the Torah, the tradition, and a more immediate authority, his mother.

When David described himself years later as having been a mama's boy, he didn't mean prissy or soft—in fact, growing to a lean six-foot-two, he thrived on sports—but preternaturally obedient. To misbehave, he understood as the child of a survivor, was not merely to anger or disappoint his mother; it was to lay more pain on a life already burdened with too much. He was the only child; he was the only link; he was the reason Erna had survived Auschwitz. So David eschewed beer and fast cars. He returned from dates before curfew and respected the virtue of girls he took out. Not a naturally brilliant student, as his SAT score in the 1200s attested, he drove himself to a perfect 4.0 grade-point and the standing of number-one rank in his class.

Instead of claiming his place in the American meritocracy by joining the Jewish influx to the Ivy League, he applied to Yeshiva University early-decision. There was a certain kind of prestige in the Modern Orthodox world to enrolling at Yeshiva when secular renown was possible; observant Jews of David's generation talked in hushed reverence about how Steven Riskin, the rabbi at Lincoln Square in Manhattan, had turned down Harvard, *Harvard*, for Y.U. David saw his own choice more in terms of comfort than status.

The summer David turned fourteen, he went for the first time to Camp Morasha, which was run by Yeshiva University. The Hebrew word *morasha* means "inheritance," and Morasha inherited its style from a Religious Zionist camp called Masad. But where Masad infused its young people with the fervor for Israel, Morasha exuded the *ruach*, the spirit, of Modern Orthodoxy. Yeshiva sent several dozen of its brightest young rabbis, including the university's future president Norman Lamm, to teach Talmud and Torah amid the Poconos' pines. The camp rang with music, whether it was the boys and girls competing in a *zimriyah*, a festival of song, or the folkies who called themselves the Rabbis' Sons. Morasha's best basketball players delighted in taking on not only other camps but the Lake Como townies, even if defeating them once brought retribution in the form of slashed tires. At Camp Morasha, being young and Orthodox was most definitely not being a nerd.

After all the isolation David had known as one of the rare Orthodox kids in Fairfield, now he found himself surrounded by a bunk of them, a softball team of them, a dining hall of them. He could choose friends by shared interests rather than on "the basis of who would tolerate me." Mostly city kids educated in Modern Orthodox day schools, the Morasha campers by their example pointed David toward Yeshiva for college.

Yeshiva expanded the Orthodox community around David from four hundred campers to eight thousand students. They saw no contradiction in wearing Converse high-tops and a *kippa*, tzitzis beneath a peacoat. You could grab pizza at Chopsie's or a burger at Parker's; you could bring your coins to

Nocki Nosh, the only kosher automat in New York. Sixty blocks north of Columbia, where the student takeover in 1968 defined an era of campus revolts, Yeshiva protested the Vietnam War with calculated self-restraint; to attack Nixon too strongly for one foreign intervention against Communism, it was understood, could undermine Israel. Just weeks after the invasion of Cambodia and the Kent State shootings, the apogee of campus radicalism, David Gottesman flew to Israel to volunteer for the summer as a hospital orderly. Instead of a chapter of the Students for a Democratic Society, Yeshiva boasted thriving branches of the Jewish Defense League and the Student Struggle for Soviet Jewry, and the refuseniks' cause united Jewish generations and denominations beneath banners that David, as Erna's son, could especially admire—"Never Again," "Let Them Go," "Weren't Six Million Enough?"

Surrounded by fellow Jews, David no longer needed to bow to *za'shtil*. He won the presidency of the sophomore class, served as secretary-treasurer of the student council. He began dating a student from Stern College, the women's division of Yeshiva, a tall, striking Venezuelan named Jenny Weinstock. Meanwhile, with the same kind of concentration that had made him high school valedictorian, he graduated a year ahead of his class and in 1971 earned admission to New York University's medical school. The homogeneity of Yeshiva, far from limiting David, had liberated him. "The best, absolutely the best," he said later of his college years. "I could be who I wanted to be. I was free."

By early 1978, with medical school complete and a residency at Bellevue Hospital ending, David was applying for fellowships in his chosen specialty of gastroenterology. He and Jenny, now married almost five years and the parents of a two-year-old daughter, intended to stay in the Northeast, close to their friends, family, and Jewish life. But one morning when Jenny was pushing Deborah's stroller across a footbridge near NYU Medical School to mail David's application to Yale University Hospital, a man robbed her at knifepoint. She had been mugged that way once before, walking with David in Riverside Park. The Gottesmans decided right then to get far away from New York.

The University Hospitals complex in Cleveland offered David a fellowship in gastroenterology. Moving to a strange place with a second daughter, Jessica, just three weeks old, David looked to the Orthodox community for a foothold. A couple of Yeshiva classmates, natives of the Cleveland area, steered the family to Cleveland Heights and the Young Israel of Cleveland, which had branches both in the Heights and South Euclid. The Gottesmans rented a home nearly a mile from the Cleveland Heights synagogue, making the Sabbath trek with children miserable during the Midwestern winters. And yet again, violence altered their path. A neighbor in Cleveland Heights was murdered on Halloween of 1978. When the time came to buy a house, David looked two towns east, in Beach-wood.

It was not the most obvious choice for an Orthodox Jew. As Jewish as Beachwood had become, David knew of only ten Orthodox families in town. The one Orthodox shul, Green Road Synagogue, was the domain of an aging congregation of Hungarian immigrants that used a Sephardic liturgy unfa-miliar to David. Besides, he couldn't afford most of the suit-able homes on the market. It looked as if he and Jenny, far from having nestled into an Orthodox community, would have to uproot themselves again when his fellowship con-cluded.

David was confessing his frustrations during a *sheva bruchot*, a party with a minyan that is held for a married couple on each of the seven days after their wedding, when a stranger named Alan Soclof said he had the perfect house. As Soclof de-scribed the place, David realized he had already seen it and ruled it out as too expensive at $148,000. Soclof proceeded to advise David how to negotiate, ultimately driving the price down to $116,000, and in April 1980 the Gottesmans moved to Beachwood.

What struck David about the episode wasn't the house as much as Soclof's instinctive kindness. He had done a favor for David simply because they were both Orthodox. Here was the type of community David had been seeking. As it turned out, Soclof's parents had run a small Orthodox synagogue colloquially known as the Redwood Shul in the old Glenville neighborhood. Now Alan's twin brother Ivan, a real estate developer, was president of Young Israel of Cleveland and lived in Beachwood. And a steady if slight number of young Orthodox families were settling along the western border, a few blocks from the Green Road Synagogue and a longer, though not impossible, walk to the Young Israel congregations in Cleveland Heights and South Euclid.

David found friends like himself, Modern Orthodox professionals in their thirties—professors of chemistry and economics, a dermatology resident, an endocrinologist. They played touch football and racquetball together; with their wives they went boating on Sunday afternoons at West Branch State Park. And, of course, they davened, often in a local rabbi's *shtibel*. Everyone had learning; everyone knew Jewish texts. Again, as at Morasha and Yeshiva, David felt the pleasure of being one among many, of not having to scan a neighborhood or a staff meeting for a knitted *kippa*, a bag lunch, a show of tzitzis, some reassurance that he wasn't the only Orthodox around.

More than luck and coincidence underlay the burgeoning Orthodox community of Beachwood. It formed part of a broader Orthodox revival in the Cleveland area. And that movement, begun during World War II, was both successor to and challenger of the earlier trend of Reform dominance that had figured so importantly in the Beachwood of Si Wachsberger and his generation.

The rebirth of Orthodoxy in Cleveland began, paradoxically, with the Nazis. When the German army invaded Russia in 1941, it closed the renowned yeshiva in Telz, Lithuania, and killed scores of its students and faculty. Two of its leading rabbis, Chaim Mordechai Katz and Elijah Meir Bloch, managed to reach the United States via Shanghai and eventually landed in the Glenville ghetto. There they reestablished the Telshe Yeshiva to perpetuate what a later rabbi called "the old ways from the other side." Like Aaron Kotler's yeshiva in Lakewood, New Jersey, Telshe grew with a rapidity that nothing in the American Jewish experience anticipated, enrolling 150 students by 1947, creating its own high school and two teachers' colleges by 1961, and three years later moving onto a 53-acre estate. Its students came from as far as Israel, South Africa, and Brazil, and, having graduated as rabbis and educators, they created yeshivot of their own from the Bronx to Chicago.

More locally, Telshe alumni opened an Orthodox day school, the Hebrew Academy of Cleveland, which grew from twenty-four students in 1943 to eight hundred a half-century later. By constructing its first permanent home in 1949 on Taylor Road in Cleveland Heights, the academy helped create the postwar epicenter of Orthodox Jewry in greater Cleveland. Oheb Zedek, more commonly known as the Taylor Road Synagogue, expanded to several hundred members as it absorbed five smaller synagogues in the fifties. Storefront *shtibels* like Shomre Shabbos and Torah U'Tefilah grew into full-scale synagogues. Along Taylor Road sprung up businesses serving a *frum* clientele—Unger's Market, the Lax and Mandel Bakery.

As central as Telshe was to Orthodox growth in Cleveland, though, it never dominated so thoroughly as to disenfranchise the Modern faction. Young Israel actually established its first synagogue in Cleveland four years before Telshe, providing an American rather than European model for Orthodox renewal. When some parents in the early eighties objected to the Hebrew Academy's refusal to celebrate Israel Independence Day, as part of Telshe's overall ambivalence about the Jewish state, they created a Modern day school in University Heights, pointedly naming it the Bet Sefer Mizrachi for the Religious

Zionist movement. Bob Stark, later to wave his *grogger* in Beachwood, largely underwrote a *kollel* that drew many of its teachers from the *hesder yeshivot* in Israel, the Mizrachi schools where students combine religious study with military service. Orthodox institutions, both Modern and *haredi*, also enjoyed millions of dollars of largesse from two local philanthropists—Irving Stone, the founder and chairman of American Greetings, a Fortune 500 company, and his son-in-law Morry Weiss, who directed the family foundation.

From within, Cleveland's Orthodox community looked varied, vigorous, healthily contentious. From outside, however, from places like Beachwood, it appeared monolithic and menacing. Non-Orthodox Jews disparaged Taylor Road as "Rue de la *Peyes.*" They blamed the Orthodox influx for the deterioration of Cleveland Heights, and thus for their own exodus from it.

Cleveland's Jewish liberals had long prided themselves on their civil rights record. At their instigation, the city in the late forties had become one of the first in America to create a Fair Employment Practices Commission to guard against racial discrimination. Jews forged political alliances early with Carl Stokes, who was elected the first black mayor of Cleveland. And yet when Jews—liberal, Democratic, Reform Jews—raced out of Glenville for the suburbs, they left a vacuum that was filled by black slums.

So Jewish progressives made the calm, orderly integration of Cleveland Heights a major cause. Under Jewish political leadership, the city in 1964 banned For Sale signs on houses to avoid the kind of block-busting and panic selling that had gutted Glenville. The Jewish commitment to public education and to the taxation required for it gave Cleveland Heights a top-rank school system. Integration advanced so gradually that in 1970 the population was just 2 percent black.

Twenty years later, however, the black population had reached 37 percent, and a white exodus from the public school

system had left it 70 percent black. Behind its veneer of tim-
bered parkland and spotless Victorians, beneath its designation
as an All-American City, Cleveland Heights by the mid-
nineties was enduring property crime, drug-dealing, and the
departure of major retailers. Only 40 percent of the incoming
students in the high school it shared with University Heights
could pass a state basic-skills test.

Decades earlier, when Anshe Chesed had first sought a
building permit in Beachwood, anti-Semites had agitated
against it partly by invoking the fear of blacks. "The Negro follows the Jew in housing," went one broadside. "No Jews, no
Negroes to follow." Now the Jews of Beachwood, many of
them expatriates from Cleveland Heights, looked at their former city in its vicissitudes and blamed not themselves for having left, but the Orthodox who took their place. The Orthodox
did not send their children to public school. It only stood to
reason, at least in non-Orthodox minds, that the Orthodox
would not vote for school tax levies, either. And with the Cleveland Heights schools already 70 percent black, how long would
it be before the city flipped residentially, too?

David Gottesman, a newcomer to the Cleveland area,
knew none of this history yet. He knew only how greatly he savored living in Beachwood. By 1989, Jenny had given birth to
three sons—Daniel, Michael, and Joshua—in addition to the
couple's two daughters. While the Gottesmans did not send
their children to public school, they enjoyed many of Beachwood's other municipal services. The boys played in softball
and basketball leagues. They received free busing to the Hebrew Academy and Bet Sefer Mizrachi. Meanwhile, David's
professional reputation soared. He taught at Case Western Reserve University's medical school and maintained a growing
private practice. When he read an article about the twenty-five
wealthiest Clevelanders, he could count about one-third of
them as patients. No longer did David fantasize about returning to New York. Instead, he expanded the Beachwood home,

more than doubling its square footage, adding a bathroom with a Jacuzzi and a master bedroom that his kids nicknamed "the Tower of Control."

All he missed was the right synagogue, and that finally seemed to be working out. In 1983, Ivan Soclof's nephew Yaakov Feitman had moved from Brooklyn to become the rabbi of Young Israel of Cleveland. Though his own time and duties were divided between the congregations in Cleveland Heights and South Euclid, Rabbi Feitman informally advised the minyan that included David, Ivan Soclof, and Bob Stark. Similarly to David, Feitman was the child of survivors, born in a displaced-persons camp, committed as an adult to reviving Jewish life. They began talking informally about starting a new Young Israel branch, based in Beachwood. Feitman was in-trigued, given one caveat: A pulpit rabbi needed a shul for his pulpit.

Taking his usual Shabbat stroll one afternoon in 1986, David spotted a For Sale sign outside a house on Green Road, near the existing Orthodox synagogue. He called Soclof that night and gushed, "Ivan, you gotta see what I saw." The very next day, Soclof bought it for $143,000. He later said of the seller, "She thought that she'd gone to heaven."

True, the house sat in a residential zone. And, true, Soc-lof had bought it through his development company, not the congregation. Still, as a developer he understood the politics and processes of land use. Beachwood's regulations allowed the residential zone along Green Road to be considered as the site for a religious institution. Any such structure, though, would require 200 feet of frontage. The house and its two-acre lot had only 134. So for three years the would-be synagogue sat idle and empty, until the house next door went on the market. Again acting through his company rather than Young Israel, Soclof bought it for $250,000. Now Young Israel had its frontage.

One member of the congregation, a carpenter named Ignatz Strulovitz, knocked down a few walls on the first floor, then painted and plastered the opened space. Someone jerry-rigged a *mechitzah* between a couple of garment racks. A former closet held the Ark, and the *shulchan*, the Torah table, pressed next to a staircase. The floor bowed, the window air-conditioners wheezed, and the fluorescent lights cast a glow that seemed neither heavenly nor eternal. But one Friday evening in the summer of 1989, David Gottesman and his companions worshipped in their own synagogue for the first time. David rejoiced in the symbolism of the timing: It was *Shabbos Nachuma*, the Sabbath of Comfort that follows the fasting and lamentations of Tisha b'Av. Just to sing *"Yedid Nefesh"* as sunset neared was to know true *ruach*, true spirit.

Within a year, the Young Israel congregation had grown to 80 families, more than filling the 125 seats in the sanctuary. The minyan had acquired a cachet, too, with its preponderance of lawyers, professors, doctors, financial analysts, and developers. "We don't fit the stereotype of the ghettoized Jew," Rabbi Feitman later told the Cleveland *Plain Dealer.* "The joke in my congregation is you need a beeper to join."

Still, their synagogue remained, strictly speaking, illegal. And just down Green Road another Orthodox congregation, one much closer to the Old World stereotype, had similarly flouting the law for nearly a decade. Back in 1982, the Lubavitcher Hasidim had purchased a private home for $270,000 and quickly transformed it into a Chabad house—installing a *mikvah*, holding Sabbath services for a hundred, using the backyard with its swimming pool for a summer camp. Among Chabad's donors was Irving Stone.

Only in 1993 did the Lubavitchers get around to applying for rezoning. A year later, with Ivan Soclof having acquired one more land parcel for $200,000, Young Israel did the same. The Hebrew Academy, it turned out, also envisioned Beachwood as the site for its Yavne High School for girls. So the mayor of Beachwood, Harvey Friedman, urged Soclof and others to combine their disparate properties and plans into a single proposal. From his perspective, both as a politician and a Re-

form Jew, it may have made perfect sense to lump all the Orthodox together.

Within the alliance of convenience, however, Mayor
Friedman's idea presented logistical headaches and theological
tensions alike. Three very different strains of Orthodoxy—Hasidim, American Modern, Lithuanian yeshivot—now had to
rearrange their twelve acres by intricately swapping bits and
pieces. They had to divvy up seats and power on the governing
board for the joint project. They had to agree on aesthetics.
They had to do all this while differing intensely on all sorts of
issues. In the past, the Hebrew Academy had refused even to
rent rooms to Young Israel for meetings of its coed youth
group. David Gottesman, like several other Young Israel members, had pulled his children out of the academy for its *haredi*
ways. As for the Lubavitchers, whenever they forgot to mow
the lawn, which was pretty much all the time, David knew he'd
be the one getting all the complaints.

Somehow, by March 1995, the Orthodox groups con-
curred on a plan and presented it to the Beachwood Planning
and Zoning Commission. It called for the existing homes on
the site to be demolished and replaced with a $2.5 million syn-
agogue for Young Israel, a $2 million Chabad center with a so-
cial hall and *mikvah*, a two-story Yavne High School with
capacity for 250 girls, and a *mikvah* open to the entire Orthodox community. At a practical level, the campus would put religious institutions within walking distance of their members,
who were, of course, *shomer Shabbos*. More symbolically, Soclof
recalled visiting the ruins of an ancient Jewish settlement in
Spain. The way you find a Jewish community, an archeologist
told him, is to look for the *mikvah*.

David believed that the Orthodox had already met
every condition Mayor Friedman had set. He had told them to
produce one plan; they produced one plan. He had told Young
Israel not to advertise its existence; it didn't put up so much as a
poster in Unger's or Lax and Mandel. The Orthodox had even
hired the city engineer as a paid consultant. Besides, Beach-

wood was a Jewish place, and a place with a memory. Surely the Reform Jews in town knew the story of Fairmount Temple and the campaign to keep it out. "How could they," as Ivan Soclof put it, "Jewishly oppose us?"

Harvey Friedman abruptly resigned as mayor in a corruption scandal in early 1995, just as the Orthodox were submitting their final proposal, and he later pleaded guilty to a charge of dereliction of duty, as ten other municipal officials also confessed to embezzling nearly $2 million in city funds. With his clout and guile, Friedman had been to Beachwood's divergent Jews something like what Tito had been to Yugoslavia's ethnic tribes, the boss enforcing coexistence if not camaraderie. He was replaced by a much younger and weaker man, City Council president Merle Gorden.

As far as David could tell, though, Friedman's fall didn't seem to harm the campus project. In June 1996, having succeeded Ivan Soclof as president of the Young Israel congregation, he hosted a meeting for all the neighbors of the proposed Orthodox site. Since he lived within a few blocks of it himself, he already knew many of them. The talk focused on lighting, fences, landscaping, garbage collection. The Orthodox group had already agreed to place an eighty-foot buffer of open land between their buildings and the nearby homes and to plant the entire perimeter with trees and shrubs. They had a solution for every problem.

For David, so much of his life a search for Jewish community, that community was at hand. There were nights that summer at the softball league field when he got just plain sentimental about it all. "You saw kids playing, their tzitzis falling out, no one cared," he said. "One parent had to bring a snack every week, and they'd always bring something kosher, because they were sensitive." And David, for his part, wanted to be sensitive, too. As Erna's son, he had had plenty of experience in not disappointing, not giving offense. "I always felt the internal pressure to be the model Orthodox," he said. "The one with the highest level of ethics. The one no one could point a finger at."

•   •

ONE SATURDAY AFTERNOON in the spring of 1996, Si Wachsberger was tending his front yard. By now, with his four boys all
grown and educated and busy with their professions, he and
Shirley had sold their home on Edgewood and moved to a
graceful ranch house on Turnbridge Lane. He had closed his
clothing store back in 1980, worked for the next decade as executive director of Fairmount Temple, and then retired from
that to devote himself wholly to community service—as a City
Councilman, Arts Council member, volunteer at the Montefiore old-age home. And Saturdays were always for the garden.
Si grew petunias and geraniums, forsythia and myrtle. On the
front yard he planted a dogwood for each of his three grandchildren. He was near them this particular afternoon, taking
clippers to the shrubbery, when two men and a woman strolled
up the sidewalk. He could tell by the dark suits, fedoras, and
long-sleeved dress that they were Orthodox, coming home
from synagogue.

"On *Shabbos* you have to work?" the woman asked.

"You come down during the week and do this work for
me," Si shot back, "and I won't have to on Saturday."

The moment passed, and the woman moved on, but the
rancor still lingered in Si. For the past several years he had felt
the Orthodox impinging on Beachwood, starting to take over
the town. The campus project merely put a public face on what
Si had been experiencing privately. He had no gripes about Orthodox Jews in general. In deference to Shirley, he had been
married by her family's rabbi from the Taylor Road Synagogue.
Shirley's cousins, still Orthodox, ate without complaint in Si's
unkosher kitchen so long as he didn't mix milk and meat.
Shirley still kept up with an Orthodox woman who'd worked
with her in an ordnance plant during World War II. The
very walls of Si's home attested to a nostalgic fondness for Orthodoxy. A line drawing of a davening Hasid, beaver hat on
head, adorned his home office; the dining room featured a lith-

ograph of an Old World rabbi with flowing beard, a Bible in his palms.

These Orthodox moving into Beachwood in the nineties, though, were another breed. As a City Councilman, an official elected to uphold the rule of law, Si had grated at the Orthodox community's stealthy way of buying land. He remembered the Chabad house when it was a private home where he'd once attended a pool party for American Field Service families. It had no business being a synagogue now. He hadn't even known that Young Israel was snapping up residential property until the congregation applied for rezoning. Lately, he had learned of another Orthodox synagogue, now located in Cleveland Heights, that was using middlemen to buy houses on the east side of Beachwood. Neighbors and constituents were calling Si to complain, "It's going to be another Taylor Road." And Si, who had seen Taylor Road evolve into "Rue de la *Peyes*," did not disagree.

For public consumption, Si favored an analogy that likened an Orthodox synagogue to strawberry shortcake. "You sit down at dinner and they give you a piece of strawberry shortcake," he put it. "And it tastes very good. Then you get another. And another. And all of a sudden, there's ten pieces of strawberry shortcake in front of you and it's overkill." Privately, he preferred a blunter analysis. "When the Orthodox began moving onto Taylor Road, the non-Orthodox felt they were being pushed out," he explained. "If you want to move in, move in. But when you bring all the baggage with you—two more synagogues, the *mikvah*, the school, the whole shtick—you're taking over."

The most disturbing aspect had nothing to do with brick and mortar. It was the sense Si had experienced so personally that morning in the front yard of being judged, scorned, found deficient as a Jew. A few weeks before the episode, on April 15, 1996, Rabbi Arthur Lelyveld died. Some twelve hundred mourners attended his funeral at Fairmount Temple; condolences arrived from President Bill Clinton, former president Jimmy Carter, Representative Louis Stokes. Yet only one Orthodox rabbi came to honor a man who had toiled alongside Orthodox colleagues as national director of the B'nai B'rith Hillel Foundation and president of the American Jewish Congress.

Of course, there was a theological reason for Orthodox rabbis to excuse themselves. The funeral was a religious service with men and women seated together in violation of *halakhah* and to attend it would be to confer legitimacy on "deviationist" practice. To Jews like Si, the absence showed disrespect for a communal hero, if not outright contempt. And it was not the first such snub. During the rabbi's last years, Beachwood had named a street Arthur Lane. Its residents, mostly Orthodox, pressed the City Council to change it to Blossom Lane.

Si hadn't even heard about what happened lately to Joshua Aaronson, one of Fairmount's assistant rabbis. Leaving the temple one balmy Friday night, he realized his car needed gas. His route to a station took him through the Orthodox section in Beachwood's northwest corner, where his headlights caught several dozen worshippers walking home from synagogue and a lone toddler lingering in an intersection. "Why are you driving through this neighborhood like a crazy person?" a parent shouted at Aaronson. "It's Shabbat."

Variations of the rabbi's encounter occurred nearly every Sabbath, at least to hear the non-Orthodox Jews of Beachwood tell it. In the typical scenario, a Jew driving on Saturday would find his path blocked by a few Orthodox women pushing baby carriages side by side in the street. And every such awkward moment on a Beachwood street was understood oppositely by different Jews. Were those *frum* mothers shoving their fundamentalism in the face of other Jews? Or were they walking in the street because the sidewalks were too narrow for several strollers abreast? Were those mothers scorning a Judaism that didn't obey Torah? Or were those Sabbath drivers ashamed at being seen?

All the aggrievement bubbled just beneath the surface of the rezoning application, waiting to spray loose. On February 10, 1997, the Beachwood Planning and Zoning Commission held a public discussion of the Orthodox campus as the prelude to a formal vote the following month. The tone, like the tone at the neighborhood meeting David Gottesman had convened, was one of reasonable men and women seeking solutions. "There are a few who don't want to see Beachwood turned into the next Taylor Road," acknowledged one speaker, Marshall Nurenberg, who had lived for thirty-five years near what would be the campus. "But the Orthodox Jews are still entitled to their own house of worship. I think that the project is doable, and that ultimately the application will and should be granted." Still, an uncommonly large crowd of 120 had attended the session. Toward its end, a member of both the zoning commission and the City Council, Martin Arsham, invited anyone with objections to register them. When no one spoke up, he asked again. Wasn't there anyone out there with a complaint?

Within days, about forty homeowners gathered to organize a campaign against the campus as the Beachwood Residents Association. Si wanted the effort to avoid religion and focus instead on residential land and public schools, two hallowed concepts in Beachwood. The twelve-acre site off Green Road was one of the last parcels of undeveloped land in the city. Didn't it make sense to build homes there, homes that would be filled with children who would attend Beachwood's schools and parents who would gratefully pay the taxes?

Inevitably, though, the opposition returned to the schism between Jews, if not overtly then covertly. Talking about the future of public schools was really a coded way of talking about Orthodox newcomers who definitely would not send their children to them and thus lacked the self-interest to support them financially. Cleveland Heights, with its overwhelmingly black system, stood as proof. A school board member sympathetic to Si's cause, Saul Eisen, told the *Cleveland*

Jewish News, "Public education will suffer. When public education suffers, property values suffer." The Beachwood Residents
Association put things just as bluntly. Its members posted yellow lawn signs against rezoning with the slogan "Preserve
Beachwood's Future." In an eight-page brochure, the association described the Orthodox campus as a threat to the "secular
nature of our city." A public-relations man active in the association, David Eden, told the City Council on March 17, "One of
the questions being asked is if this will be a little Jerusalem,
with the secular, Orthodox, and Reform Jews all trying to live
together." Asked how a city whose Reform Jews went to court
for the right to build their own temple could block an Orthodox campus, Eden replied, "Precedents are made to be
changed." Nearly six hundred residents signed a petition saying as much.

Si thought the campaign "terrible." It kept coming back
to religion. How could religion be the issue when Beachwood
already had something like twenty Jewish institutions? The
issue was the residential character of the town. The issue was the
school system, which he had played such a major role in building. Admittedly, enrollment had actually been growing over the
past decade, but the size of the last incoming kindergarten class
had fallen from about one hundred to eighty. Though Si was too
discreet to assign blame, the drop coincided with the Orthodox
influx. So there he was, back to religion again.

Any ambition Si had of steering the debate to the safely
boring realm of land use collapsed on the Saturday morning of
March 22. "Non-Orthodox Not Jews, Rabbi Group to Claim,"
read the headline of a front-page story in the *Los Angeles Times.*
It went on to print a statement being drafted by the Agudath
Harabonim, an association of about five hundred ultra-
Orthodox rabbis based in Brooklyn: "This declaration is a clar-
ion call to all that, despite their brazen usurpation of the titles
'Judaism,' 'Jewish heritage,' 'Jewish tradition' and 'Jewish con-
tinuity,' Reform and Conservative are not Judaism at all. They
are outside of Torah Jewish law and outside of Judaism." Two

days later, the *New York Times* picked up the story, and soon it went around the world in both secular and Jewish publications.

For Reform Jews like Si Wachsberger, it did not matter that the Agudath Harabonim represented a fringe of several hundred *haredi* rabbis. It did not matter that the Orthodox establishment, inside and outside Cleveland, distanced itself from the pronouncement. It did not matter that, the original headline to the contrary, the Agudath Harabonim had excommunicated the Reform and Conservative movements, not their individual members—a sort of Jewish equivalent to the Catholic dictate, "Hate the sin, love the sinner." No, Jews like Si sensed that the Brooklyn black-hats had merely spoken what most Orthodox thought.

Si need look no further than Cleveland's suburbs for proof. The chairman of the local association of Orthodox rabbis, a Telshe alumnus named Daniel Schur, especially needled Reform and Conservative Jews. In one column in the *Cleveland Jewish News*, Rabbi Schur scoffed that Jewish pluralism might as well include Christianity. When the Cleveland Indians' first postseason games in forty-one years fell on Yom Kippur in 1995, he cracked to the *Plain Dealer* that the liberal temples and synagogues would probably have televisions in their lobbies and announce scores from the pulpit. And the Orthodox insults were more than rhetorical. Back in January, non-Orthodox Jews had lost the only *mikvah* willing to accept their conversion ceremonies. The Lee Road *mikvah* in Cleveland Heights was no showplace, that was true, with its water-stained sinks and loose ceiling tiles and couches held together with duct tape. But it symbolized communal cooperation, and when the roof collapsed and forced its closure, Reform and Conservative Jews were left with no ritual bath this side of Youngstown, ninety minutes away on the Pennsylvania border. One local Conservative rabbi, Michael Hecht, resorted to a pond.*

---

* Finally, in early 2000, the Park Synagogue, a Conservative institution, opened a *mikvah* available to all Jews.

When Si entered City Hall for the zoning commission's vote on March 27, he expected a row. Even with all three sliding doors opened, the room was jammed, clusters of supporters and opponents of the campus tossed together in a patchwork. Si exchanged greetings and advice as he and Shirley made their way to seats. Turning around briefly, he caught the glance of a man with a *kippa*, who then told a companion in a voice meant for Si to hear, "Just remember him when he runs again." Si also spotted Irving Stone, and that rankled him. Sure, Irving Stone lived in Beachwood, but what was he doing at a zoning meeting except laying all his influence, backed by all his millions, behind the campus? Who would dare oppose him? Nobody who ever wanted a donation or a campaign contribution. These Orthodox in Beachwood, they sure weren't the poor scufflers Si remembered from boyhood visits to Glenville, men in dusty coats carrying tin cannisters for *tzedakah*. These days, you could tell an Orthodox family in Beachwood by its house, a garish mansion crammed to the very edge of its lot. One local architect, punning on *mishagas*, the Yiddish word for "mess," dubbed the style "misha-Gothic."

With all his political instincts, Si couldn't guess how the zoning vote would go. Only two speakers were permitted before the balloting. Sheldon Berns, an attorney for the campus, reprised the history and scope of the application. Harking back to the appellate court's language in the Fairmount Temple case, he spoke of the campus's "general benefit" to the "welfare of the community." Then the city planner, George Smerigan, addressed the meeting. Over the previous several years, he had earned $8,000 as a consultant to the Orthodox groups in developing the physical plan for the campus. Now, incredibly, he reversed course. To cries of "Betrayal" from Orthodox listeners, Smerigan dismissed the campus as "not the most appropriate use of the land." Perhaps the Orthodox could build elsewhere, along Richmond Road on the east side—well out of walking distance, though Smerigan didn't say so, of their current homes. It was Smerigan's speech, as much as the unanimous vote afterward, that conjured Bob Stark from his seat, *grogger* aloft.

The apparent defeat of the campus afforded Si little satisfaction. From his days in college, when he had seen a few fraternities dominate the homecoming queen contest by bloc voting, he had operated on this axiom of politics: An organized minority beats a disorganized majority. He could tell how well organized and how well funded the Orthodox adherents were. And the reckless rhetoric on both sides had Cleveland's Jewish establishment pushing for a settlement. Si received calls at home from various leaders seeking his vote for the campus when the City Council took it up. The regional director of the Anti-Defamation League advocated the campus in an op-ed column in the *Cleveland Jewish News*. A local group called the Jewish Unity Committee, which had been formed by Jews of all three branches after Yitzhak Rabin's assassination, urged mediation. With Passover approaching, the Jewish Community Federation of Cleveland ran a full-page ad in the *Cleveland Jewish News* with the slogan "We Left Egypt As One People." During a City Council meeting on April 7, Si heard a woman named Barbara Romm, who wasn't observant herself, plead, "We must put up a front and be united as a community."

All these efforts, of course, spoke to the tragedies of Jewish history, the exile and oppression and genocide that made unity inseparable from survival itself. And Si was not unmoved by the invocation of Jewish suffering. He could recall the emergency meeting at Fairmount Temple during the Six-Day War when he and Shirley pledged all the money they had saved for a home addition to Israeli relief. His son Jeffrey had lived on a kibbutz for a year in the seventies. While visiting him there, Si met Shirley's relatives who had survived the Holocaust. They were still so afraid of strangers that the door had swung open only after Shirley said in Yiddish, "I am Yetta's daughter."

So, yes, Si knew the ancient grip of memory, the call of bloodlines. He also knew, though, that all of these soaring testimonials to Jewish unity effectively muzzled the opposition. Who dared to speak in public against the campus after Rabbi Feitman compared foes to Nazis? Who dared put up a lawn sign when the Orthodox likened the yellow boards to the *Juden* patches Nazis forced Jews to wear? Personally, he did not intend to be silenced.

"You started to feel pushed, crowded," he said later of the Orthodox presence. "You didn't want Beachwood to be a ghetto. I hate to use that word 'ghetto' because it has so many bad connotations. People were forced to live in the ghetto; they had no choice. I feel pity for anyone who wants to live in one now. I'm a strong believer in a heterogeneous community. It's an enrichment. I want to live among Jews, but the world isn't just Jews."

As the City Council convened on June 16, 1997, for a final decision on the campus, Si did what politicians do: He counted votes. Three of the seven council members—Bob Bloom, Larry Small, Ken Kleinman—had already announced their support. At least two others were wavering. Martin Arsham had received Orthodox contributions to his reelection campaign. Fred Goodman had already been quoted in the papers as saying he could back the campus if it did not include the girls' school.

Last in alphabetical order among the council members, Si listened as every single vote went against him and for the campus. He heard his colleagues appeal to unity and neighborliness; he heard them promise Beachwood would never go the way of Glenville or Cleveland Heights. From the audience rose cheers and applause, an occasional boo. Then Si delivered his futile "no" vote and a four-page address that pointed toward the controversy's next stage. "Just giving up in anticipation of losing is unthinkable," he said. "We owe it to our Beachwood citizens to fight this issue in court. . . . I think of the money spent in court not as an expense, but rather as a logical, worthwhile investment to preserve our beautiful Beachwood community."

In the days after the vote, Si fielded compliments in the market, at the movies, through the mail. "You stood alone for your belief," wrote one woman. On a sheet of notepaper with a logo of Albert Einstein, a man hailed Si for "one of the most intelligent and beautiful speeches on a Beachwood issue I have ever heard." Then again, there was the anonymous letter that asked, "Where is your soul? Is it bankrupt?" The conversation that most stayed with Si, though, had taken place outside City Hall a few weeks earlier. An Orthodox man asked him what sort of compromises would be necessary to win Si's vote for the campus. Si's reply had nothing to do with land use or zoning or schools. "Will you recognize our female rabbi?" he asked. "Will you recognize our female cantor? Will you recognize our intermarried couples? Will you let your rabbi speak at our temple?" The answer to each question, as stipulated by *halakhah*, was no.

"We'll be good neighbors," the Orthodox man offered.

Si told him, "I already have good neighbors."

ONE EVENING in late June 1997, David Gottesman was watching his son Joshua play softball when a woman approached him with a petition. She explained that she represented a group called the Committee to Preserve Residential Zoning, and she was collecting signatures to put a referendum about the Orthodox campus on the ballot in November. David happened to be wearing a baseball cap instead of a *kippa*, so she didn't recognize him as an enemy. He decided to play along and ask why he should sign.

"I used to live in Cleveland Heights," the woman answered. "The Orthodox ruined the school system there."

"Really?"

"It went down the toilet," she said. "It'll happen here now."

David went home that night weighed down by the memory of his childhood isolation. Here in Beachwood, where he thought he'd found community, he felt just as alien as he had in Yankee Fairfield. At his son's game the next week, David trudged to the softball field, usually one of his favorite places for its easy mixture of children from all Jewish streams, with dread. Sure enough, a parent worked the sidelines and stands with a petition. Instead of watching the game, David watched the crowd to see who signed—who opposed the Orthodox campus; who, at some level, hated him.

Some of the hatred was public. There had been David Eden's comment about "Little Jerusalem." A letter in the *Cleveland Jewish News* described the zoning issue as a "holy war by Orthodox Jews." Marshall Nurenberg, who lived near David and had been so conciliatory at the zoning commission back in February, now claimed the Orthodox wanted to turn Beachwood into "another Crown Heights," the Brooklyn neighborhood that was the worldwide capital of the Lubavitcher Hasidim. More painful to David were the private comments never meant for Orthodox ears. Incognito with his baseball cap, bareheaded in his medical practice, so unlike whatever image of black-clad medievalism Orthodoxy evoked for outsiders, he was privy to many of the slurs. The woman with the petition reminded him of a doctor with whom he had moonlighted at an obesity clinic many summers earlier. David mentioned he lived in Beachwood and the doctor sighed, "Oh, boy, I feel sorry for you. The place is changing." Did he mean there was crime in Beachwood? David asked. "No," the doctor corrected. "It's the Orthodox." David had one more question. Where did the doctor live? It was in Beachwood, on Wendover, right near the Gottesmans' home. Trying to hide his hurt, David realized, *He's talking about me.*

On July 16, the opposition broke cover again, when the Committee to Preserve Residential Zoning submitted petitions signed by 1,432 residents seeking a municipal vote on the campus. Several weeks later, the Cuyahoga County Board of Elections certified 1,332 of the signatures, well over the required 10 percent of Beachwood's 9,360 registered voters. A legal challenge by the Orthodox groups failed in late August.

The campus referendum, a conflation of civic and religious life in Beachwood, headed for the November ballot.

As perhaps only a survivor's child could, David believed that somehow his own decency, his own rectitude, could repair a shattered world. Whenever he saw an Orthodox person walking in the street on Sabbath, even a *rebbetzin* with a stroller, he'd shout, "Get on the sidewalk!" If someone complained at a public meeting about how an Orthodox kid said he wasn't Jewish because he didn't wear a *kippa*, David sought out the person afterward to apologize. He winced at every show of Orthodox intransigence, however distant from Beachwood—the Agudath Harabonim decree, a Knesset bill reinforcing the Orthodox monopoly on conversion standards, the Shavuot assault by yeshiva boys against a mixed-gender minyan at the Western Wall. Sounding as plaintive as Rodney King trying to halt the Los Angeles riots that his own beating had inspired, David longed for "a way for everyone to get along." There was a Hebrew word for what he sought, *achdut*; it meant "togetherness" and something beyond togetherness, "oneness."

Yet even *achdut* had a limit. There were reasons, theological reasons, for the tensions between Jews. Accepting or not accepting patrilineal descent, for instance, wasn't merely a matter of opinion, as mutable as voting Democrat or Republican, as drinking Pepsi or Coke. In the lobby of Fairmount Temple stood a small table with a pile of *kippot* and a sign saying Optional. David believed in divine revelation. He believed that God had given the Torah to Moses on Mount Sinai. And believing that, he had to accept everything contained in the Torah and the Oral Law derived from it. Jewish disunity was caused not by those who remained faithful to the ancient mitzvot but those who took it upon themselves to "change the rules." As much as David cringed at the Agudath Harabonim's impolitic tone, he agreed with the underlying premise that only Torah "got us through 5,700 years."

So he spent the late summer and early fall preparing for the electoral battle. The Orthodox campus once more enjoyed the support of the Cleveland area's Jewish establishment. The local federation brought in speakers on Jewish unity. It convened house meetings in Beachwood—religious encounter sessions, really—where Orthodox and non-Orthodox Jews could confess and thus banish their stereotypes of each other. Nineteen local rabbis, many of them Reform and Conservative, bought an ad in the *Cleveland Jewish News* imploring Beachwood voters to "do the right thing." When the High Holy Days arrived, about a month before Election Day, no rabbi lacked for a sermon topic. The most striking oration of all came from Joshua Aaronson, who was now the acting senior rabbi at Fairmount Temple.

Rabbi Aaronson began his sermon with the story of a Reform nursery school outside Jerusalem that was bombed by Orthodox fundamentalists. He told his audience how the Orthodox Union wanted the words "religious pluralism" replaced by "Jewish unity" on all correspondence from the United Jewish Appeal. He spoke of Orthodox monopoly on conversion in Israel. In his own life, of course, Aaronson had been assailed by Orthodox worshipers for driving through their neighborhood on *Shabbos*. Privately, he said he expected Beachwood to look like Monsey, New York's *frum* suburb, in a generation. Then, with his two thousand listeners sure they could guess his position, Aaronson turned to the subject of the Orthodox campus:

> In truth, the behavior of the Orthodox has been unseemly at best. The Orthodox supporters of the Green Road campus have been unwilling to compromise and have engaged in scare tactics. In spite of behavior at odds with the Torah, our responsibility is to continue to strive to be holy. This is precisely the type of situation in which we are called to act holy. Through our actions, we have the ability to bring ourselves closer to God by doing that which is holy rather than that which is expedient or motivated by ignorance. This is the message of our sacred texts.

The sacred history of the Jewish people offers a similar teaching: Jews must take care of other Jews because no one else will. All of you can call to mind the voluminous list of incidents in Jewish history that irrefutably proves this point. . . . We cannot turn away this group of Jews. All Jews must be prepared to accept other Jews into their midst. . . .

Therefore, my friends, my teaching to you this morning is this: based solely on Jewish criteria, every Jew that is able to cast a vote on the issue of development of Green Road must vote to permit the development to proceed.

Eloquent as the sermon was, David Gottesman did not count on pastoral persuasion to win the referendum. He had spent $5,000 of his own money hiring a public-relations man for the Orthodox campus the previous spring. Now he and Ivan Soclof and Bob Stark and the other partisans were in the process of putting more than $40,000 into the election campaign. Their opponents, the Committee to Preserve Residential Zoning, would raise and use less than $2,000.

On the night of October 27, one week and twelve hours before the polls were to open, David gathered with the campus's brain trust and the two political consultants they had hired to plan the final strategy. They met in Ivan Soclof's home, despite the Orthodox stereotype a muted and graceful brick affair, in the room that featured his collection of antique Judaica—menorahs, spice boxes for *havdalah*, a wooden Torah case. Five of the seven men present wore *kippot*. The consultants, Jeff Rusnak and Leslie Grodin, were decidedly casual, he with a sweatshirt and shag haircut, she in black leggings and Doc Martens. Grodin had to keep reminding herself not to shake hands with the Orthodox men.

Their distance from Orthodoxy was, in a sense, exactly the point. The pro-campus campaign had already identified its true believers, compiling rosters of the Beachwood members of every local Orthodox shul and the Beachwood women who had visited the area's *mikvaot.* That hard core came to perhaps seven hundred votes, about one-quarter of what the campus would probably need. Rusnak and Grodin, outsiders themselves, were supposed to help deliver the rest.

So far, the campaign had called two thousand households containing three thousand voters. It had mailed out postcards, distributed lawn signs and lapel stickers, paid first-class postage to ensure that every flyer and pamphlet arrived well before Election Day. "Top Ten Reasons to Vote Yes," read one advertisement, evoking the nightly lists read by David Letterman on his TV show. Beachwood's handful of Catholics received a letter quoting their bishop's support for the campus on the grounds of religious freedom. Did anyone know a black minister, Grodin wondered, to make the same pitch to the several hundred African-Americans in town?

"We can't afford to offend anyone now," David said.

"We're going to get the most nonreligious people for poll watchers," added Miriam Berkowitz, one of two Orthodox women at the meeting.

"Have our people wear Indians caps," David said. "No one'll be able to tell the difference."

"You could shave your beard," Larry Frankel said to Harold Frolich.

The brief levity subsided as David listened to the consultants run down their latest poll data. They showed 37 percent for the campus and 35 percent against—essentially a dead heat, with 28 percent still undecided. Grodin's own mother and mother-in-law, both Beachwood residents, wouldn't tell her how they planned to vote. All the sermons, all the ads, all the appeals to Jewish unity, it was now clear, had not won over the opposition but just driven it underground.

For eight years, since the formation of Young Israel of Beachwood, David had been waiting and waiting and waiting. Families were leaving the congregation because the current sanctuary was packed so tight their children had to sit on the stairs. Even some of the founding members, who had collectively pledged $1 million, were holding off on writing their checks. Now not even a unanimous vote of the City Council had settled matters. All this talk about zoning was such sophistry. Ivan Soclof had a pet phrase about zoning battles: If your opponent screamed until his jugular vein showed, the real issue wasn't zoning at all. Beachwood had passed the jugular mark months ago. The Orthodox campus was facing the kind of innuendo and double-talk that homeowners usually save for juvenile shelters or group homes for the mentally ill. Never, David believed, not in a hundred years, would Beachwood's Jews have blocked a church the way it was blocking the campus. Only when it came to Orthodox Jews were they willing to carry on like bigots.

As the meeting moved toward its conclusion, one last matter emerged: the Spinka Hasidim. The Spinka were a sect originally from Romania, relocated since the war in Brooklyn. Once each year, scores of them descended on Beachwood to solicit donations from their relatives and landsmen in the Green Road Synagogue. They were coming this weekend, virtually the eve of the election.

"These people have fur hats," David muttered.

"Beards and black coats," Berkowitz added.

"It's like that Melanie Griffith movie," David added, alluding to *A Stranger Among Us*, a whodunit set in a Hasidic neighborhood.

"Put them in Cleveland Heights," someone offered. "Pay them to reschedule."

It was funny but it wasn't funny. Here were David and his comrades plotting how to distance themselves from other Orthodox Jews just so they could worship and learn in their own town as Orthodox Jews. The fear of losing after the years and money they had poured into the campus had them talking half-seriously about hiding their own kind. David felt a pang of remorse. For both personal and communal reasons, he knew better.

Just a few years ago, a second cousin had shown David a photograph in a book about Auschwitz. It showed a group of Jews being herded from cattle cars toward the camp gate. One of them, her face turned directly to the camera, was unmistakably Erna Gottesman. It didn't matter to the Nazis whether she was religious any more than it mattered whether the man beside her was a Marxist or a boulevardier. They were Jews. "Beachwood," David said, hanging on the word. "Hitler would've burned us all."

BY SIX IN THE MORNING on Election Day, half an hour before the polls opened, Si Wachsberger was working the perimeter of Hilltop Elementary School, wearing a Vote No button on his coat, gazing at the Orthodox canvassers down the sidewalk. Since the weekend, he'd been campaigning eleven or twelve hours a day, ringing doorbells, passing out literature, talking himself hoarse. When he'd slogged through his front door Sunday night, soaked from a cold autumn rain, Shirley had shaken her head in disbelief. Soon he was snoring on the couch.

This should have been the quietest November Si had known in decades. Before the campus issue grew so heated, he had decided not to seek reelection to the City Council in 1997; it was time, after six terms and twenty-four years, to step aside for the next generation. As much as he now regretted the promise, he had held to it, watching two leaders of the residents' association, Drew Kates and Harold Levey, run for seats on a platform against rezoning. Still, inactivity was for the "Little Corporal" a form of torture. So in the final weeks of the campaign Si had launched his own blitz on behalf of the referendum and the very future of Beachwood.

He felt weirdly exhilarated by the effort, maybe because the stakes were so great, maybe because his internal engine was burning the fuel of anger. Never in almost forty years of local politics had he seen a campaign as slick, as pricey, as unrelenting as the one the Orthodox were running. Si raised $800 to run an ad in the *Cleveland Jewish News* showing the drop in public kindergarten enrollment and the growth in the number of religious-school students Beachwood was busing at municipal expense, and then he spent $200 out of his own pocket to print up four thousand copies. But he wondered just what his efforts could accomplish against such an onslaught. Fairmount Temple's own rabbi, after all, had delivered a sermon in favor of the campus on Yom Kippur. After the service ended, Si had told Joshua Aaronson, "You're not my rabbi anymore."

Election Day began in a suitably ugly fashion. The police had been called to the polling place at Fairmount School to remove signs the Orthodox had put up in a no-electioneering area. Over at the Hamptons, an apartment complex, an anti-campus poll watcher tore down pro-campus signs and locked them in the trunk of her car. Not even Si's wife was spared suspicion. As the president of the auxiliary at the Montefiore home, Shirley sometimes helped infirm residents cast their ballots. The previous week she had received a letter from "Concerned Residents" that read: "Shirley Wachsberger and friends should know that it is a felony to tamper with another person's vote and/or to cast a vote for another person. She will be watched this election day at Montefiore."

As the hours passed, Si migrated between all five polling places, checking the turnout, hoping for a large one. He looked for senior citizens, assuming that longtime Beachwood residents were the least likely to be Orthodox. But at every poll, the pro-campus forces had eight, ten, twelve campaigners, replacing them in shifts throughout the day. As the seven o'clock end to balloting neared, the turnout remained below 70 percent, which Si reckoned as the threshold for victory. It was the lesson of the frats at Miami University all over again: An organized minority beats a disorganized majority.

After a shower, dinner with Shirley, and a change of clothes, Si drove to Merle Gorden's party to await the returns.

The mayor, like the other candidates, had been given a special phone number and access code by the county Board of Elections to receive the results. Eight and nine o'clock went by with just a trickle of numbers. Every few minutes, someone from Gorden's circle punched the redial button again as a crowd hovered, tilting their ears toward the headset. It seemed to Si that totals had come through quicker in the days of paper ballots. Then, toward eleven, the precinct totals arrived in bunches. Kates and Levey were on their way to losing, a bad sign. And the referendum? The referendum? The campus had been defeated 2,680 to 2,397.

Except that maybe it hadn't been. A janitor, it turned out, had shifted the location of a few voting booths in the Hamptons apartments just before the polls had opened. As a result, 315 residents had cast their ballots at the wrong machines and election officials had recorded those results incorrectly. Now a county judge had ordered all the flawed ballots sealed. Three hundred fifteen missing votes and the campus had lost by only 287. Si heard that the Orthodox were going to court to push for a whole new election. Two mornings after the election, he opened his copy of the *Plain Dealer* to read a quote from David Gottesman: "If you're spiritual at all, you have to wonder if the hand of God wasn't in this. Maybe He didn't like the way the vote was going and wanted a do-over."

Intervention came not from the Almighty but the Cuyahoga County Board of Elections. Recounting the sealed ballots by hand and adding them to the earlier vote totals, the board in mid-November calculated the final tally as 2,890 against the campus and 2,572 for. Whatever satisfaction Si enjoyed was tempered by the latest hate mail:

> What do Si Wachsberger, Levey, Kates and all the other "ANTI'S" have in common. You all give very little to charity, you're against everything good, and, simply put, you're just not nice people. By the way, Si, it was the solid vote of the Christian block that defeated [the campus]. The great

majority of Jews were for it. You and the "ANTI'S" are in the minority. Of course, your kind always is.

Your letter [the ad] says to enjoy peace. Once one has sinned, there is no peace.

And indeed there was not. On January 6, 1998, as Si seated himself among the audience, an unfamiliar place, the Beachwood City Council took up the campus issue again. It voted four–three to allow Young Israel and Chabad each to build a synagogue while simultaneously enacting a newer, even more stringent zoning ordinance. The compromise lasted two minutes before Mayor Merle Gorden vetoed it, saying he was honoring the results of the referendum. The *Cleveland Jewish News* succinctly reported the reaction: "Applause thundered from many of the more than 200 people crammed into Council chambers and spilling into the hallways. Many supporters of the two synagogues looked like they had just been punched in the stomach."

Si refused to join any celebration. He had won for now, but he would lose in the end. Of that he was certain. The referendum campaign had convinced him that the Orthodox had pockets deep enough to spend their opponents into oblivion. Besides, Beachwood was already changing in ways that guaranteed that in a few years, or a dozen, or whenever, the Orthodox would have sufficient votes to pass whatever they wanted. Some places hit a racial "tipping point" and went from mostly white to all-black in a blink. It had happened in Glenville; it was happening in the Cleveland Heights schools. Beachwood, Si felt, was heading for the same kind of lightning transformation, with the line drawn not between races but between different kinds of Jews. You went into the Beachwood library these days and you saw a mother with a *shaytl*, a wig worn for modesty, minding two daughters in ankle-length skirts; you went to the Jewish Community Center's health club and you saw a bearded guy with a *kippa* reading a book called *Reb Moshe* while pedaling away on his exercise bike. The kosher-style businesses that had been Jewish enough for Si's ilk were being supplanted by *glatt* establishments like Tibor's butcher shop and Abba's restaurant. A friend of Si's cracked that the Orthodox ought to just buy a few hundred acres of Beachwood and call it "Mitzvah Land."

Not even gallows humor made Si laugh. "There was a comfort level here," he said of Beachwood, referring to it like a deceased relative, in the past tense. So many of his friends, it seemed, were selling off, fleeing east to Pepper Pike or Solon. A dentist whom Si had once used as a model in a Christmas catalogue for his clothing store said he just didn't feel comfortable anymore in Beachwood. Another friend told Si about the Orthodox man who had shown up, unannounced, to offer to buy his home. When the owner said it wasn't even on the market, the would-be buyer snapped, "You don't think I could afford it? I can pay you cash." After finishing the story for Si, the friend added a postscript: "I'm so mad, I might sell to a *schvartze.*" Literally, the word meant a "black," but colloquially, as the man probably intended, it was the Yiddish equivalent to "nigger."

Si would stay; he knew that. He would volunteer at Montefiore. He would tend the dogwoods planted for the grandchildren. He would glance from time to time at the snapshots of himself in fedora and topcoat at the groundbreaking for Beachwood High, in T-shirt and ball cap coaching the Oxford Shop's Little League team, 18–1 that year. Si did not live in the past. He learned to surf the Internet and exchange E-mail, joined a *chavurah* at Fairmount Temple. But when he drove up his old block of Edgewood one day, passed the colonial with fieldstone facing where he and Shirley had raised their boys, and then spotted two For Sale signs on the street, he longed for what had once existed in Beachwood, American pluralism incarnate, and sighed, "You're going to be seeing a lot more of those."

• •

ONE SABBATH in January 1998, just after Mayor Gorden had vetoed the Young Israel and Chabad approvals, David Gottesman heard his rabbi deliver the mixture of sermon and lesson called a *d'var Torah*. The Torah portion that week was Truma, from the Book of Exodus, and to the enduring frustration of pulpit rabbis it consisted almost entirely of detailed instructions from God on how the wandering Jews should build a tabernacle—what type of wood, what sort of animal skins. From the minutiae, Rabbi Feitman plucked one atypical verse: "And let them make Me a tabernacle that I may dwell among them." He pointed out to David and the rest that God does not live in the structure but among the people. The Jews had to prove themselves worthy of the Almighty's presence. "What is it about us," Rabbi Feitman then said almost abjectly, "as Orthodox Jews and as Young Israel of Beachwood, that has engendered this kind of enmity?"

David had been wrestling with the same metaphysical question, searching for God's message in all the futility and wrath. When he first took the presidency of Young Israel back in 1996, he had expected to worship in a new sanctuary within the year. Now every time he drove past the congregation's house, it stood as reproachful as the broken walls of Jerusalem. And David had been unable thus far to play Nehemiah, the rebuilder.

It was not for lack of trying. The campus controversy had consumed his entire life. He had not attended a professional conference in two years. He'd hardly watched a "Monday Night Football" game, for that matter. During the momentary breaks in his eleven-hour workdays, he fielded calls from lawyers and politicians. He spent half of a family trip to Florida on the phone with Beachwood. "You can't relax if you don't know what's going on," David put it, "and you can't relax if you do." After all that, he still could walk into a City Council meeting and see the patients who had hired him to stop their rectal bleeding or remove polyps from their colon sitting among the campus's foes. David was good enough to clean out their bodies; he just wasn't good enough to worship in their town.

Sixteen years after Chabad had bought its land, twelve since Young Israel had purchased its first lot, five since Harvey Friedman had yoked together both congregations and the Hebrew Academy into a single project, they were defeated and dispersed. Separately now, they resubmitted less ambitious plans. In late January, a few weeks after Rabbi Feitman's sermon on tabernacles, Young Israel of Beachwood applied for a waiver from residential zoning in order to build its synagogue on three acres of land. Essentially, this was the same plan it had offered in 1994 and then withdrawn when Friedman turned matchmaker. This time, though, the matter would be heard by the Board of Zoning Appeals, the final authority on land use in Beachwood.

On April 28, 1998, the board approved the Young Israel plan by a three-to-two vote. No sooner had David crowed to the *Cleveland Jewish News*, "Justice prevailed," than Harold Levey, an attorney who had led the anti-campus petition drive, filed suit on behalf of two local homeowners. As the case gestated in the Cuyahoga County Court of Common Pleas, Chabad and the Hebrew Academy each approached the zoning appeals board with separate applications for their projects. Chabad received favorable signals from the board in November 1998, provided it was willing to scale down its proposed building from 30,000 square feet to 12,500. The Hebrew Academy request, scheduled for a vote in March 1999, appeared bound for similar assent. Despite the Levey lawsuit, it actually looked for those few months as if Beachwood might settle its civil war peaceably.

David Gottesman risked a pleasure trip to New York to watch his son Daniel compete in a tournament for yeshiva basketball teams and visit his grown daughter Deborah and his two grandchildren. He was just walking into her apartment after the game on March 18 when the phone rang. Young Israel's lawyer was calling. David couldn't believe the campus case had followed him even here, four hundred miles away, but the lawyer had tracked him down through David's medical office. And, naturally, the news was bad.

Judge Shirley Strickland Saffold of the Court of Common Pleas had struck down the zoning approval for Young Israel, ruling that the Beachwood board's decision was an "unconscionable" maneuver "to circumvent the zoning laws and referendum." A week later, when the Hebrew Academy received its variance from the zoning appeals board, Levey filed a suit challenging that decision. And when Chabad in July 1999 compromised with the board on a plan for a 15,000-square-foot center, Levey sued yet again.

Young Israel, of course, appealed Judge Saffold's decision, but it was unlikely a higher court would rule until sometime in 2000. David tried to reassure himself that all the Levey litigation was just a stalling tactic, a postponement of the inevitable. He watched as Orthodox families moved into Beachwood and joined his congregation—two lawyers, two doctors, a day school teacher, a day care center operator, a professor, all in 1999 alone. Still, the headaches crowded out the satisfactions. One night burglars broke into the Young Israel house, stealing $2,000 worth of appliances and recording equipment. It occurred to some members that the theft might have been perpetrated by their political foes until they realized the robbers had left behind a full *tzedakah* box, which any Jew would've recognized as easy loot. The fire department, meanwhile, had cited the house for code violations that would cost $30,000 to correct. Then, during the service on Tisha b'Av, neighbors called the police to gripe about the cars parked on the Young Israel lawn.

A few weeks after leading the mourning for two vanquished temples, Rabbi Yaakov Feitman moved out. Unable to build and thus to raise money from an expanded congregation, Young Israel could not afford his salary. Feitman had accepted an offer to head both a synagogue and a day school in Cedarhurst, Long Island. But money told only part of the story.

"We are leaving this city because of the baseless hatred that was directed at us, not me personally, but at Orthodox Jews in our community," he said, invoking the concept of *sinat hinam* from the destruction of the Second Temple. "Our family were victims of what happened in Beachwood."

An unlikely ally of Feitman's, Rabbi Joshua Aaronson, departed Beachwood, too, to take the pulpit of a Reform temple in Perth, Australia. Since Aaronson had been serving only as the acting senior rabbi at Fairmount Temple, it was in some respects perfectly normal for him to step aside once the position was permanently filled by a more experienced man. It was no secret, though, that Aaronson's support for the Orthodox campus had caused a mutiny in his congregation. And not even Perth, it seemed, was far enough away for escape from Judaism's rifts. When Rabbi Aaronson tried to enroll his daughter in the day school there, an Orthodox institution, he was informed that because he and his wife had been married by a Reform rabbi he would have to supply genealogical proof that his child was actually Jewish.

As for David Gottesman, he finished his term as president of Young Israel just after the High Holy Days of 1999. The synagogue of which he had dreamed, the synagogue for which he had raised money and recruited members, the synagogue that had consumed his life for a decade remained just blueprints and court documents. The bitterness it had sown, meanwhile, went on undiminished. On Sukkoth, a number of non-Orthodox Jews complained to city officials that their observant neighbors were breaking the law by putting sukkahs in driveways instead of backyards. David had come to Beachwood in a quest for *achdut*, a survivor's son trying to rebuild in his own tiny way the Jewish world decimated in Auschwitz, and Beachwood had answered his prayers with scorn. It was someone else's turn now to lead Young Israel's political and legal battles. David could only grapple with the theological question Rabbi Feitman had posed from the *bimah* months earlier.

"I've asked myself, 'How can God allow this to happen?' " David said. "Why have we had to struggle like this? What are we to have learned? There's got to be a reason. Beachwood is a microcosm of what's happening within Jewry. Nobody's getting along. And God's angry with us about it."

The Jewish Reformation

I

In the struggle for the soul of American Jewry, the Orthodox model has triumphed. To say this is not to say the Orthodox themselves have prevailed, or that only the Orthodox denomination will survive on these shores. But the portion of American Jewry that will flourish in the future—and is flourishing already against a backdrop of ever more complete assimilation—is the portion that has accepted the central premise of Orthodoxy that religion defines Jewish identity.

The Orthodox model could not have won unless America, too, had won, for the victory of religion was made possible by the demise of secular Judaism. I use the word "demise" instead of "defeat" because Jewish secularism was not slain as much as it was loved to death. America made a promise to Jewish immigrants, and to its enduring grandeur as a nation it kept that promise. It welcomed history's wanderers into a greater whole. It absorbed the wonders Jewish culture had to offer. But once intermarriage is rampant, once bagels outsell doughnuts, once "Seinfeld" is a hit even in Boise, then Jewishness as ethnicity, as folk culture, as something separate and divisible from religion, is ceasing to exist in any meaningful way.

From the time massive Jewish immigration to America began in the late nineteenth century, religious Jews feared that the new land would undermine their faith. Instead, we see now, it undermined faithlessness. When the sociologist Steven M. Cohen probed the basis of Jewish identity in the late nineties, he discovered that religious practice had remained constant, even risen slightly, among Jews over the last half-century. What had plummeted was almost every measure of Jewish ethnicity—friendships with fellow Jews, attachment to Israel, membership in Jewish institutions, commitment to social justice. Except for religion, Jews had little to hold onto that made them feel like Jews.

As a jazz fan, I might offer an analogy. From the 1900s through the 1970s, jazz was revolutionized by waves of innovation. Swing replaced the New Orleans style, bebop replaced swing, modal jazz replaced bebop, free jazz replaced modal. In the process, every rule of melody, harmony, and rhythm was shattered. And then, looking up from the wreckage, musicians realized there was nothing else left to rebel against. They could turn only in one direction: to the past, to the tradition.

The same understanding is now shaping American Judaism, and the evidence of it abounds. The rancor between the denominations, genuinely bitter as it is, has obscured a different kind of dividing line—between a core of American Jewry oriented around religion and a periphery clinging to the eroding remnants of ethnicity. The Orthodox model is, in some ways, the rebellion of that fraction of American Jews who worship on a regular basis against the vast majority who show up only for the High Holy Days or a Passover seder or send out one of those popular new on-line holiday cards featuring Santa Claus and a menorah.

American Jewry's core announced itself in 1996 with the release of "A Statement on the Jewish Future," the product of a leadership conference convened by the American Jewish Com-

mittee. The statement placed Torah atop a list of five "fundamental values" for Jewish continuity, while omitting the concept of *tikkun olam*, healing the world with social justice. It
endorsed a kind of internal evangelism to moderately active
Jews while discounting outreach to most intermarried couples
and disparaging "inclusivity [that] runs the risk of degenerating
into a vague universalism." Most importantly of all, the statement carried the endorsement of thirty rabbis, scholars, and
communal leaders, running the gamut from Reform to Modern Orthodox, from feminists to Yiddishists.

   Throughout the late nineties, both the Reform and
Conservative movements embraced traditionalism in a series
of major actions. The Conservative branch mounted a program for laity to read a chapter of the Bible every day in an obvious parallel to the Orthodox system of reading the Talmud
daf yomi, a page a day. In policies of greater symbolic than actual
impact, the movement also barred intermarried people as Hebrew school teachers in its synagogues and banned children
who are not halakhically Jewish from its Ramah summer
camps. The Central Conference of American Rabbis, the association of Reform clergy, adopted a platform that reversed
the branch's historical contempt for ritual and religious law
by commending "the ongoing study of the whole array of
mitzvot." Over months of acrimonious internal debate, it is
true, the platform was watered down and its title changed from
the provocative "Ten Principles" to the pallid "Statement of
Principles." However diluted, it stood at a vast remove from
the Reform movement's original dismissal of much rabbinic
law as "altogether foreign" to a "progressive and rational religion." Rabbi Eric Yoffie, president of the Union of American
Hebrew Congregations, devoted most of his address to the Reform group's general assembly to declaring a "worship revolution" of more prayer, more Torah study, more Hebrew literacy.
The synagogue, he told his listeners, "is first and foremost a
center of *avodah*—of worship, reverence, and awe." Not until

the eleventh page of a sixteen-page address did Rabbi Yoffie launch into a plea for gun-control legislation, the sort of liberal political stance that in the past probably would have dominated the speech.

Religious day-schools, meanwhile, are booming. Where 323 schools served 63,500 students in 1965, 670 schools served 185,000 students in 1998. In less than the last decade, enrollment in non-Orthodox schools rose by one-quarter to 37,000. As a raw number, it is modest. As an indication that certain Reform and Conservative Jews have accepted an Orthodox article of faith, it is profound. Very deliberately, American Jews long eschewed parochial schools in the belief that they would "take children out of the general American environment and train them to lead segregated lives," as a 1956 report put it. The presence of American Jews as students, teachers, and principals largely created the golden age of public education in the mid-twentieth century. So the recent influx of less observant Jews into day schools signals a stunning acknowledgment of Orthodox criticism: that the system of afternoon and weekend religious schools has failed, that Jewish knowledge and identity can be instilled only through the sectarianism of a day school, through a selective disengagement from the American mainstream.

When I look back on my years of research for this book, I think of the more ineffable, unquantifiable appeals of the Orthodox model, and how I heard them expressed by two Reform Jews. One was Rachel Adler, the feminist theologian involved in the Library Minyan in Los Angeles. Rachel herself had lived for more than a decade as an Orthodox Jew, and even after having rejected the denomination because of its limits on women's participation in worship, she spoke with unforgettable poignancy about its sense of community. "There's a template of meaning that overlays all your experience," she said. "That's something you can only have when you're in a completely intact, practicing community. If you're in an Orthodox community, you live under that protective canopy. If you're not, then it's like the ozone layer has burned off and waves of meaninglessness beat down on you."

Then there was Joshua Aaronson, the Reform rabbi in Beachwood, Ohio, where the Jewish community split so irreparably over the proposed construction of an Orthodox campus. In a Yom Kippur sermon he delivered during the height of the controversy, Rabbi Aaronson had just finished reciting a litany of Orthodox attacks, both verbal and physical, on other Jews when he turned the lash on his own congregants:

> The ignorance of progressive Jews impedes our efforts to work with Orthodox Jews as true partners. Progressive Jews suffer from a self-fulfilling inferiority complex that could be erased through the most fundamental of Jewish enterprises: Talmud Torah. Many progressive Jews lack the basic lexicon that would enable us to engage our Orthodox co-religionists on an equal basis. Too many progressive Jews are unfamiliar with the most basic Jewish concepts and ideas. Sadly, for most progressive Jews, the Torah, the single most important document in our religion, is as unfamiliar as the Rosetta stone. . . . Orthodox Jews do not take us seriously as religious equals because of our ignorance. Our ignorance does not justify the animus of the Orthodox nor our second-class status. However, we must acknowledge the validity of the Orthodox claim that we are in the main illiterate Jews.

The triumph of the Orthodox model has not come without misgivings and opposition, of course. The Ten Principles stirred outrage in some quarters of Reform Jewry, its foes denouncing them as "hypocrisy," "almost fundamentalist," and "irrelevant if not obscene." As for the "Statement on the Jewish Future," the scholar MacDonald Moore assailed it in an essay as "nouvelle tribalism" based on the fear that "American Jews cannot cope, as Jews, with our open society." The 1990 National Jewish Population Survey that calculated the intermarriage rate at 52 percent has been attacked for yielding an inflated figure due to faulty methodology. But the fact is that the rate would fall only if the survey had not counted as Jewish the adult children of mixed marriages. In other words, you can admit the intermarriage rate is soaring. Or you can admit the Jewish community in America is shrinking. You cannot claim both high numbers and high quality. One way or another, the fission of American Jewry into a core and a periphery, a thriving part and a deteriorating part, is real. And except for religion, none of the pillars of Jewish identity in America can bear its weight any longer.

II

EARLY IN 2000, the Anti-Defamation League released its list of the top ten issues and events affecting American Jewry in 1999. Leading the roster was "a summer of anti-Semitic violence and vandalism in the U.S.," including the shootings of Jews at a Southern California community center and near a Chicago-area synagogue, and the arson of three synagogues in Sacramento. Of the remaining nine items, six more concerned anti-Semitism or the Holocaust. Nowhere was there any reference to the vitriolic debates within the Jewish community over pluralism and continuity.

One takes a ranking like the ADL's with a certain skepticism. The league's raison d'etre is to combat anti-Semitism, and so its very existence depends on threats. I cannot help but remember the Jewish satirist Lenny Bruce's observation that if there were no more evil in the world, he'd be standing in the unemployment line with J. Edgar Hoover. At a deeper level, though, the ADL list attests to a perverse longing among American Jews for anti-Semitism—not a truly dangerous amount of it, just enough to bind the fragmenting community together. A little bit of anti-Semitism functions like the little bit of chicken pox or flu you get from a vaccine, never really endangering your health, but stimulating your immune system to fight off a full-blown case.

During periods of truly virulent anti-Semitism, Jews have wished for nothing more than the tolerance modern America overwhelmingly has provided. Now in modern America, where Jews enjoy social mobility and professional standing without parallel in two thousand years of the Diaspora, they claim to see enemies all around. By any measure, anti-Semitism has decreased substantially since World War II, shrinking from a socially respectable belief to the fever dream of extremists. Yet in a 1989 poll by the American Jewish Committee, 85 percent of American Jews called anti-Semitism a "serious problem," virtually twice the figure less than a decade earlier.

The vital responsibility to remember the Holocaust, to retell its story as we have retold the story of the Exodus for millennia, has become less and less an exercise in collective memory and more and more the basis of an identity built on victimization. When the film *Schindler's List* became not just a hit but a phenomenon, the Harvard professor Ruth Wisse, who herself had fled Europe as a child in the late thirties, wrote in the *Jerusalem Report:* "There is something disturbing about the way American Jews have lately appropriated the Holocaust to their own needs of self-identification, and begun to wrap themselves in its historical mantle. Commemorating the Holocaust does not require its placement at the center of Jewish experience. A community otherwise so ignorant of its sources that it becomes preoccupied with death and destruction is in danger of substituting a cult of martyrdom for the Torah's insistence on life." In my own research files, I have sad proof of Wisse's assertion. As the "Who is a Jew?" issue was flaring in Israel in 1998, the weekly Jewish newspaper near my then-home in New Jersey published a brief interview with a local community leader. By way of appealing for Jewish unity, she said, "I use the Nazi definition for a Jew—to me a Jew is anybody a Nazi would consider a Jew." Reading this, I felt she had given Hitler the posthumous victory.

Meanwhile, an anti-Semitic lynching eighty-five years ago in Georgia has become a hot property for American Jewish writers, the subject of a musical with book and lyrics by Alfred Uhry *(Parade)*, a novel by David Mamet *(The Old Religion)*, and a forthcoming history by Steve Oney. Admittedly, the Leo Frank case teems with drama. A Brooklyn native managing his in-laws' pencil factory in Atlanta, Frank was accused of murdering a thirteen-year-old Christian girl named Mary Phagan on Confederate Memorial Day in 1913. Convicted and sentenced to death by a jury on the dubious testimony of a night watchman, Frank had his punishment commuted to life imprisonment by Georgia's governor. Then, on August 16, 1915, a mob hauled him out of prison and to his death.

That Frank's murder was a horrifying and repugnant episode is self-evident. That American Jews today should know of it as part of their communal history is right. And, in fact, from a 1937 Mervyn LeRoy movie *(They Won't Forget)* to a 1987 television mini-series written by Larry McMurtry *(The Murder of Mary Phagan)*, the Frank case has been chronicled by Jews and Christians alike. The troubling part of this recent Leo Frank vogue is the message it purveys that gentile hatred is what makes Jews truly Jewish. The Leo Frank of Mamet's novel has deluded himself into thinking Atlanta, and by inference America, accepts him. Only in prison does he recognize the truth and thus recover his Jewish soul—learning Hebrew, studying Torah, observing the Sabbath. In Uhry's version, Frank is a swarthy outsider of Eastern European stock unhappily married to a belle of Atlanta's German Jewish elite. Their reconciliation, in the form of a tender reunion on a prison farm, takes place literally against the backdrop of the tree from which Frank will soon be hung. "I never knew anything at all," husband and wife sing in a duet, and it is clear that what they never knew was the foundation of their bond: Jew-haters.

As it happens, I saw *Parade* and read *The Old Religion* about the same time I met an attorney named Joseph Rackman, who knew a good deal about the strains of contemporary Jewish life in Atlanta. And those strains had nothing to do with red-neck lynch mobs. In a city with one of America's fastest-growing Jewish populations, the rabbinate had become so polarized over doctrinal differences that the American Jewish Committee dispatched Rackman to try to mediate among them and restore civility. "It's almost a form of nostalgia," he said of the Leo Frank boomlet. "It was nice and easy when the goyim was the enemy. That made it easy to know who your enemies were. But today if you're mad, who are you mad at? America is so inviting that the 'enemy' is a good."

But what about those 1999 versions of the Leo Frank murder? What about the arsonists in Sacramento? And the white supremacist, Benjamin Smith, who shot Orthodox Jews strolling home from worship in the Chicago suburb of Skokie? What about Buford Furrow, who opened fire with an assault weapon on a Jewish community center in the San Fernando Valley as a "wake-up call to America to kill Jews"? As barbaric as they were, these attacks were the product of a crackpot fringe, a fringe well worth being surveilled by law enforcement authorities, but a fringe nonetheless. The Anti-Defamation League's own survey, released in late 1998, showed that the percentage of Americans holding anti-Semitic attitudes had fallen to a new low of 12 percent. A nation that is 98 percent non-Jewish has elected dozens of Jews to Congress, including both senators from the heavily German state of Wisconsin. After the Sacramento arsons, fifteen hundred gentiles, two hundred of them clergy, rallied to support the city's Jewish community. During a spate of anti-Semitic vandalism in Billings, Montana, in 1993, ten thousand Christian households there posted logos of a menorah in solidarity. At the same time in 1984 that right-wing fanatics murdered a Jewish talk-show host in Denver named Alan Berg the intermarriage rate for the area's Jews hovered around 70 percent. A rally in Sacramento, menorahs in Billings, mixed marriages in Denver—those responses reflect the American norm. Nobody except a handful of lunatics wants to answer Buford Furrow's wake-up call.

American decency, rather than American bias, challenges American Jews. As a tiny minority in this country, as a people with two thousand years of exile and tragedy behind us, we may have ample reason to expect calamity, to see phantasms of past terrors even amid present comfort. In David Mamet's play *The Old Neighborhood*, a character who is apparently the son of a Holocaust survivor recalls, "I used to say, 'Papa, you're here now, it's over.' He would say, 'It will happen in your lifetime.' And I used to think he was a fool. But I know he was right." Orthodox foes of intermarriage dishonor the dead six million in another way when they call it the "Silent Holocaust." To insist upon viewing America as a treacherous place, to ignore or even fear the acceptance that Si Wachsberger knew in Beachwood and Bill Pluss found in his wife Anne in Denver and millions of American Jews experience on a daily basis, is more than to willfully misread reality. It is, by extension, to confess that without some common enemy we are hopelessly divided, incapable of defining ourselves.

III

ON THE NIGHT in May 1999 of Israel's national election, I wandered from my Jerusalem hotel to a trendy espresso bar called Aroma, joining a standing-room crowd to await the returns. Men with earrings, women in Lycra, the occasional soldier in olive uniform with rifle casually slung over the shoulder, they embodied the liberal, secular segment of Israeli society, and it was no accident they had gathered in a shop that had been periodically vandalized for daring to operate on the Sabbath.

Just after the polls closed at ten o'clock, the television in Aroma broadcast the first exit polls, predicting that Ehud Barak would unseat Prime Minister Benjamin Netanyahu by a double-digit margin. All through the bar, customers beamed in victory and relief. They punched numbers into cell phones to exult with friends. Drivers outside banged on their car horns and blared the radio news at boombox decibels. Only one thing stilled the celebrations. The television shifted from the poll results to a roomful of men, most bearded and clad in black, dancing in triumph. These were the leaders of Shas, the political party of Israel's Sephardic Jews, its underclass, and they had won 17 of the 120 seats in the Knesset.

The silence that settled over Aroma at that moment was the recognition that Shas was now indispensable to Barak. He had run, after all, on the One Israel banner, committed to healing the nation's rifts, and he could hardly discount the third-largest political party in assembling a coalition. Moreover, Shas had long supported territorial compromise with the Palestinians, and Barak had made it clear he intended to revive the peace process begun by his mentor Yitzhak Rabin. But Shas also represented an Orthodox constituency, and answered to a Sephardic rabbinate more fundamentalist than its followers. What the crowd at Aroma understood—what American Jews are only now beginning to realize—is that not even the election of a secular dove in Israel will solve the pluralism issue. The solution to the identity crisis of American Jewry will not and cannot come from Israel, and the reasons why not only begin with Barak's alliance with Shas.

There is a grand tradition, of course, of Israel solving American Jewry's problems. The creation of the modern state in 1948 validated decades of effort by American Zionists. Israel's arrest and trial of Adolf Eichmann in 1961 thrust the Holocaust into American Jewish consciousness. The lightning victory of Israeli troops in the 1967 war banished the stereotype of the weak, bullied Diaspora Jew. So there are historical precedents for the less observant majority of American Jews to look for Israel to resolve their battles with the Orthodox over authenticity and legitimacy. In my view, however, that will never happen.

The short-term obstacle is the political configuration of Israel. From Menachem Begin through Yitzhak Shamir through Netanyahu, every Likud prime minister has required the support of the religious parties in order to govern; and those religious parties not only endorse the Orthodox monopoly over such rites as marriage, burial, and conversion, but wish to extend that dominion more thoroughly over immigration. Barak's election shows that even a left-wing leader must make some of the same compromises. To Barak the searing lesson of Rabin's assassination was the danger of building a peace coalition so fragile it largely omitted the religious establishment and required the votes of Israeli Arab legislators. So in shaping his coalition, Barak snubbed the Israeli Arab parties as well as Tommy Lapid's anti-religious Shinui party while including Shas, the ultra-Orthodox United Torah Judaism, and the Modern Orthodox Meimad, and awarding them five ministerial appointments. The *Jewish Post*, a *haredi* monthly in the New York area, was not wrong when it gloated, "Israeli secularists . . . must be scratching their *kippah*-less pates."

Not half as much, I might add, as Reform and Conservative Jews in America. Just how deeply Barak's peace-making agenda depended on religious backing became clear during the summer of 1999, when the coalition almost collapsed over government plans to transport a giant power-plant turbine by convoy on a Sabbath. Only with the promise that non-Jews would drive the trucks did Barak hold onto Shas. United Torah Judaism pulled its five votes out of the coalition, this as Barak was trying to complete negotiations with the Palestinians and commence an even more controversial round with the Syrians.

It is not that Barak has ignored the pluralism issue as much as he has, quite rightly, relegated it to secondary status. The Modern Orthodox rabbi who is the minister of Diaspora affairs, Michael Melchior, has endorsed the joint-conversion school developed by the Ne'eman Commission. He has spoken of having the word "Jew" dropped from national identity cards and of instituting civil marriage.* The government has tried to devise a compromise allowing mixed-gender congregations to worship in one area near the Western Wall. But none of these issues approach the peace process in importance. A few months into his term, Barak dispatched a key adviser named Haim Ramon to New York to marshall support for the Oslo process among Reform and Conservative leaders. When the subject of pluralism came up in a closed-door meeting, however, Ramon evidently turned indignant. "Stop meddling in our affairs," one participant recalled him saying. (The *New York Jewish Week* reported the meeting under the headline, "Pluralism? Fuhgedaboudit!") Indeed, in December 1999, Israeli officials formally asked the Reform denomination to suspend its conversions in Israel because of their polarizing effect. The request was spurned. The Reform branch, to the contrary, went ahead with its $50 million expansion program in Israel.

Israel's internal politics, however, provide only the temporal explanation for the intractability of the pluralism issue. The larger, more permanent cause is the vast difference in the nature of Jewry in Israel and America, between being the majority population in a Jewish, Zionist state and a minority faction in an immensely diverse nation. Among themselves, Israelis vigorously debate how to sustain the secular, socialistic culture of the pioneers now that Thai immigrants work the kibbutzes and cell phones have become the symbol of consumer society. Compared to America, however, Israel instills and reinforces Jewish identity in countless ways outside religion—literature, language, history, military service, news media.

During my time in Israel, I met no one who detested the Orthodox establishment more than the journalist and former government spokesman Ze'ev Chafets. He is an American native now married to a gentile woman and he delighted in telling

---

* Natan Sharansky, the Interior Minister, later devised a system allowing civil ceremonies to be held in foreign nations' Israeli consulates.

me that after Israeli authorities refused to register the couple's baby son as a Jew he threatened to have Jesse Jackson conduct a baptism. But when Chafets spoke of his son from a prior marriage (to a Jewish woman), I could reckon the distance in experience between American and Israeli Jews. "My sixteen-year-old, who hasn't set foot in a synagogue for years, is more knowledgeable than anyone in a Reform temple," Chafets said. "What's here for him is Hebrew. An inborn Jewish life cycle. An attachment to the land. A baseline of knowledge. He can read any religious text he wants. There are high school graduation exams on the Bible and the Oral Law, on Jewish history, on Israeli history. You hear daily words that are from the Talmud. Even the pop culture—the way the TV weatherman dresses in a costume on Purim."

When several of Israel's most acclaimed writers, including Amos Oz and David Grossman, publicly joined the Reform movement in 1999, they did so as an act of political alliance, not religious conversion. Even at that, they were instantly attacked for compromising on Jewish secularism, a response unimaginable in contemporary America. Doron Rosenblum, writing in the Israeli newspaper *Ha'aretz*, ridiculed the authors for endorsing "a kind of Judaism-lite . . . that you 'sign up for' like a scout activity or a bus ride to a demonstration . . . as if Hebrew secularism were not able to stand on its own two feet, without grasping the horns of the altar of some synagogue or other."

Israeli Jews don't need pluralism to confirm their Jewish authenticity. Rather, they seek an American-style separation of church and state, a freedom *from* religion. When I visited Rabbi Uri Regev, a leader of the Reform denomination in Israel and an active player in the pluralism battles, I noticed several books on his desk—Taylor Branch's *Parting the Waters* and Richard Kluger's *Simple Justice*. These accounts of the African-American civil rights movement were for him strategy manuals, showing how a minority, outnumbered and oppressed, was able to triumph in the courts. Indeed, the Reform movement in Israel has already won a Supreme Court case allowing non-

Orthodox Jews to serve on municipal religious councils, which control budgets into the millions of dollars. Israel may officially adopt the Ne'eman Commission's compromise on conversion standards in the near future, giving Reform and Conservative rabbis some role in preparing candidates, because of the national need to integrate thousands of Russian immigrants who are ethnically but not halakhically Jewish.

It is one thing, however, to argue that as a matter of legal principle the Reform and Conservative branches of Judaism deserve parity with Orthodoxy in Israel. Personally, I happen to agree. It is quite another to delude yourself into thinking that any court ruling can provide the ineffable, soul-deep thing called "identity." Israel cannot supply the substance for American Jews whose secularism has little distinctively Jewish about it and whose Reform and Conservative synagogues abound in empty seats on all but two or three days a year. In the absence of substance, and the self-confidence it provides, insecurity thrives. I recall a cover cartoon from the *New Yorker,* hardly an organ of fundamentalism, that depicted an Orthodox Jew with beard and *peyes*, a Conservative Jew in a homburg and business suit, and a Reform Jew decked out as Santa Claus. Our own inadequacy, far more than Orthodox scorn, leaves so many American Jews futilely wishing for one more Israeli miracle.

IV

IN THE LAST FEW WEEKS OF 1999, I noticed a full-page advertisement on the back cover of the *Jerusalem Report* from a Jewish organization I had never heard of before. It was named Olam, the Hebrew word for "world," and it presented a vision of Jewish community so lacking in present-day America. At the center of the advertisement, a large photograph showed the hands of a boy and an elderly man together touching a silver pointer to the Hebrew calligraphy of a Torah scroll. Beneath that reverent image, Olam offered a list of "millennium resolutions" that were wonderfully irreverent—singing every day, questioning all dogmas, telling silly jokes to the sick, visiting Israel and not complaining about the Israelis. There also appeared Olam's slogan:

Welcome
to the
Ashkefardic-
Ultrarefoconservadox
Generation.

Intrigued by this message, I followed the advertisement's suggestion to visit the Olam Web site. There I could click on links to brief inspirational readings. I could order a T-shirt with the Olam motto. Or I could read a variety of articles packaged as appealingly as those in an on-line magazine like *Salon*. As I did so, I began to realize just whose version of Jewish community Olam actually represented. There was the memoir of a district attorney, raised unobservant, who was becoming an Orthodox *ba'al teshuva*. There was an essay about how the halakhic restrictions of women's participation in worship and mitzvot were actually "empowering." Most of the authors represented what might be called the evangelical wing of Orthodoxy—the *rebbetzin* and public speaker Esther Jungreis, the Lubavitcher leader Manis Friedman, the educator Nachum Braverman from Aish HaTorah, a group that has boasted that in three months it can turn any lapsed Jew into an Orthodox believer.

The gap between the public face and the private agenda of Olam reminded me of a real estate broker I knew years ago in Manhattan. When she had to pretty up an apartment for sale but the owner was reluctant to pay for improvements, she recommended what she called a schmear—a coat of paint that hid all the underlying faults. The T-shirt, the millennium resolutions, and the articles with headlines like "Guilt-Free Judaism" were Olam's schmear. Beneath the rhetoric of mutual respect, Olam was proselytizing for wayward Jews to adopt Orthodoxy, the one true faith.

That kind of duality is worth dwelling upon now. There are various efforts and programs afoot that seek Jewish community, and I mean ventures without the duplicity of Olam. Rabbis from different branches learn together in Westchester County outside New York City and lead public study sessions at Manhattan's 92nd Street Y. In San Antonio, Texas, the local Jewish federation, social service agency, community center, and day school amicably share a single building. A program for adult education, jointly taught by Orthodox and Conservative clergy, operates in Washington. None of these efforts would be so striking, however, if they did not stand so lonely amid the overarching climate of division. Not even the acceptance of the Orthodox model in large sections of Reform and Conservative Judaism has in any meaningful way reduced the communal tensions. If anything, a nucleus of learned, active progressive Jewry threatens Orthodoxy more than a half-hearted, self-satisfied mass of allrightniks possibly could.

What, then, might American Jewry look like in the generations to come? I have tried in this book to explore and inhabit the recent past, to restrict myself to what I have observed or researched, to listen to others rather than to speak myself. After the destruction of the Second Temple, the sages say, the gift of prophecy was bestowed only on fools. Still, at the risk of proving that premise, I believe the last forty years of American Jewish history strongly suggest the rifts and realignments ahead.

We might call them collectively the Jewish Reformation. By that I do not mean that entirely new denominations will form, although such an outcome is possible. More generally, the divides between the existing branches of Judaism on both theological and social issues are growing so vast, so irreconcilable, that in time those branches, like Christianity after Martin Luther, will be divergent faiths sharing a common deity and a common ancestry. For the sake of argument as much as prognostication, imagine American Jewry reorganizing into factions that I call Haredi, Conservadox, Reformative, and Just Jews.

Haredi: We usually think of America exerting a corrosive effect on Jewish belief, but in the case of the ultra-Orthodox it healed old wounds. In eighteenth-century Europe, the emerging Hasidic movement and the Lithuanian yeshiva theocracy were vicious enemies. The rabbinic elite were called the *Mitnagdim*, the opposers, not as one might presume because of their opposition to modernism but rather to the ecstatic, spiritual Hasidim. In America, the mutual foe of assimilation rendered the divisions within ultra-Orthodoxy irrelevant, and the emerging alliance has only grown stronger over time. The *haredim* maintain a self-perpetuating system of yeshivot, synagogues, and social service agencies. But more than that, they have begun to vie for control over the very institutions that once defined Modern Orthodoxy—day schools, Yeshiva University, rabbinical and congregational associations. All that keeps the *haredim* from entirely constituting Orthodoxy already is the continued presence of the Modern wing. And that presence, I believe, may end in the approaching decades.

Conservadox: There is a truism among the most iconoclastic of the Modern Orthodox that goes, "I'd rather be the baddest boy of Orthodoxy than the *tzaddik* ('righteous man') of Conservativism." It is a comment I have never heard, though, from an Orthodox woman, and that silence is revealing. The feminist revolution within Judaism will create a crisis of definition for the Modern Orthodox movement. The lesson of feminism in Reform and particularly Conservative Judaism is that once you start a revolution of rising expectations, you can't stop it wherever you'd like. It seems impossible to me that Modern Orthodoxy—having given women full religious education, *tefillah* groups, even some pastoral and legal duties— can dodge the ultimate decision to ordain women as rabbis and give them full roles in worship. Whenever that happens, Modern Orthodoxy will give up its already tenuous partnership with the *haredim* and find more logical partners on the right wing of the Conservative movement. That faction of Conservative clergy and laity already follows much of *halakhah* and espouses a good deal of the social conservatism of Modern Orthodoxy. It could easily share with the Modern Orthodox a synagogue with mixed seating, women reading Torah, and in all other ways a deeply traditional praxis, not unlike the Library Minyan's in Los Angeles.

Reformative: The movement toward tradition has affected Reform Judaism deeply, as the debate over the Ten Principles showed. Richard Levy, the rabbi who proposed them, has long kept kosher and walked to synagogue on Sabbath. Hasidic praise-songs have replaced Germanic hymns at many Reform temples' Friday-night services. But it would be a misreading of Rabbi Levy, and of the evolving Reform branch, to equate such practice with being either conservative or Conservative. Rabbi Levy long supported feminists in the movement, and he has spoken favorably about Reform rabbis performing commitment ceremonies for same-sex couples. The gay-rights issue is now rippling through Reform and Conservative circles the way the gender issue did twenty-five years ago, providing the battleground for the collision of religious practice and modern mores, and it promises similar results. In March 2000, the Reform rabbinate voted to bestow formal, theological approval on gay marriage, calling same-sex relationships "worthy of affirmation through appropriate Jewish rituals." While the resolution by the Central Conference of American Rabbis used the word "union" rather than "marriage," and while it supported the right of dissident members not to perform ceremonies for gay or lesbian couples, the sanction for homosexual wedlock was self-evident. Now the Conservative movement will face internal and external pressures to adopt a similar policy, and I predict the movement will split over the practice. In the aftermath, the left wing of Conservatives may well feel more comfortable linked with the neotraditional style of Reform that Richard Levy embodies, what I call Reformative, than with the Conservadox alternative.

Just Jews: Polls tell us already that roughly half of American Jewry is not affiliated with any branch. The neotraditional direction of Reform Judaism may well drive away a substantial number of its members, particularly those whose connection consists more of annual dues than any ongoing involvement. What becomes of these people—the disaffected, the secular, the ones some surveys lump together under the heading, "Just Jewish"? It is hard to work up any optimism. True, there will always be life signs of Jewishness as a culture, whether in the form of a Mandy Patinkin CD of Yiddish songs or a John Zorn performance of Judaic modern jazz, a Habonim summer camp in the Catskills or a Jewish-theme nightclub like Manhattan's Makor. The Birthright Israel program recently sent its first six thousand American students on an all-expenses-paid visit to the Jewish state, trying to rekindle the waning attachment of American Jews to Zion.

Yet the newsworthiness of these endeavors attests to their novelty. *Yiddishkeit* thrived in both formal and informal institutions, from labor unions to *landsmanschaften*, from the Second Avenue theaters to the City College cafeteria to the Borscht Belt. Nothing in secular Judaism today bears comparison. Jews still harbor a greater liberalism than other American whites, but as the sociologists Steven M. Cohen and Charles Liebman have found, they no longer consider that liberalism an expression of Jewish identity. The National Yiddish Book Center, justifiably acclaimed for finding and preserving 1.5 million Yiddish books, has only one Yiddish speaker on its staff. Some neighbors of mine in New Jersey were active in a school run by the Workmen's Circle, the Yiddish socialist group, and a few years ago they needed to hire a principal fluent in Yiddish. The only applications came from *haredim*, who are the ones keeping the language alive. Sharon Levine and her friends had good reason for sounding so mournful at their Camp Kinderwelt reunion. As the literary critic Irving Howe told a college audience six weeks before his death in 1994:

> The culture of Yiddish and secular Jewishness flourished and then declined. My own judgment is that this phase will come to be regarded as one of the most creative and vital, surely one of the most passionate in the whole history of the Jewish people. But the end of it approaches, and neither will nor nostalgia is likely to stop it. For some thoughtful Jews, those who want to remain "Jewish Jews" but in all seriousness cannot yield themselves to religion, the result is a sense of profound discomfort, perhaps desperation. I think that those of us committed to the secular Jewish outlook must admit we are reaching a dead-end.

V

IN THE TRIUMPH of the Orthodox model, there is no room for Orthodox triumphalism. Victory always comes at a price, and in the case of American Jewry the casualty is the naïve faith in equilibrium. American Jews of all stripes have shared the belief that their hyphenated identity presented no contradiction, no painful choice, that you could always be a Jew and an American simultaneously and in perfect balance. We as Jews never faced the reckoning that German Americans and Irish Americans did in World War I, that Japanese Americans and Italian Americans did in World War II, of having to take arms against the old land to prove loyalty to the new. But in a modern America of limitless possibilities, we are having to lean one way or the other, toward Jewish continuity or American dynamism, in whom we marry, in where we send our children to school, in how we spend our Saturday mornings.

"One ever feels his two-ness," W. E. B. Du Bois wrote in *The Souls of Black Folk*, and the excruciating "double-consciousness" he described in African-Americans increasingly holds for American Jews, too. The Indian-born writer Bharati

Mukherjee has likened the process of becoming an American to "murdering a former self." And she said this by way of recommending the decision. Closer to my ethnic and religious home, I am haunted by a recent essay I read by the son of two Jewish public school teachers who was now debating whether to send his own children to religious day school. The article was constructed as a dialogue between Head (day school) and Heart (public school), and it ended in stalemate.

The Jewish immigrants and their descendants who hurled themselves into Americanization were as courageous as any pioneers. In exchange for the full meaning of citizenship, a participation in the national enterprise that goes far beyond mere legal status, they infused America with the greatest treasures Jewishness had to offer—its caustic humor, its vivid vernacular, its political engagement, its passion for education and the arts. America without Jews is unimaginable, and the brave assimilationists made that possible, even if the price was much of their own distinctiveness as Jews.

Rabbi Steven Foster in Denver was correct when he told his colleagues there, as the joint-conversion program was collapsing, that you cannot have ghetto life without ghetto walls. But it is also true that boundaries, whether real or imagined, give purpose and shape to any community. Being part of the unbroken flow of Jewish history demands more than saying you are; it demands a pattern of obligations and responsibilities, a web of mutuality that many modern American Jews find imprisoning and choose to reject. So one part of American Jewry has flourished outside the old walls of identity and gazes back only in nostalgia, if at all. Another part tries to rebuild them, or at least to rescue what was valuable within them, even at the cost of a certain estrangement from America. It is tragic, yes, that American Jews have battled so bitterly, so viciously, over the very meaning of being Jewish. It is more tragic, perhaps, that the only ones fighting are the only ones left who care.

BIBLIOGRAPHY

Books, Magazine Articles, and Scholarly Publications

Adler, Rachel. *Engendering Judaism: An Inclusive Theology and Ethics.* Philadelphia: Jewish Publication Society, 1998.

———. "The Jew Who Wasn't There: Halakhah and the Jewish Woman" In *On Being a Jewish Feminist: A Reader,* edited by Susannah Heschel. New York: Schocken, 1983.

———. "Ten Women Tell . . . The Ways We Are." *Lilith,* Winter 1976–77.

———. "Tumah and Taharah; Ends and Beginnings." In *The Jewish Woman: New Perspectives,* edited by Elizabeth Koltun. New York: Schocken, 1976.

American Jewish Attitudes Toward Israel and the Peace Process. New York: American Jewish Committee, 1995.

Angel, Marc D. "Pluralism and Jewish Unity." *Responsible Orthodox Viewpoints and Editorials,* July 9, 1999.

Anonymous. "My Son's Intermarriage." *Jewish Frontier,* March 1953.

Apple, Sam. "Saving Yiddish from Itself." *Jerusalem Report,* August 30, 1999.

Axel-Lute, Paul. *Lakewood-In-The-Pines: A History of Lakewood, New Jersey.* South Orange, N.J.: New Jersey Historical Commission, 1986.

Bauer, Yehuda. *American Jewry and the Holocaust: The American Jewish Joint Distribution Committee, 1939–1945.* Detroit: Wayne State University Press, 1981.

———. *My Brother's Keeper: A History of the American Jewish Joint Distribution Committee, 1929–1939.* Philadelphia: Jewish Publication Society of America, 1974.

Bayme, Steven. *Understanding Jewish History: Texts and Commentaries.* Hoboken, N.J.: Ktav, 1997.

Becker, Ronald L. *Lasting Impressions: Greater Newark's Jewish Legacy.* Newark: Newark Public Library, 1995.

Beinart, Peter. "The Rise of Jewish Schools." *Atlantic Monthly,* October 1999.

Ben-Gurion, David. "Israel and the Diaspora." *Jewish Frontier,* March 1962.

———. Letter to Zionists. *Jewish Frontier,* February 1954.

Berkovits, Eliezer. "Time to Do: An End to the 'Who-Is-a-Jew' Symptom." *Journal of Reform Judaism,* Winter 1990.

Berman, Saul. "The Status of Jewish Women in Halakhic Judaism." In *The Jewish Woman: New Perspectives*, edited by Elizabeth Koltun. New York: Schocken, 1976.

Bernstein, Philip. *To Dwell in Unity: The Jewish Federation Movement in America Since 1960*. Philadelphia: Jewish Publication Society, 1983.

"A blooming desert ploughed back into sand." *The Economist*, April 24, 1982.

Brawarsky, Sandee, and Deborah Mark, editors. *Two Jews, Three Opinions: A Collection of Twentieth-Century American Jewish Quotations*. New York: Perigree, 1998.

Breck, Allen duPont. *The Centennial History of the Jews of Colorado, 1859–1959*. Denver: Hirschfeld Press, 1960.

Cantor, Norman F. *The Sacred Chain: The History of the Jews*. New York: HarperCollins, 1994.

Cohen, Steven M. *After the Gulf War: American Jews' Attitudes Toward Israel*. New York: American Jewish Committee, 1991.

———. "Are Reform Jews Abandoning Israel?" *Reform Judaism*, Spring 1988.

———. *The Dimensions of American Jewish Liberalism*. New York: American Jewish Committee, 1989.

———. "Religious Stability and Ethnic Decline: Emerging Patterns of Jewish Identity in the United States." New York: Florence G. Heller–Jewish Community Centers Association Research Center, 1998.

A Colorado Jewish Family Album, 1859–1992. Denver: University of Denver Center for Judaic Studies, 1992.

Crooks, James B. *Jacksonville After the Fire, 1901–1919: A New South City*. Jacksonville: University of North Florida, 1991.

Denby, David. "Passion at Yale." *The New Yorker*, September 22, 1997.

Diner, Hasia R. *A Time for Gathering: The Second Migration, 1820–1880*. Baltimore: Johns Hopkins University Press, 1992.

Du Bois, W. E. B. *The Souls of Black Folk*. New York: New American Library, 1969.

Englander, Nathan. *For the Relief of Unbearable Urges*. New York: Knopf, 1999.

Evans, Christopher, and John C. Kuehner. "The Battle for the Soul of Beachwood." *Plain Dealer Sunday Magazine*, October 26, 1997.

Ezrahi, Yaron. *Current Israeli Attitudes Toward American Jews: Contexts, Problems and Recommendations*. Los Angeles: University of Judaism, 1999.

Falk, Marcia. *The Book of Blessings: New Jewish Prayers for Daily Life, the Sabbath, and the New Moon Festival*. San Francisco: HarperSanFrancisco, 1996.

Fishman, Sylvia Barack. *A Breath of Life: Feminism in the American Jewish Community*. New York: Free Press, 1993.

Foster, Steven. "The Community Rabbinic Conversion Board—The Denver Model." *Journal of Reform Judaism*, Summer 1984.

———. "The Denver Conversion Experience." In *Central Conference of American Rabbis Yearbook*, Vol. 96, 1986.

———. "The Rabbi's Role in Counseling Converts to Judaism." Doctor of Ministry dissertation, Iliff School of Theology, Denver, 1985.

Friedman, Robert I. *The False Prophet: Rabbi Meir Kahane—From FBI Informant to Knesset Member*. Brooklyn: Lawrence Hill, 1990.

———. "The Rabbi Who Sentenced Yitzhak Rabin to Death." *New York*, October 9, 1995.

———. *Zealots for Zion: Inside Israel's West Bank Settlement Movement.* New York: Random House, 1992.

Gans, Herbert J. "Symbolic Ethnicity: The Future of Ethnic Groups and Cultures in America." In *On the Making of Americans: Essays in Honor of David Reisman.* Herbert Gans et al., editors. Philadelphia: University of Pennsylvania Press, 1979.

Gartner, Lloyd C. *History of the Jews of Cleveland.* Cleveland: Western Reserve Historical Society, 1987.

Glaser, Gabrielle. *Strangers to the Tribe: Portraits of Interfaith Marriage.* Boston: Houghton Mifflin, 1997.

Glickstein, Natalie H. *That Ye May Remember: Congregation Ahavath Chesed 1882–1982, 5642–5742.* St. Petersburg, Fla.: Byron Kennedy, 1982.

Gold, Michael. *And Hannah Wept: Infertility, Adoption, and the Jewish Couple.* Philadelphia: Jewish Publication Society, 1988.

Goldberg, Hillel. "The Denver Joint Conversion Plan: History—and Revisionist History." *Jewish Observer,* January 1998.

———, editor. "The Sea Change in American Orthodoxy: A Symposium." *Tradition,* Vol. 32, No. 4, Summer 1998.

Goldberg, J. J. *Jewish Power: Inside the American Jewish Establishment.* Reading, Mass.: Addison-Wesley, 1996.

Goldman, Ari L. *The Search for God at Harvard.* New York: Times Books, 1991.

Goldscheider, Calvin, and Alan S. Zuckerman. *The Transformation of the Jews.* Chicago: University of Chicago Press, 1984.

Goldstein, Sidney. *Profile of American Jewry: Insights from the 1990 National Jewish Population Survey.* New York: North American Jewish Data Bank, 1993.

Goodman, Allegra. *The Family Markowitz.* New York: Farrar Straus & Giroux, 1996.

———. *Kaaterskills Falls.* New York: Dial Press, 1998.

Goodman, Walter. "Bicker at Princeton." *Commentary,* May 1958.

Goren, Arthur A. *New York Jews and the Quest for Community: The Kehillah Experiment, 1908–1922.* New York: Columbia University Press, 1970.

Green, Henry Alan, and Marcia Kerstein Zerivitz. *Jewish Life in Florida: A Documentary Exhibit from 1763 to the Present.* Coral Gables, Fla.: Mosaic, 1991.

Greenberg, Blu. *On Women and Judaism: A View from Tradition.* Philadelphia: Jewish Publication Society, 1981.

Greenberg, Irving. *Will There Be One Jewish People by the Year 2000?* New York: National Jewish Center for Learning and Leadership, 1986.

Gross, Rita. "Female God Language in a Jewish Context." In *Womenspirit Rising: A Feminist Reader in Religion.* New York: Harper & Row, 1979.

Halevi, Yossi Klein. *Memoirs of a Jewish Extremist: An American Story.* Boston: Little, Brown, 1995.

———. "Will These Israelis Be Allowed to Become Jews?" *Jerusalem Report,* June 21, 1999.

Harlow, Jules, editor. *A Rabbi's Manual.* New York: Rabbinical Assembly, 1965.

———. *Siddur Sim Shalom.* New York: Rabbinical Assembly, 1985.

Hauptman, Judith. "The Ethical Challenge of Feminist Change." In *The Americanization of the Jews,* edited by Robert M. Seltzer and Norman J. Cohen. New York: New York University Press, 1995.

Heilman, Samuel. *Defenders of the Faith: Inside Ultra-Orthodox Jewry*. New York: Schocken, 1992.

Helmreich, William B. *The Enduring Community: The Jews of Newark and Metrowest*. New Brunswick, N.J.: Transaction, 1999.

Hertzberg, Arthur. "Modernity and Judaism." In *Great Confrontations in Jewish History*, edited by Stanley M. Wagner and Allen D. Breck. Denver: University of Denver, 1977.

———. *The Jews in America: Four Centuries of an Uneasy Encounter: A History*. New York: Simon & Schuster, 1989.

Hirschberg, Peter. "Murder in the Air." *Jerusalem Report*, September 28, 1998.

Hoffman, Eva. *Shtetl: The Life and Death of a Small Town and the World of Polish Jews*. Boston: Houghton Mifflin, 1997.

Howe, Irving. "The End of Jewish Secularism." New York: Hunter College Jewish Social Studies Program, 1994.

———. *World of Our Fathers: The Journey of the East European Jews to America and the Life They Found and Made*. New York: Harcourt Brace Jovanovich, 1976.

Hyman, Paula. "Ezrat Nashim and the Emergence of a New Jewish Feminism." In *The Americanization of the Jews*, Seltzer and Cohen.

In the Aftermath of the Rabin Assassination. New York: American Jewish Committee, 1996.

Isaacs, Stephen D. *Jews and American Politics*. Garden City, N.Y.: Doubleday, 1974.

Jacobs, Harold M. "Drawing the Line on Jewish Identity." *Young Israel Viewpoint*, January 1984.

Jaffe-Gill, Ellen. "Patrilineality: Creating a Schism or Updating Judaism?" *Moment*, December 31, 1998.

" 'Johns' Make War with Suits." *Connecticut Law Journal*, August 10, 1992.

Johnson, Paul. *A History of the Jews*. New York: Harper & Row, 1987.

Joselit, Jenna Weissman. *New York's Jewish Jews: The Orthodox Community in the Interwar Years*. Bloomington, Ind.: Indiana University Press, 1990.

———. *The Wonders of America: Reinventing Jewish Culture, 1880–1950*. New York: Hill & Wang, 1994.

Jospe, Raphael, and Stanley M. Wagner, editors. *Great Schisms in Jewish History*. Denver: University of Denver Center for Judaic Studies, 1981.

Kagan, Shaul. "Reb Aharon Kotler: Ten Years after His Passing." *Jewish Observer*, May 1973.

Kahane, Meir. *On Jews and Judaism: Selected Articles, 1961–1990*. Jerusalem: Institute for the Publication of the Writings of Rabbi Meir Kahane, 1993.

———. *Uncomfortable Questions for Comfortable Jews*. Secaucus, N.J.: Lyle Stuart, 1987.

Kaplan, Mordecai. *Judaism as a Civilization: Toward a Reconstruction of American-Jewish Life*. New York: Macmillan, 1934.

Karpin, Michael, and Ina Friedman. *Murder in the Name of God: The Plot to Kill Yitzhak Rabin*. New York: Metropolitan, 1998.

Klein, Woody. *Lindsay's Promise: The Dream That Failed*. New York: Macmillan, 1970.

Klinghoffer, David. *The Lord Will Gather Me In: My Journey to Jewish Orthodoxy*. New York: Free Press, 1999.

Kosmin, Barry A. et al. *Highlights of the CJF 1990 National Jewish Population Survey*. New York: Council of Jewish Federations, 1990.

Kranzler, David. *Thy Brother's Blood: The Orthodox Jewish Response During the Holocaust*. Brooklyn: Mesorah, 1987.

Kranzler, George. *Hasidic Williamsburg: A Contemporary American Hasidic Community*. Northvale, N.J.: Jason Aronson, 1995.

Landau, David. *Who Is a Jew?: A Case Study of American Jewish Influence on Israeli Policy*. New York: American Jewish Committee, 1996.

Lerner, Anne Lapidus. " 'Who Hast Not Made Me a Man': The Movement for Equal Rights for Women in American Jewry." In *American Jewish Yearbook 1977*, edited by Morris Fine and Milton Himmelfarb. New York: American Jewish Committee and Jewish Publication Society, 1976.

Lewitter, Sidney R. "A School for Scholars, The Beth Medrash Govoha, The Rabbi Aaron Kotler Jewish Institute of Higher Learning in Lakewood, New Jersey: A Study of the Development and Theory of One Aspect of Jewish Higher Education in America." Ed.D. dissertation, Rutgers University, 1981.

Lichtman, Gail. "A Page in History." *The Jerusalem Post Magazine*, May 20, 1999.

Liebman, Charles S. "Orthodoxy Faces Modernity." *Orim*, Vol. 2, No. 2, Spring 1987.

———. "Orthodoxy in American Jewish Life." In *American Jewish Yearbook 1966*. New York: American Jewish Committee and Jewish Publication Society, 1967.

Liebman, Charles S., and Steven M. Cohen. *Two Worlds of Judaism: The Israeli and American Experiences*. New Haven: Yale University Press, 1990.

Lipman, Eugene J., and Albert Vorspan, editors. *A Tale of Ten Cities: The Triple Ghetto in American Religious Life*. New York: Union of American Hebrew Congregations, 1962.

Mamet, David. *The Old Neighborhood*. New York: Vintage, 1998.

———. *The Old Religion*. New York: Free Press, 1997.

Maoz, Asher. "Religious Human Rights in the State of Israel." In *Human Rights in Judaism: Cultural, Religious, and Political Perspectives*, edited by Michael J. Broyde and John Witte, Jr. Northvale, N.J.: Jason Aronson, 1998.

———. "Who Is a Convert?" *Justice*, December 1997.

———. "Who Is a Jew?" *Midstream*, June/July 1989.

Markowitz, Ruth Jacknow. *My Daughter, the Teacher: Jewish Teachers in the New York City Public Schools*. New Brunswick, N.J.: Rutgers University Press, 1993.

Mayer, Egon. *A Demographic Revolution in American Jewry*. Ann Arbor: Frankel Center for Judaic Studies, University of Michigan, 1992.

———. "Who Is the Unaffiliated Jew?: A Demographic Profile." In *The Unaffiliated Jew*, edited by Renee Kogel and Bonnie Cousens. Farmington Hills, Mich.: International Institute for Secular Humanistic Judaism, 1997.

Meiselman, Moshe. *Jewish Woman in Jewish Law*. New York: Ktav, 1978.

Miller, Ron, and Jacob B. Ukeles. *Jewish Connections: 1997 Greater Denver/Boulder Jewish Community Study*. Denver: Allied Jewish Federation of Colorado, 1998.

Millgram, Abraham. *Jewish Worship*. Philadelphia: Jewish Publication Society, 1971.

Mintz, Jerome. *Hasidic People: A Place in the New World*. Cambridge, Mass.: Harvard University Press, 1992.

Moore, MacDonald. "Neodox Jews." *Judaism*, Vol. 49, No. 4, Fall 2000.

Morgan, Thomas B. "The Vanishing American Jew." *Look,* May 15, 1964.

Morris, Charles R. *The Cost of Good Intentions: New York City and the Liberal Experiment, 1960–1975.* New York: Norton, 1980.

Morris, Jeffrey. *Beachwood: The Book.* Beachwood, Ohio: Self-published, 1997.

Morris, Yaacov. "New Approach to American Zionism." *Jewish Frontier,* July 1962.

Neusner, Jacob. *Stranger at Home: "The Holocaust," Zionism and American Judaism.* Atlanta: Scholars Press, 1997.

1998 Annual Survey of American Jewish Opinion. New York: American Jewish Committee, 1998.

Oren, Dan A. *Joining the Club: A History of Jews and Yale.* New Haven: Yale University Press, 1985.

Peres, Shimon. *The Imaginary Voyage.* New York: Arcade, 1999.

Phillips, Bruce A. *Denver Jewish Population Study.* Denver: Allied Jewish Federation of Denver, 1981.

Pogrebin, Letty Cottin. *Deborah, Golda, and Me: Being Female and Jewish in America.* New York: Crown, 1991.

———. "Let Us Now Praise (Some) Orthodox Men." *Moment,* October 1999.

Poll, Solomon. *The Hasidic Community of Williamsburg: A Study in the Sociology of Religion.* New York: Schocken, 1969.

Ponet, James. "Too Jewish, At Yale." *CommonQuest,* Vol. 3, No. 3, May 1999.

Potok, Chaim. *The Chosen.* New York: Simon & Schuster, 1967.

Prell, Riv-Ellen. *Prayer and Community: The Havurah in American Judaism.* Detroit: Wayne State University Press, 1989.

Rabinovitch, Itamar. *Waging Peace: Israel and the Arabs at the End of the Century.* New York: Farrar Straus & Giroux, 1999.

Raff, Lauren B. *1996 Jewish Population Study of Greater Cleveland.* Cleveland: Jewish Community Federation of Cleveland, 1998.

Rawidowicz, Simon. *State of Israel, Diaspora, and Jewish Continuity: Essays on the "Ever-Dying People."* Hanover, N.H.: Brandeis University Press/University Press of New England, 1986.

Reisman, Bernard. *The Chavurah: A Contemporary Jewish Experience.* New York: Union of American Hebrew Congregations, 1977.

Rockefeller, Steven C. "Reflections on the Princeton Club System and the 1958 Bicker." Princeton University Archives, Eating Clubs collection.

Roiphe, Anne. *Lovingkindness.* New York: Summit, 1987.

Rosten, Leo. *The Joys of Yiddish.* New York: McGraw-Hill, 1968.

Roth, Philip. *American Pastoral.* Boston: Houghton Mifflin, 1997.

———. *The Facts: A Novelist's Autobiography.* New York: Farrar Straus & Giroux, 1988.

———. *Goodbye, Columbus and Five Short Stories.* Boston: Houghton Mifflin, 1959.

———. *Operation Shylock: A Confession.* New York: Simon & Schuster, 1993.

Rubin, Israel. *Satmar: Two Generations of an Urban Island.* New York: Peter Lang, 1997.

Salkin, Jeffrey K. "Jewish Macho." *Reform Judaism,* Spring 1998.

Sandberg, Neil C. *Jewish Life in Los Angeles: A Window to Tomorrow.* Lanham, Md.: University Press of America, 1986.

Sandmel, Samuel. "Hellenism and Judaism." In *Great Confrontations in Jewish History*, edited by Stanley M. Wagner and Allen D. Breck. Denver: University of Denver Press, 1977.

Schick, Marvin. "A Census of Jewish Day Schools in the United States." New York: Avi Chai Foundation, 2000.

Schoffman, Stuart. "The Ankles of King David." *Jerusalem Report*, January 4, 1999.

———. "Lettuce Was Lettuce." *Jerusalem Report*, April 2, 1998.

Shalit, Wendy. "Diversity's Limits." *City Journal*, Autumn 1997.

Shapiro, Edward S. *A Time for Healing: American Jewry Since World War II*. Baltimore: Johns Hopkins University Press, 1992.

Shapiro, Michael et al. "New York, N.Y.: The Orthodox and New Immigrants Are Changing Jewish Life." *Present Tense*, Autumn 1985.

Silberman, Charles: *A Certain People: America's Jews and Their Lives Today*. New York: Summit, 1985.

Sklare, Marshall. *America's Jews*. New York: Random House, 1971.

Soloveitchik, Haym. "Rupture and Reconstruction: The Transformation of Contemporary Orthodoxy." *Tradition*, Vol. 28, No. 4, Summer 1994.

Sontag, Deborah. "Peace. Period." *New York Times Magazine*, December 19, 1999.

Sorin, Gerald. *Tradition Transformed: The Jewish Experience in America*. Baltimore: Johns Hopkins University Press, 1997.

Spiegel, Fredelle Z. "Community Without Authority." Department of Religious Studies, California State University, Northridge, 1989.

———. "The Impact of Women's Participation on the non-Orthodox Synagogue." *CCAR Journal: A Reform Jewish Quarterly*, Fall 1992.

Sprinzak, Ehud. *Brother Against Brother: Violence and Extremism in Israeli Politics from Altalena to the Rabin Assassination*. New York: Free Press, 1999.

Stanislawski, Michael. "Back to Brother Daniel: A Legal and Ideological Analysis of the Origins of the 'Who Is A Jew' Controversy in Israel." New York: Columbia University Press, 1998.

A Statement of the Jewish Future: Text and Responses. New York: American Jewish Committee, 1997.

Sterne, Michael, editor. *Where to Live In and Around New York*. New York: Times Books, 1985.

Stone, Amy. "Gentleman's Agreement at the Seminary." *Lilith*, Spring/Summer 1977.

Trachtenberg, Joshua. "Religious Activities." In *American Jewish Yearbook 47*. New York: American Jewish Committee and Jewish Publication Society, 1948.

Uchill, Ida Libert. *Pioneers, Peddlers and Tsadikim*. Denver: Sage Books, 1957.

Van Tassell, David D., editor. *The Encyclopedia of Cleveland History*. Bloomington, Ind.: Indiana University Press, 1996.

Vickar, Shira. *Taboo Texts: Talmud Education for Women*. M.S. dissertation, Columbia University Graduate School of Journalism, New York, 1998.

Vincent, Sidney Z. *Personal and Professional: Memoirs of a Life in Community Service*. Cleveland: Jewish Community Federation of Cleveland, 1982.

Waxman, Chaim I. *America's Jews in Transition*. Philadelphia: Temple University Press, 1983.

———. "The Haredization of American Orthodox Jewry." *Jerusalem Letter/Viewpoints*, February 15, 1998.

Wertheimer, Jack. "The Orthodox Moment." *Commentary*, February 1999.

——. *A People Divided: Judaism in Contemporary America*. New York: Basic Books, 1993.

Whitaker, Mark, and Milan J. Kubic. "Israel: Last Stand in the Sinai." *Newsweek*, April 12, 1982.

——. "Sinai's Fierce Settlers." *Newsweek*, Jan. 11, 1982.

Wisse, Ruth R. " 'Schindler' and the Victim Image." *Jerusalem Report*, March 10, 1994.

Wolff, Geoffrey. *The Final Club*. New York: Knopf, 1990.

Wolpin, Nissan. "Compromise on the Great Divide: Questionable Conversions in Denver." *Jewish Observer*, January 1984.

"The Yom Kippur Jews." *American Hebrew*, August 25, 1905.

Young, James E. *The Texture of Memory: Holocaust Memorials and Meaning*. New Haven: Yale University Press, 1993.

Zelinsky, Edward A. "Are Tax 'Benefits' Constitutionally Equivalent to Direct Expenditures?" *Harvard Law Review*, Vol. 112, No. 2, December 1998.

Zohar, Zvi, and Avi Saggi. *Conversion to Judaism: An Halakhic Study*. Jerusalem: Shalom Hartman Institute, 1989.

Author's note: For the sake of consistency, I have used *Tanakh: The Holy Scriptures* (Philadelphia: Jewish Publication Society, 1985) as the source for all translations of biblical text.

Newspapers, News Services, and Web Sites

Algemeyner Dzornal (New York)
Baltimore Jewish Times
Baltimore Sun
Christian Science Monitor
Cleveland Jewish News
Cleveland *Plain Dealer*
Commentator (Yeshiva University)
Financial Times (London)
Florida Times-Union (Jacksonville)
Forward
Haaretz (Tel Aviv)
Hartford Courant
Intermountain Jewish News (Denver)
Jerusalem Post
Jewish Advocate (Boston)
Jewish Exponent (Philadelphia)
Jewish Journal of Greater Los Angeles
Jewish News (Newark, N.J.)
Jewish Post (New York)
Jewish Press (Brooklyn, N.Y.)

Jewish State (Highland Park, N.J.)
Jewish Student Press Service
Jewish Telegraphic Agency
Los Angeles Times
Minyan Monthly (Los Angeles, Calif.)
Newark Evening News
New Haven Register
New Jersey Jewish News
New York Jewish Week
New York Post
New York Times
Philadelphia Inquirer
Rocky Mountain News (Denver)
Salon
Sun-Press (Beachwood, Ohio)
Times Herald Record (Middletown, N.Y.)
Washington Post
Yale Daily News
Yated Ne'eman (Monsey, N.Y.)

Interviews

CHAPTER ONE: *Camp Kinderwelt, New York, 1963*

Azenberg, Manny—1/20/98; 8/12/98; 3/24/99
Eisenberg, Art—7/26/99 by phone
Freed, Gloria (Jackelow)—7/28/99 by phone
Gamliel, Eli—7/18/99 by phone; 7/29/99 by phone
Graubard, Myra (Canton)—6/21/99 by phone; 8/1/99 by phone; 8/10/99 by phone
Heringman, Tami (Rotem)—6/27/99 by phone; 7/27/99 by phone
Kaplan, Lorelei and Milt—7/13/99; 7/28/99 by phone
Levine, Sharon (Elghanayan)—5/6/99; 6/2/99; 7/21/99; 7/29/99 by phone; 8/9/99 by phone
Lustig, Joel—7/13/99
Petlin, Joel—7/7/99
Rosen, Yudi—8/12/98; 3/24/99
Schulman, Judi (Lederer)—6/21/99
Tumin, Esther—7/30/98 by phone
Wieder, Abraham—7/7/99

CHAPTER TWO: *Denver, Colorado, 1977–1983*

Adler, Phyllis—9/15/98
Davis, Anne—9/13/98; 9/15/98; 6/7/99; 6/99 by phone
Eisenman, Bernard—2/10/98
Foster, Steven—11/19/97; 6/1/98; 8/26/99 by phone
Goldberg, Hillel—11/18/97; 6/2/98
Goldberg, Miriam—6/2/98
Goldberger, Daniel—11/18/97; 6/3/98; 6/22/99 by phone; 7/12/99 by phone
Guthery, Jean and Peter—6/1/98; 9/13/98
Kecker, Douglas—9/15/98
Litvak, Paulina—6/2/98
Moore, Martha—6/25/99 by phone
Pluss, Bill—6/6/99; 6/7/99
Pluss, Julius—6/7/99
Rose, Herbert—1/15/98
Shreves, Helen—9/14/98; 9/15/98
Wagner, Stanley—11/19/97; 6/3/98
Zwerin, Raymond—6/3/98

CHAPTER THREE: *Los Angeles, California, 1987–1989*

Adler, Rachel—10/20/98 by phone; 1/12/99; 1/13/99; 3/15/99; 3/17/99; 7/8/99 by phone; 7/12/99 by phone
Alexander, Hanan—1/12/99; 9/2/99 by phone; 9/8/99 by phone
Braun, Bob—3/15/99
Dorff, Elliott—11/17/98 by phone; 1/11/99; 9/8/99 by phone
Dorph, Gail—1/8/99
Eisen, Alysse—9/2/99 by phone
Grossman, Fran—1/12/99; 3/17/99

Grossman, Joel—1/12/99; 3/14/99; 6/21/99 by phone
Halbert, Janet—3/16/99
Lipstadt, Deborah—5/30/99
Miller, Mitch—1/13/99
Rabin, Amy—3/14/99; 3/16/99
Rabin, Jeff—1/10/99; 3/14/99
Rembaum, Joel—3/19/99
Spiegel, Fredelle—1/13/99

CHAPTER FOUR: *Jacksonville, Florida, 1993–1997*

Baer, W. R.—12/8/97
Charter, Steve—5/19/99
Devereaux, Mark—12/8/97
Gaffney, David—12/9/97; 1/15/98 by phone; 3/18/98
Graff, Jay—3/17/98
Greenburg, Michael—3/17/98
Horovitz, Bruce—3/18/98
Jernigan, Shirley—12/8/97
Kol, Roni—5/18/99
Levine, David and Louise—12/8/97
Marcu, Phil—10/12/99 by phone
McFarland, William—12/8/97
Rapp, Dani—12/15/98
Shapiro, Harry—8/17/98; 11/23/98; 5/30/99; 5/31/99
Shapiro, Steve—3/18/98; 8/16/98
Shapiro-Moser, Juli—3/18/98; 8/16/98
Yegelwel, Evan—12/9/97
Zisser, Barry—12/8/97; 9/30/99 by phone

CHAPTER FIVE: *New Haven, Connecticut, 1995–1999*

Brodhead, Richard—3/24/98
Brown, Jerry—10/25/99 by phone
Butler, David—10/12/99 by phone
Farber, Evan—4/9/98
Goldman, Ari—10/19/99
Greer, Batsheva—1/9/98; 2/18/98; 2/19/98; 4/8/98 by phone; 5/4/98 by
     phone
Greer, Daniel—1/9/98; 2/18/98; 4/3/98 by phone; 4/9/98; 12/8/98; 12/23/98;
     3/9/99; 10/6/99 by phone; 10/12/99 by phone; 10/19/99
Greer, Dov—3/24/98
Hack, Elisha—3/25/98; 4/28/98 by phone
Hack, Harold—4/28/98 by phone
Halpern, Charles—10/7/99 by phone
Hershman, Jeremy—4/30/98
Horowitz, Michael—9/30/99 by phone
Levin, Richard—3/24/98
Lewin, Nathan—2/12/98
Oren, Dan—4/7/98 by phone
Riskin, Shlomo—5/20/99
Trachtenberg, Betty—3/25/98; 4/8/98 by phone

Whitman, Michael—3/24/98
Zelinsky, Edward—10/4/99

CHAPTER SIX: *Beachwood, Ohio, 1997–1999*

Aaronson, Joshua—10/30/97; 6/16/98
Cohen, Donna—10/28/97
Feitman, Yaakov—10/28/97; 8/3/98
Gorden, Merle—10/28/97
Gottesman, David—10/29/97; 6/14/98; 6/16/98; 8/2/98; 4/18/98; 10/24/99 by
    phone; 11/9/99 by phone
Grodin, Leslie—10/29/97
Hecht, Michael—8/4/98
Hershkopf, Ike—10/31/99 by phone
Levey, Harold—10/22/97 by phone
Oster, Marcy—10/27/97; 6/14/98
Rubinstein, Judah—6/15/98
Soclof, Ivan—10/28/97
Stark, Bob—10/21/99 by phone
Wachsberger, Si—10/29/97; 6/15/98; 6/16/98; 8/2/98; 8/3/98; 8/4/98; 4/18/99;
    4/19/99; 10/21/99 by phone; 10/27/99 by phone; 11/8/99 by phone

PROLOGUE, EPILOGUE, AND INTERSTITIAL SECTIONS

Bayme, Steven—6/5/97; 4/98 by phone
Berman, Saul—1/4/00
Botnick, Jeff—11/5/98 by phone
Chafets, Ze'ev—5/20/99
Cowan, Rachel—7/97
Diner, Hasia—4/8/99; 1/11/00 by phone
Ezrahi, Yaron—5/16/99
Greenberg, Irving—7/7/97
Guilor, Edna—11/22/99 by phone
Halbertol, Moshe—5/16/99
Halevi, Yossi Klein—5/17/99
Heilman, Samuel—6/23/99
Helmreich, William—9/10/97
Kass, Alvin—10/28/98
Kranzler, David—6/30/99 by phone; 12/3/99 by phone
Maoz, Asher—5/18/99
Marcus, Janet and David—9/29/97
Mayer, Egon—8/26/97
Moore, Deborah Dash—1/19/00 by phone
Pogrebin, Letty Cottin—12/15/99 by phone
Regev, Uri—5/16/99
Rosenblatt, Gary—10/15/97
Rosenbloom, Seymour—11/98 by phone
Sacks, Andrew—5/21/99
Salkin, Jeffrey—11/98 by phone
Schweid, Eliezer—5/17/99
Shapira, Anita—5/18/99
Sorin, Gerald—11/15/99 by phone, 1/11/00 by phone

Waxman, Chaim—4/7/98 by phone; 5/98
Waxman, Mordecai—8/27/97
Weintraub, Jeff—1/14/00 by phone
Wertheimer, Jack—11/10/98
Young, James—1/17/00 by phone

ACKNOWLEDGMENTS

Two DAYS AGO I went for my first haircut in a month, and when the barber had finished her work I could see more gray than ever in the mirror. My wife tells me that doing this book has aged me beyond the two years and nine months I spent reporting and writing it, and I'm inclined to agree with her, if only because middle age with an excuse is better than middle age without one. Whatever efforts I've made, though, I've made with the priceless assistance of many other individuals. And, as always for me, it is the special joy at my labor's end to acknowledge them.

Jew vs. Jew is dedicated to Alice Mayhew, my editor over two books and seven years. This book would not exist without her intellectual curiosity, her fascination with religion and history as subjects, her ability to transfuse energy and excitement into an author, her painstaking line-editing, and, most of all, her old-fashioned loyalty. In the turbulence of publishing today, she is a bulwark.

Rabbi Gerald L. Zelizer, who shares the dedication, sought me out as a member of his synagogue, Neve Shalom, shortly after I moved to central New Jersey in 1992. He has been a teacher, pastor, and friend to me ever since, and one of the few painful parts of returning to New York in 1999 was having to leave Neve Shalom. Rabbi Zelizer read and commented on the entire manuscript of this book, and it is surely far better for his scrutiny.

My wife, Cynthia Sheps Freedman, held our home together during my numerous out-of-town reporting trips, even as she excelled in her own legal career. She sat up late many nights reading early drafts of my chapters, and she endured the frustration, anxiety, ignorance, and depression I felt many times during this project. My children, Aaron and Sarah, breathe life back into me every day. I hope that somehow this book will inform their own Jewish identities. My father, David Freedman, is a living example of secular Judaism at its best, and he infused this project with his interest and iconoclasm. As always, I feel well loved by my stepmother, Phyllis Freedman, my sister, Carol Freedman, and my brother, Ken Freedman.

Barney Karpfinger, my literary agent, was present with Alice Mayhew at the lunch back in June 1997 when this book was conceived. More than anyone except my wife, he had to live with the oscillating moods of a writer in mid-struggle, and I'm relieved his patience was nearly infinite.

I met and interviewed several hundred people for this book, and I am grateful to all of them, but a few in particular gave so generously and unstintingly of their time that I would like to single them out—Sharon Levine Elghanayan, Manny Azenberg, and Yudi Rosen in New York; Bill Pluss, Anne Davis, Rabbi Daniel Goldberger, Rabbi Steven Foster, and Rabbi Stanley Wagner in Denver; Rachel Adler, Hanan Alexander, Joel and Fran Grossman, and Jeff and Amy Rabin in Los Angeles; Harry Shapiro, Steven Shapiro, and Juli Shapiro-Moser in Florida; Rabbi Daniel Greer, Sarah Greer, Dov Greer, and Batsheva Greer in New Haven; Si Wachsberger and Dr. David Gottesman in Beachwood.

Very early on in this project, I first met Steven Bayme, the American Jewish Committee's specialist on intra-Jewish relations and probably the national expert on that topic. Steve shared his time, insight, and knowledge with me over nearly three years thereafter, and I am indebted to him for that. A number of other scholars read and critiqued portions of the manuscript and fielded countless questions from me. For their wisdom and indulgence, I thank Chaim Waxman of Rutgers University, Hasia Diner of New York University, Riv-Ellen Prell of the University of Minnesota,

Gerald Sorin of the State University of New York, and Jack Wertheimer of Jewish Theological Seminary.

I similarly availed myself of several prominent Jewish journalists—Gary Rosenblatt, editor of the *New York Jewish Week*; J. J. Goldberg, the syndicated columnist; and Yossi Klein Halevi, senior writer for the *Jerusalem Report*. In my bibliography, I do not separately list newspaper articles, but I would be remiss if I did not indicate the extraordinary coverage done by Marcy Oster of the *Cleveland Jewish News* on the Beachwood controversy and by Hillel Goldberg, editor of the *Intermountain Jewish News*, on the joint-conversion panel. Both Marcy and Hillel opened their research files to me in a spirit of cooperation that went far beyond professional courtesy.

My friends and colleagues at Columbia University, Michael Shapiro and Ari Goldman, provided invaluable ballast, both journalistically and emotionally, as did two of my former students, J. J. Hornblass and Rabbi Shirley Idelson. And all of these people, by their example, have enriched my own Jewish life. Jonathan Kellerman and Art Cottrell read and critiqued the final version of the manuscript, saving me from my own oversights. Neil Reisner and Julian Zelizer read and commented on my proposal for this book.

My friend and fellow author Kevin Coyne read every word of this manuscript and he brought his considerable talents to bear on it. Peter Edelman, researcher extraordinaire, not only answered every inquiry of mine with alacrity but scouted out useful material unbidden. Gertrude Dubrovsky, besides being my especially beloved cousin, translated Yiddish texts for me. Sandy Edry assisted me greatly in fact-checking parts of the manuscript. Matt Weber, Arienne Noble, and Wendy Lefko contributed useful research on specific portions of the book.

Thomas L. Friedman of the *New York Times* assisted me enormously in lining up key interviews during my research trip to Israel. While I was there, the *Times*'s bureau chief, Deborah Sontag, graciously opened her office to me. Lynn Kra-oz, Noam Kra-oz, and Tal Kra-oz helped me find my way around Israel and gave me some needed R&R.

In my travels, I relied often on the kindness and sofa beds of friends and relatives. For their hospitality and good humor, I thank my aunt, Jacqueline Freedman, in Cleveland; Tom Schilling and John Rebchook in Denver; Don Samuel and family in Atlanta; and Ann and Dick Costello in Los Angeles. My visits to Harry Shapiro in prison were facilitated by Warden M. E. Ray at the Federal Correctional Institution in Edgefield, South Carolina, and Warden Gregory Parks at the Federal Correctional Institution in Coleman, Florida. Bruce Bryant-Friedland was a benevolent colleague when I was in Jacksonville.

A grant from the Freedom Forum provided vital support for my research. The Research Committee at the Columbia University Graduate School of Journalism, chaired by Professor James Carey, made a significant contribution toward my trip to Israel. My deans at Columbia—Tom Goldstein, Kate Beeby, and David Klatell—helpfully arranged and rearranged the terms of my sabbatical.

I was able to work through some of the material and ideas for this book in the form of articles, and I appreciate the help of my editors—John Darnton, Patricia Cohen, Stephen Dubner, Jack Rosenthal, and Adam Moss at the *New York Times*; Jeremy Gerard and Caroline Miller at *New York*; Joan Walsh at *Salon*; and Glen Nishimura and David Mastio at *USA Today*.

At Simon & Schuster, I benefited from the skill and attention of what I think of as Team Mayhew—Roger Labrie, Brenda Copeland, Anja Schmidt, K. C. Trommer, and a fine and unflappable young editor named Ana DeBevoise. Lydia Buechler and Carole Cook meticulously copyedited and brought order to the inexact science of transliterating Hebrew. I am also grateful for the hard work and wizardry of Victoria Meyer, assisted by Rachel Nagler, in publicizing the book. Outside S&S, Carolyn Starman Hessel of the Jewish Book Council has been a tireless advocate for this project.

Let me also thank: Alice Alexiou, Christine Baird, Janet Boss, Steve Charter, Drew Clark, Cynthia Dettelbach, Julia Goldman, Avital Louria Hahn, William Helmreich, Itay Hod, Steve Isaacs, Suzanne Keating, Rabbi Stuart Kelman, Jacob Levenson, Gene Lichtenstein, Elie Mueller, Yoni Neirman, Jim Podgers, Mark Schoifet, Haym Soloveitchik, Liz Stein, Shira Vickar, Paul Zielbauer, and Jennifer Zweben.

And for my many students at Columbia, especially those in my book-writing class, who've heard me talk the talk: All through this project your presence, whether in person or in memory, has motivated me to walk the walk.

S.G.F.
February 22, 2000

INDEX

ABOUT THE AUTHOR

SAMUEL G. FREEDMAN is an award-winning writer and professor. A former reporter for the *New York Times*, he is the author of three acclaimed books—*Small Victories: The Real World of a Teacher, Her Students and Their High School* (1990); *Upon This Rock: The Miracles of a Black Church* (1993); and *The Inheritance: How Three Families and America Moved from Roosevelt to Reagan and Beyond* (1996).

    Small Victories was a finalist for the 1990 National Book Award and *The Inheritance* was a finalist for the 1997 Pulitzer Prize. *Upon This Rock* won the 1993 Helen Bernstein Award for Excellence in Journalism. All three books have been listed among *The New York Times'* Notable Books of the Year.

    Freedman was a staff reporter for the *New York Times* from 1981 through 1987 and continues to contribute to the paper on a freelance basis. He is a member of *USA Today*'s Board of Contributors and a regular contributor to numerous other publications, including *New York, Rolling Stone*, and *Salon*.

    A tenured professor at the Columbia University Graduate School of Journalism, Freedman was named the nation's outstanding journalism educator in 1997 by the Society of Professional Journalists. His class in book-writing has developed fifteen authors, editors, and agents.

    Freedman lives in Manhattan with his wife and children.